Mentoring for Learning

Mentoring for Learning

"Climbing the Mountain"

Edited by

Harm Tillema
Leiden University, The Netherlands

Gert J. van der Westhuizen
University of Johannesburg, South Africa

and

Kari Smith
University of Bergen, Norway

SENSE PUBLISHERS
ROTTERDAM/BOSTON/TAIPEI

A C.I.P. record for this book is available from the Library of Congress.

ISBN: 978-94-6300-056-7 (paperback)
ISBN: 978-94-6300-057-4 (hardback)
ISBN: 978-94-6300-058-1 (e-book)

Published by: Sense Publishers,
P.O. Box 21858,
3001 AW Rotterdam,
The Netherlands
https://www.sensepublishers.com/

Printed on acid-free paper

TABLE OF CONTENTS

INTRODUCTION

"What is mentoring all about"? Being Telemachus' guide and resource person Mentor's prime role was to "help" the young and unskilled son of Odysseus to become a proficient and self-regulated learner, able to cope with the demands of life. This 'helping" process (Cox, Bachkirova, & Clutterbuck, 2010) was accomplished through conversation. Mentoring's typical characteristic is talk, i.e., the communicative interactive exchange between persons. This exchange is considered to be the vehicle of learning and professional development. Therefore, to tentatively answer our opening question, mentoring is about learning in conversations. For mentoring to be of any help its process (i.e., conversation) and its result (i.e., learning to become a professional) need to be carefully appreciated and scrutinized by mentors – i.e., "reflected upon" – in order to warrant a mentor's role and position as a "helping" agent.

It is precisely this appreciative inquiry into the role of conversations as a vehicle for learning, being skillfully used and placed in the hands of a 'good' mentor that lies at the heart of this volume. Moreover, a prime intention behind offering this collection of chapters is to enhance the learning potential of mentors. An observation might elucidate a concern we have:

> In evaluating student teachers' practice teaching period regarding their mentoring experiences we used the Rose Ideal Mentor scale (2003) to test appraisals with regard to: Guidance, Integrity, and Relationship in mentoring. The evaluations by students of their mentor were high (usually 4.5 of a 5 point scale). However, at a later moment, we conducted an evaluation regarding the students' appraisal of professional preparation they received through their mentoring conversations. The Kirkpatrick four levels of evaluation used were: satisfaction, learning, performance change, and sustained impact. The results of the last three evaluation levels were meager, to say it friendly. (with an average 2.5 on a 5 point scale and having a significant drop for sustained impact on professional life)

This observation meant to illustrate that although both mentors and mentees may find their conversation high in relatedness and autonomy (Decy & Ryan, 2008) the competence and insights gained from it may be less forthright. This raises a concern about the learning potential of mentoring conversations – the topic of this book.

The purpose of this book is to draw attention to the peculiar divergence or even possible divide between on the one hand the relational understanding and mutual agreed upon acceptance of support offered through conversational interaction and on the other hand the end result of professional competence development that may have fallen behind in outcomes and achievements. We feel that in positioning mentoring as a vehicle for learning mentors as guides and resource persons have a prime responsibility not only to be aware of this possible divide but also to use agency in bringing mentoring conversations up to the level of a genuine learning event.

To illustrate our position a bit further it can be referred to a comparative study by Smith, Tillema and Leshem (2011) in which mentors and students of teacher education from three different countries were asked to evaluate their communicative talks with regard to their attained learning outcomes. The main finding was that mentors believed they gave relevant feedback and guidance on professional preparation to students while students indicated a clear lack of support and absence of any strong structuring of their practice experiences.

To link process and outcome, i.e., conversation and learning, the concept of knowledge productivity will be introduced in the book. The concept of knowledge productivity (Tillema & Van der Westhuizen, 2006), as adapted from Peter Drucker's work (1999), is meant to convey the importance of building knowledge for professional action. Ultimately, learning needs to mount up to agency, at least as is the case for mentoring in the professions (Bereiter, 2002). The notion of Knowledge Productivity captures this process by identifying three elements to be present in conversations as criterions for learning: problem understanding: i.e., has insight occurred on part of the learner; perspective shift: i.e., has conversation added to change in beliefs and ideas (with regards to the content of conversation), and commitment to apply: i.e., is there a willingness to adopt advice for future action. These three criteria can act as building blocks for mentors to arrange their "learning conversations". "Mentoring for Learning", therefore, can be viewed as an agenda for highlighting both the pedagogical and accountability issue in mentoring; to ensure productivity of conversations that will surpass the basic needs for guidance, integrity and relatedness in conversations and aim for attainment of competence. The collection of chapters presented in this book provides a story line to express the promotion of enhancing knowledge productivity. Firstly by grounding the concept of knowledge building for professional preparation, and subsequently widening the arena to account for:

(1th part) Learning from mentoring conversations

(2nd part) Mentoring conversations – a two hearted affair in professional education

(3rd part) Mentor Professional development

The book is intended, in the first place, for mentors and all those involved in preparing apprentices for practice. The book draws heavily on the context of teacher preparation and teacher education although not exclusively confined to this particular context. Also, students involved in a mentoring process may find the collection of works supportive to enhance their learning experience. Additionally, the book may be of interest to teachers and instructors in conducting learning conversations (be it in the case of teaching or professional training and in-service education).

The storyline told has a strong research orientation. We feel that empirical grounding is needed on the positions taken in the subsequent chapters; it adds evidence to our argument.

THE CHAPTERS AT A GLANCE

Introductory Chapter

1. Knowledge building through conversations
   Harm Tillema, Gert J. van der Westhuizen, & Martijn P. van der Merwe

This introducing and grounding chapter for the book offers a review of different perspectives on professional knowledge development and develops a case for a distributed, i.e., shared and collaborative knowledge building in professional interactions. In this sense, mentoring conversations exemplify our position on "Mentoring for Learning" as a way to share and endorse learning in the professions (as we relate it in this book mainly to teaching). The review challenges three competing views about teacher knowledge building: i.e., the individual reflective view, the situated cognition view, and the distributed knowledge view, as different ways to bring about knowledge productivity in learning conversations/mentoring interactions. We defend and explore knowledge building in the professions as a deeply discursive and interactional activity and offer an outlook on possible conversational analytic principles that can be deployed in interactional settings for learning among professionals.

Part 1: Learning from Mentoring Conversations

2. Mentoring conversations and student teacher learning
   Harm Tillema & Gert J. van der Westhuizen

This study analyzes ways in which mentoring can enhance the quality of learning conversations in teacher education. The specific focus is on the conversational strategies used by lecturer mentors and the expected and actual impact they have on student teacher's learning. Using a case-design, 12 conversations between a student teacher and his/her mentor were analyzed in depth with regard to interactional moves by mentors to help students attain learning goals. The findings of this study suggest that: There is an overall positive effect of different conversational moves on student teacher's learning outcomes. However, we noted that almost 60% of conversational talk was non-learning goal related, but could more easily be interpreted as relational talk. Closeness in the relationship was found to positively influence student teacher's learning outcomes. No direct relation was found between specific mentor conversational moves and perceived knowledge productivity, although higher scores were found for a 'low road' approach, i.e., moves that explored and stay with the student's current learning experiences. The implication for the quality of professional (teacher) education are discussed.

3. Eliciting student teachers' practical knowledge through mentoring conversations in the practicum
Juanjo Mena Marcos & Anthony Clarke

Mentoring is being promoted as a key component in "learning to teach" because it gives student teachers an opportunity to learn for the profession under a practice teacher's guidance. Research on mentoring in teaching has largely focused on the process of mentoring (i.e., studying topics as active listening, satisfaction, reflection or classroom management) but little attention is given to the outcomes of mentoring as a tool for professional learning (i.e., building practical professional knowledge for action). This chapter calls for research attention to the content of learning conversations in mentoring (i.e., what kind of proficiency is to be acquired during conversation – labelled as *issue of substance*). The "substance" is being discussed during learning interactions (i.e., mentoring dialogues of a mentor with a learner) using a variety of methods, and leading to varied interpretations (*issue of perspective*). This chapter elucidates how these two criteria can afford mentors and students alike to focus on what is gained from conversations for professional agency.

4. Feedback in the mentoring of teacher learning
Siv M. Gamlem

Advice giving and feedback provision lie at the heart of mentoring, and when provided in the right manner it has high potential for learning. Advice and help is meant to give students 'tuned', i.e., adapted guidance respective to their needs and mastery level, and is meant to bridge the gap between current performance and goals to be achieved. Effective feedback provision in mentoring, therefore, is a) more than " telling" students what criteria there are to be met (goal orientation) or b) more than relating to a common ground and mutual agreed experiences (relatedness) but also to appraise (current) and display (future) performance. Mentors are in a position to give proposals for course of action to take to bridge performance and goals through feedback they give. The potential of feedback and advice becomes real when student accepts the feedback and is following recommendation. This chapter relates to the mechanisms involved in mentoring conversations that operate in taking advice. The primary purpose for this chapter lies in its focus on feedback and its impact on the mentee. The importance of feedback, how to give it and how it is perceived by the mentee will be addressed. How six teachers in lower secondary school taking part in an intervention study perceive external feedback as useful for developing higher levels of proficiency is analyzed.

5. Feedback provision in mentoring conversations
Bettina Korver & Harm Tillema

This chapter explores how diverging perceptions of mentors and mentees on the nature and content of feedback will have impact on learning from conversation. The study presented gauges whether different approaches to mentoring conversation promote congruency in perceptions on feedback. The focus of this research is to explore differences in mentor and student perceptions on the usefulness of feedback. For that purpose, this study compares typical mentor approaches to feedback provision across different settings. Feedback to students (Teaching assistants) in vocational education having a strong performance orientation is contrasted with a reflective oriented feedback to students in teacher education. Mentoring conversations on teaching internships of these students were analyzed. Approaches to mentors' conversation styles were identified with an observation instrument categorizing mentoring into four types. Teaching assistant students predominantly recognized their mentor's approach as having an Imperator (supervising) style, while the Teacher education students identified it predominantly as an Initiator (engaging) style. Teaching assistant students expressed a higher degree of acceptance of feedback, as compared with Teacher education students. Differences in perceptions between students and their mentors on feedback provision were found to be significant. Our findings point to the importance of mentoring approach as it impinges on the feedback acceptance in mentoring conversations.

Part 2: Mentoring Conversation – A Two Hearted Affair in Professional Education

   6. The role of knowledge in mentoring conversations for learning
     Gert J. van der Westhuizen

This chapter is about the institutional character of mentoring conversations where professors advise student teachers about their teaching practices. The purpose is to use analytic principles from Conversational Analysis Research to develop an understanding of the complexities of epistemological access, primacy and responsibility. Analytic principles were derived from studies on epistemics in interaction, on turn organization, on epistemic stance and authority, on sequencing and repair, on inter-subjectivity and shared knowledge, and on displays of understanding and knowledge in interaction.
The analysis zooms in on interaction sequences where assessments are made by mentors of access and depth of knowledge, and with recipients responding with extended accounts and explanations. Findings indicate that institutional norms seem to prioritise mentor access and inhibit stances of openness. Some evidence was found of questions which allow mentees their right to tell and explore their own depth of knowledge. These actions indicate how mentees assert themselves and claim authority of knowledge. Findings are discussed in terms of the management of knowledge congruence in mentoring conversations.

   7. The structural dimensions of mentoring conversations.
     Annatjie Pretorius & Gert J. van der Westhuizen

Although mentorship implies expertise, such expertise in teaching is not sufficient for being an effective teacher educator and thus does not guarantee effective mentoring. This chapter attempts to offer research based guidance for significant and meaningful mentoring conversations, since conversation is the vessel through which learning is mediated. The chapter clarifies the structural dimensions of mentoring conversations and how they relate to learning outcomes of student teachers.

The study presented analyzes samples of mentoring conversations and engages in three levels of analysis. On the primary level, the structure of the conversation is determined. A secondary level of analysis identifies conceptual artefacts, as outcomes of the learning conversation. A third level of analysis determines the quality of the learning by using two instruments which supplement each other. Firstly, the construction of retrospective concept maps which makes the complexity of conceptions explicit in graphical format. Secondly an index of significance of conceptual artefacts (ISCA) has been developed to further reveal the significance and meaningfulness of the student teacher's learning as a result of the mentoring conversation.

8. The learning potential of mentoring conversations
   Guido van Esch & Harm Tillema

Mentoring is an important vehicle to make 'practical knowledge explicit'. It can be maintained that mentoring conversations need to be a) supportive in 'pushing' mentees forward in maintaining (goal) direction; b) while at the same time promote learners to reflect on past performance; as well c) scaffold the necessary steps to explore or gain insights in their recent learning accomplishments. The study presented explores different patterns in conversations viewed from the perspective of student learning, asking to what extent patterned speech acts in mentoring conversations do influence the regulation of (professional) learning.

In an explorative, mixed method study mentoring conversations were video analyzed to identify episodes in conversations. Patterns were distinguished with regard to goal orientation, reflection and scaffolding of action. The conversation analysis data were linked to questionnaire data on professional learning beliefs and ideal mentor beliefs of students as well as criterion variables: student learning outcomes, and student satisfaction with mentoring conversation. The findings indicate a high variety of patterns in mentoring conversations. A predominant preference was found for a reflection oriented pattern of mentoring on part of the mentors which however was not positively related to student satisfaction or student learning outcome. For this to happen mentees preferred a pattern of talk directed towards scaffolding of action while also giving attention to goal attainment.

9. Space making in mentoring conversations
   Annatjie Pretorius

This chapter explores a particular conversational strategy which is used to reach a balance in the status-solidarity dialectic in a learning conversation where there is a significant difference between the knowledge and experience of the two participants.

This balance is facilitated through the use of utterances which display ostensible uncertainty. This strategy creates hospitable mental space in the conversation in which no fixed answers are expected or supposed. A mentoring conversation between a veteran in education and a pre-service student teacher is used as a case study.

10. Invitational conversations – a means to an end in mentoring
   Martijn P. van der Merwe & Gert J. van der Westhuizen

In managing interactions in learning situations, it is important that mentors value people, knowledge and democratic relationships (Novak, 2010). According to Novak a critical condition for learning is that one should be invited and incited to realize one's untapped potential, and to engage meaningfully and unafraid in democratic practices. Mentoring interactions are therefore in essence dialogic and underpinned by the deepest belief and value systems of the participants. Invitational education is grounded in self-concept and perceptual theory. The focus on developing positive views of self, have been extensively researched by way of the Florida Key instrument. This instrument focuses on four areas of interaction, namely: relating, asserting, investing and coping to support professional development. This chapter investigates how mentoring conversation between mentors and mentees invite professional development within these four areas.

Part 3: Mentor Professional Development

11. Understanding teachers as learners: Considering teachers' possibilities for change when designing mentoring.
   Emilio Sánchez & J. Ricardo García

A critical step in mentoring consists of collaboratively developing a shared goal orientation in conversation. However, in ensuring that goals are accessible and agreed, mentors need to take into account what teachers *usually do* before conceiving a potential goal. To explore these issues, a mentoring process on changing teachers' reading comprehension activities is analyzed. Fine-grained analysis of 34 whole-group reading lessons is offered based on four components: a) how lessons were organized, b) how teachers introduced lessons, c) how classroom interactions unfolded throughout a lesson, and d) what kinds of scaffolding were provided by mentors. Each component could be arranged from simple to complex, offering possible trajectories for professional development. This chapter highlights the importance of understanding possible trajectories in a mentoring process to bring about change in teachers' current practices, and, subsequently, to create accessible goals in mentoring in order to move current patterns to more complex ones. Our findings show different patterns of change by teachers, and indicate the challenges involved, both in professional development and in the mentoring processes.

12. Self-regulated learning and professional development: How to help teachers encourage students to use a self-regulated goal-setting process
Elena Ciga, Emma García, Mercedes I. Rueda, Harm Tillema and Emilio Sánchez

Self-regulated learning (SRL) has been advocated as a means of acquiring competence in an active inquisitive and self-determined way. However, the process that allows mentors to promote self-regulated learning in their learners is less known. Available models on SRL hardly specify (student) teachers' needs and activities when they are asked to teach according to SRL principles. This chapter attempts to understand what difficulties arise when promoting self-regulated learning in student teachers as learners as an outcome of a mentoring process. A fine-grained analysis of 32 sessions is presented from 10 mentoring processes to identify the generalizations and distortions learners make with regard to SRL teaching after being mentored on SRL. The mentoring process was aimed at learning how to help pupils in an SRL manner, i.e., (1) gaining awareness of performance; (2) finding gaps between performance and desirable standards, (3) generating goals to reduce these gaps. Subsequently, a structured mentoring intervention was designed in which student teachers were informed about the most common distortions and simplifications, and encouraged to adopt an active teaching strategy in overcoming them. Findings of the study show how important is to understand the (student) teacher learning needs in a mentoring process.

13. Mentoring – a profession within a profession
Kari Smith

The education of professionals is recently seen in a career wide perspective, consisting of three stages, initial, induction, and in-service education. In all three stages, mentoring activities are given a central role. During preparation for the profession, initial education, mentors have the responsibility of introducing the practice field to professionals-to-be. During induction, mentors become supporters and guides for the novice, whereas in the phase of in-service education, formal mentoring by appointed mentors and informal collegial mentoring within communities of practice are found to promote professional learning. In most cases mentors are chosen based on their reputation of being experienced and successful professionals, or, they are practitioners towards the end of their professional career whose work load is reduced, and mentoring is seen as a suitable activity towards the end of a long career.

The question raised in this article is if all experienced professionals can be mentors or is mentoring a different experience than practicing the profession? The claim made in this chapter is that mentoring is not the same as professional practice, it is a profession within the profession in which mentoring takes place. To illustrate and explain this view, the argument is situated within the professional education of teachers.

14. Emerging understanding of mentor's knowledge base
    Kari Smith & Marit Ulvik

The concept of Pedagogical Content Knowledge (PCK) is most commonly used in the discussion of teachers' professional knowledge. In this chapter we will expand the PCK concept in our discussion of mentors' pedagogical content knowledge. In the previous chapter, *Mentoring – A Profession within a Profession,* a claim was made that teaching children and mentoring adults are different professional practices. As we see it, in order to practice quality mentoring professional education is needed, during which mentors-to-be are introduced to the PCK of the mentoring profession. However, till today, the literature does not discuss the PCK of mentors, most of the literature relates to the role of the mentor and the activities mentors perform without extending the discussion to the knowledge and skills required to practice quality mentoring.

An attempt to develop a construct of mentors' PCK has emerged from several studies conducted in a mentor education programme at the University of Bergen, Norway. The current article presents the mentor education programme, the context, within which the model has been developed, and a suggested construct of mentors' PCK.

15. Does mentor education make a difference?
    Ingrid Helleve, A. G. Danielsen & Kari Smith

This chapter presents a study which seeks to understand the conditions under which mentors work in schools. We examine if there is a discrepancy in how mentors with and without mentor education perceive and practice their role. The findings indicate that most mentors have no mentor education and that, to a large extent, mentoring comes on top of the mentors' full job as teachers. Mentors with mentor education tend to perceive and practice their role as colleagues who are supposed to challenge the NQTs to critical reflection, while mentors without mentor education are more concerned with support and adaptation to the teaching context. All the mentors, with or without mentor education, claim that they enjoy mentoring, mainly because they take pleasure in seeing a colleague's job-confidence increase and because they, themselves, are stimulated to self-reflection .

REVIEW

16. So, how high has the mountain been climbed?
    Maureen Robinson (University of Stellenbosch)

This chapter provided a critical appraisal of the work presented in this book and an evaluation is given on the notion of mentoring as "climbing a mountain". Professor Robinson points out the problematic relation that may exist between conversation (and conversational analysis) and learning; particularly when considering the dynamics between support and challenge. As such the appraisal offers important perspectives for further consideration.

17. It is not just the talk... A rejoinder by the editors of the book.

In response to the comments made some thoughts were explored as to the future directions in mentoring for learning. Especially the need for substantiation (tools) and professionalization (education) are considered paramount in bringing mentoring conversation up to learning events.

REFERENCES

Bereiter, C. (2002). *Education and mind in the knowledge society.* Mahwah: Lawrence Erlbaum Associates.
Cox, E., Bachkirova, T., & Clutterbuck, D. (2010). *The complete handbook of coaching.* London: Sage.
Deci, E. L., & Ryan, R. M. (2008). Self-determination theory: A macrotheory of human motivation, development, and health. *Canadian Psychology, 49,* 182–185.
Drucker, P. F. (1993). *Post capitalist society.* New York, NY: HarperCollins.
Rose, G. L. (2003). Enhancement of mentor selection using the ideal mentor scale. *Research in Higher Education, 44*(4), 34–45.
Smith, K., Tillema, H., & Leshem, S. (2011). Dual roles – conflicting purposes: A comparative study on perceptions on assessment in mentoring relations during practicum. *European Journal of Teacher Education, 34*(2), 139–159.
Tillema, H. H., & van der Westhuizen, G. (2006). Knowledge construction in collaborative enquiry among teachers. *Teachers & Teaching, 12*(1), 51–67.
Zimmerman, B. J. (1990). Self-regulated learning and academic achievement. *American Educational Research Journal, 25,* 3–17.

Harm Tillema
Leiden University

Gert J. van der Westhuizen
University of Johannesburg

Kari Smith
University of Bergen

HARM TILLEMA, GERT J. VAN DER WESTHUIZEN AND
MARTIJN P. VAN DER MERWE

1. KNOWLEDGE BUILDING THROUGH CONVERSATION

Mentoring is about meaning making …

> … we shall be able to interpret meanings and meaning-making in a principled
> manner only in the degree to which we are able to specify the structure and
> coherence of the larger context in which specific meanings are created and
> transmitted. (Bruner, 1973)

> Three questions may guide our efforts to discover how people come to grasp
> conceptual distinctions

> A: How do people achieve the information necessary for isolating and learning
>   a concept?
> B: How do they retain the information gained from encounters with possibly
>   relevant events so that they may be useful later?
> C: How is retained information transformed so that it may be rendered useful
>   for testing a hypothesis still unborn at the moment of first encountering new
>   information. (Bruner: *Beyond the information given*, 1973:132)

Mentoring is an aid to go "beyond the information given" and to gain "knowledge".
Mentors, therefore, must have a conception of knowledge. This chapter explores
prevalent conceptions of professional knowledge to appraise their relevance for
mentoring. The chapter also lays the foundation for the rest of the book, given the
centrality of knowledge in mentoring.

KNOWLEDGE AND KNOWING

The process of learning to become a professional unfolds typically as immersion
into the shared knowledge among professionals, intensified by deploying agency
in the personal adaptation and renewal of that knowledge in professional practice
(Edwards, 2013). Knowledge therefore is the key to entry and retention in the
profession. And mentoring is a way to gain access to and provide maintenance of
that knowledge during professional practice. How then, is knowledge building for
the profession looked upon, and learning for the profession manifested by means
of mentoring? This chapter previews different conceptualisations of professional

H. Tillema et al. (Eds.), Mentoring for Learning, 1–19.

knowledge and develops a case for looking at knowledge through the lens of professional conversation. Knowledge building is regarded as a discursive activity enacted in interaction between people, aiming for the construction of professional knowledge. Mentoring, then, is supposed to provide the opportunities for knowledge building to flourish.

Professional Knowledge: A Reconsideration

Differing views on the nature of professional knowledge have led to diverse interpretations on how professionals act in, and learn from their practice (Edwards, 2013; Stoll & Louis, 2007; Loughran, 2004). However, most of these views on knowledge fall short, as will be argued, in the recognition of the *distributed* and *embedded* nature of professional knowledge (Eraut, 1997). In our view, being a professional is to use knowledge to produce solutions *for* action, and to continuously build (i.e., renew and improve) knowledge *in* practice. This duality (i.e., "for" and "in" practice) governs the way knowledge is viewed and enacted upon by professionals. In certain views, however, knowledge and action are seen as distinct or disconnected entities, (i.e., in teaching, as described by Day, 1999) and, consequently, the building of expertise is being divided into different acquisition paths, i.e., as it happens in teacher education (Bromme & Boshuizen, 2003). These views typically foster an education or training for the profession recognized by a division between simulation (i.e., training, theory be'for'e practice), and participation (i.e, enactment later on "in" professional practice) (Grossmann, 2009; Tillema & Orland-Barak, 2006).

Although several important educational thinkers have stressed the importance of merging '*talk and walk*', i.e., knowledge and action, for instance through advancing notions like: "wisdom of practice" (Shulman, 1987), "thoughtful teaching" (Clark, 1995), "reflection in action" (Schon, 1983) and 'situational understanding' (Bereiter, 2002), these viewpoints have nevertheless not conclusively resulted in a coherent and widely accepted understanding on how professionals become knowledgeable or develop their knowledge progressively. This inconclusiveness is especially worrying in the case of mentoring which is meant to be a space of professional learning and development. We contend therefore that in mentoring it is important for a mentor to take position on the nature of professional knowledge and to have a view on how it will be acquired in order to warrant one's role as a mentor. It is also important for a mentor to take responsibility for the way in which the mentoring process is (conceptually) organized. We adopt here a view regarding mentored learning based on the understanding that knowledge in professional action is discursive, i.e., communicative in nature (Edwards & Potter, 1992, 2012; Lehrer, 2002). From this viewpoint we highlight the shortcomings of currently prevailing cognitivist/mental models of knowledge. A discursive or "distributed knowledge" position (Clark, 2004; Edwards, 2013; Bereiter, 2004) on knowledge building argues that knowledge in the profession is displayed and modified in interactional terms and responsive to the conversational setting in which it is being used (Heritage,

2008). *Knowing* instead of knowledge (Bruner, 1973) may thus be a more adequate label to capture the nature of expertise a professional holds. Knowing unfolds by way of a *progressive discourse* among professionals and is characterized by *informed participation* (as knowledgeable action in practice situations). Both features presuppose a collaborative building of knowledge in action (Bereiter, 2002; Lipponen, 2000; Sfard, 1998). This notion of discursive practice that coincides with 'knowing' (Edwards, 1997; Wiggins & Potter, 2008; Edwards & Potter, 2012) has vivid implications for mentored learning. The view may be best explicated by three axioms:

- Professional learning (or better called, knowledge building in practice) must be regarded as a collaborative enterprise in learning partnerships (Stoll & Louis, 2007) in which conversation acts as vehicle for learning (Tillema & Orland-Barak, 2006);
- Professional perspectives and personal theories (i.e., "meanings") of individual professionals come into play in such a joint process of building knowledge, and act to embed the shared knowledge (Pajares, 1992), and
- To critically renew knowledge and knowing, professionals need practice- and solution-oriented ways of (mentored) learning which favor a progressive discourse and informed participation through conversation about practices.

(These three axioms represent our response to the three questions Bruner raises – see Introduction to this chapter.)

To further explicate our position, we would like to evaluate the prospects of competing prevailing views on the nature of knowledge and their implications for professional practice, followed by a more explicit account of our argument, that is: professional knowledge building happens in and through conversations.

THE NATURE OF PROFESSIONAL KNOWLEDGE

A View on Professional Knowledge as Individual(ly owned) Knowledge

To date, professional knowledge has been studied for the most part through the paradigm of the individual reflective practitioner (Schon, 1983). This position claims the professional to be a resource who 'possesses' personal, implicit knowledge which needs (and can!) be made explicit or less tacit through reflection. Individual reflection, then, is the main vehicle to express and build knowledge which can subsequently be distributed as 'objects of knowledge' through exchange and dialogue (or even training – i.e. Korthagen, 2002). Having this 'objectified' knowledge is a hallmark of being acknowledged as a professional (Loughran, 2004; Eraut, 1997).

This position on professional knowledge (and knowledge building by way of reflection) raises a number of concerns. For instance, although substantial research on reflection has been conducted over time, it is repeatedly being found that professionals hardly reflect, are even reluctant to do so; and training to reflect does not seem to assist in developing professional knowledge (Mena Marcos Sanchez & Tillema, 2009, 2010). Studies that advocate reflection as a vehicle of learning are mostly restricted to retrospective accounts of individual professionals who rationalize their past experiences 'on action'. These accounts constitute, as Kane, Sandretto and Heath (2002) argue, only 'half of the story'. The other, 'dark side' (Orland Barak & Tillema, 2006), however, could disclose that professionals are embedded in real practice settings, and that is where they communicate and work together with their colleagues to construe situational understandings (Bereiter, 2004) of their practice and build these into professional "knowing". Studies on reflection 'in concert', i.e., collaborative reflection in and on real settings (Engestrom, 2001) are rare and would be able to constitute an 'untold story' (Mena Marcos, Gonzalez, & Tillema, 2011).

This individualistic reflective perspective forwards the notion that professional knowledge is classifiable and 'object'ified; that is, knowledge which can be explicated, generalized and transferred. In essence, this view claims that professional knowledge is capable of being transmitted and 'transferred' among professionals through telling, explaining and externalization (Simons & Ruyters, 2004). From a discursive or distributed perspective, the limitations of such a cognitivist view of knowledge have been criticized, mainly for not accounting for the collaborative and participative nature of professional life (Edwards, 2011; Van der Westhuizen, 2012).

A View of Professional Knowledge as Collaborative Practice

The view expressed in the reflective perspective, contrasts with the view which identifies knowledge as situational understanding (Bereiter, 2002), i.e., linked to the immediate activities a professional is engaged in (Gilroy, 1993; Edwards, 2011). Such a view accentuates knowledge building from direct practice activity by means of exploration, meaning seeking in context, and most of all, specifies a (re)searching stance to understand activity. Such a view regards knowledge as largely embedded within the situational constraints in which professionals act and from which they learn by informed participation. Through informed participation, a progressive discourse between colleagues becomes possible (Palonen, 2004; Tillema & Van der Westhuizen, 2006). In this way, knowledge is distributed, will acquire its meaning and becomes truly *knowing*. This position proposes that professional learning is collaborative, i.e., shared among professionals who work together. In this sense, the literature often refers to (since learning is occurring in) communities of practice (Wenger, McDermott, & Östman, 2002). The distributed view on knowledge, in opposition to the reflective perspective, highlights an understanding of knowledge as being embedded in practice and involving agency (Tillema & Van der Westhuizen, 2006; Edwards, 2013).

However, within this distributed viewpoint on professional knowledge an important distinction has to be made between two quite different interpretations regarding the nature of learning, having to do with how knowledge is acquired or 'learned', and how communities of practice really operate. One way of viewing is that knowledge is acquired through distributed practice characterized by shared activities, along common goals, and supported by, that is embedded in, situational affordances (Lave & Wenger, 1996). This "situationist" perspective can be contrasted to a viewpoint which stresses a more deliberate and informed practice which perhaps is better labeled as "Communities of Inquiry (Baxton, 2004; Bereiter, 2004; Birenbaum, 2006). This interpretation of collaborative learning does not just look upon participants in knowledge building as "context-embedded" agents who look back on and learn from their work routines as (patterned) social behavior, but sees them act as researchers or designers of their professional environment who will build understandings of their situation to renew their practices (Huberman, 1995; Farr Darling, 2001).

The collaborative viewpoint(s) on professional 'knowledge building' (a labeling that exceeds the notion of 'learning' – see Bereiter, 2004) is in opposition to an individualistic picture of knowledge construction as reflective thinking, and stresses the complexities and embedded-ness of knowing one's practice. But at the same time the two viewpoints differ with regard to the inquisitive and deliberate nature of learning entrusted to professionals, which clearly has implications for the nature of mentoring. An illustration with regard to mentoring conversations might show how different these implications are with regard to how each of these perspectives interprets learning, for example, when a mentor asks a mentee to look back on past performance. In a reflective paradigm, verbalizations as a result of reflection most often (Mena Marcos, 2006) resemble a kind of 'rationalizations', as participants in a mentoring conversation adhere to and refer back to prior beliefs and general impressions, with little or no mentioning of knowledge that actually occurred or was present at the time of action. As a result, mentor and mentee, while staying in their 'comfort zone 'may only verbalize knowledge in terms of their own prior conceptions, i.e., "talking the talk" (Tillema & van der Westhuizen, 2006; Mena Marcos & Tillema, 2007). But when mentoring is considered as a collaborative activity, the participants most often have shared experiences as professionals about their own practice, and (afterwards in conversation) take part in a mutual activity to study and scrutinize their practice. Positioning such a joint inquisitive enterprise as a mentoring process would follow most often the specific patterns of research activity, i.e, "talking the walk", that could specifically articulate and scrutinize current performance against goals or standards set by participants in conversation (Mena Marcos et al., 2009, 2010).

To explicate our position in a more refined way, a comparison is made between the mentioned perspectives on knowledge building in terms of a specific set of criteria which include the nature of professional knowledge, the prospects of developing such knowledge, and the conceptual concerns attached to adhering to each of these views. For clarity reasons we also added another viewpoint, the Transmission View of Knowledge (which was previously dominant but still to be found in professional training, and now heavily criticized conceptually in the literature – Cochran-Smith & Zeichner, 2005 – as an essentialist view – see Table 1). The more recent discussions on professional knowledge favour a transformative, constructivist stance on learning (see Hakkarainen, Paavola & Lipponen, 2004; Fenstermacher, 1994). Table 1 summarizes the prevailing views about professional knowledge building:

Table 1. Perspectives on professional knowledge building

Nature of knowledge	Knowledge development	Critical issues
Transmission view Knowledge is objective and explicit, 'out there' – not constructed but real Knowledge can be made overt as content packages; to be codified in a knowledge base	transmission, and transfer by telling, in-service training, teaching by talking	Is there a fixed body of knowledge, is it value and context neutral; and cross culturally generalizable? How is knowledge transfer accomplished, or even possible between different settings and professionals?
A) Reflective knowledge Knowledge is tacit, hidden and not easily articulated therefore it needs explication either (be)for(e) or after action (not "in" action) Knowledge is personal and individual and 'owned'	Reflective activity on action either (be)for(e) or after action Going from implicit to explicit and vice versa Knowledge externalization is a key to learning	How can knowledge be reflected upon when it is hidden or tacit? And personal? Can knowledge be dependent on the quality of reflection? How can knowledge be reflected upon, and by what method How can explicit or articulated knowledge be used in action or stay connected to implicit direct, immediate action?
B) Contextual knowledge or situated cognition Knowledge is embedded in practice, i.e., situated and social; it is being part of a community of practice. It is shared and therefore valid (only) among colleagues	Sharing of collective understanding, Convergence of implicit and explicit meanings among stakeholders. "Peripheral approximation and socialisation" (Lave), Critical illumination	How can knowledge that is shared become externally validated and accepted beyond the individual and situational realm i.e., beyond being local, relative, and subjective?
C) Distributed Knowledge Knowledge is distributed or enacted through activity, i.e. not in the mind but rests in situational understandings and is embodied in tools of professional practice	Building knowledge through progressive discourse and informed participation Creating conceptual artefacts or tools for practice	Knowledge is embedded in tools and activity ("by doing"); but who possesses knowledge, who knows what? How 'knowledge productive' are conceptual tools i.e., different from routines

(Adapted and modified from Tillema & Orland-Barak, 2006).

In order to appraise the above perspectives on professional knowledge building for mentored learning, and to advance an understanding of the limitations of these views in the practice of mentoring, we have constructed a framework for analyzing the prospects and possibilities of each of these perspectives for professional knowledge building in mentoring. For this purpose we use three criteria to evaluate the respective viewpoints, keeping in mind the overall purpose of mentored learning, that is "climbing the mountain", or guiding and scaffolding the learner/mentee to become more proficient in his or her professional practice. The three criteria are specifications of the concept of Knowledge Productivity (Tillema & van der Westhuizen, 2006) which refers to an outcome measure of professional learning. By Knowledge Productivity we mean (Tillema, 2004): the competence of a professional to generate, adapt and renew professional tools ('solutions') for practice; which rests on the following abilities:

- 'Problem understanding' – The ability to attain and appraise relevant knowledge relative to the issue at hand.

As a criterion for evaluation, the question to ask would be: Does a viewpoint on professional knowledge explicate how an increase in knowledge of professionals is achieved? Concretely: Does the learner acknowledge that the issues spoken about during mentoring are relevant and adding to their insights?

- 'Perspective shift' – The ability to evaluate and scrutinize different points of view relative to the problem at hand.

As a criterion for evaluation, the questions would be: Does a viewpoint on professional knowledge clarify how perspectives and beliefs are modified and altered, so as to make a closer alignment with new ideas and knowledge possible? Concretely: Does the learner find the ideas, brought forward, acceptable and trustworthy?

- 'Commitment to apply' – The ability to utilize and commoditize understandings for professional practice.

As a criterion for evaluation, the question here is: Does a viewpoint on professional knowledge instigate involvement and adoption for a renewal of the learner's practice? Concretely: Is the learner interested in actively following up recommendations?

These questions are congruent with the three questions put at the start of this chapter.

Using these three knowledge productivity criteria a characterization can be given of each views on knowledge building and in this manner appraise their "knowledge productive" position in relation to mentoring.

A. Reflective knowledge. The Reflective Practitioner perspective emphasizes building of *reflective knowledge,* and in this view it is noted that prevailing knowledge can be viewed as objects of articulation to be subjected to externalization

(Nonaka & Takeuchi, 1994). According to this view, explicit articulation of knowledge is needed, since this will initiate active study (i.e., reflection) on action and will support a personal process of deliberate thought. Articulation or explication (Ruyters & Simons, 2004) triggers the unfolding of what otherwise remains implicit. Tacit knowledge then can be cognitively reinterpreted and framed into a professional more objectified language. In this way, reflections are, in essence, reconceptualizations of action (Kane & Sandretto, 2003), and as such contributed to problem understanding, preferably nurtured by 'theory' (Loughran, 2004; Day 1999; Korthagen, 2003). A sharing of ideas among professionals, for instance, in a discussion with colleagues would be in itself not necessarily fruitful and can even be a cumbersome matter, since it easily leads to misunderstandings, and suffers from a likely incommensurability of perspectives and beliefs that the different collaborators hold. In mentoring, however, it is important that shared beliefs in a dialogue lay the foundation for a fruitful talk on learning about practices.

Applying, then, the three criteria on knowledge productivity to the reflective knowledge perspective, we conjecture that in terms of '*problem understanding*', one would expect positive outcomes in mentoring because of the opportunities for deliberate articulation of expressed thoughts. Reflection can act contributive to an increase of individual knowledge. This is the kind of benefit often advocated in the reflective paradigm (Korthagen, 2002). In terms of '*perspective shift*', however, it is highly questionable to what extent a reflective practice in mentoring brings about shifts in personal views; may be a gradual modification is more often the case (Mena Marcos, 2007). We would argue that only in cases of a close alignment of 'talk and walk', the existent knowledge might 'change'. Moreover, no major shift in thinking, or for that matter in practice, is likely to occur in case of a mismatch between reflection and action. In effect, this would imply a conservative impact of reflection on knowledge development (Gilroy, 1993). In terms of '*commitment*' or willingness to change one's practice as a result of reflection, we could argue that sharing of thoughts, for instance during mentoring conversations, could potentially be beneficial under a reflective paradigm; yet this would largely depend on the fruitful input by those participating in a sharing of reflections on practice.

B. Contextual knowledge. The "situationist" view interprets professional knowledge as anchored and situated in *communities of practice*. Knowledge, according to this view, is embedded in activity which is inherently social (or socially construed). A deliberate exchange of knowledge between professionals through transfer of information would be external or alien to deep-rooted activity structures and in itself not particular fruitful when separated or disconnected from the activity itself (it would be knowing *that*, instead of knowing *how*). According to the situated view, the more knowledge becomes detached from a setting from which it originates or in which activity is embedded, the less would be gained from it. Reflective articulation and exchange of knowledge 'as such' would be unfit for action and not particularly informative for practice. Explicit knowledge would be classified as 'codified" "theoretical" knowledge which cannot be directly operated upon. Situating and enacting knowledge could indeed build an environment for interpreting events and give meaning to situations encountered, and would thus be rated in more favorable terms.

In applying the knowledge productivity criteria to this situated viewpoint, we could argue that *problem understanding* as a focus in mentoring would be less urgent or immediate and perhaps even unfavorably rated since most opportunities for learning in action remain implicit and dependent on affordances and space to attend to them. Situated learning thrives on setting-attached (i.e., directly work-related) processes of professional learning. Although "off work" discussion and exchange among professionals, for instance in a mentoring conversation, could prove to be helpful; it still entails the danger of being 'talk' instead of 'walk'. In terms of *perspective shift*, real and lasting change in thinking (and action) would occur when mentor and mentee are working closely together on a regular basis, preferably sharing the same setting/practice since it provides a common ground for talk and would trigger conversation about jointly encountered problems (Engestrom, 2003). In terms of *commitment*, we would argue that working closely together under similar work-based conditions would lead to high involvement and raise interest in the outcomes of a conversation. In this respect, mentoring conversations can provide an authentic platform for raising the level of 'situatedness' and create an awareness for learning.

C. Distributed knowledge. The distributed knowledge view focuses on professional knowledge as being acquired through *progressive discourse and informed participation*. Characteristic is the importance attached to scrutinizing one's practice for the sake of creating tools for (an improved) practice. Collaborative inquiry would be a valid route to generate, adapt and renew 'knowing' under the condition that there is a sufficiently grounded professional language or knowledge base available to help participants frame their thoughts and identify key issues for discourse and conversation. Aim of conversation and sharing is to build artifacts for improved agency which ultimately can be used for practical action. Articulation and inquiry are sources of knowledge building. The resulting success would vary depending upon the conceptual frames or constructs delivered throughout the exchange. Conversation, then, provides a crucial condition for discovering and exploring situational understandings that emerge from and prevail in the group. Conversation would primarily focus on seeking tangible solutions, and on finding a common shared core of interpretative concepts to understand or inform one's practice.

In terms of the three knowledge productivity criteria, it can be maintained that *problem understanding* is facilitated through inquisitive collaboration and by working together. Mentoring would constitute an ideal setting to do so. Its conversational approach could enhance the creation of artifacts, i.e., solutions for practice. Conversation would, in addition, add to the attainment of new insights and create understanding of situations and problems encountered in practice. *Perspective shift* would in this view be the primary target of a mentoring process. Mentors would, for example, select cases or instances which offer a clear or explicit structural problem or offer a framework to evaluate encountered problems, all meant as a source of mutual learning during the discourse. In the case of *commitment*, the distributed view would stress a real investment in mentoring in scrutinizing one's practice and establish a critical involvement in solution oriented group discussions. In this sense mentoring conversations are the main vehicle for learning.

We then could summarize the way mentoring conversations are likely to contribute to the enhancement of professional knowledge in the following way (Table 2). In addition to the three outcome criteria of knowledge productivity we also gauge: adhering to prior knowledge and importance attached to interaction, as of interest to a mentoring conversation. It shows that the three views on professional knowledge differ in the way they would arrange mentoring conversations and value in distinct ways the interactional and implicit nature of professional knowledge.

Table 2. Appraisal of mentoring conversations based of different views on professional knowledge building

	Resulting evaluation on the three knowledge productivity criteria	Prior knowledge base of individual learner	Process of exchange and communication
A) Reflective knowledge	Problem Understanding (PU) = positive Perspective Shift (PS) = negative Commitment to apply (CA) =negative	• helpful in looking back, making explicit what occurred • articulation of what was considered • valuable for clarification	• not particular useful, occurrence of misunderstanding, interpretation problems, negotiations
B) Situated, cognition	PU = negative PS = negative CA = positive	• not helpful as it is disengaged, too far away from actual practice • knowledge difficult to articulate; misunderstandings • not particularly essential for practice	• important to clarify thoughts, needed for working towards a common understanding
C) Distributed knowledge	PU = positive PS = positive CA = positive	• only relevant for creating mutuality in personal understandings • focus on core ideas	• only when agreement on shared concepts, based on informed participation

Key: PU = problem understanding; PS = perspective shift; CA = commitment to apply

The abovementioned table distinguishes clearly the differing views on the nature of professional knowledge building and how it affects learning through conversations. Therefore, we like to explore in more detail what prospects a collaborative, inquiry oriented, and participative mode of learning, i.e., our position on distributed knowledge, has for mentoring as offering learning conversations.

KNOWLEDGE BUILDING IN COMMUNITIES OF INQUIRY

How professionals learn from each other through professional interactions can be understood by studying learning in communities of inquiry (Lipponen, 2000; Stoll & Louis, 2007; Birenbaum, Kimron, Shilton, & Sharaf-Barzilay, 2009). These studies on collaborative learning examine how conversations as vehicles of exchange, particularly those in which study and deliberate (re)search are used, scaffold a process of gaining insights from the challenges of practice (Palonen, 2004). Participants in such communities – and we like to see mentoring as such a community – typically engage one another with deliberate notions about improving practice and have thoughtful solutions in mind when they address challenges in their practice, all for the sake of developing and implementing tools and artifacts that can help to improve performance (Bereiter, 2002; Tillema & Van der Westhuizen, 2006). Evident from different approaches to collaborative learning (Stoll & Louis, 2007) is that the arrangement of conversations is crucial to lead to fruitful, tangible and prospective solutions, i.e. becoming knowledge productive (Lipponen, 2000).

The way, then, conversations are arranged establishes how participants will be brought to scrutinize and articulate their practice. Functioning as a community of inquiry, participants will develop among themselves multiple connections (Edwards, 2013). As conversations evolve, the 'community' members (e.g. in mentoring conversations the two members involved) adopt each other's solutions to practices that become 'distributed', i.e., that reflect their joint personal connections. As a result, conversation in such communities mounts up to knowledge building from multiple perspectives. For this we coined the metaphor "Climbing the Mountain" (see Chapter 2).

We contend that this kind of professional knowledge building, i.e., mentoring as a community of inquiry, is particularly beneficial for the improvement of professional action; in that participants exhibit a strong drive to generate, modify and apply knowledge in practice, and to learn from each other (Tillema & Orland Barak, 2006). "Mentoring for learning", as this may be called, is characterized by interactions in communities of inquiry that provide a physical or virtual space for scrutinizing practices (Stoll & Louis, 2007). Such mentoring also allows for exploring joint goals, providing availability for help and advice; creating encounters that bring about occasions for applying skills, designing solutions (tools for practice), making decisions, using creativity, and for developing collegial interactions in the larger professional community (Stoll & Louis, 2007; Birenbaum et al., 2009).

We could summarize, then, our position as follows:

Professional knowledge building is initiated and sustained through on-going, progressive discourse, developed by informed participation, and leading to knowledge productivity. We consider conversation to be the main vehicle for knowledge building in that it encourages professionals as learners (and mentors) to make their knowledge productive.

This position stresses the notion of 'articulate' knowledge, i.e., one of search and inquiry on knowledge 'in use', while at the same time attributing importance to the discourse on knowledge that is expressed through interactions and conversations with others. Specifically, emphasizing the role of conversation in knowledge building illuminates a number of critical elements that may open further thinking towards reconsidering some of the premises on mentoring for learning. We can ask, for example: 'How does conversation generate productive knowledge?', 'Why is articulation of concepts and beliefs hard to specify and lead to change in professional work?' 'How does talk, i.e., advice, lead to following recommendations'? And also address issues in mentoring like: 'How does conversation put knowledge into action?' or 'match beliefs to practice?'.

To concentrate further on the critical role of conversation in knowledge building, we borrow the notion of *situational understanding* (Bereiter, 2002) to capture what professionals encounter during a process of mentoring for learning. In this notion, knowledge building in conversation is not interpreted as moving packages of objectified knowledge (i.e., transfer of explicit knowledge), but rather as an active search for and (de)construction of valuable meanings through inquiry and progressive discourse between colleagues based on experiences drawn from practice contexts. The notion of situational understanding helps to interpret more explicitly how professionals come to (re)value their work-related experiences (Wang & Odell, 2002). In contrast to the notion of situated cognition (see Table 1), *situational understanding* adds the idea of a *progressive inquiry of performance in situ*. This view aligns with Shulman's notion of 'wisdom of practice' (Shulman, 1987), as 'contextual understanding': from which we conclude that professionals 'know' in an embedded and distributed sense. Based on this conceptualization, we look in more depth at the discursive nature of mentoring conversations.

APPROACHING MENTORING AS CONVERSATION

An appropriate entry point for exploring the discursive nature of conversations lies in the tradition of conversation analysis research. This tradition draws on social interaction theory (Goffman, 1974; Rawls, 1984) and contends that meanings are created through what Goffman (1969a) calls "interactional performance". Meaning making, as for instance is the case in mentoring, is shaped by social and cultural resources in which professionals operate (see also Drew & Heritage, 1992). Such meaning making in interactions is dialogic in nature, i.e., negotiating meaning in interaction. Participation in dialogue signifies the importance of a collective search for meaning. From this position we can pursue how professional knowledge building is developed in interactions with a mentor. This position states that conversation is the vehicle for knowledge building as well as the framework thereof. A closer conversation analysis look can reveal how meaning making and situational understanding unfold.

It is becoming clear from studies on Conversation Analysis (CA) that what participants say in conversations is not a mere reflection of internal mental representations, i.e., a virtual window into their cognitive state (Edwards, 1993: 211); rather, professional knowledge is displayed discursively (in communication), and demonstrated through concepts used during exchange that represents "flexible components of situated talk" (Edwards, 1993: 209). How knowledge building comes into play during interaction is a function of the actual setting and participants involved, and constructed and oriented to, in interaction, along the way (Wiggins & Potter, 2008: 79; see also Heritage & Raymond, 2005). In a discursive practice, discourse and conversational interaction have a meaning-construing nature (Edwards, 1997). As such, mentoring is a mindful process where, as noted by Edwards, 1997: 33, the apparently private process of learning and thinking of learners are realised in interaction and openly. Unfolding this argument further we draw, in particular, on five major insights from the conversational analysis literature to identify 'knowledge productive' learning conversations that, as is the case in mentoring, may help to structure talking together.

A) Talk in conversation are *open*, varied, and done in accountable ways – open in the sense of disclosing positions and recognizing roles; varied in the sense that each utterance is a response on what was said previously, and with participants responding in accountable ways to pursue the relevancy of talk at hand. As such, conversation is an inquisitive knowledge making procedure (Edwards and Potter 1992; Birenbaum et al., 2009). When mentors and mentees are in conversation about practices for example, they make their knowledge open by responding to what the other says, and by using the conversation as vehicle to articulate what they know (Engestrom, 1994).

B) Conversational interaction is *intersubjective,* and shared knowledge is a performative category, i.e, must lead to solutions for practice; be knowledge productive. This implies that talk is not just mediated interaction, but social action which involves assumptions, beliefs, understandings, that "are attended to, implied, made relevant, etc., as part of whatever business talk is doing" (Edwards, 2004b: 41). Intersubjectivity is a feature of talk characterised by turn taking, uptake, and how participants design their responses (Edwards, 2004a). Knowledge building in mentoring conversation should therefore be looked at as a collaborative and reciprocal enterprise, and conducted in what Engestrom (1994) called, their language of conversation.

C) During conversations, participants do not simply draw on and exchange "predetermined categories of speech" (Pike, 2010: 164) but engage in an *advancement of knowing* or a 'progressive discourse'. This means knowledge building happens gradually in terms of turn-by turn interactions; ultimately to climb to higher levels of understanding. Learning is contextualised in the mentoring setting, a joint activity that relies on presuppositions participants have of utterances made by the other in the interactional development zone a mentoring setting constitutes (Mercer, 2000; Pike, 2010: 164; Addison Stone, 1993). In such zones, knowledge becomes apparent as essentially embedded in unique episodes of interaction. Knowledge building draws on these sequences of verbal interactions – i.e., turn-taking, responding and exchanging utterances – not simply to duplicate experiences and conceptualisations, but taking the form of constructive and reconstructive rich understandings shaped and adjusted by participants (Lindfors, 1999; Rodgers & Raider-Roth, 2006; Magano, Mostert, & Van der Westhuizen, 2010).

D) Knowledge building through conversation entails a *moral domain* with clear implications for conversational relationships among participants (Stivers, Mondada, & Steensig, 2011). Specific moral dimensions of knowledge in conversations can be identified (Stivers et al., 2011):

• *epistemic access;* that is: who owns knowledge (described in terms of who determines what constitutes knowing vs not knowing; by what degree of certainty are solutions for practice adopted; who provides knowledge resources; what is accepted as knowledge);
• *epistemic primacy;* that is: who decides on goals or direction of talk (described in terms of relative rights to know; relative rights to claim; relative authority of knowledge); and
• *epistemic responsibility;* that is: who concludes about the relevancy of talk (described in terms of what is knowable to act upon, how recipients design their actions and turn-taking).

Epistemic access is about 'gate-keeping' the information that will be talked about. By eliciting and claiming knowledge entries in a conversation and it presupposes willingness to interact (Stivers et al., 2011). In knowledge building, this plays out in the engagement of participants to interact for example working together in mentoring as a study team, (Tillema & Orland-Barak, 2006). Epistemic primacy in conversational interactions involves allowing recipients their relative rights to tell, inform, assert or assess something, and acknowledges asymmetries in the depth, specificity, or completeness of their knowledge (Stivers et al., 2011). In mentoring settings this would mean that conversations are shaped by prevailing norms of alignment and affiliation. In practice this may be observed in the ways in which professionals account for what they know, how certain they are about their knowledge, and how they exercise their right and responsibilities as contributors to the knowledge conversation (see Stivers et al., 2011: 9). Epistemic responsibility refers closure and opening; to conclusion and prospects of a talk, which entails a recognition of the fruitfulness and productivity of conversations for further action.

Advice and guidance offered in mentoring need to be recognized as such in order to follow recommendations.

E) Conversation creates a *participative* ground for sharing knowledge. Drew's analyses of cognitive states in interaction offer evidence for the ways in which individual knowledge comes to the "interactional surface" (Drew, 2005: 176). In conversational interactions, utterances may be associated with recurrent and systematic patterns of merging 'cognitive states'. In professional interactions this means participants would use the conversation to stay tuned to the shared understanding, and allow for confusion to be clarified. Participation requires following the flow of communication in an attentive manner.

To abridge these highlights from Conversation Analysis research into a kernel characterization it can be posited that knowledge productive 'learning' conversations are constituted by:

a. a progressive discourse (have A, B, C), and
b. an informed participation (have C, D E).

To recognize such conversations additional analysis is needed (and one of the main purposes of this book and following chapters). Edwards' (1997: 45) notion of "analytical moves" may guide a more detailed and analytical inquiry into how mentoring conversation are conducted and how interactions evolve. Such moves in talks would involve for instance: identifying a topic of inquiry; allowing for explication; moving towards another theme. Studying knowledge building in mentoring conversations also would call for questions such as: What are the typical discourses in mentoring settings? How do they unfold? What patterns occur? How is a higher level in understanding attained? An inquisitive look at mentoring conversations as learning conversations (i.e., those which 'climb the mountain') would require for example detailed analysis of: What are the practices discussed? Where or when do they occur in a conversation? How do they vary across episodes, how are they organised in interaction, as part of participant accountability for participation in discourse? Analyses of moves in conversation might help (a mentor, for instance) to screen interactions and to focus on how utterances are constructed in a course of a conversation, and how it relates the practices under scrutiny (Edwards & Potter, 2012).

CONCLUSION

This chapter explored how knowledge building develops through conversation. Although differing views exist on the nature of knowledge building for professional practice, we put forward that the discursive nature of knowledge and 'knowing' is pertinent to understanding how professionals use conversations for building knowledge. Mentoring conversation is a vehicle for creating such a situational understanding. We have attempted to establish that knowledge building in mentoring practice is interactional and collaborative, responsive to situational context, takes professional beliefs and perspectives into account, and need to be knowledge productive, i.e., solution oriented. Knowledge productivity appears not to be an innate individual's possession, which is reflected on and transferred through merely by telling, explaining and externalization. On the contrary, professional knowledge building leading to knowledge productivity is a function of the situated talk occurring in an actual setting between participants, i.e., in our case, between mentors and mentees, who should be intent on responding in varied and unique ways in creating professional knowledge. Ultimately, the knowledge built is framed and constituted through the way the participants manage and design and execute the conversation (Stoll & Louis, 2004). Mentors and mentees engaged in knowledge building through conversations are thus accountable to engage in constructing and reconstructing rich and meaningful conceptualisations that go 'beyond the information given' and shape unique episodes of knowledge productive interaction.

REFERENCES

Addison Stone, C. (1996). What is missing in the metaphor of scaffolding? In E. A. Forman, N. Minick, & A. C. Stone (Eds.), *Contexts for learning: Sociocultural dynamics in children's development* (pp. 169–185). New York, NY: Oxford University Press.

Bakhtin, M. (1986). *Speech genres and other late essays* (Vern W. McGee, Trans.). Austin, TX: University of Texas Press.

Bereiter, C. (2002). *Education and mind in the knowledge society*. Mahwah, NJ: Lawrence Erlbaum Associates.

Birenbaum, M., Kimron, H., Shilton, H., & Shahaf-Barzilay, R. (2009). *Cycles of inquiry: Formative assessment in service of learning in classrooms and in school-based professional communities*. Paper prepared for presentation at the 2009 AERA Annual Meeting (Division A-Administration, Organization and Leadership/Section 3: School Improvement), San Diego, CA.

Bruner, J. S. (1973). *Beyond the information given*. New York, NY: Norton company.

Cazden, C. B. (1988). *Classroom discourse: The language of teaching and learning*. Portsmouth, NH: Heinemann.

Clandinin, D. J., & Connelly, F. M. (2000). *Narrative inquiry, experience and story in qualitative research*. San Francisco, CA: Jossey Bass.

Clark, C. M. (1995). *Thoughtful teaching*. New York, NY: Columbia University, Professionals College Press.

Cochran-Smith, M., & Zeichner, K. M. (2005). *Studying professional education: Report of the AERA panel on research and professional education*. Mahwah, NJ: Lawrence Erlbaum.

Drew, P. (2005). Is confusion a state of mind? In H. te Molder & J. Potter (Eds.), *Conversation and cognition*. Cambridge: Cambridge University Press.

Drew, P., & Heritage, J. (Eds.). (1992). *Talk at work: Interaction in institutional settings*. Cambridge: Cambridge University Press.

Edwards, A., Gilroy, P., & Hartley, D. (2002). *Rethinking professional education: Collaborative responses to uncertainty*. London, England: Routledge Falmer Press.

Edwards, D. (1993). But what do children really think? Discourse analysis and conceptual content in children's talk. *Cognition and instruction, 11*(3&4), 207–225.

Edwards, D. (1997). *Discourse and cognition*. London, England: Sage.

Edwards, D. (2004). Discursive psychology. In K. Fitch & R. Sanders (Eds.), *Handbook of language and social interaction* (pp. 257–273). Mahwah, NJ: Lawrence Erlbaum.

Edwards, D. (2006). Discourse, cognition and social practices: The rich surface of language and social interaction. *Discourse Studies, 8*(1), 41–49.

Edwards, D., & Potter, J. (1992). *Discursive psychology.* London, England: Sage.

Edwards, D., & Potter, J. (2012). *Pre-conference workshop: Discursive psychology: Psychology as an object in and for interaction.* DARG Conference, University of Loughborough, England.

Elbers, E. (2004). Conversational asymmetry and the child's perspective in developmental and educational research. *International Journal of Disability, Development and Education, 51*(2), 201–215.

Engeström, Y. (1994). Professionals as collaborative thinkers. In I. Carlgren (Ed.), *Professionals' minds and actions.* London, England: The Falmer Press.

Engeström. Y. (2001). Expansive learning at work. Toward activity theoretical reconceptualization. *Journal of Education and Work, 14*(1), 133–156.

Farr Darling, L. (2001). When conceptions collide, constructing a community of inquiry for teacher education in British Columbia. *Journal of Education for Teaching, 27*(1), 7–21.

Fenstermacher, G. D. (1994). The knower and the known: The nature of knowledge in research on teaching. *Review of Research in Education, 20*, 3–56

Gilroy, P. (1993). Reflections on Schon, an epistemological critique. In P. Gilroy & M. Smith (Eds.), *International analysis of professional education.* London, England: Carfax.

Goffman, E. (1969a). *Interaction ritual.* New York, NY: Doubleday Anchor.

Goffman, E. (1969b). *Strategic interaction.* Philadelphia, PA: University of Pennsylvania Press.

Goffman, E. (1974). *The presentation of self in everyday life.* Middlesex: Penguin Books.

Goffman, E. (1981). *Forms of talk.* Philadelphia, PA: University of Pennsylvania Press.

Hakkarainen, K., Paavola, S., & Lipponen, L. (2004). From communities of practice to innovative learning communities. *Life Long Learning in Europe, 6*(2), 74–84.

Heritage, J., & Raymond, G. (2005). The terms of agreement: Indexing epistemic authority and subordination in talk-in-interaction. *Social Psychology Quarterly, 68*(1), 15–38.

Hiebert, J., Gallimore, R., & Stigler, J. (2002). A knowledge base for the teaching profession: What would it look like and how can we get one? *Educational Researcher, 31*, 3–15.

Huberman, M. (1995). Networks that alter teaching, conceptualizations, exchanges and experiments. *Teaching & Professionals, 4*(1), 193–212.

Kane, R., Sandretto, S., & Heath, C. (2002). Telling half the story; A critical review of research on professional beliefs. *Review of Educational Research, 72*(2), 177–229.

Koole T. (2010). Displays of epistemic access: Student responses to professional Explanations. *Research on Language and Social Interaction, 43* (2), 183–209.

Korthagen, F. A. (2002). *Linking practice and theory; the pedagogy of realistic professional education.* Mahwah, NJ: Lawrence Erlbaum.

Lehrer, K. (2002). Discursive knowledge. *Philosophy and Phenomenological Research, 60*(3), 637–653

Lindfors, L. (1999). *Sloyd education in the cultural struggle. Part VIII. An outline of a sloyd educational theory* (Reports from the Faculty of Education, No. 4). Vasa: Abo Academic University, Department of Professional Education.

Lipponen, L. (2000). Towards knowledge building: From facts to explanations in primary students' computer mediated discourse. *Learning Environments Research, 3*, 179–199.

Magano, M. D., Mostert, P., & van der Westhuizen, G. J. (2009). *Learning conversations. The value of interactive learning.* Cape Town: Heinemann Publishers.

Mchoul, A. 1978. The organization of turns at formal talk in the classroom. *Language in Society, 7*(2), 183–213.

Mena Marcos, J., Sanchez, E., & Tillema, H. H. (2009). Professionals' reflection on action: What is said (in research) and what is done (in teaching). *Reflective Practice, 10*(2), 191–204.

Mena Marcos, J., Sanchez, E., & Tillema, H. H. (2010). Grounded professional reflection. Does professional reflection research support professional professional development in reflection? In I. Saleh & M. S. Khine (Eds.), *Teaching professionals: Approaches in improving quality of education.* New York, NY: Nova Publishers.

Mercer, N. (2000). *Words and minds: How we use language to think together.* London, England: Routledge.

Mercer N. (2007). *The sociocultural analysis of classroom dialogue.* London, England: TLRP. Retrieved July 5, 2009 from http://www.bera.ac.uk/the-sociocultural-analysis-of-classroom-dialogue/

Mercer, N. (2008). Talk and the development of reasoning and understanding. *Human Development, 51,* 90–100.

Olson, D. R., & Bruner, J. S. (1996). Folk psychology and folk pedagogy. In D. R. Olson & N. Torrance (Eds.), *Handbook of education and human development: New models of learning, teaching and schooling* (pp. 9–27). Oxford, England: Blackwell.

Olson, M. R., & Craig, C. J. (2001). Opportunities and challenges in the development of professionals' knowledge: the development of narrative authority through knowledge communities. *Teaching and Professional Education, 17,* 667–684.

Orland-Barak, L., & Tillema H. H. (2006). Collaborative knowledge construction; the dark side of the moon. *Professionals & Teaching, 12*(1), 1–12.

Paavola, S., Lipponen, L., & Hakkarainen, K. (2004). Models of innovative knowledge communities and three metaphors of learning. *Review of Educational Research, 74*(4), 557–577.

Pajares, M. F. (1992). Professionals' beliefs and educational research: Cleaning up a messy construct. *Review of Educational Research, 62,* 307–332.

Palonen, T. (2004). Best practices of professional competence development. *Life Long Learning in Europe, 2,* 95–102.

Palonen, T., Hakkarainen, K., Talvitie, J., & Lehtinen, E. (2004). Network ties, cognitive centrality and team interaction within a telecommunication company. In H. P. A. Boshuizen, R. Bromme, & H. Gruber (Eds.), *Professional learning: Gaps and transitions on the way from novice to expert.* Dordrecht: Kluwer.

Peräkylä, A. (2004). Traditions of interaction research. *British Journal of Social Psychology, 43,* 1–20.

Pike, C. (2010). Intersubjectivity and misunderstanding in adult-child learning conversations. In H. Gardner & M. Forrester (Eds.), *Analysing interactions in childhood. Insights from conversation analysis.* West-Sussex: Wiley-Blackwell.

Potter, J., & Hepburn, A. (2008). Discursive constructionism. In J. A. Holstein & J. F. Gubrium (Eds.), *Handbook of constructionist research* (pp. 275–293). New York, NY: Guildford.

Rawls, A. W. (1984). Interaction as a resource for epistemological critique. *Sociological Theory, 2,* 222–252.

Rodgers, C. R., & Raider-Roth, M. B. (2006). Presence in teaching. *Professionals and Teaching: Theory and Practice, 12*(3), 265–287.

Sacks, H., Schegloff, E. A., & Jefferson, G. (1974). A simplest systematics for the organization of turn-taking in conversation. *Language, 50*(4), 696–735.

Scardamalia, M., & Bereiter, C. (1999). Schools as knowledge-building organizations. In D. Keating & C. Hertzman (Eds.), *Developmental health and the wealth of nations: Social, biological, and educational dynamics* [On Line]. Retrieved from http://csile.oise.on.ca/abstracts/ciarunderstanding.html

Schön, D. A. (1983). *The reflective practitioner: How professionals think in action.* New York, NY: Basic Books.

Sfard, A. (1998). On two metaphors for learning and the dangers of choosing just one. *Educational Researcher, 27*(2), 4–13.

Shulman, L. S. (1987). Knowledge and teaching: Foundations of the new reform. *Harvard Educational Review, 19*(2), 4–14.

Simons, R., & Ruyters, M. (2004). Learning professionals: Towards an integrated model. In R. Bromme & Boshuizen (Eds.), *Professional learning: Gaps and transitions on the way from novice to expert* (pp. 231–251). Boston, MA: Kluwer.

Stivers, T., Mondada, L., & Steensig, J. (2011). *The morality of knowledge in conversation.* Cambridge: Cambridge University Press.

Stoll, L., & Louis, K. S. (2007). *Professional learning communities: Divergence, depth and dilemmas.* Maidenhead: Open University Press/McGraw Hill.

Tillema, H. H., & Orland-Barak, L. (2006). Constructing knowledge in professional conversations; The role of beliefs on knowledge and knowing. *Learning & Instruction, 16*(6), 592–608.

Tillema, H. H., & van der Westhuizen, G. J. (2006). Knowledge construction in collaborative enquiry among professionals. *Professionals & Teaching, 12*(1), 51–67.

Van der Westhuizen, G. J. (2012). The conversational dimensions of classroom and social media learning interactions. *Communitas,* 17, 137–160.

Wang, J., & Odell, S. J. (2002). Mentored learning to teach according to standards-based reform: A critical review. *Review of Educational Research, 72*(3), 481–546.

Wenger, E. (1998). *Communities of practice: Learning, meaning and identity.* Cambridge: Cambridge University Press.

Wenger, E., Mc Dermott, C., & Snyder, B. (2002). *Cultivating communities of practice.* Cambridge: Harvard University Press.

Wiggins, S., & Potter, J. (2008). Discursive psychology. In C. Willig & W. Stainton Rogers (Eds.), *The Sage handbook of qualitative research in psychology.* Los Angeles, CA: Sage.

Wickman, P. O., & Östman, L. (2002). Learning as discourse change: A sociocultural mechanism. *Science Education, 86,* 601–623.

Harm Tillema
Leiden University, The Netherlands

Gert J. van der Westhuizen
University of Johannesburg, South Africa

Martijn P. van der Merwe
University of Johannesburg, South Africa

PART 1

LEARNING FROM MENTORING CONVERSATIONS: DO WE?

Does mentoring make a difference? We know that knowledge construction in real contexts by engaged mentors can highly contribute to one's learning (from practice). But how is it accomplished? Reflection, for one, is said to be the effective tool.

But one could ask, then: is this reflective or "explicating paradigm' a sufficiently appropriate framework for interpreting what (student) teachers as (beginning) professionals actually learn from their practice or learn from the feedback they receive during mentoring sessions? Specifically, a number of critical elements can be noted inherent in the reflective paradigm on professional learning.

We could critically ask, for example:

- 'Does reflection generate useful knowledge (for practice) ?',
- 'Why is reflection at conceptual levels so hard to articulate/to tap by professionals?' and
- 'Why does not "talk" lead to "walk"? (Mena Marcos & Tillema, 2006).

The reflective rhetoric talks about matching beliefs to practice by starting with the beliefs. But on the other hand, how can practical knowledge emerge in (mentoring) conversation without (beginning) professionals deliberately having to enact and situate it first?

To take position:

The reflective premise holds that professionals as learners can or should articulate their knowledge as evidence of their learning.

But, findings suggest that participants in mentoring claim to have learned 'what really matters to them as professionals', by being able to enact them.

How then do we learn from mentoring? This is the overarching query of this part of the book.

TOWARDS PROFESSIONAL SITUATIONAL UNDERSTANDING

To address the above concern, an alternative viewpoint would be found in the concept of *professional situational understanding* which states that professionals grow on what they encounter in and from their daily action. In this vein, knowledge is not viewed as distributable and objectified knowledge to be exchanged during mentoring (see the position taken in chapter 1), but rather as actively constructed in and from contexts through continuing and progressive discourse between "colleagues" who interpret and (re)value work-related situations.

The notion of situational understandings is further explored in the current part of the book. The question to be addressed in the upcoming chapters is how mentoring conversation and discourse could function to foster an improved understanding of practice. Chapter 2 by Tillema and Van der Westhuizen explores the knowledge productivity of mentoring conversations. Chapter 3 by Mena and Clarke critically review the reflective paradigm and stress the importance of validity of practical knowledge. Chapters 4 by Gamlem and 5 by Korver and Tillema take up feedback as the informative tool that provides the content in learning conversations.

HARM TILLEMA AND GERT J. VAN DER WESTHUIZEN

2. MENTORING CONVERSATIONS AND STUDENT TEACHER LEARNING

To foster a mentee's learning, mentoring comes to aid as a 'helping' process to attain higher levels of proficiency but… the main lesson is that the high ground can not be approached hastily. Even the most difficult problems can be solved and even the most precipitous heights can be scaled, if only a slow step-by-step pathway can be found. Mount improbable can not be assaulted; gradually, if not always slowly, it must be climbed. (R. Dawkins (1996:365) *Climbing Mount Improbable*. New York: W.W. Norton Company)

Knowing how to proceed is one thing. Knowing what to address another….

Think of what a small proportion of thought becomes conscious, and of conscious thought what a small proportion gets uttered, what a still smaller fragment gets published, and what a small proportion what is published is used. (Campbell, 1987, p. 105 "Blind Variation and Selective Retention in Creative Thought as in Other Knowledge Processes". In: Radnitzky, G./Bartley, W. W., III. (eds). *Evolutionary Epistemology, Rationality, and the Sociology of Knowledge*. La Salle, IL: Open Court, 91–114)

Mentoring conversation is the mechanism through which both mentee and mentor get to know. We need therefore to understand how the mechanisms of conversation work.

INTRODUCTION

This chapter focuses on the mentor's conversational strategy during mentoring and its impact on what student teachers learn. The notion of knowledge productivity is put forward to highlight the nature of exchange between a mentor and a mentee as one of preparation for the profession and attainment of high(er) levels of proficiency. Using a case-design in the context of teacher education, twelve conversations between a student teacher and his/her mentor were video-analyzed with regard to the conversational moves of the mentor. An instrument for the description of conversational moves is described. Conversational moves were contrasted with respect to their resulting knowledge productivity (i.e., analyzed as behavioural intentions to change one's practice). The findings suggest that:

H. Tillema et al. (Eds.), Mentoring for Learning, 23–45.

- A mentor's conversational approach consists of different conversational moves, signifying different strategies in conversation.
- Conversational moves, per se, do not significantly influence the student teacher's perceived knowledge productivity. We noted, however, three dominant types to occur in conversations: a scaffolding and prescriptive one, which in combination we called a 'high road' approach, and an exploring one which we called a 'low road' approach.
- Student teachers who were having a regular, closer and positive relationship with their mentor were associated with higher knowledge productivity.

Our findings indicate an overall small effect of differing conversational moves on student teacher's learning outcomes. To position this finding we have to bear in mind that almost 60% of conversational talk consisted of non-learning or goal related, but instead of relational remarks. Markedly, closeness in the relationship was found to positively influence student teacher's learning outcomes. Although no direct relation was found between specific mentor moves and perceived knowledge productivity, higher attainment scores were found for the 'low road' approach. This is discussed in relation to the aim of mentoring conversations as learning conversations.

Mentoring for Proficiency

Mentoring plays an important part in the professional education of a student teacher. It refers to the collaboration of a more experienced teacher with a novice teacher to provide 'systematic and sustained assistance' to the learner (Huling-Austin, 1990). Mentoring is believed to support and facilitate the professional development of student teachers (Loughran, 2003). Research suggests that mentoring is a highly effective method for supporting and facilitating student teachers in their professional development (Tomlinson, Hobson & Malderez, 2010; Orland & Yinon, 2005).

To a large extent, student teacher's professional knowledge is developed and framed within conversations with a mentor (Edwards, 1995; Hobson, 2004). The mentor's approach taken during mentoring conversations therefore might influence the learning outcomes profoundly. In a mentoring conversation a mentor can use different approaches to help the student teacher in his/her learning process (Huling-Austin, 1990; Smithey & Evertson, 1995). Analysis of mentoring conversations shows that a mentor predominantly determines the format and topics of conversation, its start, finish and flow (Strong & Baron, 2004). In the literature several ingredients of successful mentor conversational approaches have been outlined. According to Daloz (1986) support and challenge are key ingredients. Franke and Dahlgren (1996) point out the benefits of a reflective approach to mentoring. Edwards (20041995?) stresses the importance of relational and interpersonal skills in conversation. Garvey (2011) acknowledges the significance of meaning making and relevancy of conversation.

In their review Hennissen, Crasborn, Brouwer, Korthagen and Bergen (2008) constructed an explicit framework to categorise different approaches (styles they called them) that mentors may use in conversations. They distinguish especially between directive and non-directive approaches. A directive approach is characterized as informative, critical, instructive, corrective and advising. Its constituting conversational moves are: assessing, appraising, instructing, confirming, expressing one's own opinion, offering strategies, and giving feedback. An opposite non-directive approach is defined as reflective, cooperative, guiding and eliciting. The corresponding moves in the non-directive style are: asking questions, guiding to developing alternatives, reacting empathetically, summarising and listening actively.

Conversational moves, also known as speech acts (Seedhouse, 2004) serve the essential purpose of mentoring, that is, "systematically and sustainably assist" the learning and expertise development of the mentee. Mentoring comes to aid in the attainment of higher levels of proficiency. In line with Ericsson's (2002) theory on developing expertise, a mentor may accelerate the attainment process by giving feedback on the basis of knowing what aspects of performance are 'ready' to be improved at a next level of proficiency (Ericsson, 2007). Ericsson's work states that such deliberate practices lead to enhanced improvement in performance. A "mentored" deliberate practice in essence builds representations of desired performance goals, knowledge on how to execute the performance, and provides monitoring of performance. This interactive process is depicted in Figure 1.

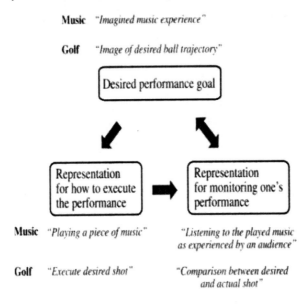

Figure 1. Model of deliberate practice by Ericsson (2002)

We can take this model of deliberate practice to gauge real mentoring conversations in order to establish what speech moves a mentor utilize to scaffold and support the learner in the attainment of high(er) levels of proficiency. In our view the purpose and function of mentoring can be depicted as "climbing mount improbable', to paraphrase R. Dawkins (1996), in such a way that a "skilled mentor' as described by Crasborn and Hennissen (2009) will bring the mentee up to a level of attainment previously believed to be hard or difficult to reach. This view of "mentoring for learning" is represented in a slight rearrangement of the model on deliberate practice and shown in Figure 2 to capture in a concise way by the phrase "Climbing the Mountain".

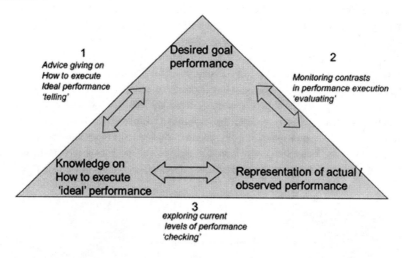

1=prescriptive move
2=scaffolding move
3=exploring move

Figure 2. Climbing mount improbable: relating three mental representations

The metaphor Climbing the Mountain stands for the idea that a seemingly complex goal becomes achievable by way of many, gradual, and supportive steps that point out the relevant paths to pursue which were most often previously unseen by the mentee. This metaphor may be of help to interpret mentoring conversations as vehicles of deliberate practice.

A mentoring conversation's purpose is to help to bridge the gap between the prior beliefs, unfamiliar theoretical knowledge, and the still unattained states of proficiency of the student teacher; and guide the student through the necessary or requisite knowledge on action (Edwards, 2011). Moves in mentoring conversation can be of different kinds:

- Moves that stay at the level of exploring (focus on 3 in Figure 2) i.e., talking about personal tacit beliefs as they relate to the existing knowledge base to be learned for a student, or
- Moves meant to be accommodating and supportive (focus on 2 in Figure 2) to scaffold learning i.e., starting from the student's position (in beliefs or performance) and aligning it with a learning goal perspective, or
- Moves that deliberately guide the student toward the to-be-attained end result, i.e., providing directed feedback on relevant knowledge functional to the performance goal (focus on 1 in Figure 2).

Typically, these three moves taken together resemble an instructional orientation, as Sadler (1995) has put forward, which is constituted of: 1: knowing where you are, 2: deciding where to go; 3: specifying the steps to get there.

Especially in teacher education, the mentors' position and role is to raise the level of proficiency of their students with conversation as their main vehicle. We are interested to learn how mentors select the conversational moves to "climb the mountain", i.e., to attain learning goals. Is a mentor aware of the risks of guiding the student teacher on a path that is steep (focus on 2)? Or alternatively, select moves to reach a certain level of attainment too brisk and early (focus on 1)? Or stay at length on the low road (focus on 3) of exploring one's positions without any new learning occurring? To reach the desired goal performance: i.e., the summit of 'mount improbable', the mentor may need to take a 'high road' in conversation from time to time. That is, to push forward in the right (goal) direction as is typical for mentoring in the professions (Garvey, 2011) as it is, also, for sustaining Ericsson's (2002) deliberate practice (Strong & Baron, 2004). Or alternatively, stay, for some time, at the 'low road' of exploring to get acquainted with held beliefs by a mentee.

We position this framework as helpful in detecting and interpreting mentoring approaches in conversations. For instance: a mentor who intends to help the student teacher to 'monitor his performance' by scaffolding and guiding towards the end goals set and by asking persistent reflective questions about the student teacher's performance in reference to the desired goal is in our view combining moves 1 and 2 (Figure 2). This "high road" approach or 'challenging approach' (Daloz, 1986) can be compared with a 'reflective approach' as mentioned by Franke and Dahlgen (1996) and also be related to the non-directive approach as described by Hennissen et al. (2008); in contrast to a mentor who stays on the 'low road', to build acquaintance and comfort; with moves that consist of discussing and eliciting comments.

Learning as a Result of Conversation

Mentoring in the professions (Garvey, 2004), as is the case in teacher education (Hobson, 2004), is directed toward attainment of (higher) levels of proficiency. In teacher education, mentoring aims to support and facilitate the professional development of student teachers (Loughran, 2004). New insights in the professional development of teachers (Edwards, 2011) point to the interactional and collaborative nature of teacher knowledge which is developed and modified through shared understandings and gradual approximations in performance (Orland Barak & Hinon, 2006; Tillema & Van der Westhuizen; Chapter 1 of this book). Ultimately, professional development and knowledge advancement in the profession rests on the ability to gain insight from past performance and learn to create (improved) tools/ solutions for future practices (Tillema, 2006). In the study we report in this chapter, knowledge attainment for the profession, regarded as an outcome of conversation in mentoring, is analyzed from the perspective of knowledge productivity (Tillema & Van der Westhuizen, 2006). Knowledge productivity is defined as the creation of conceptual artefacts to improve professional practice (Bereiter, 2002). Conceptual artefacts (i.e., tools useful for professional practice) are the outcomes of shared understandings and (often) are collaborative approximations of practice that can be argued about and shared among professionals (Tillema & Orland Barak, 2006). These artefacts become productive (i.e., tangible and useful) through conversation (as laid out in plans, protocols and action schemes, for instance; see Tillema, 2005). Knowledge productivity is a notion which captures the 'learning' outcomes (see Bereiter, 2002). Challenging (or "climbing") conversations (Farr-Darling, 2001) can stimulate knowledge productivity (Baxter Magolda, 2004) which means they can lead to learning outcomes that evidence themselves in conceptual artefacts. The notion of knowledge productivity is used in this study to appraise outcomes of conversations, and is in more detail specified by three evaluative (perceptive) criteria:

- Raising problem understanding. This criterion relates to an increased awareness, better understanding and insights gained as a result of collaborative exchange, i.e., conversation. The most important question of this criterion is: is the dialogue related to the practice of the student and does the student acknowledge the issues spoken about as relevant?
- Shifting perspective. This criterion relates to a conceptual change in the beliefs of the student by listening to the viewpoints of the mentor. Most important question of this criterion is: does the student find the ideas, brought forward during conversation, important enough to adopt?
- Commitment to apply. This criterion relates to how the student was involved in the conversation and showed interest in the discussion. Engagement and participative interaction with the mentor is regarded as important for a subsequent follow-up of advice given and recommendations made. The most important question is whether the student is interested in actively following up recommendations (Tillema, 2005).

The central question we like to pursue is: to which extent does the mentor's moves in conversation relate to the perceived learning outcomes of the student teacher? More specifically:

- To what extent does the mentor's selection of three different moves during conversation relate to perceived "understanding", "perspective shift" and "commitment to apply"? Conceptually speaking: is taking a 'high road' approach in mentoring conversations leading to higher perceived learning outcomes?
- As a rival perspective: To what extent do student (prior experience based) expectations on (the mentor's approach to) conversations influence student teacher's learning outcomes? Conceptually speaking: do established relationships in mentoring have impact on the choice of conversational moves?

THE STUDY

Respondents

In the study we report on 12 dyads of student teachers and their mentors. Eight student teachers were enrolled in a teacher education program for secondary education and four attended teacher education for primary education. Students were between 18 and 28 years old and took courses in their first to their fourth year of education.

Four out of the 12 mentors were the regular mentors of the student teachers; both working together in teaching practice classes. Six mentors were involved as supervising teacher educators. They visited the students at their internship-schools and met for mentoring conversations. Two mentors were working as mentor coordinators; they regularly visit, observe, and evaluate student teachers at different sites. The twelve mentors differed in their experience and position as a mentor (on average 6.5 years). Relationships between a mentor and a mentee varied in closeness, i.e., the length or duration of the relationship. This circumstance was used as a framework for analysis.

Design of the Study

A comparative case design (Linn, 1998) was used in this study to explore within different school settings the nature of interaction in the dialogues between a mentor and a student teacher. In a case comparative design it is possible to explore framed contexts both in a qualitative and quantitative way (Druckman, 2005). The framing, i.e., selection of settings, consisted of varying the "closeness" variable i.e., the personal mentoring relationship established between the stakeholders over an extended period of time. The moderator variable in this study is the mentors' moves in the conversations, determined by analyses of propositions from the transcribed mentoring conversation, using content analysis methods (Bovar & Kieras, 1985). As outcome variable, student expectations with regard to the conversation as a learning event was measured using a questionnaire, as well as by in depth interviewing, using the Memorable Event method (Tillema, 2005). To determine the learning outcomes of mentoring the questionnaire on perceived knowledge productivity was used. (see Table 1 for an overview and instrument.)

Table 1. Concepts, variables, instruments, and research expectation in this study

Concept	Variable	Instrument	Conjecture
Mentor's approach	Mentor's moves	Content analysis coding on prescriptive, scaffolding and exploring propositions by mentor	Prescriptive and scaffolding propositions are related to high road approach and exploring propositions are related to low road approach
Mentoring relationship	Mentoring expectations	Adjusted Ideal Mentoring Scale (IMS)	High expectation is related to positive relationship
	Perceived Learning impact	Memorable events interview	High experienced effects are related to positive relationship
Learning outcomes	Knowledge productivity	Questionnaire on perceived knowledge productivity on – understanding, – perspective shift and – commitment to apply	High perceived knowledge productivity is related to high perceived learning outcomes

Procedure

The selected 12 pairs consisted of a mentor and a student teacher in a mentoring relationship. They were invited by mail to join the study and accepted on willingness to participate. Beforehand they received a short introduction to the nature of the study and its procedure. If both student teacher and mentor gave consent to the process, an appointment was made for videotaping their upcoming mentoring conversation. Before the mentoring conversation, students were asked to fill out the questionnaire on Mentoring Expectations. When the regularly scheduled mentoring conversation took place, the researcher visited the site (most often at the internship school) and gave a short repetition of the procedure and answered possible questions. With the camera was installed, the researcher left the room and waited outside during the conversation room not to interfere the process. After the conversation had ended, the researcher administered the questionnaire on perceived Knowledge Productivity and administered the Memorable Events interview.

Instruments

Student teacher's mentoring expectations. Student teachers' expectations represent the way a student teacher values a mentoring conversation as contributing to his or her learning. For this purpose, a questionnaire was developed based on the Ideal Mentoring Scale by Rose (2000). The Ideal Mentoring Scale measures mentor abilities a student appreciates most in a mentoring conversation. Three scales evaluating the student's appreciation with the mentor are: Integrity, Guidance, and Relationship. The original questionnaire by Rose was adjusted to appraise the current expectations before conversation with the mentor took place. Therefore the opening question of the IMS was changed from 'My ideal mentor would ...' to 'What I would like to occur in this conversation with my mentor is ...' The items of the original IMS were not changed. The adjusted instrument was used to measure student's satisfaction with the existing mentor relationship. Before the mentoring conversation, the student teacher filled out the questionnaire that consisted of 34 statements on a five point Likert scale (ranging from not true at all to very true).

- Integrity consisted of 14 items l (e.g. 'What I see in my mentor is that he values me as a person').
- Guidance consisted of 10 items (e.g. 'What I see in my mentor is that he helps me plan a timetable for my research').
- Relationship consisted of 10 items (e.g. 'What I see in my mentor is that he helps me realize my life vision').

The internal consistency for these items in three categories was measured with Cronbach Alphas: for integrity $r = .87$, for guidance $r = .75$ and for relationship $r = .78$.

Interview: Memorable events. After the conversation took place students received an open interview format with nine evaluative questions pertaining to their satisfaction with the conversation as a learning event. The interview questions asked to specify (by writing) the "memorable events" during conversation as instances of what was said that matters most or was highly relevant to the student on three aspects (with regard to the knowledge productivity of the conversation):

- Problem understanding: three questions evaluating whether the student teacher accepted and learned from the messages expressed in the discussions (e.g. 'what have you learned and gained from the examples your mentor expressed?').
- Perspective change: two questions evaluating whether the conversation led to insightful new knowledge (e.g. 'how the talk you had have changed your way of approaching matters in teaching?').
- Commitment to apply: four items evaluating whether the student teacher took active part in the process (e.g. 'what kind of consequences would you draw as a result of the mentoring conversation?').

The answers of the student teachers on each question were coded as positive, negative or neutral. The reliability of this instrument was tested by an inter-rater reliability test. This resulted in an agreement of 89%.

Questionnaire of perceived knowledge productivity. Knowledge productivity represents the valuation of learning outcomes by the student teacher, i.e., did the mentoring support my professional practice? This variable is measured using a questionnaire developed by Tillema (2005; Orland Barak & Tillema, 2006). The questionnaire was administered to the student teacher after the mentoring conversation and consisted of 20 evaluation questions with respect to three categories on a five point Likert scale (ranging from not true at all to very true).

- Problem representation: seven items evaluating whether the student better understood the topic under discussion and gained insights from the conversation (e.g. 'I found the problems being discussed authentic and real').
- Perspective taking: seven items evaluating the ideas the mentor expressed that contributed to learning (e.g. 'my thinking changed during the discussion').
- Commitment: six items evaluating whether the student teacher was actively involved in the conversation (e.g. 'I took ideas to practice further').

The internal consistency for these items in the three categories was measured with Cronbach Alphas: for problem representation $r = .71$, for perspective taking $r = .64$ and for commitment $r = .97$. To increase homogeneity of the scale Perspective taking one item on the scale is deleted (I was able to grasp interesting ideas), rises Alpha to .71.

Data: Content Analysis

Mentor's moves during conversation were measured with a self-developed coding instrument. The instrument is used for a propositional analysis of the transcribed video registration of the conversation. The propositional method in a conversational analysis (Goodwin & Heritage, 1995: Holsti, 1968; Mazur, 2004) was chosen to increase rater reliability in scoring the unit of analysis, i.e., moves. Moves are speech acts used by the mentors during conversation which, following our conceptual framework, is categorized as either:

1. Prescription: a move containing a reference to the present or referenced knowledge base and directed toward a performance goal. Speech acts can be: explanation, referencing, guiding, remarking. A prescription is intended to give an advice based on previously taught or instructed content knowledge to warrant a recommendation for future action.
2. Scaffold: a move referring to present student performance linking it to a performance goal. Speech acts can be: giving hints, providing examples, prompting. Scaffolding is meant to monitor and highlight actions taken by the student in reference to possible improvements that could be made.
3. Exploration: a move referring to a knowledge base relating it to present student performance. Speech acts can be asking for explication, acknowledgments,

invitation. Exploring is meant to investigate actions performed and provide perspectives for future action.

A fourth category contained miscellaneous comments. A guideline was developed for raters to support a reliable scoring (Mazur, 2004). Definitions and examples of scoring are;

- Prescription: statement in which the mentor tells the student teacher how to act in a certain situation, how to execute, in order to reach the desired goal (e.g. 'the best option is sending him to his seat to reflect').
- Scaffold: statement in which the mentee by is invited to reflect on classroom behaviour in order to reach the desired goal (e.g. 'what can you do to prevent this?').
- Exploration: statement in which the mentor explores student teacher performance in a certain classroom setting (e.g. 'were all pupils focused on your instruction').
- Other: statement not typically fit into one of the categories (e.g. 'I liked your lesson I saw today').

The unit of analysis we worked with, is a proposition, i.e., a subject – predicate relation (Holsti, 1994). In case of unfinished sentences (because of interruptions or pauses), a group of adjacent propositions were used as unit of analysis. The video registration was transcribed into a meaningful enumeration of units of propositions in order to establish (i.e., score) whether a category has occurred in that particular unit. Only one category was assigned to one proposition.

Example:
To give an example on the coding of mentoring conversations in this study, part of a mentoring conversation's coding is shown step by step.

Step 1: transcribing the conversation

Mentor: 'How could you prevent that for instance? You now say: at the start of the lesson I did not wait for the class to be quiet. You did not check if it was completely clear to the students what your intention was. What your goal for the lesson was, what you expected from the students'.

Step 2: dividing the conversation into propositions

- How could you prevent that for instance?
- You now say: at the start of the lesson I did not wait for the class to be quiet.
- You did not check if it was completely clear to the students what your intention was.
- What your goal for the lesson was, what you expected from the students.

Step 3: coding the propositions

How could you prevent that for instance?	Scaffolding (question to help the student reflect on the situation)
You now say: at the start of the lesson I did not wait for the class to be quiet.	Other (citation of the student teacher by the mentor)
You did not check if it was completely clear to the students what your intention was.	Exploring (exploring the current performance)
What your goal for the lesson was, what you expected from the students.	Exploring (exploring the current performance)

Step 4: assigning a category

The number of specific codes under each category is counted after coding the conversation. The frequency count for each category provides the 'footprint' of the conversation. This footprint indicates how many propositions in the conversation are prescriptive, scaffolding, exploring or other. In the above example the footprint of this little part of the conversation is: prescriptive: 0, scaffolding: 1, exploring: 2, other: 1.

The reliability of coding was tested by multiple raters. Initial coding agreement on 50 propositions was 46%. Raters then received training; two raters were employed afterwards resulting in inter-rater reliability of sampled transcripts of $k = .86$.

Data Inspection

Scoring of propositions of mentor moves consisted of frequency counts of the three categories to arrive at a 'footprint' of each conversation. A footprint consists of categories: scaffolding (n); prescription (n), and exploration (n).

Scores on questionnaire of Mentoring Expectations were obtained by calculating the mean scale score on the three questionnaire scales: Integrity, Guidance and Relationship.

Scores on Memorable Event interview are obtained by counting the amount of positive answers on the nine interview questions. Twelve student teachers answered the scale Problem Understanding with a positive instance of 30 out of the 36; Perspective Change were answered positive in 10 of the 24 cases, for Commitment to Apply the positive instances were 25 out of the 36 answers. In overview, student teachers answered more than half of the questionnaire items positively

The scores on perceived Knowledge Productivity are obtained by calculating the mean score on the three questionnaire scales. The questionnaire consists of scales: Problem Representation, Perspective Taking and Commitment to Apply. There were no missing values.

Analysis

To answer the first question on the relation between mentor's conversational moves and knowledge productivity, the knowledge productivity scale scores are compared on type of 'footprint" i.e., the combination of categories of mentor moves. Especially we were interested in the effects of a 'high road approach' or footprint and a 'low road' approach. A high road being dominated by prescription, and/or scaffolding vs a low road being dominated by exploring moves. Taking into account the small amount of conversations (n=12) a Mann-Whitney U-test was used.

To answer the second question on the relation between mentoring expectations and knowledge productivity, two analyses were conducted. Firstly, scores on knowledge productivity are compared for the high and low expecting students and analysed with a Mann-Whitney U-test. Secondly, the influence of 'closeness' in mentoring relationships on knowledge productivity is contrasted for dyads that are unfamiliar or familiar in their relationships. The scores were analysed with a Mann-Whitney U-test.

RESULTS

Description

A descriptive account of findings shows the following findings:

Conversational moves. Content analysis of the 12 conversations indicates that there is considerable variation in selected moves by the mentors; grouping them under footprints or type of approach it reveals that 3 conversations are considered to have a 'high road' approach and 9 are considered to have a 'low road' approach. Table 2 shows the frequencies for coded categories of all 12 conversations.

Mentoring expectations. The questionnaire on student teacher's Mentoring Expectations contains three scales. The scale Integrity has a mean of 4.14 (N = 11, $SD = 0.49$), the scale Guidance has a mean of 3.55 (N = 11, $SD = 0.50$) and the scale Relationship has a mean of 3.27 (N = 11, $SD = 0.61$). The total mean is 3.71 (N = 11, $SD = 0.46$). Taking a scale mean of 3.50 to be high on expectations indicated that 7 out of 11 respondents had high expectations.

Knowledge productivity. The Knowledge Productivity questionnaire contains three scales. The scale Problem understanding has a mean of 4.35 (N=12, $SD=0.43$), the mean of Perspective taking is 3.94 (N = 12, SD = 0.59) and the Commitment to apply scale has a mean of 4.23 (N=11, $SD=0.40$). The mean score on all of the scales is 4.16 (N=12, $SD = 0.37$).

Table 2. 'Footprint' for all conversations

Conversation	Prescriptive	Scaffolding	Exploring	Other	High or low road
1	87*	64	118	155	High
2	64	8	84	240	Low
3	13	20	38	60	Low
4	13	43	65	122	Low
5	56	19	132	127	Low
6	23	11	11	50	High
7	23	18	89	320	Low
8	10	15	36	112	Low
9	2	5	27	53	Low
10	16	16	39	25	Low
11	47	32	66	54	High
12	27	15	61	46	Low

* Table contains frequencies of propositions

Conversational moves and knowledge productivity. To answer the first question student teacher's scores on knowledge productivity are compared under a 'high road' approach (n=3) and 'low road' approach (n=9). Median score in the 'high road' approach was 3.94 and median score in the 'low road' approach was 4.03. The distributions in the two groups did not differ significantly (Mann–Whitney $U = 8.00$, n = 12, p = .31 two-tailed). There is no significant difference in knowledge productivity for students who had a 'high road' conversation or a 'low road' conversation.

Mentoring expectations and knowledge productivity. Based on their expectation score, student teachers are divided (around the scale median score) into two groups: high and low expectations. The knowledge productivity scores were compared for these two groups with a Mann-Whitney U-test. Mean score in the high group was 4.37 and mean score in the low group was 3.82. The distributions in the two groups differs significantly (Mann–Whitney $U = 3.00$, n = 11, $P = .04$ two-tailed). Student teachers having high expectations have higher perceived knowledge productivity.

With respect to closeness in the mentoring relationship, student teacher's scores on Knowledge Productivity were compared for a high closeness relationship (n = 6) and low closeness (n = 6). It was expected that students under a high closeness relationship would perceive higher knowledge productivity. For this analysis a Mann-Whitney U-test is executed. The median score in the high closeness group was 4.52 and the median score for low closeness was 3.92. The distributions in the two groups differs significantly (Mann–Whitney U = 5.00, n = 12, P = .04 two-tailed). Student teachers under high closeness perceive higher knowledge productivity. Both analyses related to mentoring relationship indicate a positive relationship with higher knowledge productivity.

DISCUSSION

This study meant to explore the relation between mentoring conversation and student teacher's learning, taking into account the student's relationship with his/her mentor.

Mentoring Relationship and Learning Outcomes

Using a comparative case design we found support for the influence of student – mentor relationship on learning outcomes. The student's learning in a mentoring relationship was gauged with respect to: student teacher's expectations, and perceived knowledge productivity of the conversation. When knowledge productivity is compared for student teachers with high and low expectations our analysis showed a significant difference. Student teachers who were satisfied with their mentors had a higher mean perceived knowledge productivity. The same applies when comparing student teachers having a close (i.e., extended) relationship with their mentors.

Conversational Approach and Learning Outcomes

A clear relation between specific mentor moves and student teacher's learning outcomes was not found. We particularly gauged a 'high road' approach vs a 'low road' approach taken by the mentor; expecting that prescriptive and scaffolding moves (i.e., 'high road' or 'pushing' approach) by the mentor would lead to higher knowledge productivity compared to exploring moves i.e., 'low road' or 'laissez faire' approach. In fact, the mean knowledge productivity was higher for conversations with a 'low road' approach, although no significant differences were found.

In interpreting our findings several reasons can be mentioned why taking a 'low road approach' in mentoring conversations has higher knowledge productivity. A conceptual reason is that prescriptions and scaffolding by the mentor may not have been adequate, or accepted as stepping stones towards the desired goal. Exploring current performance, on the other hand, may have been considered informative to the student to orient them towards the desired goal. The results in our case-study show that exploring current performance had a high frequency of moves as well as miscellaneous moves, indicating that the conversations provided less time for guiding or prescribing routes, but invested ample time in monitoring performance, i.e., "covering ground".

It is also possible that the identified moves are incomplete in responsiveness to the mentee's intent to use the conversation as a vehicle toward a desired learning outcome. A crucial factor in mentoring that was not included in our selection of moves is the need of the mentee (Garvey, 2011). It can be claimed that student teacher's learning outcomes will be determined by their motivational needs (Deci & Ryan, 2004). In this respect a conversation with low knowledge productivity would not have sufficiently addressed motivational needs of students. In our study, we did not cover for mentor moves that address different motivational needs or "background states" of students (i.e., "prior knowledge" could have been another), but then again the moves we identified did show a different footprint (a specific combination of three constituting categories), indicating different patterns of conversation affecting learning outcomes. It would seem that in a mentoring relation a mentor's intent to arrange the conversation in a certain way would imply a deliberate connection to the learner('s motivation or background). This would constitute an interesting line of study to pursue. One way of looking into this, i.e., to satisfy the needs of students, would be to take into account or differentiate between the phase or stage of conversation as it relates to the progression in learning needs of the student (Ormond, 2011) since it might have a positive impact on learning outcomes; i.e., needs of a more experienced student teacher required a different mentor's approach to maximize the learning outcomes.

Another reason for our findings is the sensitivity of our 'model' i.e., detecting moves in conversations. The instrument we used to measure moves can be improved; not only by training to improve reliability, but also by improving on the content analysis that was used. A propositional analysis converts a conversation as a speech activity into a transcript, which might lose intent and purpose, as well as interactional cues (Mercer, 2004). In favour of a propositional; analysis speaks rigor and control of coding but may be at the expense of information and relevancy. In addition, a propositional approach analyzes the smallest units possible but in a conversational analysis larger, i.e., meaningful units might be a better frame of analysis. In support of this we found that the frequent occurrence of sequences of propositions with a common tread or pattern of moves i.e., a scaffolding or a prescriptive proposition is often preceded by several exploring propositions. The coding we used in this study, however, counts only the number of propositions in each category; not their sequence or pattern. It might be of interest to look for patterns, for instance we found that exploring propositions are often introductory for scaffolding or prescription moves (see further extentions in Chapter 7).

Another observation with regard to our analysis of moves is the high amount of propositions that could not be assigned to one of the three categories recognized by our model. More than half of the studied conversations had 50% or more 'other', miscellaneous propositions. Mena Marcos, Sanchez and Tillema (2010) who distinguished in their study between learning oriented moves such as rules and artefacts which were low in frequency of occurrence also found a high amount of 'other or non learning related propositions which could be characterized as "positive appraisals", i.e., comments of reassurance. This might indicate that a considerable amount of time in conversations is needed to provide for emotional and interactional alliance. The "high road" moves (which were more seldom) include giving feedback, providing information and suggesting practical advice, which only constituted a small (but we believe essential) part of the conversations. Emotional support was more predominant and includes the explorative moves characterized by giving sympathetic and positive support, attention and empathy.

In fostering the vital function of conversation as a vehicle to promote learning (Van der Westhuizen, Van der Merwe & Tillema, 2012) a mentor's approach, in our opinion, will need to have an impact on students' personal setting of standards (i.e., by the mentor's expression of high expectations) and on reassurance of the fruitfulness of discussion (to achieve knowledge productivity). This could imply that mutual understanding and a common interpretation on goals and attainment levels are of key importance in a talk between a mentor and a mentee. Zanting Verloop and van Driel (2007) point to the importance of 'explicating practical knowledge' as a common understanding in mentoring and argue that (in our words) "taking a high road" can be advantageous to student teachers for four reasons: student teachers obtain new information about teaching; they understand the nature of teaching better; they understand their mentor's mentoring better, and integrate theory with practice. There may be several approaches in conversation but some of them are better suited to make knowledge explicit than others. Our study indicates that at least three 'moves' are useful in capturing a conversation and analyzing its potential for learning.

IMPLICATIONS

It is of interest to note that the results of our case analysis of twelve conversations indicates that student teacher's relationship with his mentor highly influenced perceived learning outcomes. If this result can be generalized, it would indeed be recommendable to pay more attention to the matching process of students and to their mentors. What seems common practice now is that most student teachers and mentors are matched based on circumstantial considerations, e.g. availability, group composition, distance or class membership. Investing in a proper matching between mentor and mentee, for example established by using the Ideal Mentoring Scale by Rose (2000), could benefit the learning process.

Our study further shows that mentor's moves in a conversation influences the learning outcomes of the student teacher, but not significantly. Students who experienced a low road approach in the mentoring conversation have higher perceived learning outcomes. This probably has to do with the relative proficiency already attained by these students (all were in their 4th year of the program). It could imply that 'experience' has an impact on the relevancy of a particular approach. It would suggest that our 'low road' is beneficial for those student who already possess sufficient knowledge for practice and that a 'withholding', i.e., non prescriptive mentoring approach in these cases would be more beneficial to facilitate learning. If this finding can be generalized to mentoring programs, mentors can deliberately select combinations of moves as an approach to increase student teacher's learning outcomes.

39

ACKNOWLEDGEMENT

We like to thank Femke Gerretzen (MSc.) for her part in the coding and collection of data.

REFERENCES

Baxter Magolda, M. B. (2004). Evolution of a constructivist conceptualization of epistemological reflection. *Educational Psychologist, 39*(1), 31–43.

Bereiter, C. (2002). *Education and mind in the knowledge society*. Mahwah, NJ: Lawrence Erlbaum.

Bibby, T. (2009). How do children understand themselves as learners? *Pedagogy, Culture and Society, 17*(1), 41–55.

Bornstein, R. F. (1989). Exposure and affect: Overview and meta-analysis of research, 1968–1987. *Psychological Bulletin, 106*(2), 265–289.

Bovair, S., & Kieras, D. E. (1985). A guide to propositional analysis for research on technical prose. In B. K. Britton & J. B. Black (Eds.), *Understanding expository text*. Hillsdale, NJ: LEA.

Crasborn, F .J. A. J. (2010). *The skilled mentor. Mentor teachers' use and acquisition of supervisory skills* (Dissertation). Technische Universiteit Eindhoven, The Netherlands. Retrieved from http://alexandria.tue.nl/extra2/675808.pdf

Daloz, L. A. (1986). *Effective teaching and mentoring*. San Francisco, CA: Jossey-Bass.

Dawkins, R. (1996). *Climbing mount improbable*. New York, NY: W. W. Norton & Company.

Druckman, D. (2005). *Doing research*. Thousand Oaks, CA: Sage.

Edwards, A. (1995). Teacher education: Partnerships in pedagogy? *Teaching and Teacher Education, 11*(6), 595–610.

Ericsson, K. A. (2002). The path to expert golf performance: Insights from the masters on how to improve performance by deliberate practice. In P. R. Thomas (Ed.), *Optimising performance in golf* (pp. 1–57). Brisbane, Australia: Australian Academic Press.

Ericsson, K. A., Prietula, M. J., & Cokely, M. T. (2007). The making of an expert. *Harvard Business Review, 85*(7/8), 114–121.

Farr-Darling, L. (2001). When conceptions collide: Constructing a community of inquiry for teacher education in British Columbia, *Journal of Education for Teaching, 27*(1), 7–21.

Feldmann, A. (1999). *Conversational complexity*. Paper presented at the Annual Meeting of the American Educational Research Association, Montreal.

Franke, A., & Dahlgren, L. O. (1996). Conceptions of mentoring: An empirical study of conceptions or mentoring during the school-based teacher education. *Teaching and Teacher Education, 12*, 627–641.

Garvey, B (2011). *A very short fairly interesting and reasonably cheap book about coaching and mentoring*. London, England: Sage.

Garvey, B. (2014). *Fundamentals of coaching and mentoring*. London,England: Sage Publications Ltd.

Garvey, B., Stokes, P., & Megginson, D. (2009). *Coaching and mentoring, theory and practice*. London, England: *Sage*.

Goodwin, C., & Heritage, J. (1990). Conversational analysis. *Annual Review of Anthropology, 19*, 283–307.

Hargreaves, E. (2010). Knowledge construction and personal relationship: Insights about a UK university mentoring and coaching service. *Mentoring & Tutoring: Partnership in Learning, 18*(2), 107–120.

Hawkey, K. (1998). Mentor pedagogy and student teacher professional development: As study of two mentoring relationships. *Teaching and Teacher Education, 14*, 657–670.

Hennissen, P., Crasborn, F., Brouwer, N., Korthagen, F., & Bergen, T. (2008). Mapping mentor teacher's roles in mentoring dialogues. *Educational Research Review, 3*, 168–186.

Holsti, O. R. (1968). Content analysis. In G. Lindzey & E. Aronson (Eds.), *The handbook of social psychology* (Vol. 2). Reading, MA: Addison-Wesley.

Huberman, M. (1995). Networks that alter teaching, conceptualizations, exchanges and experiments. *Teaching & Teachers, 1*, 193–212.

Huling-Austin, L. (1990). Teacher induction programs and internships. In W. R. Houston, M. Haberman, & J. Sikula (Eds.), *Handbook of research on teacher education* (pp. 39–50). Reston, VA: Association of Teacher Education.

Leone, L., Perugini, M., & Ercolani, A. P. (1999). A comparison of three models of attitude-behavior relationships in the studying behavior domain. *European Journal of Social Psychology, 29*, 161–189.

Loughran, J. (2003). *Knowledge construction and learning to teach.* Keynote address for the International Association of Teachers and Teaching conference. Leiden University, Netherlands.

Martin, S. (1996). Support and challenge: Conflicting or complementary aspects of mentoring novice teachers? *Teachers and Teaching: Theory and Practice, 2*, 41–56.

Mazur, J. (2004). Conversation analysis for educational technologists: Theoretical and methodological issues for researching the structures, processes and meaning of on-line talk. In D. Jonassen (Ed.), *Handbook of research for educational communications and technology.* New York, NY: McMillian.

Nespor, J. (1987). The role of beliefs in the practice of teaching. *Journal of Curriculum Studies, 19*, 317–328.

Orland-Barak, L., & Tillema H. H. (2006). Collaborative knowledge construction; The dark side of the moon. *Teachers & Teaching 12*(1), 1–12.

Orland Barak, L., & Yinon, H. (2005). Sometimes a novice and sometimes an expert. Mentors professional expertise as revealed through their stories of critical incidents. *Oxford Review of Education, 31*, 557–578.

Ormond, C. (2011). Tailoring mentoring for new mathematics and science teachers: An exploratory study. *Australian Journal of Teacher Education, 36*(4), 53–72.

Pajares, F. (1992). Teachers' beliefs and educational research: Cleaning up a messy construct. *Review of Educational Research, 62*, 307–332.

Ragins, B. R., Cotton, J. L., & Miller, J. S. (2000). Marginal mentoring: The effects of type of mentor, quality of relationship, and program design on work and career attitudes. *Academy of Management Journal, 43*, 1177–1194.

Rodger, F. (2006). The ideal mentor? *Professional Learning Today*, 29–37.

Rolfe, A. (2007). *The mentoring conversation.* Kincumber, NSW: Synergetic People Development Pty Limited.

Rose, G. L. (2000). What do doctoral students want in a mentor? Development of the ideal mentor scale. *Dissertation Abstracts International, 60*(12B), 6418.

Smithey, M. W., & Evertson, M. W. (1995). Tracking the mentoring process: A multi-method approach. *Journal of Personnel Evaluation in Education, 9*, 33–53.

Strong, M., & Baron, W. (2004). An analysis of mentoring conversations with beginning teachers: Suggestions and responses. *Teaching and Teacher Education, 20*, 47–57.

Tillema, H. H. (2005). Collaborative knowledge construction in study teams of professionals. *Human Resource Development International, 8*(1), 81–99.

Tillema, H. H., & van der Westhuizen, G. (2006). Knowledge construction in collaborative enquiry among teachers. *Teachers & Teaching, 12*(1), 51–67.

Tomlinson, P. D., Hobson, A. J., & Malderez, A. (2010). Mentoring in teacher education. In P. Peterson, E. Baker, & B. McGaw (Eds.), *International encyclopedia of education* (pp. 749–756). Amsterdam, The Netherlands: Elsevier.

Zajonc, R. B. (1968). Attitudinal effects of mere exposure. *Journal of Personality and Social Psychology, 9* [Monograph supplement No. 2, Pt 2].

Zanting, A., Verloop, N., Vermunt, J. D., & van Driel, J. H. (1998). Explicating practical knowledge: An extension of mentor teacher's roles. *European Journal of Teacher Education, 21*(1), 11–28.

Harm Tillema
Leiden University, The Netherlands

Gert J. van der Westhuizen
University of Johannesburg, South Africa

Appendix 1. Scores on Measured Variables per Conversation

| Conversation | Mentor's approach | | | | | Satisfaction with mentor | | Relationship | | Learning outcomes |
| | Content analysis | | | | High or low road | M | Satisfaction | Closeness | | Knowledge productivity |
	Prescriptive	Scaffolding	Exploring	Other				Mentor's social position	Closeness	M
1	87 (21%)	64 (15%)	118 (28%)	155 (37%)	High	No score	No score	1	High	3.94
2	64 (16%)	8 (2%)	84 (21%)	240 (61%)	Low	4.53	Satisfied	1	High	4.67
3	13 (10%)	20 (15%)	38 (29%)	60 (46%)	Low	3.53	Satisfied	2	High	4.75
4	13 (5%)	43 (18%)	65 (27%)	122 (50%)	Low	3.88	Satisfied	1	High	4.00
5	56 (17%)	19 (6%)	132 (40%)	127 (38%)	Low	4.21	Satisfied	2	High	4.72
6	23 (24%)	11 (12%)	11 (12%)	50 (53%)	High	3.38	Not satisfied	3	Low	3.71
7	23 (5%)	18 (4%)	89 (20%)	320 (71%)	Low	3.65	Satisfied	3	Low	3.98
8	10 (6%)	15 (9%)	36 (21%)	112 (65%)	Low	3.38	Not satisfied	3	Low	4.13
9	2 (2%)	5 (6%)	27 (31%)	53 (61%)	Low	3.09	Not satisfied	3	Low	3.86
10	16 (17%)	16 (17%)	39 (41%)	25 (26%)	Low	4.09	Satisfied	3	Low	4.03
11	47 (24%)	32 (16%)	66 (33%)	54 (27%)	High	3.94	Satisfied	1	High	4.37
12	27 (18%)	15 (10%)	61 (41%)	46 (41%)	Low	3.15	Not satisfied	3	Low	3.78

Instruments
Instrument: Questionnaire on Student Teacher's Satisfaction With His/her Mentor
Please indicate your view by means of a number next to each statement. Choose on scale 5 to 1:
True for me 5 – 4 – 3 – 2 – 1 Not true for me

What I see in my mentor is that he/she:

Treats me as an adult who has a right to be involved in decisions that affect me	1	2	3	4	5
Values me as person	1	2	3	4	5
Respects the intellectual property rights of others	1	2	3	4	5
Believes in me	1	2	3	4	5
Recognizes my potential	1	2	3	4	5
Generally tries to be thoughtful and considerate	1	2	3	4	5
Works hard to accomplish his/her goals	1	2	3	4	5
Accepts me as a junior colleague	1	2	3	4	5
Inspires me by his or her example and words	1	2	3	4	5
Gives proper credit to students	1	2	3	4	5
Is a role model	1	2	3	4	5
Advocates for my needs and interests	1	2	3	4	5
Is calm and collected in times of stress	1	2	3	4	5
Prefers to cooperate with others than compete with them	1	2	3	4	5
Provides information to help me understand the subject matter I am reflecting on	1	2	3	4	5
Helps me plan a timetable for my reflection report	1	2	3	4	5
Helps me to investigate a problem I am having with my reflection report on school experience	1	2	3	4	5
Helps me plan the outline for my reflection report on school experience	1	2	3	4	5
Helps me to maintain a clear focus on my reflection report	1	2	3	4	5
Gives me specific assignments related to my reflection report	1	2	3	4	5
Meets with me on a regular basis	1	2	3	4	5
Is generous with time and other resources	1	2	3	4	5
Brainstorms solutions to a problem concerning my reflection report	1	2	3	4	5
Shows me how to employ relevant teaching methods	1	2	3	4	5
Relates to me as if he/she is a responsible, admirable older sibling	1	2	3	4	5
Talks to me about his/her personal problems	1	2	3	4	5

Is seldom sad and depressed	1	2	3	4	5
Is a cheerful, high-spirited person	1	2	3	4	5
Rarely feels fearful or anxious	1	2	3	4	5
Helps me realize my life vision	1	2	3	4	5
Has coffee or lunch with me on occasions	1	2	3	4	5
Is interested in speculating on the nature of the universe or the human condition	1	2	3	4	5
Takes me out for dinner and/or drink after work	1	2	3	4	5
Keeps his or her workspace neat and clean	1	2	3	4	5

Instrument: Questionnaire on The Experienced Learning Effect Of Mentoring

1.1 How do you evaluate your learning experiences in the mentoring conversation?

....

1.2 What have you learned and gained from the examples of the things that you expressed?

....

1.3 Can you identify some ideas expressed in the talk that you think contributed to your understanding of the issues in your reflection report?

....

2.1 Can you think of examples of things that were talked about which challenged the beliefs about teaching you have?

....

2.2. What experiences have changed your way of approaching matters and how have they influenced you?

....

3.1. Have the points you mentioned above in 1 in any way affected your thinking? How?

....

3.2 What kind of consequences would you draw as a result of the mentoring conversation?

....

3.3. Describe what you regard as memorable in the conversation. Why was it memorable for you?

....

3.4. If you were to think of a metaphor to describe the conversation you had with the mentor, what would you choose and why?

....

Instrument: Questionnaire On Perceived Knowledge Productivity
Please indicate your view by means of a number next to each statement. Choose on scale 5 to 1:
True for me 5 – 4 – 3 – 2 – 1 Not true for me

Problem understanding

I found the problems being discussed authentic and real	1	2	3	4	5
I think the discussion was fruitful and interesting	1	2	3	4	5
I could recognize from my own practice the issues that were dealt with	1	2	3	4	5
I found the discussion productive and leading to conclusions	1	2	3	4	5
I felt we dealt with problems that really mattered	1	2	3	4	5
I was cognizant and aware of the issues being discussed	1	2	3	4	5
I could contribute to the discussion in a productive way	1	2	3	4	5

Perspective shifting

I was able to grasp interesting ideas from my mentor	1	2	3	4	5
I think there were a lot of thoughts that set me thinking	1	2	3	4	5
I often experienced being confronted with new ideas in the discussion	1	2	3	4	5
I often led my thinking change during the discussion	1	2	3	4	5
I enjoyed listening to my mentor's contributions	1	2	3	4	5
The contributions my mentor made were very important	1	2	3	4	5
There were a lot of important ideas generated in this talk	1	2	3	4	5

Commitment to Apply

I let my mentor have the opportunity to air ideas	1	2	3	4	5
I refrain from pushing my own ideas too strongly	1	2	3	4	5
I experience great satisfaction partaking in the discussion	1	2	3	4	5
I participated to foster a process of mutual understanding	1	2	3	4	5
I sought to encourage an interactive communication at a high level	1	2	3	4	5
I think it is important to be understood in the discussion	1	2	3	4	5

JUANJO MENA AND ANTHONY CLARKE

3. ELICITING TEACHERS' PRACTICAL KNOWLEDGE THROUGH MENTORING CONVERSATIONS IN PRACTICUM SETTINGS

A Propositional Discourse Analysis (PDA)

INTRODUCTION

Student teacher: Sara asked me for the definition of "condensation" and I replied: It is like the humidity we feel in the air… I made a mistake and I feel terrible for it.

Mentor Teacher: In the case where a classroom student asks you for a further explanation and you do not know how to do it, you can tell her/him to look up the word in her/his own dictionary. First, you will not commit a mistake and mislead the student. Secondly, you will show Sara, or any other pupil, how to make use of that specific skill. Remember that using the dictionary is one of the procedural skills for most of the teaching units and this one is no exception. (May, 2013)

This interaction is a fragment taken from a mentoring conversation that took place in a Primary school in Salamanca (Spain). The Student Teacher was giving a lesson about the states of matter to 5th graders (11 years old). After the explanation, when classroom pupils were working in pairs, Sara, a student, asked aloud for clarification of the term "condensation". Since it was a pivotal concept for the lesson the Student Teacher had carefully read the definition of the textbook to the whole class minutes before: The inverse process of vaporization in which a vapor turns into liquid when there is a contrast of temperatures. However, as Sara seemed not to understand the previous explanation the Student Teacher's reply to Sara's question was to incorrectly equate condensation to air humidity. That was wrong and the advice the mentor teacher provided was to redirect the student to a dictionary the next time as an alternate strategy for dealing with the situation.

The learning contained in this example may be relatively unsubstantial in the 'bigger picture' of schooling but, in essence, it illustrates a genuine teaching strategy about how to proceed when the teacher vacillates about the right answer to a question. This kind of knowledge is evident in schools but is often neglected in Teacher Education Programs. Suggesting that the student use the dictionary may

H. Tillema et al. (Eds.), Mentoring for Learning, 47–78.

be not among any canonical response to the above problem, namely, the correct explanation of the concept of *condensation* in terms that an eleven year old student can easily understand. Some may have thought that it would be better to tell the Student Teacher to prepare more consciously her knowledge of the key concepts of the lesson. We agree that this is one possible response. But we also believe that other strategies or formulation should be considered valid as far as it is useful when dealing with practical situations. We have in this example an expert teacher's *rule of thumb* suggestion for addressing a problem quickly—as a kind of *in-situ* response that might be useful the next time the Student Teacher might face a similar situation. If the mentor teacher, as expert, recommends using that particular rule it is because it serves a purpose (i.e., not misleading the student), although it might be a temporary one. Using the dictionary in this situation is a strategy that serves as a halfway step until the Student Teacher learns a more standard response: a strategy that implies the best solution of the teaching problem in terms of pedagogical adequateness.

Therefore, the sum of guiding *in situ* strategies, such as the one described above, constitutes part of the practical knowledge repertoire that expert teachers use in their daily teaching, and may be determined by different professional roles and identities over the course of one's career.

The important issue therefore is finding ways to make this valuable knowledge explicit and communicable to others, especially the newcomers to the profession. Apart from that, it is also important to articulate this knowledge into theories *of* and *for* practice that may be utilized in classroom settings (both in-service and pre-service). Practical knowledge is often tacit knowledge (Verloop, Van Driel & Meijer, 2001) not readily accessible or verbalized unless those teachers are triggered to reflect upon or problematize their practice (Shulman, 1986, 1987). In this case, the classroom teacher may have not thought about the use of the dictionary until witnessing the student teacher's pitfall. The elicited expert teachers' tacit knowledge could provoke, in turn, a particular learning process for the apprentice and consequently affect future performance and style of teaching (Clarke, 2001).

The purpose of this chapter is therefore to highlight the importance of revealing the teachers' practical knowledge that plays a determinant role in ordinary decision-making processes at schools through a research approach called Propositional Discourse Analysis (PDA). This methodology allows for systematically identifying meaningful units of knowledge and organizing them into action-oriented formats that could make knowledge utilizable in other in-service, novice and prospective teachers' contexts.

Our objective is twofold: on the one hand we aim at (1) stressing the relevance of seizing the practical knowledge that emerges in mentoring conversations (as in the one contained in the above example), leaving other aspects of the interaction aside for the moment (i.e. context, personal engagement, emotional commitment, roles, etc.); and, on the other hand, (2) describing a possible procedure that may help researchers, teachers, and teacher educators to make such practical knowledge not only explicit but accessible for other teachers.

Along these lines, and according to the objectives, the chapter is structured into two major sections: (1) theoretical underpinnings in teacher mentoring (three main viewpoints) aimed at clarifying the nature of this process in educational research. To this end, we develop the argument that practical knowledge not only needs to be made public, but also be articulated into theories which can be shared in real settings of practice; (2) a discussion of how to make the practical knowledge explicit stressing one method in particular: Propositional Discourse Analysis (PDA).

MENTORING AS A GENUINE PRACTICE OF TEACHING TO TEACH

Over the last two decades teacher mentoring has been regarded as a key activity that plays a crucial role for the improvement of the quality of the educational practices (Clarke, 2001; Packard, 2003). Basically, mentoring is understood as the process of mediating professional learning in practice settings (Osula & Irvin, 2009). Mentors Teachers (MTs) are the ones who supervise Student Teachers (STs) in the schools with the purpose of helping them learn how to teach (Clarke, 2006, 2007).

Many education programs worldwide have begun to invest in teacher mentoring as an important way of enhancing the profession because it implies a direct connection to actual practices (Zollo & Winter, 2002). At the same time, a substantial body of research has shed light on relevant dimensions of mentoring and has proposed ways to facilitate its improvement (Hudson, 2013). If these are provided, then the practicum experience would become one of their most significant sources of learning support for STs (Marable & Raimondi, 2007).

More specifically, Teacher Education has stressed mentoring as a professional relationship that activates critical learning (Bradbury & Koballa, 2008) and effectively assesses practice (Tillema, 2009); a process that supports the development of knowledge and skills (Hudson, 2013) and ensures social transformation (Orland Barak, 2001). Nonetheless the intricate details of the work of mentoring are difficult to determine because it is an activity that takes place in both formal and informal situations often carried out on a voluntarily basis, and is time-consuming (Weinberg and Lankau, 2011). Besides, MTs "are regarded as little more than ad hoc overseers [and] often neglected in terms of their potential role as teacher educators (Nielsen, Triggs, Clarke, & Collins, 2010, p. 840).

Three relevant meta-analysis studies (Hansford, Ehrich & Tennent, 2004; Hobson, Ashby, Malderez & Tomlinson, 2009; Clarke, Triggs, & Nielsen, 2013) have revealed the state of art in mentoring by reviewing a substantial sample of studies of more than 300 original research papers. The following conclusions were reached:

- There are hidden and highly complex dimensions associated with the mentoring process;
- The literature on mentoring is disjoint and disparate which limits the construction of solid theoretical frameworks.
- The learning that emerges from the mentoring interactions is especially relevant when teaching to teach.

49

Research Perspectives on Mentoring and the Place of Practical Knowledge

However, there was no explicit addressing of the weight of practical knowledge as an object of study in the reviews referred to. For that reason, we chose a random selection of 50 studies from the studies reported in the three meta-analyses (which had deemed them both substantive and relevant) and organized them according to their focus of research. Two criteria were followed: first, the studies selected were all in peer-reviewed education journals that were published throughout the last 30 years and appear in major databases such as ERIC, EBSCO, Science Direct and PsycINFO; second, all the works refer to mentoring as a formal professional activity supported by teaching institutions (as opposed to informal mentoring). A matrix was created including the title of the article, author, date of publication, descriptors, object of study and a short statement of major results. Our review resulted in the appreciation of three latent research trajectories (see Table 1):

1. Mentoring as a way of constructing a professional identity
   A substantial body of research states that mentoring leads to the construction of particular teacher identities (Connelly & Clandinin, 1999; McLean, 1999; Chong, Ling & Chan, 2011; Danielewicz, 2001) because only by the assimilation of routines and professional ideas can STs and MTs identify themselves as classroom teachers. Table 1 shows that 44% of the selected research studies (22 out of 50) highlight that mentoring contributes to enhancing personal attributes, assuming certain roles and beliefs which, in the end, determine professional growth (Killian & Wilkins, 2009). The identification (in research) and promotion (in practice) of those attributes is the epicentre of this perspective.

2. Mentoring as a form of establishing a supporting relationship.
   STs' learning of the profession happens through successive interactions that promote active participation in a community of practice (Lave & Wenger 1991). According to Table 1, 34% of studies defend that the mentoring communicative process is crucial to understand the teaching profession. Furthermore, the mentoring relationship extends beyond the MT and the ST dyad to include the administration, school staff and families (Clarke & Jarvis-Selinger, 2005). The key functions of the mentoring relationship according to Clarke *et al.* (2012) and Daloz (2012) are: challenge, motivation, and support. Johnson (2006) stresses the distinction between professional and personal dimensions whereas Feiman-Nemser & Floden (1999) refers to psychological support and instruction-related support.

3. Mentoring that discloses practice-based learning that emerges in school settings.
   The meanings that are negotiated by mentors and mentees in particular situations constitute the repertoire of knowledge that needs to be learnt. Those meanings arise through engaging in cognitive process such as critical reflection, think aloud, analysis of lessons or systematic observations and are represented in 22% of the studies in Table 1. Often what is discussed and reflected upon reveal

Table 1. Review of teaching mentoring research outcomes. Based on studies listed in Hobson et al., (2009); Hansford et al. (2004) and Clarke et al. (2013) reviews

Main idea	Dimension	Results reported		Nr. of studies
		For mentors	For mentees	
Mentoring a as a way of constructing a professional *identity*	Self	- Mentoring provides additional non-contact time to prepare for their role (Abell, Dillon, Hopkins, McInerney & O'Brien, 1995) - Consolidation of teacher identity (Bodoczky & Malderez, 1997) - Contributing to the personal development of mentors (Danielewicz, 2001) - Mentors feel less isolated (Hagger & McIntyre, 2006); or feel more isolated (Graham, 1997) - Mentors are models for good professional practice (Foster, 1999) - Mentoring increases mentors' professional self-esteem (Evans & Abbott, 1997). - Mentoring develops professional beliefs (Rajuan, Beijaard & Verloop; 2007) - Mentoring increases confidence and self-esteem (McIntyre & Hagger, 1996) - Mentoring practice is sometimes constraining and not enough "freedom to innovate" (Beck & Kosnick, 2000). - Mentors do not grow professionally from mentoring (Tauer, 1998) - Mentors help mentees to construct particular teacher identities (McAdams, 2001; Chong, Ling & Chan, 2011)	- Teachers who are mentored are less likely to leave teaching because they assume a particular identity (Ingersoll, 2004) - Assumption of professional beliefs (Haser & Star, 2009). - Individual well-being (Ballantyne, Hansford & Packer, 1995; Kessels, Beijaard, Veen & Verloop, 2008) - Mentoring promotes identity transformation within the work environments and organization (Mullen, 2011) (Bullough, 2005) - Mentoring reduces STs' feelings of insecurity, nervousness by being observed (Orland Barak, 2001) - STs depend on mentoring for their well being (Hardy, 1999). - Insufficiently challenged by mentors (Edwards, 1998)	22
Mentoring as a form of establishing a supportive *relationship*	Interaction	- The mentoring relationship (MR) increases mentor teachers' job satisfaction and confidence (Douglas, 1997) - The MR is a way of improving mentors' communication skills (Moor, Halsey, Jones, Martin, Stott, Brown & Harland, 2005) - The MR promotes support and connection to external networks (Whisnant, Elliott & Pynchon, 2005) - The MR leads to increasing workloads (Lee & Feng, 2007) - Difficulties in accommodating all their mentees' needs (Maynard, 2000) - The MR provides a chance to engage with STs (Glenn, 2006)	- The MR advances psychosocial support (Kram 1985) - The MR increases collaboration and enjoyment (Murray & Owen, 1991) - The MR helps the socialization of preservice teachers (Johnson, 2006) - The MR helps preservice teachers to adapt to the school norms (Wang &Odell, 2002) - Mentees have access to support in external networks (Brady, 1993) - The MR is framed under a structured programme of mentor preparation (Crasborn, Hennissen, Brouwer, Korthagen & Bergen, 2008) - The MR facilitates the development of a shared discourse (Carroll, 2005) - Great source of comfort characterized by collegial cultures (Bush & Coleman, 1995) - The MR assistance and support socialization (Crow & Matthews, 1998; Lipton & Wellman, 2001; Ballantyne, Packer and Hansford, 1995)	17
Mentoring as a way of practice-based *learning.*	Knowledge	- A way of improving critical reflection (Lopez-Real & Kwan, 2005) - A way of gaining new ideas and perspectives (Davies, Brady, Rodger & Wall, 1999). - A way of validating ideas with university tutors or re-engaged with the profession (Hobson, Malderez Tracey, Giannakaki, Kerr, Pell, Chambers, Tomlinson & Roper, 2007) - A way of fertilizing new ideas (Brady, 1993) - Helping mentors to understand the potential benefits of discussing pedagogical issues (Lindgren, 2005) - Mentoring stimulates mentees to reflect on their actions (Dunne & Bennet, 1997) - Observing lessons (of and by mentee) and analyzing them (Heilbronn, Jones, Bubb & Totterdell, 2002)	- A way of learning content knowledge in many areas (Hardy, 1999) - A way of learning new ideas from mentors' feedback (Tin, 1995) and reflecting on one's own teaching (Spargo, 1994) - It leads to rethinking beliefs and prior knowledge (Baumert & Kunter, 2006)	11

uncertainties or contradictory information (Daloz, 1986). However they constitute the platform for understanding teaching practice. It is a way of gaining new ideas and perspectives. In this sense, ideally, the knowledge that expert teachers gather throughout years of practice is shared with apprentices to initiate their learning of the profession. (Tillema & Van der Westhuizen, 2013; Orland-Barack, 2010)

Table 1 shows that most of the research assumes that teachers' styles are rooted in particular professional and personal attributes that result in more or less supportive mentoring relationships (a total of 78% of the studies). Fewer studies focus their attention on the practical knowledge learnt in mentoring conversations, and it is typically associated to processes such as reflection, critical thinking or action-research (Russell, 1987).

However, practical knowledge has been extensively promoted in Teacher Education as the knowledge of how to do things (*techne*) which is not subjected to scientific procedures (*episteme*) but needs to be studied and exposed to standards of justification because it is of crucial importance for the teaching practices (Fenstermacher, 1986, 1994). Elbaz (1983) extends the notion of practical knowledge not only to knowing how but also to being aware of different aspects of teaching activities (i.e. pupils' learning styles, social school dynamics, community policies, etc.). Connelly, Clandinin and Fang He (1999) as well as Meijer, Verloop & Beyaard (1999) expand the definition of personal practical knowledge as the body of beliefs, thoughts and attitudes found in the teacher's practice which finally result in a combination of practical understandings and principles. Practical knowledge is therefore bound to specific situations and oriented to action (Feiman-Nemser & Floden, 1986) because it serves as a platform for making decision on future classroom objectives, instructional strategies or curricular materials (Tillema, 2006; Tillema & van der Westhuizen, 2013).

Articulation of Practical Knowledge from Teacher Mentoring

As can be confirmed in the literature reviewed, Teacher Education has accumulated a corpus of evidence around mentoring which has been structured into coherent theories to guide practice. Current educational research usually follows four predetermined stages to articulate evidence (Sánchez, 2001), although they do not always unfold in the strict order as shown in Figure 1:

• Typically, new ideas (stage 1) impact practice after research shows that they are valid (stage 2). Through the dissemination of those results in specialized journals or Educational programs (stage 3), teachers are typically left with the responsibility of accomplishing the implementation process on their own (Stage 4) sometimes with the help of specialized literature. As a result, they are expected (but not researchers) to transform research evidence into instruments or know-how knowledge that may be useful for their practice.

- Alternatively, we propose another possible path to overcome this constraint and better articulate research findings. In the search to find spaces to elicit teachers' practical knowledge, and give it a leading role in educational research, we suggest that this path entails the accomplishment of four stages (see Figure 2):

1. Description of real practices: Instead of creating theories from the university we propose to follow a naturalist (grounded) approach and start by describing what is done in the teaching practice (i.e. through field observation; video-recordings, etc.)
2. Validation: Data gathered from the previous stage have to be subjected to regular educational research data analysis procedures.
3. Implementation: Educational research—and this should be underlined—has to provide the means by which the validated data can be implemented in the contexts of practice. In order to do this, the research outcomes must be transformed into practice-ready knowledge for teachers that can be used in regular teaching situations. We propose the use of Action Oriented Knowledge (AOK) units. Those units are know-how sets of strategies and techniques that help practitioners

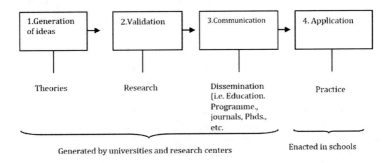

Figure 1. Stages followed in Traditional Educational Research in the articulation of Teacher Education evidence (Adapted from Sánchez, 2001)

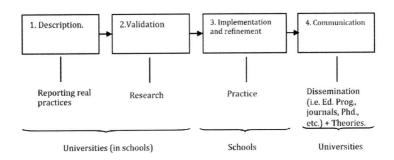

Figure 2. Alternative path to articulate research evidence in Teacher Education

to make sense of practice (Urzúa &Vásquez, 2008; Lougrhran, Berry & Mulhall, 2012). They bring together "..all profession-related insights that are potentially relevant to the teacher's activities" (Verloop, van Driel, & Meijer, 2001, p. 443). Those AOK units can be polished and refined once they are tested in practice as more teachers explore and experiment with them.
4. Communication: Schools would directly benefit from the results of research projects in the form of new knowledge, tools (i.e. handbooks and teaching practice guidelines) or knowledge management systems (i.e. on-line mentoring system) which, in turn, will facilitate teacher professionalization (with a direct impact on pupil learning and ST mentoring).

Steps 1 and 2 represent a way of assembling professional knowledge into *theories of practice*. Knowledge gathered from particular mentoring situations are further structured into a set of principles and ideas that serve to describe phenomena around teaching practice (Carr, 1986). In short, a "knowledge base for teaching" (Shulman, 1987, p. 4). On the other hand, steps 3 and 4 are a means of embedding practical knowledge into other practices *(theories for practice)*. Practical knowledge should not be only described as theories of practice but also framed in such ways that it can be implemented in real teaching needs, goals, and contexts (Cochran-Smith & Lytle, 1999).

A DISCOURSE ANALYSIS FRAMEWORK TO ARTICULATE PRACTICAL KNOWLEDGE

With a deliberate focus on the practice-based learning that mentoring provides (third research perspective, Table 1), in this section we want to clarify how practical knowledge can be made explicit from mentoring interactions and also communicated to other teachers. Universities and higher education institutions need to support teachers in eliciting and communicating their valuable ideas, thoughts and insights that facilitate teacher learning. We propose the use of research discourse analysis techniques for the identification and articulation of teachers' practical knowledge as opposed to action-research or narrative inquiry since this methodology admits the precise identification of practical knowledge units in regular discourse interactions.

Preliminary Considerations

Problem of substantiality. However, prior to making practical knowledge explicit educational research needs to prioritize what pressing aspects would firstly need to be known by STs and others, which may be complementary. Often many aspects are considered (see Table 1) without often realizing the local limitations and short time frames to act and learn to be a teacher. Thus, which learning would be more substantial to guarantee that STs learn the basics of the teaching profession during the practicum experience?

54

To better answer this question, imagine another professional learning context where an expert surgeon has to teach a novice surgeon how to suture a wound on a patient. What knowledge should the expert surgeon share with the apprentice in an attempt to better teach him/her how to perform this medical process?

By making a hypothetical transposition of some evidence from Teacher Education (see Table 1) to the field of medicine, the following would be part of what the expert surgeon must do to improve the learner's capacities:

1. Reduce feelings of isolation of the Student Surgeon (SS).
2. Increase SS' confidence and self-esteem.
3. Manage SS' time and workload.
4. Improve the BS's ability for critical reflection.
5. Share new perspectives and ideas with the SS.
6. Increase collaboration and enjoyment.
7. Identify SS conceptions about surgery.
8. Undertake an appropriate program to be a good surgeon mentor.

[...]

According to the actual procedure followed in surgery the knowledge to be shared would be similar to this (Aluwihare, 2002):

1. Insert the needle at right angles to the tissue and gently advance through the tissue avoiding shearing forces.
2. As a rough rule of thumb, the distance from the edge of the wound should correspond to the thickness of the tissue and successive sutures should be placed at twice this distance apart, i.e. approximately double the depth of the tissue sutured.
3. All sutures should be placed at right angles to the line of the wound at the same distance from the wound edge and the same distance apart in order for tension to be equal down the wound length. The only situation where this should not apply is when suturing fascia: the sutures should be placed at varying distances from the wound edge in order to prevent the fibers parting.
4. For long wounds being closed with interrupted sutures, it is often advisable to start in the middle and to keep on halving the wound [...] (p. 14–15).

In the first mentoring situation the format of knowledge is based on abstract principles and good intentions to improve professional learning. In contrast, in the second mentoring situation the format of knowledge is based on rules that break down the procedure into manageable and easy to access steps and their conditions (= if you find "x"... then you should do "y"). Therefore while the two examples are extreme and the contexts different, the point that we wish to make is that the first is grounded in *intentions,* the second one in *actions.* We argue that, the most efficient way for STs to make the most of their practicum is to start by learning the set of procedures and strategies that help to deal with practical situations (similarly to the medical procedure above) and, once the protocols are mastered (i.e. techniques to manage classroom, strategies to deliver a lesson, etc.) then they can also reflect on what is done, to share perspectives, work collaboratively, etc.

The problem of perspective. The use of discourse analysis, as a methodology that collects, transcribes and analyzes data to further find significant sequences of meaning (Schiffrin, Tannen & Hamilton, 2003), is crucial to systematically approach the representative events that are occasioned by and through mentoring interactions. Nonetheless, different types of discourse analysis may be undertaken depending on the units chosen (i.e. episodes, topics, critical incidents, utterances, etc.). Any of these are suitable for in-depth study of mentoring conversations depending on the research questions. However not every one can be potentially relevant to capture practical knowledge.

To illustrate this point, we take an example already published in literature by Crasborn, Hennissen, Brouwer, Korthagen and Bergen (2011, p. 322) to determine how it might be analyzed differently by using different units of discourse analysis:

MT: Ella, in the reading comprehension lesson you carried out, I saw you had a correct diagram on the blackboard. Very good!

ST: Yes, thank you!

MT: But, I saw that Paula wrote on a small piece of paper. You know, the agreement is that she must use her notebook. You should have told her to do so.

ST: Yes, I wanted her to write it in her notebook, but I forgot to give special attention to her, because a few other pupils were asking questions.

If utterances are used to analyse the conversation above the speech should be divided into statements, defined as a group of words that are demarked by two pauses. Henissen, Crasborn, Brouwer, Kortaghen and Bergen (2011) identify utterances by the principle of turn-taking. This unit may coincide with one or several sentences within the same participant's conversational turn (Schegloff, 2000). Therefore, in this interaction four utterances are identified coinciding with four turns of discussion, two for each of the participants (see Table 2).

In the case of using critical incidents the researcher has to analyse only significant events that are important for both the ST and MT (Fanagan, 1954; Orland-Barak, 2005). In the above fragment the critical incident may be designated as the broad theme-name that identifies it: (Not the) use of the notebook by one student (see Table 2). Critical events may underpin either positive or negative teaching experiences (Husu, Toom & Patrikainen, 2008) and trigger meaningful mentoring conversations in which questions about when, what and why happened are asked (Carnot & Stewart, 2006).

Table 2. A mentoring conversation fragment analysed according to different discourse analysis methods. Note: Talk Rubrics. Yes = Rubrics that were discussed in the fragment. No = Rubrics that were not discussed

Verbatim text	Utterances	Topical analysis	Critical incidents	Interaction units	Talk rubrics
MT. Ella, in the reading comprehension lesson you carried out, I saw you had a correct diagram on the blackboard. Very good!	U1. Ella, in the reading comprehension lesson you carried out, I saw you had a correct diagram on the blackboard. Very good!	Correct information on in the blackboard	(Not) use of the notebook by one student.	Unit of interaction 1. -Judgment given by MT: " Your reading comprehension lesson was good" -Meaning attributed by the MT. "It was good because you had a correct diagram on the blackboard".	Rubric1:Visual information (Yes) Rubric 2:Teacher's Eye contact (No)
ST: Yes, thank you! MT: But, I saw that Paula wrote on a small piece of paper. You know, the agreement is that she must use her notebook. You should have told her to do so.	U2. Yes, thank you! U3. But, I saw that Paula wrote on a small piece of paper. You know, the agreement is that she must use her notebook. You should have told her to do so.	Paula did not use the notebook.		-Formalization of the rule: "a diagram on the blackboard" is valuable in circumstances…"of reading comprehension" and leads to… "success". Unit of interaction 2. -Judgment given by MT: " Paula wrote on a small piece of paper"	Rubric 3: Individual attention to students (Yes) Rubric 4: Clear instructions to class students (No)
ST. Yes, I wanted her to write it in her notebook, but I forgot to give special attention to her, because a few other pupils were asking questions.	U4. Yes, I wanted her to write it in her notebook, but I forgot to give special attention to her, because a few other pupils were asking questions.	Not giving attention to students.		-Meaning attributed by MT: "You should have told her to… use her notebook". Meaning attributed by ST: -"I forgot to give special attention to her because other students were asking questions". -Formalization of the rule: "using the notebook"…is valuable in circumstances …"when students wrote from the blackboard" and leads to…"better understanding"	

Topics are also often used in discourse analysis. This technique reduces primary data into different levels of categories following a grounded process of analysis (Straus & Corbin, 1994) enriched by relevant theories on mentoring. A topic seizes an essential piece of information with regard to the research question and "represents some level of patterned response or meaning within the data set" (Braun & Clarke, 2006, p. 82). It generally coincides with data categories at a certain level of analysis. In the example given above, there are three topics therefore (Table 2): (t1) Correct information in the blackboard; (t2) Paula did not use the notebook; and (t3) Not giving attention to the students.

Interaction units represent the meaning each participant attributes to the events that have been discussed in a mentoring interaction. Usually a unit of interaction is created each time the object of meaning (or topic) changes and it is labeled strictly using the participants' vocabulary (Challies, Bruno, Méard & Bertone, 2010). Each interaction unit is represented by a structural pattern where the sequence of meaning is defined as: (a) the judgment given by the either the MT or ST to a particular event, (b) the meaning attributed to that event, and (c) the formalization of a rule, or principle of learning for the situation analyzed (Challies, Escalié, Bertone & Clarke, 2012). In the example above there are two units of interaction (see Table 2).

Finally, talk quality rubrics may be used for the analysis of any mentoring conversation. However they are based on a predetermined list of criteria or categories (i.e., objectives, class organization, etc.) about what is important for a teaching episode or interaction. Additionally, rubrics establish a rating scale for the behaviours observed: for example, from excellent to poor (Jonsson & Svingby, 2007). Usually rubrics are used as a top-down analysis tool, where preset indicators are first introduced to look through the data (Junker *et al.*, 2004). In the selected example, if this unit of analysis is chosen it requires selecting instructional rubrics beforehand and then further identifying them in the mentoring conversation as it unfolds. Four rubrics might be included but it entirely depends on the listed categories chosen.

Each technique entails a different sort of analysis and, consequently, a different account of knowledge for the same mentoring conversation excerpt. Depending on the analysis, there are four utterances, one critical incident, three topics, two units of interaction, and two talk rubrics. Besides, according to Table 3 each unit has a different nature: *syntactical* if it is based on formal linguistic indicators (i.e. words, sentences, utterances); or *semantic* if it is based on inferred meanings. Semantic units seem to be more suitable for describing practical knowledge. Each unit also represents different ways of conducting the analysis (inductive: bottom up vs. deductive: top-down) and scales in levels of scrutiny depending on the size of the unit (data examination can be more or less rigorous according to it). Inductive and more specific sorts of analyses would be preferable to precisely depict shared understandings of practice.

The Propositional Discourse Analysis (PDA)

Since we propose to describe what MTs and STs do (stage 1 in Figure 2) we need to consider how to extract the substantial components of what constitutes practical knowledge (problem of substantiality) following a technique that more precisely allows accounting it (problem of perspective). The analysis of the mentoring interactions should be also performed in a way that it may be validated (stage 2 in Figure 2). In order to meet those criteria, we propose a research discourse methodology anchored in propositional analysis to describe the social representations of the conversations.

Table 3. Comparison of five discourse units of analysis in relation to their nature, type of analysis, level of scrutiny and contingent features

Unit of analysis (method)	Nature	Type of analysis	Level of scrutiny (according to the unit size)	Contingent features
Utterances	Syntactical	Inductive	High	- They allow seeing who brings the topic to the conversation. - Good for analysing the level of participation.
Critical incidents	Semantic	Inductive	Low	- Broader than topics they also allow to organize the contents of the conversation. - Good for making first-order categories.
Topics	Semantic	Inductive	Medium	- They allow to condense the information into comprehensible units of meaning: i.e. *"The ST had problems with the student' use of notebook (no use)"*. - Good for making categories.
Units of interaction	Semantic and syntacticAL	Inductive	High	- They give a common frame to every interaction making the dialogue predictable. - Good for extracting structures/schemes of knowledge.
Talk rubrics	Semantic	Deductive	Medium	- They start from an agreed frame of categories to analyse practice. - Good to compare different mentoring performances out of the same dimensions.

Propositional analysis as the baseline to analyze mentoring interactions.   Originally used in the field of reading comprehension (Kintch & Van Dijk, 1978; Kintsch, 1988; Sánchez, Rosales, & Suárez, 1999) propositional analysis is a methodological approach that provides insights on how knowledge is generated through the examination of text generated by the participants in professional conversations (Tierney & Mosenthal, 1983). A proposition is a statement that contains one single predicate (Kintsch & Van Dijk, 1978; Sánchez, Rosales, & Suárez, 1999). A predicate is an expression that can be true of something and usually includes the predicate or relational term (often verbs and auxiliaries) and the arguments of that predicate (i.e. the subject and object noun phrases) (Kroeger, 2005). From our perspective, and following Bovair and Kieras (1985), we define a proposition as "a unit of information containing a single predicate that, when isolated from its wider text, allows for a clear identification of its meaning (Mena, García, & Tillema, 2012, p. 5).

59

Making use of the same example used by Crasborn *et al.* (2011, p. 322), Table 4 shows briefly how the propositional analysis may work:

The verbatim text is divided into eight propositions or ideas (p1 to p8), each of them corresponding to a grammatical predicate. There are two levels of propositions: first order propositions (e.g., p1; p2, p3, etc.) when the idea is commonly stated within a main clause; and second order propositions (e.g., p8.1) when the idea usually comes in the form of a subordinate clause (e.g., a causal proposition in the case of p8.1; but they can also be conditional, modal, circumstantial or final propositions).

Secondly, a proposition, as we define it, has an independent meaning on its own without depending to a large degree on the context is taken from. Therefore they can be listed in order to infer categories in later stages of the analysis. For that reason we use square brackets to indicate that a piece of information has been repeated by the analyst in order to keep the meaning of the idea when the agent is omitted or when anaphoric elements have been used (i.e. "it" "that" "he/ she", etc.)

On the other hand we use curly brackets to indicate that a piece of information has been moved from its original wording position or slightly modified by the analyst in order to keep a single, non context-dependent predicate while preserving the original meaning.

According to Table 3, the criteria used for the propositions meet the requirements of being:

a. semantic units that reflect sociocognitive processes (necessary for looking for meanings or ideas in the conversation)—not syntactical units as words, sentences or utterances;
b. they arise after a bottom-up inductive analytical process is conducted (Grounded Theory Analysis, Strauss & Corbin, 1994)—this is important because what matters is what MTs and STs originally think and not the heuristics or predetermined set of categories researchers may apply to data;

Table 4. Example of propositional analysis. Following Mena, Sánchez and Tillema, 2008

Verbatim transcription	Analysis (propositions)	
MT. Ella, in the reading comprehension lesson you carried out, I saw you had a correct diagram on the blackboard. Very good!	P1.	Ella, you carried out {a reading comprehension lesson}
	P2.	I saw you had a correct diagram on the blackboard.
	P3.	[The diagram on the blackboard] was good.
ST: Yes, thank you!		
MT: But, I saw that Paula wrote on a small piece of paper. You know, the agreement is that she must use her notebook. You should have told her to do so.	P4.	I saw Paula wrote on a small piece of paper.
	P5.	The agreement is: she must use her notebook.
	P6.	You should have told her to do so.
ST. Yes, I wanted her to write it in her notebook, but I forgot to give special attention to her, because a few other pupils were asking questions.	P7.	I wanted her to write in her notebook.
	P8.	I forgot to give special attention to her
	P8.1.	(CAUS) Few other pupils were asking questions.

c. the level of scrutiny is high since the unit size of analysis is small (one proposition equals one predicate)—they are similar to utterances but with the difference being that propositions are aligned with ideas shared and not simple defined in terms of conversation turns; and

d. they are accurate as they generate an exact number of ideas that represent teachers' practical knowledge derived from the conversation.

Furthermore, propositional analysis should also be validated. Validating the knowledge that is extracted from mentoring interactions implies, as suggested by Cho & Trent (2006), that we should take into the account that a level of certainty needs to be reached. They refer to it as transactional validity,

> an interactive process between the researcher, the researched, and the collected data that is aimed at achieving a relatively higher level of accuracy and consensus by means of revisiting facts, feelings, experiences, and values or beliefs collected and interpreted. The role and use of transactional validity in qualitative research varies to the extent the researcher believes it achieves a level of certainty. (p. 321)

In gaining that level of consistency we need to subject propositions –as with any other unit of analysis—to at least two criteria if we want to focus our attention on the professional knowledge that emerges from mentoring conversations:

Fitness for purpose (Strauss & Corbin, 1998). Any work in research needs to plausibly meet "the relationship between the methods chosen and the process studied" (Mena & Tillema, 2006, p. 114). The last implies choosing the means that best expresses what is being searched for. For instance, if we want to analyze teachers' classroom performance, then topics from field notes or video-tape transcriptions could be more aligned to that purpose than excerpts from the answers given to a questionnaire; the latter talks more about teachers' beliefs while the former is more clearly tied to teachers' actions. Similarly, if we want to analyze the level of participation then topical analysis would be less useful than utterances.

Standard of unambiguity. Researchers also need to think about the unit of analysis that results in less ambiguous outcomes. In other words, we need a unit that leads to fewer interpretations of the data. We specially need to meet this criterion when quantitative data is offered or when reliability checks are to be undertaken. For instance, "turns" are a straightforward unit with a very small error-of-interpretation margin but they do not help to capture the shared understandings in mentoring conversations: They do not *fit* for that intention. Critical incidents or topics can respond for the last but they may include more than one teacher's thought, idea or belief (i.e. a wider unit). In this sense, the semantically longer the unit is the more difficult is to find unambiguity in its categorization.

We consider that propositional analysis to be an eligible approach to effectively deal with both criteria because it fits for the purpose of analyzing practical knowledge: it seeks for "meanings" contained in the predicates (Criterion 1). Secondly propositions are less ambiguous units of analysis than others described above since one unit only can contain one predicate. Therefore the smaller the unit is the less the interpretation margin (Criterion 2). Furthermore, the process of research data validation (step 2; Figure 3) can be undertaken by using Cohen Kappa reliability checks. Propositional analysis allows reaching higher levels of data replication according to ad hoc methodological verification processes (Denzin & Lincoln, 2000). Reliability scores from propositional analysis in previous works demonstrated k=.70 to k=.90 (Mena *et al.*, 2012).

Extended procedure of the PDA. Relying on propositional analysis means that the analysis of mentoring interactions follows two processes: (a) segmentation of information and (b) categorization.

A. Segmentation of Information

Primary segmentation will consist of dividing the transcribed dialogues into propositions following the process described above (Please refer to Appendix A, column 4). A secondary and broader segmentation, according to Emilio Sánchez's work (Sánchez, Rosales, & Suárez; 1999; Sánchez & Rosales, 2005; Rosales, Iturra, Sánchez, & De Sixte, 2006) propose the use of larger units of discourse analysis such as episodes (coherent sequences of sentences or paragraphs that globally organize the mentoring dialogue into broad segments, for example, an episode of evaluation; Schegloff, 1987) and cycles (fragments of the discourse that often end up in conversational agreement; Wells, 2001) in order to scale the segmentation of the text transcriptions from wider to smaller bits of information (e.g., episodes-cycles-propositions). Please see Appendix A, columns 1 and 2.

B. Categorization

B1.Pairing propositions with knowledge types. Once the transcribed conversations are divided into propositions, the next step is to identify the types of practical knowledge by pairing each proposition with a type (see Appendix A; column 5).

According to previous works, we have identified at least four distinctive knowledge types that are present in most mentoring dialogues and that we argue help MTs to assist PTs in analyzing their practice: Recalls, Appraisals, Rules and Artifacts (Mena, García, Clarke and Barkatsas, *accepted*; Mena *et al.*, 2012; Mena, García & Tillema, 2009; Mena & García, 2011). These four types of practical knowledge scale in complexity or level of re-description (Karmiloff-Smith, 1992) from a compilation of facts and events (i.e., recalls), to evaluation and judgment of those events (i.e., appraisals) culminating in a higher level of sophistication whereby those experiences are sorted into overarching strategies or know-how (i.e., rules and mobilization and/or incorporation of artifacts). In short they move from narrative knowledge through to inferential knowledge where rules and artifacts constitute a refined and more complex understanding of practice (Bruner, 1991).

Narrative Knowledge is characterized by being concrete (subjected to the experience lived) and less generalizable (its format of representation is usually stays at the descriptive level). It usually takes two distinguishable forms:

1. Recalls

Recalls are direct reproductions of what has been experienced, that is, images that STs extract from the lesson, as collected from memory, in the form of events or incidents. For example, "I organized the classroom in two groups" or "Ana shouted at Enrique" (Mena *et al., accepted*).

Those teaching actions are the basis of what teachers reflect upon and the first step to scale into more complex forms of knowledge construction (Schön, 1983, 1987; Elliot, 1991; Kemmis & McTaggart, 1988). According to Gholami & Husu, (2010) any teaching action is understood in terms of situational knowledge (actions and reactions to different facts) and routines (repeated actions repeated over lessons). They are part of what is done (actions) whereas reflection is about what is thought. However we want to draw the attention to the fact that the first step of any reflective process is to recount (remember) what has been done. Those representations can be more or less accurate depictions of actual experiences. Some authors do not often consider recalls as a form of practical knowledge (Engstrom, 2009) since they are roughly included within the realm of the experience itself.

2. Appraisals

Appraisals constitute evaluations or value judgments of the action that is being recalled. The function of appraisals is differentiating which episodes of practice were successful from the ones that were not. As such, we can divide appraisals into two groups: Positive appraisals are aspects of practice that are satisfactory and productive for STs (i.e., "They [Pupils] chose quickly a partner to work with) and negative appraisals are aspects of practice that turned out to be inadequate and detrimental to pupil learning (i.e., "The classroom size was very small for the activities").

From the field of philosophy, Engstrom (2009) equates appraisals to "practical judgments in which certain actions are deemed good or bad" (p. 56). However, practical judgments should be distinguished from "judgments of appraisal actions", that is to say "our approval or disapproval of particular actions and conducts which has been often recalled as moral judgments" (p. 56). Husu and Tirri (2003) referred to this as moral reflection.

Inferential knowledge, on the other hand, is more abstract in nature and therefore more generalizable to the broader context of one's practice. Two different sorts of knowledge are to be found within this category:

3. Rules (to guide practice)

Rules are defined in this study as inferences extracted from experience that constitute practical principles for teachers (for example, "controlling the time students spend in classroom tasks is important"). That is, it is a manner of re-describing particular facts and transforming them into global ideas (abstracting the general from the particular) that can be used in future situations. They are usually framed after memorable facts are recalled or when becoming aware of a classroom routine. In that sense they can be representations of tacit knowledge displayed in teachers' skills and competences (Toom, 2006, 2012).

The term rule has been used in research on practical knowledge. Elbaz (1981, 1983) and Conelly, Clandinin and Fang (1997) differentiate two different generalizations of practice: rules as expressions of actions (e.g., listening to students) and practical principles as wider conceptions than rules (e.g., "students learn more when they pursue their interests"). Connelly, Clandinin and Fang He (1997) add another category: personal philosophy. Personal philosophy represents engagement of a broader nature in which the teacher connects their own experiences, rules or principles, with theories.

4. Artifacts

According to Shulman (2002) "artifacts are things –objects, tools, instruments, that human beings construct because they are needed but don't exist in nature" (p. 62). Artifacts have two main characteristics: (1) they are products generated after reflecting on practice; and (2) they are considered in a wider sense as a generalization of experience: "… I would argue that these principles can be generalized, that learning from experience entails learning from, with, and through the artifacts that are generated to capture, display and preserve the experience" (Shulman, 2002, 62).

In our view, artifacts constitute instruments, physical supports, or tools and also mental representations of any procedure or strategy that can be applied in practice. Besides, we think that not all generalizations of experience may be considered as artefacts. Artefacts are made explicit as procedures whereas rules are conceptual representations of experiences. In other words, artifacts constitute ways of transposing rules to the practice setting thereby making them usable within the context of one's teaching practice, for example, "I will use the *Class Sojo* program for students to visualize the timing for the lesson activities." In this example using the *Class Sojo* program denotes an instrument the teacher will use according to a previous inferred rule: "It is better controlling the time students spend in classroom tasks". Both represent generalizations of a previous experience.

B2. Pairing propositions with knowledge precision. Additionally, another dimension can be applied to the types of knowledge outlined above: precision (see Appendix A; column, 6). Precision is useful because it differentiates which types of knowledge are more useful to teaching depending on how univocal and certain is the meaning contained in them. We generally consider that a type of knowledge is *imprecise* when information conveyed is vague or unspecified (e.g., Kids liked the activity) and *precise* when the predicate contains detailed information about the knowledge generated (e.g., Kids remained silent in the auditorium). With both these notions in mind (types of knowledge and precision of knowledge) each single proposition can be coded accordingly and thereby allowing for the transformation of speech statements (e.g., ideas) into frequency counts (e.g., using descriptive statistics).

In a recent study (Mena *et al.*, *accepted*) we tested three different sorts of mentoring interactions: dialogue journaling; regular conferences, and stimulated recalled conferences in order to explore which of them potentially elicited more types of practical knowledge and the level of precision associated with each. Overall 4,534 propositions were coded (see Table 5).

Results indicate, according to Log-linear analysis, that major statistical differences in the elicitation of inferential knowledge (rules and artifacts) were found when

Table 5. Propositions found in mentoring interactions that were classified according to the practical knowledge types. Taken from Mena et al. (accepted)

Mentoring interaction	Knowledge type		Imprecise		Precise		Totals	
			f	*%*	*f*	*%*	*f*	*%*
(1) Dialogue journaling (Text)	Narrative	Recalls	101	5.8	108	6.3	209	12.1
		Appraisals - Positive	570	32.9	359	20.8	929	53.7
		Appraisals - Negative	100	5.8	280	16.1	380	21.9
	Inferential	Rules	84	4.8	104	6.0	188	12.8
		Artifacts	8	0.4	16	0.9	24	1.3
Sub-totals			*863*	*49.9*	*867*	*50.1*	*1,730*	*100*
(2) Regular conferences (Face-to-Face)	Narrative	Recalls	92	6.4	144	10.0	236	16.4
		Appraisals - Positive	315	21.9	204	14.1	519	36.0
		Appraisals - Negative	181	12.5	110	7.7	291	20.2
	Inferential	Rules	93	6.4	219	15.2	312	21.6
		Artifacts	36	2.5	45	3.1	81	5.6
Sub-totals			*717*	*49.8*	*722*	*50.2*	*1439*	*100*
(3) Stimulated -recall conferences (Face-to-Face)	Narrative	Recalls	39	2.9	327	23.9	366	26.8
		Appraisals - Positive	81	5.9	58	4.2	139	10.1
		Appraisals - Negative	151	11.0	192	14.1	343	25.1
	Inferential	Rules	108	7.9	294	21.5	402	29.4
		Artifacts	43	3.1	72	5.3	115	8.4
Sub-totals			*422*	*30.9*	*943*	*69.1*	*1365*	*100*
All three types of interaction combined (#1, #2, #3)	Narrative	Recalls	232	5.1	579	12.8	811	17.9
		Appraisals - Positive	966	21.3	621	13.7	1587	35.0
		Appraisals - Negative	432	9.5	582	12.8	1014	22.4
	Inferential	Rules	285	6.3	617	13.6	202	19.9
		Artifacts	87	1.9	133	2.9	220	4.9
Total			*2,002*	*44.2*	*2,532*	*55.8*	*4,534*	*100*

comparing text-based journal interactions (14.1%) to regular conferences (27.2%) and stimulated recall conferences (38.2%). On the other hand stimulated recall conferences displayed the highest number of precise propositions: 69.1% compared to 50.2% found in the other two conditions. In previous work (Mena *et al.*, 2012) Chi square statistics also demonstrated that inferential knowledge was habitually stated in precise terms which helped STs not only to understand experience but also to start changing it.

B3. Grouping knowledge types into content categories. The next step would be to generate content categories out of the knowledge types following a Grounded Theory Analysis approach (Strauss & Corbin, 1994). This is a crucial issue to be considered if we do not want to remain at a syntactical level where the content of the conversations is reduced to formal classifications (i.e. recalls, appraisals, rules and artifacts).

For instance, Gholami and Husu (2010) state that some of the overarching crucial content-categories for practical knowledge are "classroom management" "instructional strategies" and "learner, learning and teaching". Mena et al. (2012) propose as major content categories, that are subdivided into three levels of hierarchy: student learning, teaching strategies and family-school relationships. We claim that the content categories give us the "concept map" of particular mentoring conversations that help to easily visualize the contents of the dialogues.

B4. Including content categories in the domains of professional practical knowledge. Not all teachers' declarations belong to a unique domain or field of thought. For example the above categories by Gholami & Husu and Mena et al. (2012) belong to the domain of "pedagogical knowledge". According to Elbaz (1983) the main domains of practical knowledge would be knowledge of subject matter, curriculum, instruction, self and the milieu of schooling. Shulman's (1987) proposes: content knowledge, general pedagogical knowledge, curriculum knowledge, pedagogical content knowledge, knowledge of learners, knowledge of educational contexts, and knowledge of educational ends, purposes and values. Mishra & Koehler (2006) and Koehler & Mishra, (2008) in refining Shulman's (1987) categories, suggest three main domains of professional knowledge:

1. Content Knowledge (CK). The content of the subject that needs to be taught. The content to be taught in science is different from the one that is taught in History.
2. Pedagogical Knowledge (PK). The knowledge about teaching techniques and "… strategies of classroom management and organization that appear to transcend subject matter" (Shulman, 1987, p. 8).
3. Technical knowledge (TK). It is the knowledge about the use of educational technologies (i.e.Internet, Digital Whiteboards, tablets, videos, e-mail, software, or textbooks) and its integration in teaching dynamics (Cuban, Kirkpatrick & Peck, 2001).

It is important to note that the four sub-categories overlap (see Figure 3):

1 and 2. Pedagogical Content Knowledge (PCK). It is the type of knowledge that blends content and pedagogy of a given subject matter (Shulman, 1986; Lougran, et al., 2012).

1 and 3 Technological Content Knowledge (TCK). The way the technological content is related to disciplinary content.

2 and 3. Technological Pedagogical Knowledge (TPK). This is the knowledge about how teaching can change through the use of different technologies (i.e. webquests, blogs, chats, etc.).

1, 2 and 3. Technological Pedagogical Content Knowledge (TPCK). This kind of knowledge integrates the three major forms of knowledge at the same time.

We suggest that either the three main domains or the four combinations (or both) are useful to situate each piece of practical knowledge type (see Appendix A, column 8).

Construction of action oriented knowledge units: Implementation of research evidence into practice. The last part of the analysis coincides with stage 3 (Figure 2). Once the practical knowledge has been described and validated through

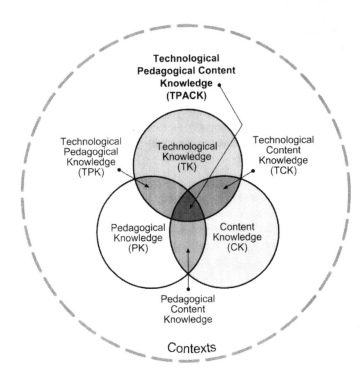

Figure 3. Depiction of the types of professional knowledge (Koehler & Mishra, 2008)

research processes there is still a need to encapsulate propositions, categories and domains within a comprehensible format that is readily accessible for use by teachers and other professionals (i.e. STs, Faculty Advisors, administrators, etc.). In other words, the evidence gathered from research needs to be organized according to teaching practice demands. One way to do this, we propose, is to construct Action-Oriented Knowledge (AOK) units that show in an organized way what others have learnt from particular practical situations.

AOK units may be defined as learning outlines that depict coherent know-how sets of knowledge contained in mentoring situations and that have previously been analyzed by following well-defined and validated research methods. Drafting those research results into a practice-oriented tool (AOK unit) will make explicit expert teachers' tacit knowledge that can be accessed by others (MTs and STs) as aids for making sense of such within the context of their own teaching.

AOK units could be generated from three contexts regarding the mentoring process:

1. Teaching situation. Brief summary information about the classroom and the event(s) of the lesson taught.
2. Mentoring interaction. Referring to the mentoring dialogue from which the knowledge was extracted. This part would contain: (2.1) identification information about the MT, the ST and the type of mentoring situation: Formal setting: *practicum* for STs or *practice year* for beginner teachers; Non-formal: *peer guidance* or *school supervision* (i.e. promotion); and (2.2.) a verbatim transcription of a significant episode of the conversation.
3. Mentoring outcomes. Description of the practical knowledge as extracted from the PDA: types of knowledge; content categories; and domains of knowledge. Additionally, the MT's explanation of the importance of that knowledge could be included along with the conditions he or she thinks to be put in consideration when applying the knowledge.

Below is an example of what an AOK unit may look like:

This AOK unit would be a readily accessible knowledge that other STs or MTs could use in the context of their practice. The five rules in Figure 4 could also be tested in other classroom contexts in a search for consistency (i.e., to know if they can successfully work when generalized to other situations) following the mentor's envisaged conditions. This would be the phase of refinement indicated in stage 3, Figure 2.

Finally, when these action-oriented units are verified by a number of practitioners it would be ideal to have them published under a handbook format or guidelines to show future teachers what actually works for a majority of professionals (stage 4; Figure 2).

1. TEACHING SITUATION.	*1.1. Classroom information.* Teaching level and grade Subject and topic	Primary (3th grade) Spanish Language: Synonyms and antonyms.
	Class size *1.2. Event information.* Event title	25 pupils Bad writing on the blackboard.
	Event description	At 10: 15 a.m. Sheila, a student teacher was delivering the content of synonyms and antonyms to 3rd graders in an urban Primary Education school. She tried to write the definitions of categories, uses and examples while she was further explaining it. The final writing seemed to be blurry, messy and disorganized. She uses blackboard and classroom IDB.
2. MENTORING INTERACTION	*2.1.Identification.* Preservice teacher Mentor teacher Mentoring Situation	Female, 21 Female, 42 Formal (Practicum).
	2.2.Conversation. Verbatim transcript.	*PT:I did not feel comfortable with what I wrote on the blackboard* *MT: you will need to practice the letter font on the blackboard. Pressing more the chalk would be a first step. Secondly, learn the correct graphical drawing [for this letter style] and third, organize better the information displayed on the blackboard, and not too much, to reach a higher level of visual comprehension".*
3. MENTORING OUTCOMES	*3.1. Analysis* Knowledge types	RULE#1: Need to practice the letter font on the blackboard (Generalization) RULE#2: Pressing more the chalk RULE#3: Learn the correct graphical drawing. RULE#4: Organize better the information displayed on the blackboard RULE#5: Not {to write} too much information.
	Content category Domain of knowledge	Teaching strategies (Type of letter; Organization of information) Pedagogical Knowledge (PK)
	3.2. Additional information Explanation	MT: Writing properly on the blackboard is crucial since much of the information pupils catch and write in their notebooks are through the visual channel. They see what teachers write on the blackboard as the final production to be learnt.
	Conditions	MT: Apply this (i.e. all 5 rules) when: a.- there is no alternative source of offering visual information in the classroom (i.e. digital whiteboard; posters with the content, etc.). b.- Always when the students are between 6 to 10 years old. When they are older than that they usually catch the information through oral dictation and explanation.

Figure 4. Illustration of an AOK unit

CONCLUSION

Mentoring in education focuses on characterizing teaching practices as related to domains of expertise, to interpersonal relationships and to knowledge development (Orland-Barack, 2010). Any account of the ways in which teachers conceptualize their practice represents a complex process because much of teachers' practical knowledge remains as non-verbalized constructs. For example, professional routines are deeply rooted in personal teaching styles and are socially embedded (Eraut, 2004). As a result teachers know more than they can tell (Polanvi, 1967).

This chapter highlights the importance of describing the experience-based knowledge that STs learn from their MTs when discussing classroom-based actions. We demonstrate by the use of PDA that much of this practical knowledge can be captured into propositional knowledge by following language operations that relates actions to ideas. Our proposal relies on disclosing those ideas that have arisen in mentoring conversations and seeking if there is any content that is more supportive in improving teachers' practice in terms of the teaching strategies that turn out to be more substantial for teaching. Formal criteria, as outlined above, suggests that PDA is an eligible methodology for disclosing practical knowledge because it plausibly fits for the purpose of accounting for the number of ideas that are shared in formal interactions and it also turns out to be less ambiguous because it operates with a small unit size.

The analysis of teachers' practical knowledge from this methodology leads us to confirm at least three major assumptions:

Teaching Professional Knowledge Needs to Be Learnt Progressively

In an early learning stage, such as the one where STs are immersed in the practicum setting, specific instructions, rules and procedures are needed to first engage in and move within the complexities of teaching. Once these elements are assimilated, the ST can attend more fully to higher levels of professionalization (i.e. critical reflection, sharing new ideas, feeling confident, etc.). In other words, if novice teachers do not master, for instance, basic classroom procedures (e.g., planning for instruction), whatever heuristic, scheme or protocol is agreed upon (e.g., establish the objectives, recapitulation, class management, etc.) it is unreasonable to expect them to critically reflect on their practice, envisage social consequences in the act of teaching or assuming certain roles and attributes.

Practical Knowledge Should Be Oriented as a Form of Gaining Expertise (Not Only as a Way of Gathering Experience)

Main findings from our studies indicate that ST's dedicate more of their speech to recall and appraisal events, therefore they are more episode-oriented (gathering experience). The easiest way to redescribe experience is by recalling and judging facts and events that occurred in their teaching. More complicated is the effort to codify those experiences into practical principles, rules or instruments. The last requires a more skill-oriented disposition to practice (gaining expertise) but it also guarantees extracting more regularities of practice (rules and artefacts) and redefining teacher actions into more precise terms (Mena et al., accepted).

Practical Knowledge Described in Research Should Be Redirected to Practice

The third implication is that *in-practice* knowledge that is described by research needs to be articulated as knowledge *for-practice* (Cochran-Smith & Lytle, 1999), a readily accessible knowledge for teachers. AOK units are offered in this chapter as a possible tool to move towards the redescription of practical knowledge into knowledge for practice or action-oriented knowledge. The combination of AOK units would help in developing a joint set of criteria (guidelines) for the practicum supervision in the university programs. These criteria have the advantage of being based on validated research outcomes from transcriptions, observation, and evaluation of teaching and therefore they are aligned to schools' actual practices.

We claim that these considerations are crucial in order to advance the professionalization of mentoring (Clarke, 2007) and PDA allows not only for precisely describing teachers' practical knowledge but also for the recognition of different patterns of mentoring in the form of most frequent behaviours (e.g., it is usual that PTs do not establish the objective of the lesson at the beginning of the session).

But, if describing MTs' mentoring techniques and procedures is a must, then it is also a pre-requisite to convey that learning to MTs and STs in a professional oriented format. In other words, if we want to improve the profession, we need to arrange the research outcomes into the language and procedures used in schools. Therefore, and based on the results from this approach, we suggest that the practicum and Educational Programs should provide opportunities for STs, SAs and Fas to make use of the knowledge that is been generated and accumulated from other teaching practices because it is a genuine way to replicate, contrast and make use of different valuable teachers' strategies.

In conclusion, the line of research we postulate in this chapter claims that future studies should take into consideration two moves: First, *understanding practice* (knowledge of practice) by scientific means and second, *changing practice* (knowledge for practice) by attending to teachers' needs (i.e., creating understandable and communicable instruments or tools that may be used by practitioners in their school settings).

REFERENCES

Aluwihare, A. P. R. (2002). Self and distance learning in surgery: A collaborative venture [CD]. In T. Mays & A. Kwan (Eds.), *Transformation education for development*. Proceedings of the Commonwealth and Open Learning Conference. Durban, South Africa: Technikon SA.

Bovair, S., & Kieras, D. E. (1985). A guide to propositional analysis for research on technical prose. In B.K. Britton & J. B. Black (Eds.), *Understanding expository text*. Hillsdale, NJ: LEA.

Bradbury, L., & Koballa, T. (2008). Borders to cross: Identifying sources of tension in mentor-intern relationships. *Teaching and Teacher Education, 24*(8), 2132–2145.

Braun, V., & Clarke, V. (2006). Using thematic analysis in psychology. *Qualitative Research in Psychology, 3*, 77–101.

Bruner, J. S. (1991). The narrative construction of reality. *Critical Inquiry, 18*, 1–21.

Carr, W. (1986). Theories of theory and practice. *Journal of Philosophy of Education, 20*(2), 177–186.

Chaliès, S., Bruno, F., Méard, J., & Bertone, S. (2010). Training preservice teachers rapidly: The need to articulate the training given by university supervisors and cooperating teachers. *Teaching and Teacher Education, 26*, 764–774.

Chaliès, S., Escalié, G., Bertone, S., & Clarke, A. (2012). Learning 'Rules' of practice within the context of the practicum triad: A case study of learning to teach. *Canadian Journal of Education, 35*(2), 3–23.

Cho, J., & Trent, A. (2006). Validity in qualitative research revisited. *Qualitative Research, 6*, 319–340

Chong, S., Ling, L. E., & Chuan, G. K. (2001). Developing student teachers' professional identitites – An Exlploratory Study. *Internal Education Studies, 4*(1), 30–38.

Clarke, A. (2001). Characteristics of cooperating teachers. *Canadian Journal of Education, 26*(2), 237–256.

Clarke, A. (2007). Turning the professional development of cooperating teachers on its head: Relocating that responsibility within the profession. *Educational Insights, 11*(3), 1–10.

Clarke, A., & Jarvis-Selinger, S. (2005). What the teaching perspectives of cooperating teachers tell us about their advisory practices. *Teaching and Teacher Education, 21*, 65–78.

Clarke, A., Triggs, V., & Nielsen, W. S. (2013). Cooperating teacher participation in teacher education. *Review of Educational Research*, 1–40. Retrieved from: http://rer.sagepub.com/content/early/2013/09/23/0034654313499618

Clarke, A., Collins, J., Triggs, V., Nielsen, W., Augustine, A., Coulter, D., … & Weil, F. (2012). The mentoring profile inventory: An online professional development resource for cooperating teachers. *Teaching Education, 23*(2), 167–194.

Cochran-Smith, M., & Lytle, S. L. (1999). Relationships of knowledge and practice: Teacher learning in communities. *Review of Research in Education, 24*, 249–305.

Connelly, F. M., & Clandinin, D. J. (Eds.). (1999). *Shaping a professional identity: Stories of educational practice*. New York, NY: Teachers College Press.

Connelly, F. M., Clandinin, D. J., & Fang He, M. (1997). Teachers' personal practical knowledge on the professional knowledge landscape. *Teaching and Teacher Education, 13*(7), 665–674.

Crasborn, F., Hennissen, P., Brouwer, N., Korthagen, F., & Bergen, T. (2011). Exploring a two-dimensional model of mentor teacher roles in mentoring dialogues. *Teaching and Teacher Education, 27*, 320–331.

Daloz, L. A. (1986) *Effective teaching and mentoring: Realizing the transformational power of adult experiences*. San Francisco, CA: Jossey-Bass.

Daloz, L. A. (2012). *Mentor: Guiding the journey of adult learners*. New York, NY: Wiley.

Danielewicz, J. (2001). *Teaching selves: Identity, pedagogy, and teacher education*. Albany, NY: State University of New York Press.

Denzin, N. K., & Lincoln, Y. S. (2000). Introduction: The discipline and practice of qualitative research. In N. K. Denzin & Y. S. Lincoln (Eds.), *Handbook of qualitative research* (2nd ed., pp. 1–28). Thousand Oaks, CA: Sage.

Elbaz, F. (1981). The teacher's "practical knowledge": Report of a case study. *Curriculum Inquiry, 11*(1), 43–71.

Elbaz, F. (1983). *Teacher thinking: A study of practical knowledge*. London, England: Croom Helm.

Elliott, J. (1991). *Action research for educational change*. Buckingham: Open University Press.

Engstrom, S. (2009). *The form of practical knowledge: A study of the categorical imperative*. Cambridge, MA: Harvard University Press.

Eraut, M. 2004. Transfer of knowledge between education and workplace settings. In H. Rainbird, A. Fuller, & A. Munro (Eds.), *Workplace learning in context* (pp. 201–221). London, England: Routledge.

Flanagan, J. (1954). The critical incident technique. *Psychological Bulletin, 51*(4), 327–358.

Feiman-Nemser, S., & Floden, R. (1986). The cultures of teaching. In M. Wittrock (Ed.), *Handbook of research on teaching* (3rd ed., pp. 505–526) New York, NY: Macmillan.

Fenstermacher, G. D. (1986). Philosophy of research on teaching: Three aspects. In Merlin C. Wittrock (Ed.), *Handbook of research on teaching* (3rd ed., pp. 37–49). New York, NY: Macmillan.

Fenstermacher, G. D. (1994). The knower and the known: The nature of knowledge in research on teaching. *Review of Research in Education, 20*(1), 3–56.

Gholami, K., & Husu, J. (2010). How do teachers reason about their practice? Representing the epistemic nature of teachers' practical knowledge. *Teaching and Teacher Education, 26*, 1520–1529.

Hansford, B. C., Ehrich, L. C., & Tennent, L. (2004). Formal mentoring programs in education and other professions: A review of the literature. *Educational Administration Quarterly, 40*(4), 518–540.

Hennissen, P., Crasborn, F., Brouwer, N., Korthagen, F., & Bergen, T. (2011). Clarifying pre-service teacher perceptions of mentor teachers' developing use of mentoring skills. *Teaching and Teacher Education, 27*, 1049–1058.

Hobson, A. J., Ashby, P., Malderez, A., & Tomlinson, P. D. (2009). Mentoring beginning teachers: What we know and what we don't. *Teaching and Teacher Education 25*, 207–216.

Hudson, P. (2013). Mentoring as professional development: 'Growth for both' mentor and mentee. *Professional Development in Education, 39*(5), 771–783. Retrieved from http://www.tandfonline.com/doi/abs/10.1080/19415257.2012.749415

Husu, J., & Tirri, K. (2003). A case study approach to study one teacher's moral reflection. *Teaching and Teacher Education, 19*, 345–357.

Husu, J., Toom, A., & Patrikainen, S. (2008). Guided reflection as a means to demonstrate and develop student teachers' reflective competencies. *Reflective Practice, 9*(1), 37–51.

Jonsson, A., & Svingby, G. (2007). The use of scoring rubrics: Reliability, validity and educational consequences. *Educational Research Review, 2*(2), 130–144.

Junker, B., Weisberg, Y., Matsumura, L. C., Crosson, A., Wolf, M. K., Levinson, A., & Resnick, L. (2006). *Overview of the instructional quality assessment* (CSE Technical Report 671). Los Angeles, CA: Center for the Study of Evaluation, National Center for Research on Evaluation, Standards, & Student Testing. Retrieved December 10, 2013 from http://www.cse.ucla.edu/products/reports/r671.pdf

Karmiloff-Smith, A. (1992). *Beyond modularity: A developmental perspective on cognitive science.* Cambridge, MA: MIT Press/Bradford Books.

Kemmis, S., & McTaggart, R. (Eds.). (1988). *The action research planner* (3rd ed). Victoria: Deakin University.

Killian, J. E., & Wilkins, E. A. (2009). Characteristics of highly effective cooperating teachers: A study of their backgrounds and preparation. *Action in Teacher Education, 30*(4), 67–83.

Kintsch, W. (1988). The use of knowledge in discourse processing: A construction-integration model. *Psychological Review, 95*, 163–182.

Kintsch, W., & Van Dijk, T. A. (1978). Toward a model of text comprehension and production. *Psychological Review, 85*(5), 363–394.

Koehler, M. J., & Mishra, P. (2008). Introducing technological pedagogical knowledge. In The AACTE Committee on Innovation and Technology (Eds.), *The handbook of technological pedagogical content knowledge for teaching and teacher educators* (pp. 3–29). New York, NY: Routledge.

Kroeger, P. (2005). *Analysing grammar: An introduction.* Cambridge, UK: Cambridge University Press.

Lave, J., & Wenger, E. (1991). *Situated learning: Legitimate eripheral participation.* Cambridge: Cambridge University Press.

Loughran, Berry, A., & Mulhall, P. (2012). *Understanding and developing science teachers' pedagogical knowledge.* Rotterdam, The Netherlands: Sense Publishers.

Marable, M. A., & Raimondi, S. L. (2007). Teachers' perceptions of whatwas most (and least) supportive during their first year of teaching. *Mentoring and Tutoring: Partnership in Learning, 15*(1), 25–37.

McLean, V. (1999). Becoming a teacher. In R. P. Lipka & T. Brinthaupt (Eds.), *The role of self in teacher development.* Albany, NY: State University of New York Press.

Meijer, P. C., Verloop, N., & Beijard, D. (1999). Exploring language teachers' practical knowledge about teaching reading comprehension. *Teaching and Teacher Education, 15*, 59–84.

Mena, J., & Garcia, M. (2011). *Action-oriented knowledge: How student teachers get professional expertise from reflection.* 14th Biennial EARLI Conference for Research on Learning and Instruction, Exeter, England.

Mena, J., & Tillema, H. (2006). Studying studies on teacher reflection and action: An appraisal of research contributions. *Educational Research Review, 1*(2), 112–132.

Mena, J, García, M. L., & Tillema, H. (2012). Student teacher reflective writing: What does it reveal? *European Journal of Teacher Education*, 1–17. Retrieved from http://www.tandfonline.com/doi/abs/10.1080/02619768.2012.713933

73

Mena, J., García, M., & Tillema, H. (2009). *Constructing knowledge from problem-solving in teaching practice: An action-research project.* Paper presented at the EARLI 13th Biennial Conference, Amsterdam, The Netherlands.

Mena, J., García, M. L., Clarke, A., & Barkatsas, A. (Forthcoming). An analysis of three different approaches to student teacher mentoring and their impact on knowledge generation in practicum settings. *European Journal of Teacher Education.*

Mishra, P., & Koehler, M. J. (2006). Technological pedagogical content knowledge: A framework for teacher knowledge. *Teachers College Record, 108*(6), 1017–1054.

Nielsen, W. S., Triggs, V., Clarke, A., & Collins, J. (2010). The teacher education conversation: A network of cooperating teachers. *Canadian Journal of Education, 33*(4), 837–868.

Orland- Barak, L. (2001). Reading a mentoring situation: One aspect of learning to mentor. *Teaching and Teacher Education, 17*(1). 75–88.

Orland-Barak, L. (2005). Lost on Translation: Mentors learning participate in competing discourses of practice. *Journal of Teacher Education, 56*(4), 355–367.

Orland-Barak, L. (2010). *Learning to mentor as Praxis: Foundations for a curriculum in teacher education.* New York, NY: Springer.

Osula, B., & Irvin, S. (2009). Cultural awareness in intercultural mentoring: A model for enhancing mentoring relationships. *International Journal of Leadership Studies, 5*, 37–50.

Packard, B. W. (2003). Student training promotes mentoring awareness and action. *Career Development Quarterly, 51*, 335–345.

Polanyi, M. (1967). *The tacit dimension.* London, England: Routledge.

Rosales, J., Iturra, C., Sánchez, E., & De Sixte, R. (2006). El análisis de la práctica educative. Un studio de la interacción profesor-alumnos a partir de dos sistemas de análisis diferentes. *Infancia y Aprendizaje, 29*(1), 65–90.

Russell, T. (1987). Research, practical knowledge, and the conduct of teacher education. *Educational Theory, 37*(4), 369–375

Sánchez, E. (2001). Ayudando a ayudar: El reto de la investigación educativa. *Cultura y Educación, 13*, 249–266.

Sánchez, E., & Rosales, J. (2005). La práctica educative. Una revision a partir del studio de la interacción profesor-alumnos en el aula. *Cultura y Educación, 17*(2), 147–173.

Sánchez, E., Rosales, J., & Suárez, S. (1999). Interacción profesor/alumnos y compression de textos. Qué se hace y qué se puede hacer. *Cultura y Educación, 14/15*, 71–89

Schegloff, E. A. (1987). Analyzing single episodes of interaction: An exercise in conversation analysis. *Social Psychology Quarterly, 50*, 101–114

Schegloff, E. A. (2000). Overlapping talk and the organization of turn-taking for conversation. *Language in Society, 29*, 1–63.

Schiffrin, D., Tannen, D., & Hamilton, H. E. (2003). *The handbook of discourse analysis.* Malden, MA: Wiley-Blackwell.

Schön, D. A. (1983). *The reflective practitioner: How professionals think in action.* London, England: Temple Smith.

Schön, D. A. (1987). *Educating the reflective practitioner toward a new design for teaching and learning in the professions.* San Francisco, CA: Jossey- Bass, Inc.

Shulman, L. S. (1986). Those who understand: Knowledge growth in teaching. *Educational Researcher, 15*(2), 4–14.

Shulman, L. S. (1987). Knowledge and teaching: Foundations of the new reform. *Harvard Educational Review, 57*, 1–22.

Shulman, L. (2002, January). *Forgive and remember: The challenges and opportunities of learning from experience.* Launching the next generation of new teachers Symposium Proceedings. New Teacher Centre at the University of California, Santa Cruz, CA.

Strauss, A., & Corbin, J. (1994). Grounded theory methodology: An overview. In N. K. Denzin & Y. S. Lincoln (Eds.), *Handbook of qualitative research* (pp. 273–285). Thousand Oaks, CA: Sage.

Strauss, A., & Corbin, J. (1998). *Basics of qualitative research.* Thousand Oaks, CA: Sage Publications.

Tierney, R. J., & Mosenthal, J. H. (1983). Cohesion and textual coherence. *Research in the Teaching of English, 17*, 215–229.

Tillema H. H. (2006). Constructing knowledge in professional conversations. The role of beliefs on knowledge and knowing. *Learning and Instruction, 16*(6), 592–608.

Tillema, H. H. (2009). Assessment for learning to teach appraisal of practice teaching lessons by mentors, supervisors, and student teachers. *Journal of Teacher Education, 60*(2), 155–167.

Tillema, H., & Van der Westhuizen, G. (2013). Mentoring conversations and student teacher learning. *South African Journal of Higher Education, 27*(5), 1305–1323.

Toom, A. (2006). *Tacit pedagogical knowing: At the core of teacher's professionality* (Research Reports 276). Finland: University of Helsinki, Department of Applied Sciences of Education.

Toom, A. (2012). Considering the artistry and epistemology of tacit knowledge and knowing. *Educational Theory, 62*(6), 621–640.

Urzúa, A., & Vásquez, C. (2008). Reflection and professional identity in teachers' future-oriented discourse. *Teaching and Teacher Education, 24*, 1935–1946.

Verloop, N., van Driel, J., & Meijer, P. (2001). Teacher knowledge and the knowledge base of teaching. *International Journal of Educational Research, 35*(5), 441–461.

Wells, G. (2001). The case for dialogic inquiry. In G. Wells (Ed.), *Action, talk, and text: Learning and teaching through inquiry* (pp. 171–194). New York, NY: Teachers College Press.

Weinberg, F., & Lankau, M. (2011). Formal mentoring programs: A mentor-centric and longitudinal analysis. *Journal of Management, 37*, 1527–1557.

Zollo, M., & Winter, S. G. (2002). Deliberate learning and the evolution of dynamic capabilities. *Organization Science, 13*, 339–351.

Juanjo Mena-Marcos
Department of Education
University of Salamanca, Spain

Anthony Clarke
Department of Curriculum and Pedagogy
University of British Columbia, Canada

APPENDICES

Appendix A. The Propositional Discourse Analysis (PDA). Example about a mentoring conversation excerpt transcription (Primary school classroom. Age: 6 years).

Transcription	(1) Segmentation			(2) Categorization (PK)			
	Episodes	Cycles	Propositions	Types	Precision	Content	Domain
[...] P: Did you succeed with the objectives you planned for the lesson?	Ev	C1					
A: Not completely. Overall, they understood the tale plot when I first played the video in the iPad. They were highly motivated because they liked the animations. They wanted to interact with the device...But the app suddenly shut down and I had to start over...[laughs]. Anyway the activity works. P: I agree.			P1. {I did not succeed} completely {with the objectives for the lesson}	AP-	0	T2	PK
			P2. They understood the tale plot P2.1. (MOD) {with the use of the iPad}	AP+	1	T10	PK
			P3. [The pupils] were highly motivated. P3.1. (CAUS) they liked the animations {on the iPad}.	AP+	1	T14	PK
			P4. [The pupils] wanted to interact with the device.	RC	1	T31	PK
			P5. The app suddenly shut down.	AP-	1	T43	TK
			P6. I had to start over {the reading}	RC	1	T22	PK
			P7. The activity works.	AP+	0	T1	PK
P: What about the second part? A: In the second part, some pupils seemed not to understand the passages of the story mainly because some students were slower at reading; some others felt ashamed, etc. P: Correct.		C2	P8. Some pupils seemed not to understand the passages of the story. P8.1. (CAUS) {some students} were slower at reading P8.2. (CAUS) {some students} felt ashamed.	AP-	1	T10	PK
A: They were tired because it was Friday... Besides the text sentences were long and some of them contained unknown words for the pupils. P: Yes, indeed. But maybe you should have modified the text according to 6-year -old students' vocabulary. They were unable to follow the story told by their mates. Additionally, notice that pupils this age cannot pay attention for long periods. And they need to rest in between those periods.			P9. {Pupils} were tired P9.1. (CAUS) it was Friday.	AP-	1	T8	PK
			P10. The text sentences were long sentences	AP-	1	T12	CK
			P11. [The sentences] contained unknown words for the pupils.	AP-	1	T13	CK
			P12. You should have modified the text P12.1. (MOD) according to 6-year-old students' vocabulary.	RL	1	T12	PK
			P13. [Pupils] were unable to follow the story.	AP-	0	T10	PK
			P14. Pupils this age cannot pay attention for long periods.	RL	0	T4	PK
			P15. {Pupils} need to rest between periods.	RL	1	T4	PK
A: Besides, the kids did not know when to stick the picture on the board. I should explain the pictures content before reading the text next time P: And also give them a clue, for instance pointing at the students, to indicate the association between the read text and their image. A: Aha.			P16. The kids did not know when to stick the picture on the board.	AP-	1	T16	PK
			P17. I should explain the pictures content next time. P17.1. (CIR) before reading the text	RL	1	T16	PK
			P18. [You should] give them a clue P18.1. (PUR) indicate the association between the read text and their image.	RL	1	T16	PK

Context:

"Ainhoa's objectives for the lesson were practicing pupils' reading aloud skills and oral comprehension. She chose a tale: "La castañera" [The chestnut seller]. First, she told the story playing a video on her iPad. In a second stage she handed out a piece of cardboard for each pupil containing a paragraph with two or three short sentences of the story. The cardboards were numbered following the story line. She also gave each student a picture with scenes or characters of the story. Pupils had to read aloud individually their fragment of text to the rest of the group and the kid that hold a picture related to the text read had to go to the board and stick it.

Abbreviations

Transcription: P= Pilar, the Mentor Teacher; A= Ainhoa, the Student Teacher.
Segmentation
    Episodes: EV= Episode of Evaluation; PL= Planning; PR= definition of a problem; SL= Solutions for practice.
    Cycles: C1= Activities done during the lesson; C2= Improvements and changes.
Propositions:

a. Propositions. Ideas that are shared in the dialogues. Pn= Number of proposition (p1, p2, p3, etc.)

b. Connectors. Connectives relate propositions in the text and provide it with coherence. According to traditional propositional analysis (Kintch and Van Dijk, 1978) eight categories are specified: Conjunction ("and"), disjunction ("or"), causality ("because"), purpose ("in order to"), concession ("but"), contrast ("more than"), condition ("if) and circumstance ("when"). In the analysis presented just 6 of them are used within the proposition introduced in the connected clause to indicate second order –subordinate- ideas. (CAUS)= Causal proposition; (COND)= Conditional proposition; (MOD)=Modal proposition (introduces a means to achieve something); (PUR)= Final proposition.; (CIR)= Circumstantial proposition (when). They are coded as p1.1.; p1.2. etc. and are dependent of a main previous proposition. 'Conjunction' and 'disjunction' connectors are not used because both ideas related are considered as first order propositions.

c. Formal keys. Symbols used to represent repeated or modified information by the analyst:

    [...]= *Repeated information.* When the agent is omitted in the discourse and it is necessary to rescue it to make the proposition semantically independent outside the paragraph.
    {...}= *modified information.* Simplification of an expression while preserving the meaning.

Categorization (PK = Practical Knowledge)

Types of practical knowledge:

RC = Recall, AP+ = Positive appraisal, AP– = Negative Appraisal, RL = Rule, AR = Artifact.

Precision:

0 = Imprecise proposition; 1 = Precise proposition.

Content.

Topics. i.e. T10 = not understanding the lesson; T8 = Pupils tired

Domains.

CK = Content knowledge; PK = Pedagogical Knowledge; TK = Technological knowledge

SIV M. GAMLEM

4. FEEDBACK IN THE MENTORING OF TEACHER LEARNING

Lisa, a lower secondary school teacher in Norway participating on an in-service education course at a University College said she finally understands how feedback can be a great support for improving her teaching and students' learning. Taking part on an in-service education course over six months gave Lisa and other teachers the opportunity to explore teachers' feedback practice and how it might be improved to support students' learning and their own teaching. Lisa and five more teachers experienced how quality feedback makes a difference for the students and their own practice. In an interview held after the in-service education course Lisa said:

> I now have tests to see how far my students have come, not only to measure what they know. Yes, I believe that there is a difference in this. I need to know where they are to give the best feedback. If someone stands out positively or negatively I can find this out and give them the extra help they should have. Earlier I thought; someone is always lagging behind, they'll never learn. But it's not at all certain that it needs to be this way. I've begun to think that maybe it is us teachers who reinforce that someone doesn't get it right, because we take away tasks or lower the learning aim instead of providing feedback and support for learning so they can accomplish more. Yes, I have become more aware of this, since I teach both low and high achieving students and I see clearly that some students are not 'allowed' to do anything academically challenging. As I have learned more of how feedback might support or preclude students' learning it has become more difficult to give feedback to my students. Difficult in a positive way, because I may have become better to identifying where they are and then helping each of them further which is hard work. Earlier I wasn't aware of what I really was doing when using feedback in school. (Lisa, June 2010)

In this chapter, teachers' perceptions of feedback in the mentoring of teacher learning and how feedback can improve teaching and students learning, are described. A study of teachers' perceptions of feedback will be valuable, since feedback can be one of the most powerful tools for increasing student and teacher learning, but only if it is conducted in accordance with the research on effective feedback (Hattie & Timperley, 2007; Nicol & Macfarlane-Dick, 2006).

H. Tillema et al. (Eds.). Mentoring for Learning, 79–97.

FEEDBACK FOR TEACHERS

Feedback is a powerful tool in student learning, and it is important for teachers' professional development too. Although feedback is generally considered to be beneficial, there is debate as to the nature of 'good feedback', with numerous typologies and theorizations (e.g. Hattie & Timperley, 2007; Nicol & Macfarlane-Dick, 2006; Shute, 2008).

Feedback is essential in mentoring, but not all kinds of feedback have the power to support learning. Quality feedback can be a significant contributor to academic success (Hattie & Timperley, 2007), if it is conducted in accordance with the research on effective feedback. The lived experience of academic teachers as they engage in feedback has received relatively little research attention compared to student perspectives on feedback. This paper explores teachers' lived experience of feedback and thus contributes a focus on feedback in mentoring teacher learning as a social practice. There has been a tendency in recent decades to view feedback through the lens of higher education students' experience, with a focus on student learning rather than teaching (Haggis, 2006; Tuck, 2012). Academic teachers' presence in the feedback literature is felt primarily through textual feedback comments and only occasionally through teachers' own reflections on their experiences. Consequently, the emphasis in research has been on feedback as a textual product rather than on feedback-giving as a complex social practice (Tuck, 2012). Within this paper, feedback in mentoring is defined as:

> Information given or sought by an agent (e.g. mentor, teacher, him-/herself) concerning/regarding quality aspects of the agent's (or other's) performance and/or understanding on the basis of work done (retrospective), with the purpose to point out a direction for further development/improvement (prospective).

In this chapter, when I use the term mentor, I refer to a teacher (e.g. external expertise, colleague) who is engaged in supporting the learning of another teacher. Moreover, when I use the term mentee I mean the teacher receiving feedback through participation in e.g. an in-service education course, while when using the term learner teacher I mean any teacher at any point in their life/career.

The quantity/quality of feedback provided and its helpfulness to the mentee, appears to range widely, and can give rise to uncertainty and confusion. Mentoring is a help to guide the learner teacher in the building of proficiency, and can be done as a regular practice among teachers and their principal in a school or through participation in an in-service education course. In compulsory school (in e.g. U.K. and Norway), there is a renewed emphasis on using teacher evaluations not only to rate teachers but also to give them formative feedback that might help them improve classroom instruction. A backdrop is that research findings and expert opinions about how traditional feedback from classroom observations affects instruction and student achievement are not encouraging (DuFour & Marzano, 2009).

Feedback can be understood as the hinge that joins teaching and learning (Pollock, 2012), and yet the concept remains largely undeveloped in the literature on the mentoring of teacher learning. Research points to a variation in what is (and should be) emphasized when giving feedback (Harris, Harnett, & Brown, 2013; Hattie & Timperley, 2007; Shute, 2008; Sternberg & Grigorenko, 1997), but the manner of how individual teachers perceive feedback messages as useful in their professional learning has not received much attention in research. The purpose of this chapter is to clarify knowledge of lower secondary school teachers' perceptions of feedback received and sought while taking part in an in-service education course at a University College during the school year 2010. The aim of the in-service education course was to develop teachers' understanding on how feedback can be a tool for improving their teaching and student learning focusing on Assessment for Learning (AfL) (Black & Wiliam, 2009). In this context, the mentees are six lower secondary teachers from Norway. The mentoring was conducted by a lecturer/researcher at a University College with special expertise on AfL and feedback, who was a former teacher from lower secondary school.

Further literature about the importance of feedback, how to give it and how it is perceived by these teachers taking part in an in-service education course, will be reviewed.

THE POWER OF FEEDBACK IN LEARNING

Several researchers identify core principles and strategies of feedback to support learning and development: Feedback must be an integral part of the learning process, be understandable to the receiver, and the learner must be allowed to act on the feedback (refine, revise, practice and retry) (Hattie & Timperley, 2007; Shute, 2008). Furthermore, feedback should be linked to learning intentions, and should cause the mentee to practice self-reflection (Black & Wiliam, 2009; Nicol & Macfarlane-Dick, 2006).

Quality feedback is recognized as being information that can be used for further learning and development; and involving teachers as partners in the teacher evaluation and development process. Quality feedback gives information that helps and guides the learner towards better understanding and performance. To accomplish those goals, feedback to teachers must be focused, specific and constructive.

Focused Feedback

Focused feedback is characterized by qualities, such as:

- centring around a limited number of specific aspects or indicators of teacher performance
- connecting specific evidence from classroom observations to words and phrases in the teacher evaluation instrument (e.g. learning intentions for activity) (Nicol & Macfarlane-Dick, 2006; Wiliam, 2011).

As a mentor wanting to support teacher learning it is easy to overwhelm the learner teacher with a list of every performance indicator from an evaluation instrument on which the learner teacher could possibly make improvements. This might instead end up as "killer-feedback" (Askew & Lodge, 2000). The results from killer-feedback are often a form of cognitive paralysis that produces little or no growth of any kind (Dweck, 2008). Focused feedback contributes to teacher learning on a manageable number of growth goals over the entire period of the evaluation cycle. It is "less is more" and "neat and beautiful" if communicated from a clear description of effective teaching.

In a mentoring situation teachers must become familiar with the definitions or descriptions used for instruction and feedback. For example, after an informal classroom visit a teacher (or principal) might give the feedback: "The use of frequent feedback loops between you and your students and among the students seems to lead students to obtain deeper understanding of material and concepts", or "The way you and your students often build on student responses seems to expand students' understanding". The language is taken from a content analysis tool for mapping the quality of feedback interactions to support students' learning in classrooms (Gamlem & Munthe, 2014). Tying language to the learning intentions with the observations of the mentee's practice and an evaluation instrument gives a mentee a sense of success criteria, and the mentee's proficiency can be built through understanding, established practice and new knowledge.

The use of dialogue(s), instead of monologue(s) may be considered the hinge for formative feedback to support learning. Several aspects of formative feedback in dialogical learning interactions (Alexander, 2006) stand out: The mentor and mentee both need to be aware of the learning intentions (goals) to know where they are heading. This interaction occurs in supporting climates that enable frank discussions for learning. The mentor should build on the mentee's experiences, thoughts and ways of thinking in order to help and guide the learner teacher to build knowledge and skill from what is done to what can be done in the future to increase the mentee's performance (Borko, 2004; Bransford, Brown, & Cocking, 2000; Tharp & Gallimore, 1988).

Specific Feedback

Specific feedback is important to help a learner teacher to improve teaching, understanding and/or misconceptions (Carless, Salter, Yang, & Lam, 2011; Hattie & Timperley, 2007). A challenge is that specific feedback might be fuzzy, rather than effective. Specific feedback becomes effective when it:

- emphasizes how strategies are used, not how many strategies are used,
- includes both student and teacher evidence, and/or
- focuses on evidence, not interpretation.

Specific feedback can be fuzzy if it contains a checklist, simply documenting and commenting on use of strategies, rather than on how appropriate a strategy was to the particular teaching situation and the skill level at which the strategy was employed (Wiliam, 2011). Feedback such as "I really enjoyed this class, you are clever!" or "this was a good lesson" are frequently found in feedback to learner teachers and might be acceptable if a goal is to make the learner teachers feel acknowledged, but this feedback offers no information for promoting teacher proficiency on improving teaching. This feedback can be understood as personal praise or an interpretation, and being targeted towards a personal level and not the task, it can be counterproductive (Hattie & Timperley, 2007). Although interpretation may be appropriate at certain points (e.g. "students showed a lack of engagement"), greater emphasis should be placed on the evidence leading to an interpretation (e.g. "three students were texting on their cell phones and at least a half dozen others were web browsing"). Such information allows a teacher to be a partner in the interpretation process, and discussions for what to change might be a topic in the mentoring conversation.

While feedback information through mentoring should provide learner teachers/mentees with information enabling them to increase their own and students' performance, it can potentially be detrimental to learning if it is vague (i.e. easy to misinterpret or misunderstand), is not related to the learning focus of the activity, is inaccurate, or directs learner attention away from the task (Parr & Timperley, 2010).

Constructive Feedback

Feedback should give the learner teacher a sense of where he or she is on a continuum; what to improve, why and how (Hattie & Timperley, 2007; Sadler, 1989). This feedback can be understood as *constructive feedback* if it contains more than telling and praising. Constructive feedback is dialogue and sharing views and perspectives in a professional conversation. Constructive feedback can be seen as feedback that:

- helps the learner teacher construct his or her own options for using feedback to move forward / improve teaching and students' learning
- features manageable action recommendations that give learner teachers clear directions on how to improve
- encourages self-assessment and reflection on practice, based on evidence (e.g. notes from students, video recordings from lessons)
- promotes focused, deliberate practice

Constructive feedback to learner teachers following classroom observations (or video recordings) can be one of the most powerful tools for increasing student learning, but only if it is conducted in accordance with the research on effective feedback (Carless et al., 2011; Gamlem & Munthe, 2014; Hattie & Timperley, 2007).

Hattie and Timperley (2007) promote four major levels at which feedback is aimed. The levels are: Task (i.e. whether work is correct or incorrect), Process (i.e. comments about the processes or strategies underpinning the task), Self-regulation (i.e. reminders to learners about strategies they can use to improve their own work), and Self (i.e. non-specific praise and comments about effort). Feedback on the self-level is found to be the least effective, feedback on the process- and self-regulation level are powerful in terms of deep processing and mastery of task, and feedback on the task level is powerful when task information in retrospect is useful for improving strategy processing or enhancing self-regulation (Hattie & Timperley, 2007). The level at which feedback is directed influences its effectiveness for learning and development. The authors argue that self-regulation feedback may be the most powerful type because it can lead to greater engagement, effort, and self-efficacy (ibid.).

Learner teachers also seek different type of feedback – some ask for advice and hints, while others ask for an answer ('how to do it') or evaluative feedback. Evaluative feedback is information about how well an assignment is done, as e.g. how successful a lesson has been based on the teacher's work. Evaluative feedback such as "You did a great job!", or "This was a good lesson" is less powerful for development processes than descriptive feedback (e.g. specific feedback about task and process). Evaluative feedback is concerned with e.g. how well a learner performs, and less about how to improve and why.

In higher education students report that the extent to which feedback is confidential are important for their use of the feedback (King, Schrodt, & Weisel, 2009). This might also become an issue for learner teachers. Not only might feedback be "potentially threatening, yielding a sensitive dimension, but the usefulness (utility) of feedback forms a unique perceptual dimension, along which students may vary" (ibid., 254). In practical terms, when feedback information leads to awareness of an improvement gap (e.g., the learner teacher needs to provide his/her students with improved assistance, hints, or prompting when participating in classwork) the mentee (or learner teacher) might feel pressure to change practice to reduce the gap. However, improvement of behaviour (e.g., feedback practice) is only one way in which the gap between desired performances and improved feedback practice can be addressed. The mentee (learner teacher) may instead of improvement decide to change or abandon the standard for what quality teaching should be like, or reject the feedback received by derogating the source of the feedback (Boekaerts & Corno, 2005; Hattie & Timperley, 2007).

TEACHER LEARNING AND FEEDBACK

It is accepted in academic circles that feedback is an essential component in the learning cycle, stimulating reflection and development. Several researchers state that feedback has one of the most powerful influences on learning and achievement when promoted in the service of supporting academic needs and to guide (e.g. a learner teacher) in the attainment of higher levels of proficiency (Hattie & Timperley, 2007; Hounsell, McCune, Hounsell, & Litjens, 2008; Sadler, 1989, 1998; Shute, 2008). It is important to state that feedback is just as important for teachers in adjusting their teaching practice as it is for students to support their learning. Nevertheless, we see from studies in e.g. Norway that compulsory school teachers report that they rarely receive targeted external feedback from their leaders or colleagues on how to improve their teaching to better support students' learning (Vibe, Aamodt, & Carlsten, 2009).

Norms that promote supportive yet challenging conversations about teaching are one of the most important features of successful learning communities (Borko, 2004; Westerberg, 2013). Major influences on learner teachers' success in development and learning are related to the degree to which they perceive and receive academic and social support from their mentors, leaders and colleagues, and the degree to which they receive support to become active (self-regulated) teachers for ongoing development (Borko, 2004; Timperley, 2008).

Feedback is not external knowledge the learner merely 'takes in' rather the learner constructs his or her own understanding and this construction will be based on the learner's prior experiences, mental structures, external support and beliefs (Brown, 2004; Smith, 2011). Teachers generally welcome the opportunity to discuss ideas and materials related to their work, and work-related conversations in professional development settings are easily fostered. Yet, a challenge is that discussions and feedback that support critical examination of teaching are relatively rare (Putnam & Borko, 1997; Vibe et al., 2009).

Mentors who investigate and build on teachers' experiences, understanding, and thinking can better support the learner teachers' development of understanding and engagement, by functioning as scaffolding for the mentee (Bransford et al., 2000; Tharp & Gallimore, 1988). Perhaps some of the most potent feedback is received within a setting in which the learner teacher interacts with some problem he or she is trying to solve, with feedback resulting as a natural phenomenon of the context of instruction. A mentor can present learner teachers with new possibilities, and challenge the social norms by which teachers operate, wherever these norms constrain professional learning (Borko, 2004; Desimone, 2011; Timperley, 2008).

Effectively designed learning environments are assessment centered, where feedback is given, received and sought. An assessment centered approach draws attention to three key instructional processes: establishing where the learners are in their learning, where they are going, and what needs to be done to get there (Hattie & Timperley, 2007; Sadler, 1989). Thus, the concern with feedback should be less about whether it is given and more about how it is received, perceived and used (Hattie & Gan, 2011; Perrenoud, 1998). Learner teachers also need to know what to do when trying to improve practice, and have the will to work towards a goal, in order to be successful in classrooms (Boekaerts, 2002; Pedder & Opfer, 2012).

In the next part, I will describe a research study conducted in 2010 based on six lower secondary school teachers who took part in an in-service education course for developing feedback practice to improve teaching and students' learning.

PARTICIPANTS, METHODS AND ANALYSES

The participants in this study were six teachers from four lower secondary schools in Norway. They volunteered to take part in an in-service education course over six months at Volda University College to learn more about feedback to support students' learning. Like the majority of Norwegian teachers, the participating teachers have more than 10 years of teaching experience, and teach in classes with 20–29 students.

The in-service education course lasted for a school semester, consisting of group courses together with individually work. An expert on AfL and feedback from the University College was the mentor for the learner teachers taking part in the in-service education course. The in-service education course was designed from a professional learning model (Timperley, 2011). This model was implemented over a two month period, and re-engaged three times (three cycles) as the in-service education course lasted for six months (see Figure 1). Each cycle was structured by three levels: level 1 (1st, 3rd, 5th course) a two-hour common workshop for all teachers participating, level 2 (observing period[s]) teachers trying out new ideas; videotaping teachers' lessons (á three lessons each teacher), and level 3 (2nd, 4th, 6th course) an individual workshop for teachers with video stimulated reflective-dialogues (VSRD) (Moyles, Paterson, & Kitson, 2003).

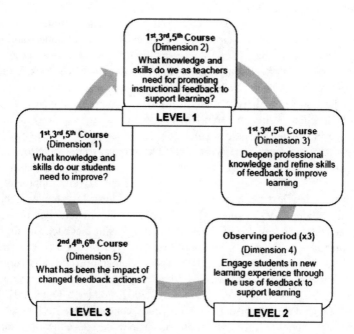

Figure 1. Teacher inquiry and knowledge building cycle for improving instructional feedback – one cycle (model based on Timperley 2011)

The knowledge building cycle (Figure 1) held five dimensions which were systematically introduced for the mentees by the mentor throughout the in-service education course. Each cycle started with a common workshop with an emphasis on the first of five dimensions in the knowledge building cycle: How to determine what knowledge and skills students have and need for further improvement, and how classroom feedback can assess and improve learning by providing information at what the students should be aiming.

What knowledge and skills teachers need for promoting and improving instructional feedback to support learning was the second dimension in the knowledge building cycle. In the course (held at the University College) the mentees were asked to identify what they need to know and do to be more effective in the areas of students' needs when providing instructional feedback. The mentees elaborated on their choices with the participating learner teachers and the mentor. In this situation the mentor avoided the trap of dispensing what would be 'best practice' for teachers and telling them what to do, since a development focus (dimension 2) has to be built from the teachers' beliefs about how feedback can be used to improve teaching and students' learning towards research on effective feedback. In the 1st course (and 3rd and 5th) theory on AfL and feedback were introduced by the mentor with the objective to build teachers' awareness of how assessment and feedback practice can be useful for improving their teaching and students' learning. The deepening of professional knowledge and refinement of skills comprised dimension 3 in the knowledge building cycle.

Further, classroom observations were video-taped by the mentor (researcher) between three and five weeks after the 1st course (and 3rd and 5th course). In this observing period (see Figure 1) mentees engaged their students in new learning experience through the use of feedback to support learning, by practicing practical techniques discussed at the in-service education course (dimension 4). At this point the mentees, in partnership with the mentor (researcher), had identified skills (e.g. questioning practice, building feedback loops, building on student responses, looking for misconceptions) to develop in their own practice. An aim was to enhance the learner teachers' capability to use, reflect upon and answer the assessment questions: 'Where am I going, How am I going, Where to next?' (Hattie & Timperley, 2007; Sadler, 1989; Timperley, 2011). Topics for development were e.g. feedback in relation to learning targets/learning intentions, feedback on task-/process-/self-regulation-/self-level, feedback as encouragement and affirmation, cumulative content driven exchanges, and evaluative and descriptive feedback.

The fifth and last dimension in the knowledge-building cycle was to reflect if there had been a change in the mentee's classroom feedback practice, and if so what had been the impact of the changed actions. This fifth dimension was emphasized at 2nd/4th/6th course and video recordings and video stimulated reflective-dialogues (VSRD) were used as tools for mentoring. The mentees' elaborated on own feedback practice and how their students responded to new practices. The 2nd/4th/6th course lasted one hour each time, and was arranged as an individual VSRD workshop. At these courses (workshops), the individual mentee together with the mentor studied sequences from their video-recorded lessons to identify successful feedback practice and important issues to develop.

Through conducting this professional learning model (Timperley, 2011) the mentees' got feedback from the mentor and their colleagues who took part in the in-service education course, at the same time as their own feedback practice in classrooms gave scope for development.

Data and Analyses

Data for this study are video recordings from the in-service educations course held January to June 2010 (see Figure 1), and individual post-interviews with the six teachers at the end of the in-service education course. The post-interviews were held to ascertain the teachers' perceptions of the provided feedback from the mentor and colleagues during the in-service education course. Interviews lasted from 49 to 170 minutes (M=82 minutes), and were recorded. An interview guide was used and the interviews were semi-structured (Kvale, 2001). The author of this chapter conducted the interviews, and it was stressed that anonymity would be maintained.

Individual interviews were conducted since the study focuses on the mentees experience of feedback in an in-service education course, and the awareness that feedback seems to be learner sensitive (Hattie & Timperley, 2007; King et al., 2009). In the interviews, the interviewees were asked to describe what kinds of feedback they received when participating in the in-service education course, what kinds of feedback they appreciated, what type of feedback was useful for their learning – and why. In addition to this, they were asked to elaborate on particular feedback from the mentor and their colleagues taking part in the in-service education course, or feedback they had sought during this process.

The three teachers that demonstrated the highest engagement throughout the in-service education course conducted the longest interviews. Still it is the kind of rapport, as well as the amount, that is critical for deriving information. Interviewees can be highly engaged in a topic (i.e. feedback practice) in an interview, but not reveal personal opinions. Conversely, interviewees may be very open about personal matters, but not willing to engage in any critical reflection on the matter (Maxwell, 2005).

All data are transcribed verbatim, and inductive coding was used for the analysis. Inductive codes are defined as codes that are generated by the researcher by directly examining the data during the coding process (Johnson & Christensen, 2011). Data are analyzed from a person- and content approach (Thagaard, 2009). All the courses (Figure 1) were video recorded, something that made it possible to transcribe the information to text. Using a person- and content approach for analysis means that the researcher has analyzed the text from the mentees' perceptions (e.g. how they mean feedback becomes useful for their teaching/student learning, what he/she finds necessarily to improve, what he/she appreciates when receiving/seeking feedback), and from their observed feedback practice (e.g. task-/process-/self-regulation/self-level). Data are thus analyzed from an inductive approach according to how mentees perceive feedback as useful for their own development and learning. Three dimensions with nine elements emerged from data through careful reading the transcribed text. These dimensions and elements (in brackets) were personal level (trust, encouragement, and proficiency), feedback content (evaluative, descriptive, task-level, process level), and feedback mode (oral, audio-visual).

TEACHERS' PERCEPTIONS OF USEFUL FEEDBACK IN MENTORING TEACHER LEARNING

An aim of this study was to derive more knowledge about what feedback learner teachers taking part in an in-service education course perceived as useful help and guidance in mentoring of building proficiency of their own feedback practice to improve teaching and support students' learning.

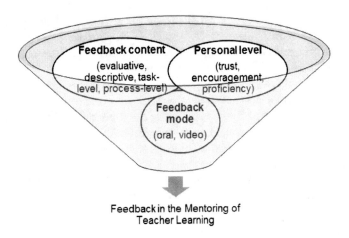

Feedback in the Mentoring of Teacher Learning

Figure 2. Dimensions and elements of feedback perceived as useful feedback in mentoring teacher learning

The three dimensions: personal level (trust, encouragement, and proficiency), feedback content (evaluative, descriptive, task-level, process level), and feedback mode (oral, audio-visual) were results from the coding process on useful feedback in mentoring teacher learning (see Figure 2), and will further be presented.

Personal Level

The first dimension *personal level* has three elements: trust, encouragement, and proficiency. These three elements were stated by the mentees as a necessarily baseline for quality feedback, and for their will to interact upon the feedback. The teachers taking part in the in-service education course said that a mentor needs a high level of proficiency according to the task under development (i.e. AfL and feedback), and there is need for a relationship between the participants built on trust. Statements by mentees such as "feedback is dependent on a good relationship between sender and receiver", "I appreciate a mentor with a high level of proficiency, since he might be able to help me to attain a higher level" and "a mentor that keeps it between us is valued, since I don't have to worry about making a fool of myself", reflect mentees' perceptions of why a personal level becomes important when seeking and receiving feedback in mentoring. These participating teachers had all more than 10 years of teaching experience, but still there seems to be a challenge/vulnerability for these lower secondary teachers to show other teachers (e.g. colleagues, a mentor) a 'failure' in their practical work or lack in understanding of feedback in teaching.

All six teachers who took part in the in-service education course communicated throughout the courses a strong emphasis on how important it is that they receive approval and encouragement from the mentor. The mentees said they appreciated encouragement, and were longing for someone to tell them that they did a good job; they wanted to be "good teachers". A challenge for giving feedback on a self-level is that feedback as extrinsic rewards often leads a learner to place more emphasis on incentives, which results in greater evaluation and completion, rather than enhanced engagement in learning (Deci, Koestner, & Ryan, 1999).

The study also revealed that these six mentees seem to perceive approval feedback equally, while corrective feedback is perceived differently. When the mentor was giving approval for strategy use at the individual $2^{nd}/4^{th}/6^{th}$ course, the six participating teachers (mentees) seem to perceive this as approval for skill and proficiency in using feedback, while feedback that questioned practice (might be understood as corrective feedback) was perceived with different valence by these six mentees. Valence, as used in psychology, especially in discussing emotions, means the intrinsic attractiveness (positive valence) or aversiveness (negative valence) of an event, object or situations (Frijda, 1986). Four of the six mentees perceived corrective feedback (e.g. questioning why peer work was not used in class when students were working on assignments) as feedback for developing practice, while two of the six mentees perceived such feedback as negative (critique) and placed it on a self-level. How learner teachers perceive feedback valence might be hard to get hold of, but in this study the teachers (mentees) took part in an interview at the end of the in-service education course where their perceptions of valence were a focus of the interview. An approach used in former research (King et al., 2009) was used to get hold of this type of data in the interviews. Examples of this result are statements by Anne and Tom, two lower secondary school teachers taking part in the in-service education course. Anne said: "I have felt that I at times have been useless in this in-service education course. I felt that the focus have been on improvement and less on acknowledging. The feedback always seemed to contain something that could be developed, always a question about improving practice. I felt that everything was something that could be done differently. It was not motivating. However, it is not certain that everything I do is perfect; it's not what I mean. I know this is also about how I am as a teacher, and I have been exhausted. The other teachers were awesome motivated and enthusiastic because they felt they learned so much. I didn't – I felt somewhat unsuccessful. However, I have learned throughout this in-service education course that my students might think the same about the feedback they receive. It is not certain that they bear to change something to improve." (Anne, June 2010), while Tom said "I think it has been very nice to get feedback because then I know what I can improve, what I manage and stuff like that. It has felt good to discover aspects of my own practice that can be improved. Many pieces have fallen into place through what I have heard, read and seen these last months. I have e.g. become concerned with the timing and content of feedback, and find that oral feedback should be continuous, and written feedback should be given as fast as possible so students can use it for further learning. I have also gone from asking in whole class, 'do you understand?' to use dialogue with my students. I have changed my teaching because you [mentor] have questioned and helped me to understand what really I was doing" (Tom, June 2010). These statements made by teachers might indicate that feedback in mentoring teacher learning is perceived differently by teachers taking part in an in-service education course based on the receiver's willingness to change and understanding for what counts as 'good teaching', a finding that seems to coincide with research by Sternberg and Grigorenko (1997) and Pedder and Opfer (2012). E.g. Sternberg and Grigorenko find that teachers give feedback and assess students' work and behaviour based on their own preferences for what is valued in education (Sternberg & Grigorenko, 1997).

To add up, feedback directed on task level seems to be perceived as feedback on a self-level by some mentees taking part in the in-service education course due to their preferences and beliefs. This finding is something one should be aware of when giving feedback in mentoring teacher learning, due to the challenge that personal comments (feedback on self-level) seem to reduce volitional strategies (Boekaerts & Corno, 2005). Volitional engagement is essential if a learner teacher is to remain resistant and overcome threats to self-esteem that may cause her/him to divert resources away from their active participation in the development process and expend resources on efforts to avoid interaction with a mentor and withdraw from the situation (Black & Wiliam, 2009; Dweck, 2008).

Feedback Content

The second dimension *feedback content* has four elements: Evaluative, descriptive, task level, and process level. Evaluative feedback is about how well a task is performed, for example on what are 'right or wrong answers' and any deficiencies in the performance, while descriptive feedback is on specifying attainment and improvement, constructing achievement, and constructing the way forward (Gamlem & Smith, 2013; Tunstall & Gipps, 1996). Task level is understood as how well tasks are understood/performed, and process level is understood as the main process needed to understand/perform tasks (Hattie & Timperley, 2007). Hattie and Timperley (2007) say that feedback related to task level will have the greatest impact on learning when it can help to make learners (e.g. learner teachers) aware of misinterpretation, higher quality, and point out a direction for further work.

A finding in this study is that the mentees who took part in the in-service education course seek different feedback types from their mentor, and a challenge is that not all types of feedback might be of help and support for a development process (Hattie & Timperley, 2007). In the in-service education course some mentees asked for evaluative feedback from their mentor, while others sought a descriptive type where the focus was on how to improve. The mentee(s) seeking evaluative feedback, were concerned with how well they performed and less about how to improve their teaching through feedback interactions. The challenge for a mentor in such a case is to re-conceptualize a mentee's understanding for how feedback becomes useful for their improvement, and how it can be used to the attainment of higher levels of proficiency for teaching and giving feedback to support students' learning.

Of the many goals of feedback, research has elaborated on how it can guide students in how to accomplish the learning aim/intention, provide information about misconceptions, and motivate students to invest more effort in the task (Dweck, 2008; Hattie & Gan, 2011; Hattie & Timperley, 2007). This is also a goal for learner teachers. To be able to construct a direction for attainment of higher levels of feedback practice in classroom to improve teaching and student learning, the feedback provided has to be specific on the retrospective and more general for the prospective (Sadler, 2010). An example on such feedback to a mentee is: "By observing your class I see there are some attempts to elicit and acknowledge students' background knowledge or misconceptions and that previously learned material is integrated, but these moments are limited in depth and not consistently provided. By consistently linking new concepts/procedures/broad ideas to students' prior knowledge their understanding might advance and/or misconceptions can be clarified." Feedback information provided by a mentor needs to be based on the mentee's prior experiences, mental structures and beliefs (Brown, 2004; Mory, 2004). A mentee can and will only use information that is understood and perceived as useful, since she/he constructs his or her own reality from the information provided.

When feedback from e.g. task level is given orally by a mentor for a group of mentees (e.g. the group of teachers taking part in an in-service education course), the individual mentees' understanding/knowledge of topic communicated and opinion on relevance can decide to what extent this feedback is used to further learning (Hattie & Timperley, 2007). If a mentee does not understand what is being said in the feedback message, or why (i.e. has not preferences/knows the qualities in a performance), the mentee cannot take benefit of the feedback. Alternatively, he/she may perceive that the feedback message is directed towards the public group ('the others'), and thus does not see the relevance in using the information the mentor provides. As such, feedback on task level is most effective when it is directed towards the individual, is specific on the basis of what one has been doing and more general about what can be done further (Sadler, 2010). In addition, much feedback at task level may encourage a mentee to focus on the immediate goal, and not the strategies/processes to achieve the goal.

A result in this study was that not all mentees taking part in the in-service education course asked for feedback on the process level. This might be critical for the mentee's opportunities to build and sustain higher levels of feedback practice to improve teaching and support students learning, if also a mentor does not become aware of the lack of this level of feedback information. This is because feedback on the process level has the strength to give a mentee an understanding of his/her own learning and performance, so that she/he can initiate the right processes to come further in the work. Feedback at the process level is important for development since it deals with information about processes that are assumptions for the implementation of the assignment, which is related to the assignment or transfer learning from this task to another, i.e. the use of strategies and teaching methods (Hattie & Timperley, 2007). This result from the study points to a need for a mentor's awareness for what feedback is given, and asked for by a mentee in the in-service education course.

Feedback Mode

The third and last dimension, *feedback mode* has two elements; oral and audio based information. These two elements emerged based on tools for receiving external feedback in the in-service education course. Feedback from the mentor (i.e. lecturer from the University College) was based on orally dialogic feedback. The mentor built the feedback messages from the mentees' practice, questions and responses. One of the lower secondary school teachers taking part in the in-service education course told in the post-interview that useful feedback can be explained by looking at a Swiss cheese. He said: "Earlier my practice was like a 'Swiss cheese' with lots of holes in it, but gradually by receiving feedback the holes get filled on the sides, so now I can fill in without it slipping out. The information makes meaning" (Tom, June 2010). The challenge (and advantage) with an orally dialogic approach is to make sure that the sender of feedback (e.g. mentor) and receiver (e.g. mentee) are tuned into the same understanding for what they are aiming for (Alexander, 2006; Sadler, 1989).

All six lower secondary teachers taking part in the in-service education course explained that they appreciated being able to discuss their own practice with the mentor, and said that a quality sign for good oral feedback was that they could build deeper understanding through conversations of what they "were really doing when using feedback". Statements such as "to receive relevant questions which guide me in the attainment of higher understanding of what I'm doing and what impact this have on my students, has been helpful" and "feedback related to my practice, my challenges has been great – finally I can get help in the attainment of becoming a better teacher" reflect the value of targeted dialogic oral feedback by these mentees' taking part in the in-service education course.

Still, results indicate that there are differences in conceptual distinctions between the six mentees on the purpose of feedback. One of the mentees participating in the courses said: "By discussing what to improve I feel that what I am doing is not good enough". This statement shows how feedback to a mentee might preclude development and improvement of teaching practice. To understand this statement better, we can look at research by Kluger and DeNisi (1996). They have proposed two axioms for feedback: feedback cues that draw attention to meta-task features (such as threats) retard performance, while feedback cues that draw attention to motivation or learning processes enhance performance (Kluger & DeNisi, 1996). A question will be how learner teachers (and/or mentees) perceive feedback on their learning process differently, and from this how feedback might support or preclude their development process (King et al., 2009). An additional perspective to this is that feedback as hint might be perceived differently depending on the performer's level of achievement (Shute, 2008). This boils down to the awareness for how feedback in the mentoring of teacher learning is received and used. Research results points out that feedback leads to learning gains only when it includes guidance about how to improve, when the receiver (mentee) understands how and why to use it, and is willing to dedicate effort (Boekaerts & Corno, 2005; Hattie & Timperley, 2007; Kluger & DeNisi, 1996). Quality feedback gives information which helps and guides the learner teacher/mentee to better understanding and performance. To accomplish those goals, feedback to teachers must be focused, specific and constructive.

Knowing whether the feedback a mentee receives responds to his/her needs and beliefs is important information for a mentor to be able to give support for learning and development, something that argues for the value of using dialogue when providing feedback in mentoring teacher learning.

The second element in the third dimension, feedback mode, is feedback from audio-visual information. This was video recordings from the teachers' (the mentees) lessons. This audio-visual feedback was derived by the use of video stimulated reflective-dialogues (VSRD) in $2^{nd}/4^{th}/6^{th}$ course in the in-service education course. To watch videos from their own teaching was perceived as useful by five of the mentees, while one struggled to watch the recorded videos from her classroom. This lower secondary school teacher said her voice was strange and stated her feedback interaction with her students as less attractive. She kept assessing herself from a self-level throughout the in-service education course and stated her practice in negative terms; what was 'wrong' more than what she found interesting for development. By analysing her statements in this study, results show that this mentee had a strong focus on evaluative feedback, and less on the descriptive type. It has to be informed that the mentees did only watch videos of their own teaching, and the $2^{nd}/4^{th}/6^{th}$ course was arranged individual for the participating teachers in the in-service education course. What might be interesting for knowledge building on feedback in mentoring teacher learning is that a mentee might perceive external feedback at task- and strategy level as feedback at the self-level. This result seems to coincide with former research by Kluger and DeNisi (1996), where feedback on task might be perceived as a threat to a mentee's self, something that might retard performance and development.

CONCLUSION

Results from this study indicate that feedback to improve teaching is something teachers want and are longing for, but that feedback messages can be perceived differently by a mentee based on his/her preferences and beliefs about what feedback should be given.

Three dimensions are described as useful feedback in the mentoring of teacher learning (see Figure 2), and the combination of these dimensions seems to be perceived as most helpful for the mentee in mentoring conversations as e.g. in this in-service education course.

Feedback content, feedback mode, and a personal level are important facets for a mentee taking part in an in-service education course and should be considered separately as well as interactively with personal characteristics. A result from this study is that the same type of feedback is not helpful guidance for all mentees in the attainment of higher levels of feedback to improve teaching and support students learning. Feedback can be made more effective in the support of improvement if it can be adapted to the needs of the mentee – cognitive and noncognitive characteristics – as well as different types of knowledge and skills. Results in this study also reveal that feedback in the mentoring of teacher learning should be derived at a personal level, such as giving encouragement, being based on trust and being given by an 'expert'. The question for feedback in the mentoring of teacher learning is: What dimensions and elements of feedback complexity seems to be most useful to support a mentees' learning and improvement?

As a final remark, the purpose for this chapter was to promote knowledge of how teachers taking part in an in-service education course perceive feedback as useful in the mentoring of teacher learning. As evidenced throughout the analyses, there might not be 'a best' type of feeback in mentoring for all mentees. However, feedback can enhance teacher learning to the extent that the mentee is receptive and the feedback is on target, specific, focused, and constructive.

REFERENCES

Alexander, R. (2006). *Towards dialogic teaching: Rethinking classroom talk* (3rd ed.). Cambridge, UK: Dialogos.

Askew, S., & Lodge, C. (2000). Gifts, ping-pong and loops: Linking feedback and learning. In S. Askew (Ed.), *Feedback for learning* (pp. 1–17). London, England: Routhledge.

Black, P., & Wiliam, D. (2009). Developing the theory of formative assessment. *Educational Assessment, Evaluation and Accountability, 21*(1), 5–31.

Boekaerts, M. (2002). Motivation to learn. *International Bureau of Education, 27.* Retrieved from http://www.ibe.unesco.org/publications/EducationalPracticesSeriesPdf/prac10e.pdf

Boekaerts, M., & Corno, L. (2005). Self-regulation in the classroom: A perspective on assessment and intervention. *Applied Psychology, 54*(2), 199–231.

Borko, H. (2004). Professional development and teacher learning: Mapping the terrain. *Educational Researcher, 33*(8), 3–15.

Bransford, J. D., Brown, A. L., & Cocking, R. R. (2000). *How people learn: Brain, mind, experience and school.* Washington, DC: National Academy Press.

Brown, G. T. L. (2004). Teachers' conceptions of assessment: Implications for policy and professional development. *Assessment in Education, 11*(3), 301–318.

Carless, D., Salter, D., Yang, M., & Lam, J. (2011). Developing sustainable feedback practices. *Studies in Higher Education, 36*(4), 395–407.

Deci, E. L., Koestner, R., & Ryan, R. M. (1999). A meta-analytic review of experiments examining the effects of extrinsic rewards and intrinsic motivation. *Psychological Bulletin, 125*(6), 627–668.

Desimone, L. M. (2011). A primer on effective professional development. *Kappan, 92*(6), 68–71.

DuFour, R., & Marzano, R. J. (2009). High-leverage strategies for principal leadership. *Educational Leadership, 66*(5), 62–68.

Dweck, C. S. (2008). *Mindset. The new psychology of success.* New York, NY: Ballantine Books.

Frijda, N. H. (1986). *The emotions.* Cambridge: Cambridge University Press.

Gamlem, S. M., & Munthe, E. (2014). Mapping the quality of feedback to support students' learning in lower secondary classrooms. *Cambridge Journal of Education, 44*(1), 75–92.

Gamlem, S. M., & Smith, K. (2013). Student perceptions of classroom feedback. *Assessment in Education: Principles, Policy & Practice, 20*(2), 150–169.

Haggis, T. (2006). Pedagogies for diversity: Retaining critical challenge amidst fears of dumbing down. *Studies in Higher Education, 31*(5), 521–535.

Harris, L. R., Harnett, J. A., & Brown, G. T. L. (2013). *Exploring the content of teachers' feedback: What are teachers actually providing to students?* Paper presented at the AERA 2013, San Francisco, CA.

Hattie, J., & Gan, M. (2011). Instruction based on feedback. In R. E. Mayer & P. A. Alexander (Eds.), *Handbook of research on learning and instruction* (pp. 249–271). New York, NY: Routhledge.

Hattie, J., & Timperley, H. (2007). The power of feedback. *Review of Educational Research, 77*(1), 81–112.

Hounsell, D., McCune, V., Hounsell, J., & Litjens, J. (2008). The quality of guidance and feedback to students. *Higher Education Research & Development, 27*(1), 55–67.

Johnson, R. B., & Christensen, L. B. (2011). Chapter 19: Data analysis in qualitative and mixed research. In R. B. Johnson & L. B. Christensen (Eds.), *Educational research methods: Quantitative, qualitative, and mixed approaches* (4th ed., pp. 515–545). Los Angeles, CA: Sage.

King, P. E., Schrodt, P., & Weisel, J. J. (2009). The instructional feedback orientation scale: Conceptualizing and validating a new measure for assessing perceptions of instructional feedback. *Communication Education, 58*(2), 235–261.

Kluger, A. N., & DeNisi, A. (1996). The effects of feedback interventions on performance: A historical review, a meta-analysis, and a preliminary feedback intervention theory. *Psychological Bulletin, 119,* 254–284.

Kvale, S. (2001). *Det kvalitative forskingsintervju* [The Qualitative Interview]. Oslo: Gyldendal Akademisk.

Maxwell, J. A. (2005). *Qualitative research design. An interactive approach* (2nd ed., Vol. 41). Thousands Oaks, CA: Sage.

Mory, E. H. (2004). Feedback research revisited. In D. H. Jonassen (Ed.), *Handbook of research on educational communications and technology* (2nd ed., pp. 745–783). London, England: Lawrence Erlbraum Associates.

Moyles, J., Paterson, F., & Kitson, N. (2003). It wasn't as bad as I thought: Learning from reflective dialogues. In J. Moyles, L. Hargreaves, R. Merry, F. Paterson, & V. Esarte-Sarries (Eds.), *Interactive teaching in the primary school* (pp. 141–154). Maidenhead, PA: Open University Press.

Nicol, D. J., & Macfarlane-Dick, D. (2006). Formative assessment and self-regulated learning: A model and seven principles of good feedback practice. *Studies in Higher Education, 31*(2), 199–218.

Parr, J. M., & Timperley, H. (2010). Feedback to writing, assessment for teaching and learning and student progress. *Assessing Writing, 15*(2), 68–85.

Pedder, D., & Opfer, V. D. (2012). Professional learning orientations: Patterns of dissonance and alignment between teachers' values and practices. *Research Papers in Education,* 1–32.

Perrenoud, P. (1998, March). From formative evaluation to a controlled regulation of learning processes: Towards a wider conceptual field. *Assessment in Education: Principles, Policy & Practice, 5*(1), 85–102.

Pollock, J. E. (2012). *Feedback: The hinge that joins teaching and learning.* Thousand Oaks, CA: Corwin.

Putnam, R., & Borko, H. (1997). Teacher learning: Implications of new views of cognition. In B. J. Biddle, T. L. Good, & I. F. Goodsen (Eds.), *The international handbook of teachers and teaching* (pp. 1223–1296). Dordrecht, The Netherlands: Kluwer.

Sadler, R. (1989). Formative assessment and the design of instructional systems. *Instructional Science, 18*(2), 119–144.

Sadler, R. (1998). Formative assessment: Revisiting the territory. *Assessment in Education: Principles, Policy & Practice, 5*(1), 77–84.

Sadler, R. (2010). Beyond feedback: Developing student capability in complex appraisal. *Assessment & Evaluation in Higher Education, 35*(5), 535–550.

Shute, V. J. (2008). Focus on formative feedback. *Review of Educational Research, 78*(1), 153–189.

Smith, K. (2011). Professional development of teachers – A prerequisite for AfL to be successfully implemented in the classroom. *Studies in Educational Evaluation, 37*, 55–61.

Sternberg, R. J., & Grigorenko, E. L. (1997). Are cognitive styles still in style? *American Psychologist, 52*(7), 700–712.

Thagaard, T. (2009). *Systematikk og innlevelse. En innføring i kvalitativ metode (3.utgave)* [Systematic approach and empathy. An introduction to qualitative methods]. Bergen: Fagbokforlaget

Tharp, R. G., & Gallimore, R. (1988). *Rousing minds to life. Teaching, learning, and schooling in social context.* Cambridge: Cambridge University Press.

Timperley, H. (2008). Teacher professional learning and development. *Educational practices series-18. International Bureau of education, 31.* Retrieved from http://www.ibe.unesco.org/fileadmin/user_ upload/Publications/Educational_Practices/EdPractices_18.pdf

Timperley, H. (2011). *Using student assessment for professional learning: Focusing on students' outcomes to identify teachers' needs* (p. 34). Melborne: State of Victoria, Department of Education and Early Childhood Development.

Tuck, J. (2012). Feedback giving as social practice: Teachers' perspectives on feedback as institutional requirement, work and dialogue. *Teaching in Higher Education, 17*(2), 209–221.

Tunstall, P., & Gipps, C. (1996). Teacher feedback to young children in formative assessment: A typology. *British Educational Research Journal, 22*(4), 389–404.

Vibe, N., Aamodt, P. O., & Carlsten, T. C. (2009). *To be a lower secondary teacher in Norway. Results from OECD first Teaching and Learning International Survey (TALIS)* (Report No. 23). Oslo: NIFU STEP.

Westerberg, T. R. (2013). Feedback for teachers: Focused, specific, and constructive. *Principal Leadership, 30–33.*

Wiliam, D. (2011). *Embedded formative assessment.* Bloomington, IN (USA): Solution Tree Press.

Siv M. Gamlem
Faculty of Humanities and Teacher Education
Volda University College, Norway

BETTINA KORVER AND HARM TILLEMA

5. FEEDBACK PROVISION IN MENTORING CONVERSATIONS

Differing Mentor and Student Perceptions on Learning from Mentoring

INTRODUCTION[1]

The case of a (not too unlikely) feedback session:

> Mentor: "You were irritated by a student. What happened?; what were you thinking at that moment. Why did you react the way you did?
> Student: "Yes, she really caused irritation." I thought it was sufficient to react nonverbally to it. I thought it would be best"

Possible ways to give feedback:

1

> Mentor: "and when you look back on it now? You could have done something else. Looking back now; are there arguments or ideas or feelings why what you did was the best way you did it?"

> Student: "I think it is because...."

2

> Mentor: "Okay, your core purpose in maintaining attention in the class is: stimulating your students to stay involved and to address them on this. How are you going to assure that?

> Student; "yes but...."

3

> Mentor: Tell me more what you want personally in handling the class, and discussing with pupils. How would you like to function here as a teacher...

> And tell me how you will become more the teacher you would like to be....

> Student: "What I like is ...."

H. Tillema et al. (Eds.), Mentoring for Learning, 99–115.

In mentoring it is all about providing and accepting feedback. In this case we illustrate possible different ways a mentor could provide feedback which in turn might lead to different perceptions on part of the student that will, most likely, give rise to different kinds of student learning.

MENTORING AND FEEDBACK; AN INTRICATE RELATION

This chapter explores how diverging perceptions between a mentor and a mentee on the nature and content of feedback given in mentoring conversations have an impact on the mentee's learning from conversation. Our study gauges whether approaches to mentoring relate to congruency in perceptions on provided feedback. The aim of this research is to explore differences in mentor and student perceptions of feedback during mentoring sessions. For that purpose, this study compares typical mentoring approaches across different settings.

Sixty eight students (37 Teaching Assistant (TA) students in secondary vocational education and 31 Teacher Education (TE) students in Higher Education) and their mentors participated in this study. Mentoring conversations on teaching internships of these students were analyzed. A questionnaire instrument was used to gauge 1) acceptance of feedback from a mentor as well as 2) following recommendations after feedback provision. Mentors' conversation styles were identified with an observation instrument categorizing four types. We found that TA students predominantly recognized their mentor's approach having an Imperator (supervising) style, while the TE students identified it as an Initiator (engaging style). As a result, TA students expressed a higher degree of acceptance of feedback, as compared to TE students. Differences in perception between students and their mentors on feedback provision were found to be significant.

Our findings point to the importance of mentoring approach as it impinges on the feedback acceptance in mentoring conversations. In discussing our findings we note the diverging perceptions students have on effective mentoring.

Providing Feedback

In mentoring, feedback provision is a process of fundamental importance (Wiliam, 2011). Providing and using feedback, however, are strongly dependent on the way both the deliverer and the receiver of feedback perceive the mentoring conversation (Mena Marcos & Tillema, 2006). This study intends to uncover the alignment in feedback (mis)perceptions between mentors and their students, in relation to the differing mentoring approaches used in conversation. We expect that congruency, i.e., shared mentoring goals, adds to the utility of feedback (Shute, 2008).

The process of providing feedback is meant to enhance a student's achievement (Hattie, 2009) and can be viewed as a two staged, reciprocal activity of: on the one hand *monitoring* and on the other hand, *scaffolding*. Monitoring or focus on "assessment for learning" (Wiliam, 2011) deals with evaluating the students' learning process, which, on part of the student, requires acceptance of evaluative information. *Scaffolding* as a process of guiding and enhancing further learning deals with giving advice and suggestions for planned action that, on part of the student, which may lead to following recommendations (see Pat- El, Tillema, Segers, & Vedder, 2012) for a more detailed account of this twofold process). The reciprocity of assessment/evaluation and enhancement/guidance is typical for mentoring (Tillema & Van der Westhuizen, 2013); and, in a mentoring conversation, occurs within a high frequency of interexchange (Boshuizen, Bromme, & Gruber, 2004, pp. 164–166). During conversation, both mentor and student search for understanding and confirmation with regard to interpreting past performance and are "meaning making" on attainments of the student, for the purpose of amendments and identification of further needs of the student (Dochy, Heylen, & Van de Mosselaar, 2002, p. 22; Black & Wiliam, 1998). The process underneath an effective feedback provision (Sadler, 1989) may include the following key features: (1) diagnosis of current state; (2) evaluation of progress made relative to standards set; (3) providing informative feedback that motivates the students to accept the assessment; and (4) giving advice on how to follow recommendations for the acquisition of required skills and knowledge (James & Fleming, 2004; Hattie & Timperley, 2007).

The impact these features have on student's learning from feedback depends highly on the way they are communicated during conversation (Shute, 2008). Brinko (1993) captured this concisely into four W-questions (and an H-question) to characterize the feedback process in mentoring: What (the information that is fed back), When (the occasion upon which the information is fed back), Where (the location in which the information is fed back is psychologically safe), and How (the manner in which the information is given and received). These 'W/H' questions, however, can be very differently interpreted by participants?. Carless (2006) explored possible different interpretations of students and their mentors with regard to feedback giving and noted how divergent viewpoints in goals and plans act as barriers to distort the acceptance of feedback and its subsequent following of recommendations. In order for an alignment in perceptions to occur, Carless (2006) conceived giving and interpreting feedback in mentoring as consisting of three interlocking components: (1) Discourse: the way feedback is communicated must be fully understood; (2) Power: the (often) authoritative position of the feedback giver, i.e., mentor, must help to facilitate acceptance of feedback; and (3) Willingness: the mentee as recipient of feedback must be personally involved and willing to invest time and effort in following recommendations.

Our contention then is: As conversation is the major vehicle of exchange between a mentor and a mentee, it may be highly vulnerable to misinterpretation, since different perceptions may arise on what to accept and how to follow recommendations. How then, i.e., by what mentoring approaches, are mentoring conversations being conducted to reinforce the mentee's acceptance and following recommendations, and make feedback work?

Mentoring Approaches in Conversation

Mentoring can be a highly powerful learning environment to promote learning because of its close and direct interaction between one who "teaches" and one who "learns" (Garvey, Stokes & Megginson, 2009). Delivering feedback during a mentoring session builds on tailored comments to the learner, in close connection to the student's zone of proximal development. Characteristic of a mentoring relationship (Clutterbuck & Megginson, 2009) is mutuality in: honesty, openness, sensitivity, self-awareness, and reflexivity, which supports student's learning and motivates. Feedback should, therefore, be provided with clarity of intents (to accept advice), feasibility of comments made (to follow recommendations), and trust in the relationship (to have a conversation) (Tillema, 2009).

The complexity of effective feedback provision in a mentoring relationship lies, among other things, in the intricate alignment of perceptions regarding a) what to attain; b) what has been achieved, and c) how far one has progressed from a to b (Sadler, 2010). Feedback provision in a mentoring relationship can be looked upon as a double-edged sword, with on one hand the mentor acting as a scaffold, while at the same time keeping evaluative standards high. A mentor may then select different strategies or approaches to cope with this duality. Following Tillema & Kremer-Hayon (2005) there are three dilemmas or strategic choices to be made in selecting a mentoring approach in conversation: (1) Reflection versus Action, that is, offering space for experiencing or questioning to stimulate reflection as opposed to promoting planned action and resolve; (2) Supervising versus Facilitating, i.e., talking together in or as a community of learners, as opposed to advice giving under scrutiny of performance; (3) Delivery or Inquiry, i.e., giving support by using a telling-method, or by waiting to discover, accepting students' initiatives, thus dealing with students differently (Garvey et al., 2009). Resolving these dilemmas results in different mentoring approaches that can be recognized in conversations (Crasborn, Hennissen, Brouwer, Korthagen, & Bergen, 2011).

Tillema and Smith (2007) identified the following approaches: (1) Instructive/ prescriptive approach, as giving directions, with its prime focus on progress made, evaluated against targets being set, (2) Relational approach, which rests highly on self-regulated learning and input given by the student, (3) Situational approach, in which the mentor acts as a (performance) coach to stimulate learning, using articulation of shared goals. These mentoring approaches in conversation may highly influence the student's acceptance and use of given feedback. This study then particularly looks at differences in mentoring approaches and how it affects perceptions of feedback provision by the mentee. We conjecture that ways in which conversations are conducted by the mentor will result in different outcomes when it comes to acceptance of advice and its subsequent following of recommendations by the mentee. For this purpose we studied mentoring conversations in student teacher learning and compared mentoring approaches both in a performance oriented teacher education program and a reflective oriented program teacher education program. We were interested to see how these different settings in which mentoring was conducted would affect student perceptions of feedback (i.e, interpreted as acceptance of advice and following recommendations)

The main research question of this study is: *to what extent do feedback perceptions of mentees relate to the mentoring approach of their mentors?*

METHOD

This study was conducted within the internship courses of two teacher education programs. The total sample was comprised of four third-year groups of student teachers, two at the level of secondary vocational education (TA – teacher assistant program) and two at the level of professional higher education (TE – teacher education program) in The Netherlands. The programs differed in two important ways as far as mentoring is concerned: in the TA program mentors have individual sessions with their students to assess the degree to which a set of pre-specified competences are attained/completed during the internship period (both assessed formatively/process based as well as summative/outcome based), whereas the TE mentors appraise their students internship activities formatively during group sessions and provide reflective support (formatively), while external assessors/supervisors assess the attainment levels separately and in a summative way. The mentoring quality in the TA is dependent upon explicit coverage of predefined appraisal criteria, i.e., "protocolled" in the TE setting it is highly dependent on conversational and relational skills of the mentor.

A total of 68 students participated together with their mentor: 37 Teaching Assistant students (26 female, 11 male) with age ranging from 19 to 22, and 31 Teacher Education students (31 female, 1 male) with age ranging from 20 to 24. The four group related mentors (2 female, 2 male) with age ranging from 44 to 50 (Sd 2.5) had working experience as a mentor of 2 to 6 years (mean 4.67, sd 2.3).

Instruments

This study used a survey questionnaire design. Questionnaire instruments were administered after the internship program by the corresponding mentor to their students. The questionnaires contained both pre-specified instruments as well as a number of open questions. All questionnaire items were measured on Likert scales ranging from 1 to 5 (1= strongly disagree, and 5= strongly agree), to measure students' appraisal of feedback provision (dependent variables: acceptance of feedback and following recommendations) and as well as assessment orientation of mentor and mentee (as presage variable). Mentor approach in conversation was used as a moderator variable.

Assessment Orientation Questionnaire

The assessment orientation questionnaire measures student and mentor orientation towards assessment and evaluation of learning. It consists of a Teacher and Student

Assessment for Learning Questionnaire version, i.e., the TAFL-Q and SAFL-Q. Explorative and multivariate factor analyses of the instruments were performed by Pat-El, Tillema, Segers, and Vedder (2012) resulting in a stable solution of two factors. Both instruments determine perceptions with regard to a) feedback provision as evaluation and b) support from feedback for further action. The TAFL-Q questionnaire consists of 28 items divided into two scales: (1) Assessment as an aid to Monitor performance; and (2) Assessment as a Scaffold for further learning. In the corresponding SAFL-Q for students 28 items are divided into two scales: (1) Receiving Feedback; and (2) Using Feedback. *Receiving Feedback* measures the students' perception of feedback acceptance from their mentor whereas *Using Feedback* measures the students' intent to follow recommendation. Reliability of the scales in this study is high: alpha. 92 and. 80 respectively (corresponding to the reliabilities found by Pat-El et al., 2012).

Appraisal of Feedback Instrument

A questionnaire instrument was constructed to appraise the nature of feedback provision after mentoring conversation to the student, having 29 questions. The instrument previously developed and used in a study by Tillema & Smith (2006; reliability alpha. 87), measures three criteria with respect to the way a mentor conducts a mentoring conversation. The instrument gauges a) clarity (degree of problem understanding gained from conversation by the mentee), b) feasibility of feedback provided (practicality of comments made by the mentor), and c) trust, (degree of confidence in the relationship with the mentor). The *Clarity* scale (9 items) measures the overall rating of the feedback given (with respect to communication and goals to be attained), i.e., "The feedback I receive is clear ...". The *Trust* scale (10 items) refers to the degree of relatedness. i.e., "I rely on the advice of my mentor ..." and the *Feasibility* scale (10 items) refers to the do-ability of expressed advice to comply to the recommendations given, i.e., "The goals don't discourage me, because I know I can reach them...". Reliability of the scales is: Clarity. 85, Trust. 87, and Feasibility. 82.

Mentoring Approach Questionnaire

Mentoring approach in conversation was measured with a questionnaire originally developed by Crasborn, Hennissen, Brouwer, Korthagen, and Bergen (2011) and modified for the purpose of this study to adapt to the setting of mentoring in teacher education for primary education. The questionnaire contained 24 questions, identical for mentor and students, having four scales corresponding to four types of mentor approaches identified in the study by Crasborn et al. (date): (1) Initiator; (2) Imperator; (3) Encourager; and (4) Advisor. *Initiator* refers to the use of non-directive skills and an active, stimulating, implicit way of advice giving. *Imperator* refers to use of a high degree of directive and active, prescriptive advice giving.

Encourager refers to use of non-directive questions and passiveness in discussing topics, and *Advisor* refers to the use of directive skills, combined with passive suggestions for further actions.

Open Questions

The student questionnaire booklet also contained a number of open questions asking about student motivation, gauging interest to become a teacher, as well as intentions to finish the program. These questions were meant to give a background perspective on the students' opinions on learning from advice giving and their prospects for further learning. It could provide a figure ground contrast to the questionnaire data. Furthermore some descriptive control variables were measured with regard to student background: birth year, gender, nation of origin, prior completion of the teacher education program.

Procedure

To make sure that students' perception regarding mentoring conversation was measured and not the concerns (and fears) for actual assessment of their performance, the dates of the questionnaire administration were set at the end of the school year, yet after the actual final performance assessment of the students had taken place.

The participating student groups (TE and TA) had been approached previously by the researcher to obtain consent for participation. Students and their corresponding mentors were asked to complete the questionnaires after a short introduction by the main researcher. Respondents were assured about anonymity.

Data Analysis

Homogeneity and reliabilities of questionnaire scales was tested. Results are given in Table 1.

Differences in perception of feedback and mentoring approach between student groups, and between students and their mentor were analyzed with independent two-tailed t-tests. A Factorial design using multivariate analysis of variance was used to scrutinize group differences in Trust, Clarity, Feasibility. Discrepancy scores (z-scores using the mentor's mean score) were calculated between the mentor and their students with regard to mentoring approach in feedback use.

RESULTS

Descriptive findings on collected data (means and standards deviations) are presented in Table 2.

Correlations between data collection instruments are presented in Table 3. Table 2 indicates that TA students rated high on mentor approach: Imperator, and mentor

105

Table 1. Reliability of student questionnaires, with examples of items, number of items, and Cronbach's Alpha

Scale	Examples of items	No.of items	Cronbach's Alpha
SAFL-Q *Receiving feedback*	My mentor encourages me to look back on my learning process and to think about what I can do differently next time.	16	.918
SAFL-Q *Using Feedback*	I know which points I need to work on to improve my results.	12	.803
Mentor appraisal			
Clarity	The feedback I receive from my mentor is clear.	9	.853
Trust	I rely on the instructions and advice of my mentor, because for me they indicate the right course.	10	.872
Feasibility	The goals, as mentioned by my mentor don't discourage me, because I know I can reach them.	10	.817
Mentoring approach			
Initiator	During the feedback session my mentor asks me to reflect on my actions, so I come to insights by myself.	5	.592
Imperator	My mentor asks me, with regard to the assignment, how I think I will perform the task.	6	.845
Encourager	My mentor steers me in no way through instructions or advice.	6	.702
Advisor	During the feedback session I mostly come with the topics discussed and my mentor responds strongly by steering guidance and advice regarding my development.	6	.769

appraisal Trust, Clarity, as well as Feedback acceptance, compared to their TE counterparts. Pearson correlation coefficients show moderate significant (at $p < .01$) associations between variables, with an exception on variable Encourager, which correlates significantly negatively ($p < .01$) with all other variables.

Feedback and Mentoring Approach

A main research expectation concerned the relation between mentor approach and feedback provision. A significant difference was found between TA and TE students on their acceptance of feedback, having a medium effect size (Cohen's d = 0.62) with (t (66) = 2.29, $p < .05$). However, no significant differences between groups TA and TE were found for mentor approach on following recommendations (see Figure 1).

Table 2. Table of means and Sd for TA (N=37) and TE (N=31) on measured variables

Scale	Mean		Sd	
	TA	TE	TA	TE
Receiving Feedback	3.49	3.17	.72	.75
Using Feedback	3.71	3.52	.53	.56
Mentor appraisal				
Clarity	3.64	3.34	.67	.62
Trust	3.65	3.33	.71	.76
Feasibility	3.47	3.34	.58	.68
Mentor approach				
Initiator	3.58	3.30	.67	.54
Imperator	3.67	2.97	.81	.69
Encourager	2.41	2.73	.77	.64
Advisor	3.50	2.85	.67	.57

Table 3. Correlation of variables for TA group (MBO) and TE group (HBO)

		Rec FB	Using FB	FB Acc	Foll Rec	Clarity	Trust	Feasibility	Initiator	Encourager	Imperator	Advisor
Rec FB	MBO	1										
	HBO	1										
Using FB	MBO	.742**	1									
	HBO	.791**	1									
FB Acc	MBO	.741**	.758**	1								
	HBO	.661**	.621**	1								
Foll Rec	MBO	.572**	.690**	.840**	1							
	HBO	.694**	.652**	.928**	1							
Clarity	MBO	.702**	.790**	.937**	.909**	1						
	HBO	.678**	.702**	.897**	.901**	1						
Trust	MBO	.542*	.634**	.877**	.942**	.858**	1					
	HBO	.673**	.590**	.931**	.954**	.794**	1					
Feasibility	MBO	.687**	.673**	.884**	.894**	.871**	.822**	1				
	HBO	.615**	.580*	.964**	.941**	.855**	.908**	1				
Initiator	MBO	.469*	.533*	.642**	.628**	.656**	.607**	.656**	1			
	HBO	.316	.468*	.578*	.553*	.638**	.462*	.578*	1			
Encourager	MBO	-.555**	-.533**	-.818**	-.747**	-.820**	-.747**	-.720**	-.654**	1		
	HBO	-.559*	-.474*	-.739**	-.765**	-.613**	-.806**	-.732**	-.521*	1		
Imperator	MBO	.721**	.734**	.775**	.701**	.817**	.647**	.739**	.766**	-.779**	1	
	HBO	.671**	.522*	.788**	.715**	.743**	.713**	.708**	.501*	-.611**	1	
Advisor	MBO	.555**	.640**	.776**	.739**	.762**	.761**	.727**	.602**	-.746**	.743**	1
	HBO	.635**	.528*	.844**	.787**	.728**	.796**	.838**	.578*	-.622**	.738**	1

** Pearson two-tailed significance at p <.001
* Pearson two-tailed significance at p <.01

Furthermore, a significant difference between TA and TE students was found for their appreciation of the Imperator mentoring approach, having a large effect size (Cohen's d = 1.29), with (t (66) = 3.78, p < .001). This was also the case for the

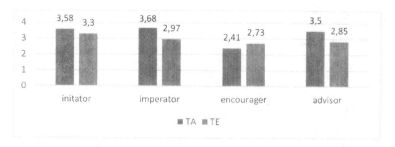

Figure 1. Means of TA and TE for 4 types of mentoring conversations

Table 4. Frequency table of mean differences in perception of feedback with regard to mentoring approach between mentor and mentee within four mentoring groups

Scale	Discrepancy Means Imperator approach TA group 1	Discrepancy Means Imperator approach TA group 2	Discrepancy Means Initiator approach TE group 3	Discrepancy Means Initiator approach TE group 4
Receiving Feedback	.55*	.17	1.02**	.72**
Using Feedback	.40*	.08	.37	.33
Acceptance Following	.52*	−.33	.25	.08
Recommendations	.45*	−.09	.29	.75**
Clarity	.38	−.33	.41*	.51*
Trust	.56*	−.05	.80**	.36
Feasibility	.58*	−.31	−.38	.38
Initiator	−.13	−.63**	−.04	−.52*
Imperator	.20	.04	.43*	1.17**
Encourager	.89**	.96**	.43*	.61**
Advisor	.19	−.03	.47*	.79**

(* >.4 points difference; ** >.6 points difference)

mentoring approach Advisor (t (66) = 4.25, p < .001) (Cohen's d = 1.17). In this case the TA students expressed a higher appreciation for Advisor approach than TE students.

The variance in appreciation of a mentoring approach was used to analyze each of the four mentor groups in more detail using the discrepancy between the mentor's favored approach against the student's appreciation of the practiced approach by a mentor as a predicator of feedback acceptance and following recommendations. Table 4 gives the mean discrepancies for each of the four mentored groups.

The mentor's approach in Group 1 (TA) was analyzed using the student questionnaire on mentor appraisal, which indicated an outspoken Encourager style by the mentor, i.e., using non-directive questions and passiveness in discussing topics. The results on student questionnaire data on feedback provision resulted in significant discrepancies on all feedback related dependent variables. This indicates that the mentor perceived high outcomes on part of the students, more than his students indicated this to be the case on feedback receiving and use. However in Group 2 (TA) also having an Imperator approach no mean z-score discrepancies were found. It needs to be noted in this case that students acknowledged also an Initiator mentoring approach in conversation (i.e., mentor asking open questions). Group 3 (TE) was found having a mentoring approach characterized by a blend of styles. This mentoring approach showed hardly any discrepancies in perceptions on feedback between students and their mentor. Remarkable in this case are the strong differing perceptions regarding receiving feedback and trust, meaning that the mentor held a more favorable view on these matters than his students. Group 4 (TE), also characterized by students by a blend of mentoring approaches, demonstrated a difference on mainly receiving feedback and following recommendations, and to a lesser degree clarity of recommendations. Apparently, the mentor regards himself as more directive and active than his students.

Overall Table 4 shows that most differences occur with regard to receiving feedback, following recommendations, and clarity of advice. In general, our data indicated that mentors tend to overrate their effort in the feedback process (higher mean scores), while the students' present clearly lower scores on received feedback.

Belonging to either a TA or TE Student group (Table 5) was not significantly related to mentoring approach Initiator, however, it was on Encourager ($F (1,62)$ = 6.160, p < .05, .090), Imperator ($F (1,62)$= 20.187, p < .001, .246), and Advisor ($F (1,62)$= 20.016, p < .001, .244).

Feedback Acceptance and Use

To further scrutinize possible differences between mentor groups with regard to measured variables, the TA and TE groups were studied in more detail. They differed significantly (p < .01) both on acceptance and use of feedback. Two interaction effects were noted, on receiving feedback ($F (1,62)$= 9.070, p < .01, .128), and on

Table 5. Differences in mentoring approach
perceptions between TA and TE students

Scale	F	p	Δ^2
Initiator	3.583	.063	.055
Imperator	20.187	.000	.246
Encourager	6.160	.016	.090
Advisor	20.016	.000	.244

using feedback (F $(1,62)$= 6.029, p < .05, .089). The students' motivation to learn (measured as a background variable) was found to be significantly related (p < .05) to acceptance and use of feedback. Student motivation had a significant correlation (p < .05) with trust, clarity, and feasibility. Regression analysis was then utilized to test the influence of each mentored group on variables: Trust, Clarity, and Feasibility of Feedback provision. For TA students a predictive value (R^2) was found of 0.632, indicating 63.2% was explained by appraisal of mentor conversation. Clarity was the strongest predictor (β = .942, t (33) = 3.773, p < .01). Trust and Feasibility showed no significant impact on Using Feedback.

For the TE students Trust, Clarity, and Feasibility accounted for 50.8% of explained variance. Clarity again is, the strongest predictor of the three predictor variables (β = .744, t (27) = 2.851, p < .01). Again, Trust and Feasibility shows no significant impact.

Looking at our research expectation on variation in mentor approach, we found for the TA students that mentoring approach accounts for 58.3% of explained variance. Imperator is a significant predictor of Using Feedback (β = .532, t (32) = 2.322, p < .05). The mentoring approach Initiator, Advisor, and Encourager did not significantly show impact on Using Feedback, while Initiator and Encourager showed a non-significant negative contribution.

For the TE students mentoring approach accounted for 35.8% of explained variance. However, none of the mentoring approaches are significantly related to Using Feedback.

DISCUSSION AND CONCLUSION

This study meant to explore how mentoring approaches used in conversations affects acceptance of feedback and how a mentor's way of providing feedback differentially influences its usage with respect to following recommendations. We contended that student perceptions of the mentor (appraisal) and alignment between mentor and mentee in preference of a mentoring approach would enhance the utilization of feedback.

First it was analyzed whether *differences in perceptions on feedback provision were related to mentoring approach (across two settings), and if possible differences were related to appraisal of mentoring approach.*

The dominant mentoring approach in both the TA and TE setting was of an Imperator (prescriptive/directive) and Initiator (non-directive/stimulating) style. Our students perceive the Encourager (non-directive/passive) approach the least present in the feedback they receive. A significant discrepancy (however, small) was found between mentors and their students in their perception of the actual mentoring approach used. Of interest here is the large difference found in perception with regard to the mentoring approach Encourager: while mentors meant to deploy this approach, their students perceived this otherwise. Apparently, mentors using this approach did not communicate their intentions clearly to their students.

Furthermore, a substantial difference between TA and TE setting was found with regard to acceptance of feedback, with TA (having a performance oriented program) expressing a higher mean on degree of acceptance of feedback. And again we found that students and mentors differed in their perception of feedback use; while mentors overrated its impact/use, their students were more negative. Especially perceptions regarding receiving feedback, trust, and following recommendations were overrated by the mentors.

Secondly, we analyzed whether *differences in appreciation of mentoring conversation, i.e., with regard to Feedback, Trust, Clarity, Feasibility, were related to mentoring approach.*

Difference in appreciation of mentoring with regard to setting as well as students' motivation (measured as background variable) had a significant interactive effect on the mentoring approaches Imperator and Initiator. While the TE students (i.e., reflective oriented program) expressed a low degree of appreciation for the Encourager or Advisor approach they favored a high degree of the Initiator approach. In contrast, the TA students (i.e., performance oriented program), irrespective of students' motivation, showed no major difference in preference for either an Imperator or Initiator approach. We also found that students' motivation to learn has a substantial influence on, in particular, the TE student's appraisal of conversation. Apparently these students favor receiving feedback in a non-directive and stimulating manner. In particular, TE student motivation was highly related to all three variables on feedback provision in mentoring conversation: trust, clarity, and feasibility. TE students having a negative motivation showed low scores on receiving feedback; and also low scores on following recommendations. Apparently, students' motivation to learn has a great impact on feedback utilization (Dweck, 1986).

Thirdly, we analyzed whether *Feedback provision in conversation: with Trust, Clarity, Feasibility, was related to mentoring approach, and if this varies between settings.*

Clarity of conversation, in both settings, is the most important factor in utilization of feedback, with a stronger effect showing in the TA setting. Hattie (2009) points out the importance of clarity, meaning to explicate what is meant, how it is conveyed, and when it is to be delivered during mentoring conversations. Both the TA and the TE students indicated that the mentoring approach Imperator has the most positive effect on Clarity of conversation.

With regard to the TA students we found that the mentoring approach Imperator has a significant effect on actual utilization of feedback, while the Initiator and Encourager approach, both being non-directive, contribute in a negative way to utilization of feedback. With regard to the TE students none of the identified mentoring approaches were significant indicators of feedback utilization. The TE students valued the Initiator mentoring approach as most dominant during mentoring sessions, with its low directedness and high stimulation.

For both students groups we found that the Advisor mentoring approach has a positive effect on Trust, while the Encourager approach has a negative effect on

B. KORVER & H. TILLEMA

Trust. The TE students expressed this effect in a much stronger way than the TA students. Furthermore, we found that the approach Encourager has a negative effect on Clarity. This holds for the TA students in the same way as for the TE students. Also, the TE students indicated that the Advisor approach has a positive influence on Feasibility, while the Encourager approach is regarded as more negative with regard to Feasibility of following recommendations.

The outcomes of this study raise some questions about the nature of feedback provision in mentoring conversations. We found that students perceive the nature of feedback provision, as well as the mentoring approach being used, in a different way as their mentors do; which causes some concern. The finding was present irrespective of teacher education setting/program, but with some notable differences. TA students perceive their mentors as highly directive in their mentoring approach, while their mentors think they are not; and the TE students perceive mentoring approach of their mentors as low in directedness. The TE mentors however recognize themselves in another type of mentoring, i.e. Initiatior. The question then can be raised how differing perceptions between mentors and their mentees work out on feedback utilization, i.e., does, for instance, a mentor's openness or non-directedness during mentoring conversation result in experiencing a corresponding willingness to accept and follow up of recommendations?, or does a non-alignment negatively influence feedback utilization?

Our findings give some indication on the direction of this mechanism. We assume that importance of alignment in perceptions between mentor and mentees as it relates to feedback use varies with mentoring approach. With regard to the mentoring approach Imperator we found, for instance, that it significantly influenced utilization of feedback for TA students (working in a performance oriented setting), while the approaches Initiator and Encourager, both being strongly non-directive, contributed in this setting in a negative way on use of feedback; while this was not the case for the TE students (who work in a reflective oriented program). This implies that the TA students, more than TE students profit from active, directive feedback input during their mentoring sessions, combined with clear and concrete advice on how to proceed. They indicate that the Imperator mentoring approach is what they would like more (than their mentors), and close alignment would prove to work well for their motivation to learn and utilization of received feedback. In support of this case, we found that the TA students also expressed a higher degree of accepting feedback, as compared to the TE students. However, a question still can be raised whether these findings indicate that feedback under alignment of mentoring approach leads to higher degrees of feedback acceptance.

Also, as previously noted, it needs to be noted that actual perceptions of mentors and their mentees regarding feedback provision showed discrepancy, i.e., with mentors overrating the impact of their feedback provision. Trust seems to be especially overrated by mentors. To narrow a gap in perceptions and have a better grip on how the feedback is perceived, conversational input by the mentee to the mentor could definitely add to an effective feedback process.

Overall this study pointed out some issues of concern regarding the provision of feedback in mentoring conversations. Differences between mentor approaches and (non-)alignment in perceptions between students and their mentors have been highlighted, as well as some factors, both in conducting a conversation as well as in style and approach, which may contribute to a more effective utilization of feedback. One of our main conclusions is, that the clarity of conversational intent and approach taken makes the difference. Also our study's setting characteristics (i.e., program orientation of mentoring, either performance based or reflection oriented teaching) highly influenced mentoring approaches being used, with its subsequent impact on the outcomes of feedback. Of relevance in this comparison is the impact we found on diverging perceptions students have on effective mentoring. Therefore, we conclude that context matters in mentoring.

REFERENCES

Black, P., & Wiliam, D. (1998). *Inside the black box: Raising standards through classroom assessment.* London, England: School of Education, King's College.

Boshuizen, H. P. A., Bromme, R., & Gruber, H. (2004). *Professional learning: Gaps and transitions on the way from novice to expert. Innovation and change in professional education.* Dordrecht: Kluwer Academic Publishers. Retrieved from http://dx.doi.org/10.1007/1-4020-2094-5

Brinko, K. T. (1993). The practice of giving feedback to improve teaching. *Journal of Higher Education, 64*(5), 574–592. Retrieved from http://dx.doi.org/10.2307/2959994

Carless, D. (2006). Differing perceptions in the feedback process. *Studies in Higher Education, 31*(3), 219–233. Retrieved from http://dx.doi.org/10.1080/03075070600572132

Clutterbuck, D., & Megginson, D. (2009). *Further techniques for coaching and mentoring.* Amsterdam: Butterworth-Heinemann.

Crasborn, F., Hennissen, P., Brouwer, N., Korthagen, F., & Bergen, T. (2011). Exploring a two-dimensional model of mentor teacher roles. *Teaching and Teacher Education, 27,* 320–331. Retrieved from http://dx.doi.org/10.1016/j.tate.2010.08.014

Dochy, F., Heylen, L., & Van de Mosselaar, H. (2002). *Assessment in onderwijs* [Assessment in Education]. Utrecht, The Netherlands: Lemma.

Dweck, C. S. (1986). Motivational processes affecting learning. *American Psychologist, 41,* 1040–1049. Retrieved from http://dx.doi.org/10.1037/0003-066X.41.10.1040

Garvey, R., Stokes, P., & Megginson, D. (2009). *Coaching and mentoring: Theory and practice.* London, England: Sage Publications Ltd.

Hattie, J. (2009). *Visible learning: A synthesis of over 800 meta-analyses relating to achievement.* New York, NY: Routledge.

Hattie, J., & Timperley, H. (2007). The power of feedback. *Review of Educational Research, 77*(1), 81–112. Retrieved from http://dx.doi.org/10.3102/003465430298487

James, D., & Fleming, S. (2004). Agreement in student performance in assessment. *Learning and Teaching in Higher Education, 1*(05), 32–50.

Mena Marcos, J. J., & Tillema, H. (2006). Studying studies on teacher reflection and action: An appraisal of research contributions. *Educational Research Review, 1,* 112–132. Retrieved from http://dx.doi.org/10.1016/j.edurev.2006.08.003

Pat-El, R. J., Tillema, H. H., Segers, M., & Vedder, P. (2013). Validation of assessment for learning questionnaires for teachers and students. *The British Journal of Educational Psychology, 83,* 98–113. Retrieved from http://dx.doi.org/10.1111/j.2044-8279.2011.02057.x

Sadler, D. R. (1989). Formative assessment and the design of instructional systems. *Instructional Science, 18*(2), 119–144. Retrieved from http://dx.doi.org/10.1007/BF00117714

Sadler, D. R. (2010). Beyond feedback: Developing student capability in complex appraisal. *Assessment & Evaluation in Higher Education, 35*(5), 535–550. Retrieved from http://dx.doi.org/10.1080/02602930903541015

Shute, V. J. (2008). Focus on formative feedback. *Review of Educational Research, 78*(1), 153–189. Retrieved from http://dx.doi.org/10.3102/0034654307313795

Tillema, H. (2009). Assessment in learning to teach. Appraisal of practice teaching lessons by mentors, supervisors, and student teachers. *Journal of Teacher Education, 60*(2), 155–167. Retrieved from http://dx.doi.org/10.1177/0022487108330551

Tillema, H., & Kremer-Hayon, L. (2005). Facing dilemmas: Teacher-educators' ways of constructing a pedagogy of teacher education. *Teaching in Higher Education, 10*(2), 203–217. Retrieved from http://dx.doi.org/10.1080/1356251042000337954

Tillema, H., & Smith, K. (2006). *Portfolios for professional development: A research journey.* New York, NY: Nova Science Publishers.

Tillema, H., & Smith, K. (2007). Portfolio appraisal: In search of criteria. *Teaching and Teacher Education, 23*, 442–456. Retrieved from http://dx.doi.org/10.1016/j.tate.2006.12.005

Tillema, H., & Van der Westhuizen, G. (2013) Mentoring conversations and student teacher learning. *South African Journal of Higher Education, 27*(5), 1305–1323.

Wiliam, D. (2011). What is assessment for learning? *Studies in Educational Evaluation, 37*(1), 3–14. Retrieved from http://dx.doi.org/10.1016/j.stueduc.2011.03.001

Bettina Korver
Consultant
Oudorp, The Netherlands

Harm Tillema
Leiden University, The Netherlands

USE OF FEEDBACK INSTRUMENT – EVALUATION SCALE:

(Administered in the context of mentoring) (Rating scale is of a 5 point Likert type)
(Source: Tillema, H.H & Smith, K. (2007). Portfolio assessment, in search of criteria. *Teaching & Teacher Education*. 23(4), 442–456).
The items measure three criteria:

- Clarity: is the information given understandable?
- Feasibility: is the advice given do-able?
- Trust: is the feedback trustworthy?

Feedback Acceptance

The information about goals and intentions given at the feedback session was clear to me- *clarity*
The dialogue partner (my mentor) was aware of my goals. – *trust*
The feedback session was a non-threatening one–*feasibility*

I was taking part in deciding when and what to bring forward—*trust*
The organization of the feedback session was attuned to my needs. – *clarity*
I was able to talk about the process of my activities in the feedback session. –*feasibility*
I was able to express my own viewpoints during the feedback session- *trust*

During the session I had the opportunity to indicate my strong and weak points –*feasibility*
I could accept the assessment comments on my professional qualities I receive- *trust*

Following Recommendations

The mentoring process has been illuminative for me (e.g. the comments made are clear). – *clarity*

My opinions were taken into consideration when the overall comments were given –*feasibility*
The feedback was specified and detailed enough for me to act upon -*feasibility*

My qualities were being reviewed fairly – *trust*
I know what to do with the feedback given to me by my mentor – *clarity*

PART 2

MENTORING CONVERSATION; A TWO HEARTED AFFAIR

Mentoring when situated in professional education (e.g., in teacher education or other professional education programs) is somewhat different from mentoring in a profession. We took the metaphor "Climbing the mountain' to express this difference. It highlights that in education not only goals and intentions of the mentee are prevailing but also the goals or standards set by the program in which the mentee participates. This means, in essence, that mentors have a dual role or bridging position: bringing the mentee up to the level of attainment that is required.

This two hearted orientation will mirror in the mentoring conversations, no doubt. It is not only that the mentoring conversation will provide space for explicating intentions and reflection upon experiences or exploring perspectives of mentees, but mentors in professional education also have to consider achievement goals that have to be met as an end result of the mentoring process.

Specifically, teacher educators as mentors need to bring conversation up to a level of explicated, program related knowledge. From a mentoring 'helping' perspective this may lead to a conflict, i.e., an overly and early introduction of models of codified knowledge disconnected from students' previous or practice experiences.

How then do mentors in professional education reconcile this double hearted position in conducting a conversation? By what strategies, tactics, or moves are conversations "organized"? This is what the current part of the book explores.

Mentoring conversations are, on the one hand, involving both mentor and mentee in elaborating the issue under hand and developing a shared language for describing experiences, jointly analyzing classroom practices in light of the 'situated understandings' testing alternatives and exploring solutions, suggesting alternatives for classroom action, and scrutinizing their effects as well as reviewing what is learned

On the other hand, however, teacher educators have a responsibility as mentors to bring the conversation in relation to validated knowledge covered by the program. This requires testing or assessing past learning, referencing to knowledge in a way that is shareable with other practitioners, analyzing or inquiring about alternative hypotheses based on theories and other sources. A conversation in professional education has a mix of mentor intentions. Put differently, we could say that mentors in education, by virtue of their role, need to favor and forward a more explicit and informed professional language (Freeman) for articulating knowledge as well as favor reflection on personal knowledge by the mentees for explaining themselves and talking about their teaching experience.

The chapters in this part of the book address issues of conversational arrangements and provide ways of analyzing and understanding them. Chapter 6 by Van der Westhuizen explores the interactive nature of conversations and the asymmetries between students and mentors. Chapter 7 by Pretorius highlights the structure mentors create in conversations with mentees, and how this relates to knowledge productivity. Chapter 8 by Van Esch and Tillema analyze in a detailed way how conversations can "climb the mountain". In chapter 9 Pretorius and Van der Westhuizen draw attention to the social norms and authority issue in mentoring that may govern learning conversations. In chapter 10 Van der Merwe and Van der Westhuizen introduce the notion of an invitational style of mentoring, and clarify the interactional nature of such a style to benefit learning.

GERT J. VAN DER WESTHUIZEN

6. THE ROLE OF KNOWLEDGE IN MENTORING CONVERSATIONS

INTRODUCTION

This paper is concerned with the role of knowledge in mentoring interactions. It reports on analyses of mentoring conversations on topics of teaching practice, and the purpose is to understand how the knowledge of both mentors and mentees come into play in learning interactions.

Conversation Analysis studies have contributed much to our understanding of the role of knowledge in social and institutional interactions (see Edwards, 1997, 2006; Heritage, 2005; Maynard, 2006; Koole, 2012). Various studies have shown for example how asymmetry in knowledge shapes interaction and sequence organisation (Heritage, 2012), how knowledge authority is established conversationally Heritage and Raymond (2005), and how people orientate themselves to asymmetries in knowledge in a conversation (Enfield, 2011). Similarly, in learning conversations, i.e. conversations set up for purposes of learning, such as in mentoring, knowledge participants draw on their knowledge when they interact.

Various factors determine the role of knowledge in mentoring for learning. As in other learning interactions, these include diversity in participants' language and socio-cultural background (Goodwin, 2007), and the "epistemic positions" taken by participants through their embodied action and language (Stivers, Mondada, & Steensig 2011: 8). The latter implies that both mentors and mentees participate in an interaction drawing on what they know, and on the conversational norms they are familiar with (see Sidnell & Enfield (2012). In mentoring interactions, similar to other learning interactions, diversity and ethnographic detail influence the differences in and use of knowledge (Rintel, Reynolds, & Fitzgerald 2013: 3).

The purpose of this chapter is to contribute to the understanding of the interactional nature of knowledge, by exploring how participants in mentoring use knowledge to orientate what they say and do in the interaction (i.e. 'epistemic primacy') for purposes of learning. Following the studies by Heritage (2012, 2013), the chapter explores how students exercise their relative rights to tell, inform, assert or assess something, given the asymmetries in their knowledge. Epistemic primacy is about the depth, specificity, or completeness of knowledge (Stivers et al., 2011:13; Heritage, 2013) and is at the heart of mentoring interactions where knowledge building is the purpose (Tillema & van der Westhuizen, 2014, this volume).

H. Tillema et al. (Eds.), Mentoring for Learning, 119–138.

This chapter reports on video-analyses of interactions between a diversity of participants (two professors and their student teachers from different language and cultural backgrounds) on topics of teaching practice. It draws on analytic principles from Conversation Analysis research to study the use of knowledge in episodes of learning interactions, on the levels of utterances and sequences of utterances. Learning is observed in terms of assessments and 'claims of change of state' ranging from extreme/explicit to denying a change of state and neutral assessments of distancing self from a position taken (Paulus & Lester, 2013; see also Koschmann 2013).

In this exploratory study, evidence indicates how mentors and mentees orientate themselves differently in terms of questions and response preferences, the incongruence in the stances they take in relation to the topic of the mentoring session, and how mentees/students avoid accounts of insufficient knowledge. Students seem avoid assessing mentor utterances openly. Tentative interpretations are offered of how conversational norms are evident in what Heritage and Raymond (2005) and Heritage (2013) described as claims of access and the indexing of independent opinion. Findings are discussed in terms of both institutional and pedagogical norms at play in epistemic primacy and what Heritage (2010, 2012) calls the management of knowledge congruence.

PROBLEM ISSUE AND ITS RELEVANCY

It is characteristic of mentoring interactions that they display institutional norms of practice: the mentor is the knower, and the mentee the learner. Such norms shape social interactions and conversations to be typical of the institution (Drew & Heritage, 2006; Heritage & Sefi, 1992). For example, mentoring interactions in a teacher education programme would involve talking appropriate to the setting, with the mentor teaching and mediating the understanding and knowledge development need of the mentee (Orland-Barak, 2010). In such institutional interactions, knowledge is used in ways that are congruent with the purpose and institutional form of the conversation, often 'scripted' (Edwards, 2006). One would however, expect mentoring interactions to be dialogical, interactive, and, in Vygotskian terms, involving the development and mediation of semiotic tools of understanding and learning (Kozulin, 2003). In addition, mentoring interactions are also shaped by the nature of the relations among participants: it is assumed that a certain openness, distance/familiarity, ascribed authority co-determine learning (Tillema & van der Westhuizen, 2013), and that a certain quality of conversation is required (Tillema & Orland Barak, 2006).

Studies of everyday talk have gone a long way to help us understand the role of knowledge in social interaction. Conversation Analysis research is clarifying the role of knowledge in everyday interactions, as has been shown by the milestone studies of Sacks (1992), and others. Such interactional perspectives refer to 'epistemics in interaction', and assume that knowledge is socially shared and distributed in epistemic communities (Heritage, 2013). This perspective distinguishes between epistemic *stance* and *status*. According to Heritage (2013), in everyday talk, participants have their own 'territories of knowledge' which can be depicted in terms of an 'epistemic gradient': ranging from the more knowledgeable "K+" to the less knowledgeable "K-", in terms of which status is presumed (see Heritage 2010, 2012; Heritage, 2013:376).

Research into the role of knowledge in mentoring is key to the challenges of improving professional learning. In the mentoring of teachers for example, knowledge about teaching is one of the main objects of mentoring. This would include knowledge of pedagogy and of practice. In teacher education research, professional conversations have been the focus of recent studies attempting to understand the discursive nature of professional preparation (Tillema, Van der Westhuizen & Van der Merwe, this volume), guided by studies in sociology and discursive psychology on the nature of everyday social interaction (see summaries by Koole (2013) and Edwards and Potter (2005). This study follows the strand of research on the epistemics of social interaction, which include the prominent studies by Heritage, 1990; Drew, 1991; Maynard, 2006; Edwards, 1996 and others.

Keogh (2010) reviewed studies on the "the interactional achievement" of mentoring, with reference to landmark studies by Orland Barak and Klein (2005) who showed how mentoring relationships work, and how they are "conversationally co-constructed". This implies that the relationship element is crucial for the effectiveness of mentoring, as has been emphasised by Korver and Tillema (2014) (this volume) who showed how levels of familiarity impacts actual mentoring conversations. Power elements of such relations however, are not to be underestimated (Keogh, 2010).

The focus of this inquiry is on the primacy of knowledge, i.e. the relative right of participants to know and to share what they know. The Afrikaans for primacy is 'vooropstelling', which, in the context of social interactions and conversations, is about how participants put their knowledge 'up front', make it primary for the conversation at hand. This *making your own knowledge primary* in a social interaction is also about the social/cultural norms of leading/dominating the conversation. In terms of the definitions offered by Stivers et al. (2011), primacy is about how participants orient themselves to asymmetries, i.e. the differences in knowing, and how they exercise their relative rights to know and to talk/tell their views about state of affairs (Stivers et al., 2011:13).

In mentoring, epistemic primacy would involve the mentor and mentee displaying what they know, and using conversational opportunities to share/ claim what they know. In mentoring, the authority to know is with the mentor, with the mentee the learners, with less authority, perhaps just in terms of practical experience. The question in this study is how epistemic primacy plays out in mentoring settings – if the mentor explains something, does that mean he is accurate in assuming that the mentee does not know? And alternatively, if a mentor requests information, e.g. by asking a question, it does not necessarily mean that the mentee has an answer. This is where learning need comes into play, and where mentor takes up the teaching/mediating responsibility.

In mentoring, in institutional context, both participants share the responsibility for knowing what they know, and for taking into account how recipients will recognise what they say (Stivers et al., 2011:18, 19). This means that they would use turns to account for what they know and in doing so, adhering to the social norms of interaction and making morally accountable choices with informational and relational consequences (following the arguments by Stivers et al., (2011:19) in this regard).

From this outline it should be clear that knowledge plays an important part in mentoring. It is used *in-action*, and *as-action* (Rintel et al., 2013). The analysis of epistemic primacy would help clarify the dynamics in the micro-context of turn organisation in mentoring. Such an analysis will help clarify the stance taken by participants, and the rights participants have and how they exercise, claim and index their rights, relative to the status and stance of the other, and given the content topic of the interaction. In this analysis, primacy of knowledge would need to be related to interactional learning, defined as displays of regularities/change over time (Koschmann, 2011; Koschmann, 2013).

Epistemics and the Interactional Nature of Knowledge in Mentoring

Mentoring, as social interaction, is characterised by conversational practices and norms (Tillema & Van der Westhuizen, this volume). Herbert Clark (1996) described conversation as joint activity, cumulative and incremental – when people participate in a conversation, they bring with them knowledge, beliefs, and assumptions which they use to find "common ground" (Stalnaker 1978:39, quoted by Clark 1996). This means participants use their knowledge in a responsible way for the purpose of the conversation and for the moral obligations they have in interaction with one another (Stivers et al., 2011).

Interactional perspectives on epistemics in conversations assume that knowledge is socially shared and distributed, and that people form 'epistemic communities' based on what they share (Heritage, 2013). In everyday talk, epistemic status is about the presumed knowledge of the participant as well as the rights to possess it (Raymond & Heritage, 2006). It embraces what is known, how it is known and a person's rights, responsibilities and obligations to know (Drew, 1991); Stivers et al., 2011 quoted by Heritage, 2013:377). The primacy of *status* in an interaction features in for example requests for information and is a fundamental element in the construction of social action, more important than the form, i.e. the language in which a question is asked (Heritage, 2012). In contrast, epistemic *stance* is more of a moment by moment expression of knowledge relationships in the context of an interaction (Heritage, 2013:377). This distinction between 'stance' and 'status' would be useful for this study since they help clarify how knowledge is used "in action".

The interactional perspective on the role of knowledge in mentoring requires a conceptualisation of asymmetric relation between the mentor and mentee, and the stances being taken by participants congruent with the institutional purpose of mentor interactions. Mentoring practices are, however shaped by at least two other sets of conditions. The one is the assigned roles and the institutional norms of mentors and mentees. The other is the task context, and the learning purpose which participants adjust their participation to. The latter is about the task structure, i.e. what the mentoring is about. This means that interactional learning works on a macro-episodic level (i.e. bigger sections of the interaction), and the micro of specific sequences (Appel, 2010). Learning from participation is vested the academic task structure, i.e. the content that has to be learned (Erickson, 1996; Appel, 2010; see Van der Westhuizen, 2011). Participation depends on the "cognitive state" of participants used as resource when and where they are interactionally relevant (Mercer, 2004: 171).

The interactional perspective on the role of knowledge in professional mentoring encourages a refined view of learning, as displayed during the interaction, and as outcome. Tillema and van der Westhuizen (this volume) noted that indicators of learning in mentoring would include a new/better/improved understanding, change in perspective, or willingness to try something new. From an interactional perspective, participants take responsibility for what they know, and use the knowledge they have to advance towards what is called 'epistemic congruence', i.e. when the status of a speaker is compatible with the epistemic stance taken (Heritage, 2013: 379; see Stivers et al., 2011).

Learning in interactions is also displayed in terms of a change of 'state' i.e. the position taken by a participant indicating a change in view (Paulus & Lester, 2013). have described evidence of an 'extreme change of state' where a participant makes announcements such as "I was amazed", and: "I can't believe". Other displays of learning include a more neutral assessments of news received as informative, interesting, helpful or enjoyable, or denying a change of state where a participant may claim that not much was learned, and aligning claims with personal experience (Paulus & Lester, 2013).

In conceptualising learning from an interactional perspective, the distinction between understanding and learning is useful. Central to conversations is "the orderly unfolding of sequences of actions in time" (Mondada, 2011:542). This unfolding can happen because of the possibility of understanding – which is "a collective achievement, publicly displayed and interactively oriented" (Mondada, 2011:542). Understanding is situated, contingent, embodied and intersubjective (Mondada, 2011:542). It is "not treated as a mental process but is related to the next action achieved by the co-participant and demonstrating her understanding (Mondada, 2011:543). The original studies by Sacks (1992) has clarified how speakers "do understanding" embedded in next turns in a sequence of interaction, and is as Schegloff (1992) put it, a by-product of conversational actions such as agreeing, answering, assessing, responding. Understanding is "a collective achievement, publicly displayed and interactively oriented to within the production and the monitoring of action" (quoted by Mondada, 2011:550).

In summary, depicting the interactional nature of knowledge seems to involve a distinction between epistemic access, primacy and responsibility (Stivers et al., 2011). Epistemic *responsibility* is played out conversationally through social actions such as claiming, accounting, questioning (Sidnell & Stivers, 2012). Epistemic *primacy*, is about how participants claim their right to knowledge and how the congruency/lack of congruency in epistemic stance of participants is managed (Raymond & Heritage, 2006); see also Heritage, 2012, 2013). Epistemic *authority* is claimed when participants assess the 'state of affairs' in the conversation and index their independent opinion in different ways (Heritage & Raymond, 2005). A claim of epistemic primacy inherently suggests asymmetrical, differentiated epistemic stances between interactants (Hayono, 2010:31). In this regard, social norms of alignment and affiliation influence understanding in conversations: interactants "show themselves to be accountable for what they know, their level of certainty, their relative authority, and the degree to which they exercise their rights and fulfil their responsibilities" (Stivers et al., 2011:9).

THIS INQUIRY

We explore actions of epistemic primacy in mentoring by means of an analysis of interactions between University lecturers and student teachers in their final year. The guiding question was how epistemic primacy is interactionally achieved by both mentors and mentees, and made consequential for student mentee learning.

Epistemic primacy, for the purpose of this study, has been defined as the orientation of participants to the asymmetries in their rights to know; their knowledge authority and claims; and the asymmetries in depth and completeness of knowledge. From this definition analytic principles were derived and used, as described below, to analyze selections of interactions.

The study involved two mentors interacting each with one student teacher in their final year of study. The mentors were both teacher educators with at least 20 years of experience. The mentor-mentee pairs were diverse in respect of language, culture, school subject domain, and how well they knew one another.

The mentors participated in planning sessions where the purpose of this inquiry was confirmed as a project of practice research aimed at understanding mentoring conversations, how they are conducted, and how they benefit student learning of practices. Mentors recruited students before they went to schools for six weeks on school experience/teaching practice. Recruitment included the request that students would write a reflection report on school experience, to be submitted to the Mentor. The Mentors then arranged for a mentoring session after they have studied the reflection reports and noted the issues they wanted to focus on during the mentoring session. The actual mentoring sessions were around 30 to 45 minutes in duration, video-taped and transcribed.

Table 1. Selection of learning episodes per Mentor – Mentee pair

Topic	Mentor/Mentee dyad	Frequency of contact/ interaction between mentor and mentee	Duration
Note taking in a high school classroom	Dyad 1: Mentor: Lecturer L, male, Afrikaans home language and Student S, female, Sotho home language	Infrequent	Lines 20–60
Classroom discipline	Dyad 1: Lecturer L, male, Afrikaans home language Student S, female, Sotho home language	Infrequent	Lines 150–200
Teacher reflections on practice	Dyad 2: Lecturer J, male, Afrikaans home language Student G, female, Afrikaans home language	Frequent	Lines 69–86

Reflection reports by the students varied and covered topics of teaching methods, discipline, student learning, and interactions with teachers in the school. Four episodes were purposefully selected from two of the mentoring interactions. They were examples of interactions focused on one specific topic, involved extended participation, and included a closure of learning attained – see Table 1.

Data was analysed in terms of Conversation Analysis principles, derived from studies on epistemics in interaction, including Sacks, Schegloff, and Jefferson (1974) on turn organization, Schegloff (2007) on sequence organisation, Heritage (2012) and Heritage and Raymond (2005) on epistemic stance and authority, Drew (2012) on sequencing and repair, Edwards (1996, 2006) and Edwards and Potter (2005, 2012), and (Mondada, 2011) on intersubjectivity and shared knowledge, and Koole (2010) on displays of understanding and knowledge in interaction (see Van der Westhuizen 2012).

The focus on epistemic primacy required analyses of utterances and sequence organisation in the selection of learning episodes. We noted specifically

a. the approach of participants in terms of their epistemic status, and how they positioned themselves relative to the other as knowledgeable/less knowledgeable;
b. the *stances* taken by mentor/mentee, i.e. their moment by moment actions as expression of knowledge and how they allowed for the asserting, claiming of, and accounting for knowledge (Heritage, 2012), and
c. *primacy* actions of

+ *orienting* themselves to difference/asymmetry in knowledge, e.g. supporting vs downgrading knowledge claims;

+ *assessing* knowledge (own and another's)
+ *claiming* the right to know and to say and *asserting* their own;

d. *Learning* – following Paulus and Lester (2013): learning as assessing utterances; claiming change of state by accepting, denying, or staying neutral by distancing self from utterances made by the mentor.

FINDINGS

1. Epistemic Primacy in an Episode of Learning on Note Taking

In this learning episode the Mentor L (Afrikaans first language speaker, with more than 30 years of experience in teacher education) interacts with S, (a Sotho speaking female student teacher in her final year or professional preparation) on the topic of note taking in a high school class (Dyad 1). The Student talks about her observation during school experience where the teacher wrote extensive notes on the board on the lesson topic, and required of learners to copy.

The episode of interaction took around 49 turns, and eight sequences were observed, mostly question answer sequences on what the student observed in lines 20–39, the problem the student sees with note taking in lines 35–57, an explanation of the assessment of the problem 58–73, solutions offered 74–87, extended solutions 88–102; the skills involved in note taking 103–113 and a conclusion/closing in lines 114–121.

The sequence organisation and progression seem to reflect the roles and epistemic status of participants. The mentor's status is confirmed by utterances of questioning such as in lines 33, 46, 103, and requesting and probing clarity in for example lines 56 and 74. These utterances communicate status of the mentor as teacher educator. The status of the student is confirmed by for example accounting for observations and offering such accounts for the mentor to consider, such as in the turns starting with lines 66, and 95.

In this extract the Mentor L, after introductions, starts with an announcement in line 20/21 of one of the points made by the student in her reflection notes. The role of Mentor is acted out by this announcement of what the first part of the conversation should be about line 21. S is invited by L in line 33 to assess her observations in one teacher's class during school experience, taking stance that the observed practice is problematic. This happens after S informed L of her observations, encouraged/ confirmed by L in turns lines 56 and 66. S gives an extension of her observations of children copying notes from the board in the teacher's class in lines 35 to 39. The utterance by L in 40 seems to be an assessment in the form of a reflective summary of what S said in the previous turn, and is followed by the affirming 'Yes' in 41, the assessment by S in 43 that the teacher could have been more interactive, and the extended account of what she meant in 48 onwards.

Table 2. Learning episode on note taking, Dyad 1

20	L	You're talking about (.) your expectations:: befo::re but then also
21		finding children ahm (.) ah (.) making notes all the <u>time</u>?
22	S	Ye::s ((nodding)) ahm I think just writing all the time because it
23		wasn't an actual ((gesture both hands)) handout (.) >if you get
24	L	me< especially in LO all they ha::ve is what they're ((right hand
25	S	gesture)) given (.) if you get me (.)=
26	L	[Ja::]
27	S	=for tasks
28		[Ja::]
29		=and all their work they wrote out.
30		[Ja::]
31		There're no worksheets for them. So they spent many hours
32		writing.
33	L	[So what was the:: (.) issue for you <u>there</u>?
34		(1.0)
35	S	I think in a sense maybe expecting ((right hand gesture)) the
36		teacher as <u>well</u> to interact with the children ↑more and to speak to
37		them because literally (.) the children would come to class and
38		then (.2) "↑Morning, ↑afternoon class. Okay:: your work is on the
39		board↓. Just write it out.↓" ((right hand waving gesture))
40	L	So they would sit and copy all the time.
41	S	[Yes
42	L	Okay.
43	S	[Sit and copy so that's why that ((right hand open palm
44		gesture)) troubled me:: feeling that maybe she needed to interact
45		with them more so °ja°
46	L	So what would be ↑bet↓ter than just sit and eh eh (.) and copy
47		notes from the bo::ard?
48	S	(0.4) I feel that maybe even if she <u>did</u> ((right hand gesture)) write
49		all those notes↑ (.) maybe:: be more interactive with the:m and
50		((gestures)) trying to teach the:m what's going on because even
51		when she did stand up it was "Oh this is what's on the boa::rd↓
52		((right hand pointed gesture)) okay" you know feeling that she
53		should interact ((both hands swirling gestures)) with them more
54		>trying to get them< invo::lved. You know it's more like a free
55		period it's more like a free (0.2) period in cla:ss
56	L	So it's not hard work to sit nn <u>copy</u> notes=
57	S	=No not at all

(Continued)

Table 2. (*Continued*)

58	L	Jah::: Its als it's also so ah ahm:: maybe establishing some kind
59		((left hand gesture)) of ah >relationship< where you don't have to
60		work hard, you can just come here and make notes ((left hand
61		through hair)) uhm and I think you're ↑right (.) the ah (.) the
62		alternative is >to be much more interactive< and ahm to let the
63		learning happen in the ((left hand gesture)) interaction. (.) And
64		then where would the ah note taking fit such interactions? Ahm
65		would you say?
66	S	I think (0.2) maybe firstly explaining what ((gesture both hands))
67		it is that they're doing. They can't take notes:: (.) coming to cla::ss
68		"This is what we're doing↑ This is what it's about↑." Ahm telling
69		the students >what they're doing<. Then ↑they can write their
70		notes ((gesture both hands)), because they know what it is and
71		they know what they're ↑doing or alternatively letting them write
72		the notes and the next day (.) ((gestures)) explaining everything to
73		them.
74	L	[Ye:s ye:s so you're saying that they can do the interaction
75		around the notes=
76	S	[Yes ((nodding))
77	L	=But then the notes can also be used (.) as a learning (.) as a
		learning tool↑
78	S	Mmmm ((nodding head))↑
79	L	Because ah ah::m taking notes is (.) is a ↑skill
80	S	[yes]
81	L	(.) is a skill↓ Have you >seen a teacher doing that<? letting (.) you
82		know (.) letting ah (.) children taking notes from class? Or was
83		was=it mostly copying from the board? ((left hand touching
84		head))
85	S	Yes it was mainly ((nodding))
86	L	[Mostly that. Oh okay. Okay.
87	S	Yes it was mostly tha:t.
88	L	How would a lesson like that wo:rk where you encourage (.) ah
89	S	note taking? (1.0) But not copying from the board ((gesture left
90		arm)) but have interaction and then do notes. How would such a
91		lesson work?
92		((nodding))
93	S	Do you mean in the doing of the (.) the lesson?
94	L	[Ja] [yes]
95	S	Ah::m (0.2) I feel that (0.2) maybe in a sense >integrating the
96		two< ((gestures both hands)) (1.0) so you can have your lesso:n
97		speaking to the students and then↓ in a sense ↑asking them to
98		write it after they've written so that it's a bit of both ahm (1.0)
99		((gestures))

(Continued)

Table 2. (Continued)

100 101	L	Ye:s ((left arm gesture)) so first the lesson and then let them make notes about what they are (.) about what they observe.
102	S	((nodding)) Ye:s.
103 104	L	Okay. What about writing (.) ah notes ↑while ah the ↑lesson is going on↓?
105 106	S	Oh yes that as well >what we do< ahm <u>here</u> at varsity. That also works.
107	L	That's how it works here.
108	S	Yes ((nodding))
109 110	L	So what do you teach them? What <u>skill</u> would you teach learners ah note taking during a lesson.
111	S	Mmmmm I think maybe it's the skill ((right hand gesture)) of being able to listen↑ (.) and to also write↓.
112	L	Yes
113	S	It's a very good skill to <u>do</u> that ((right hand gesture))=
114 115 116 117	L	[=So its listen and <u>write</u> but its also ((left hand gestures)) identifying the <u>main</u> idea a:nd you distinguish >what's good, what's not good<. I should write this and not tha::t ((left hand gestures)) and not copy everything.
118	S	((nodding)) It's like reasoning as well in a sense.
119	L	Ye:s ((nodding))
120 121	S	You're thinking about what you're writing and you're thinking about (.) what you're hearing instead of mere (.) just copying.
122 123 124 125 126 127	L S L	((nodding)) Ye:s You were also saying in your reflection notes ((left hand pointing to notes)) that you (.) you were surprised by the problems that uh the children have with the reading and writing. Uhm ((nodding)) Tell me a bit about that?

From this interaction, it seems that the mentor actions of primacy consist of assessing the student's knowledge (for example lines 33, 46), extending (58, 79), and supporting student views (58 onwards). Mentee actions of epistemic primacy include informing the mentor of experiences (22, 27), assessing observations (34, 43) and asserting own views of the observations (22–28 and again in 44 and 48).

In lines 58 to 65 the mentor extends the view of the mentee that the note taking required by the teacher she observed, may be problematic. He then offers an invitation to the mentee to consider alternative. In 66 S responds by claiming her understanding, confirmed in 76 that note taking can have interactional value. This claim can be taken as representing learning on the part of the mentee, i.e. positively assessing the suggestions by L.

The sequences from 77 onwards zoom in on the question how note taking can be used for learning. L invites S to respond with the question 77 and extension of the question in 81 to 84 and 88 to 91. S claims her views in the turn of 95, summarised by L in 100, 191. L's challenge in 103 is a push for alternative/extended views and S confirms her agreement in 105.

2. Epistemic Primacy in an Episode of Learning on Classroom Discipline

In this second episode, the mentor raises questions on discipline, referring to by the Mentee in her school experience report.

Table 3. Learning episode on classroom discipline, Dyad 1

150 151	L	So from you:r uhm schoo:l experience what else came out for you (.) that are ah uhm (.) that are points you want to talk about↓?

152
153
154
155
156
157
158
159
160
161
162
163
	S	(.) So I think the last thing that I wrote which I said was a concern ((right hand gesture)) a question when I'd find that in a cla::ss let's say (.) five students were outside (.) for four days. So (.) I understand ((gestures)) they sometimes didn't do their work or if they're absent they must bring a letter↓ to say why it ↑is but for me there was a problem of (0.2) how I think >it was the last question< I wrote how do I tackle that ((right hand gesture)) if I'm in the school environment. I don't think they're learning by sitting outside↓=
		    [Yah
		    =and some students don't wanna learn (.) so its like "Oh it's cool. I just will do it 'cause I can sit outside (.)

164 165 166	L	Was (.) was that an opportunity where ah ah ah::m:: where you had to do ↑discipline with the learners? Ah:: that was interesting↑ in your notes he::re (.) tell me about that↑.
167	S	Ah you mean (.) in terms of them being quick to hit the children?
168	L	Ye::s (.) ye::s
169 170 171 172 173 174 175 176	S	Yes that too was a problem for me because I think it was more (…) ((right hand gesture)) outside being (.) not a (.) "Why are you doing this". A student would (.) do something and >the first instinct was the teacher will hit them< or (.) or it also troubled me that ↑once I was left alone ((right hand gesture)) with the children and then I was just like (.) "I'm not gonna shout at you. What's wrong? Why are you making such a noise?" One of the children was like >"you must hit us or just swear at us< or something"
177 178	L	[Ja:: ja::: give me an example of the hitting. How did the hitting happen?

(Continued)

Table 3. (Continued)

179 180 181 182 183	S	(.) So a teacher was gone (.) a teacher was gone for some reason and then I was asking them to hand in their work ((gestures)) and I'm like "why did you not do your work? And half the class didn't do their work. "why did you do it?" and then they're like uhm I think the best way to get through to us is hitting us."
184	L	Oh:::: okay.
185 186 187 188	S L S	["Just hit us and we'll listen." And I found that (the) unruly like if I say "if you don't do your work, <u>stand</u>. " So you tried something ↑else. Ye::s. Tried something ↑else.
189 190	L	Okay So what are your views about this idea of hitting? Hitting children.
191 192 193 194 195 196 197	S	[Ahm for me personally I don't agree:: definitely don't agree especially the context (.) that ahm so many of those children came from because some are being abu:sed at home some aren't being listened to. So I think its more (.) a (.) "I care ((right hand gesture)). It should be from that perspective. Trying to find out what the problem is rather than "I'll just hit you "'cause that's probably what happens at ↑home.
198	L	Ye:::s
199 200	S	....A child doesn't listen... "I'm just gonna hit you." ((tight hand gestures))
201 202	L	Ye:::s That's just continuing the practice of ahm scolding and ah ja:: ja:::
203	S	Mm hm:::
204 205 206 207	L	Well you're saying that there should be a more ↑positive response and I think I agree with tha:t I <u>think</u> ahm it is more <u>constructive</u> you know to (.) work out the ↑discipline ah (.) in class in a <u>different</u> way.
208	S	Yes ((nodding))
209 210 211	L	Ah (.) ah rather than being ah:: punitive. Its better to: ahm try to be more constructive and have other ways of establishing (.) the discipline ja::, ja::
212	S	Yes ((nodding))
213 214 215	L	Ahm you ahm ((clearing throat)) you also ah made one you referred in your notes to a method of spelling tests? ah:::m ah:: let's ah:: talk about that please↑.

This extract is from a later episode of the mentoring interaction of Dyad 1. In this extract the Mentor L continues to confirm his status as mentor by steering the interaction with questions. The focus of this episode is classroom discipline and the student gives an account of what she observed in class. In this episode, the stance of the Mentor is one of assessing (164) and exploring (166), and claiming the stance of wanting to know more in 168. The Mentee uses her turn in 174 and 175 to give an account of her response to learners' demands, extended further in 179 and 185. In 191 she takes the position of not giving in to learners' demands. This stance is supported by L in 204–207 and 209–211.

In this extract evidence is found of L requesting S to state and account for her views on discipline, based on what she observed in class. It seems L holds back on his views, allowing S to use the space for taking and claiming her stance. In 204 onwards the mentor offers an assessment of the student's views by summarising the views noted by the mentee, and confirming agreement in views, i.e. epistemic congruence. This assessment may be taken as a summary of the learning on the part of the mentee based on her observations during school experience.

3. Epistemic Primacy in an Episode of Learning on Teacher Knowledge

This episode is an interaction of Dyad 2 between Mentor J and student G, both Afrikaans speaking, who agreed to have the session in English.

Table 4. Learning episode on teacher knowledge

52 53 54	J	What do you think of the knowledges that a teacher need to have↓? ( ) a teacher who's been teaching for a while. What do you thi:nk (.) of the different types of knowledge that a teacher needs to have↓?
55 56 57 58	G	Uhm (.) Definitely, obviously <u>content knowledge</u> ↑<u>and</u> like we've learned the pedago.pedago(.)gical ((laugh)) <u>content knowledge</u>. Uhm you have to be able to (1.0) >in a way< <u>sum up↑ (.) children (.)</u> and where they come from:: and how they wo::rk and
59	J	[a little bit of contextual knowledge=
60 61 62 63 64 65 66	G	=Yes a contextual knowledge. So definitely you need to know your contextual knowledge <u>and</u> your content knowledge and how the two work together (.) and skills of multitasking↓ like I <u>said</u> and <u>being flexible</u>↑ >is also an important thing< about (.) you might have planned a lesson to:: (.) You're gonna do this and this and this but when you start the lesson you see that its not gonna work and then you have to be able to (.) think on your feet and be flexible and change it so that it=
67 68	J	=[Oooh… Two important issues. So what you're saying you need a bit of <u>self</u>-knowledge
69	G	[Mmm
70	J	and then you also need to have (being reflective)
71 72 73 74	G	Yes definitely (.) Ja. self knowledge is <u>very important</u>.knowing what <u>you</u> are capable of doing. If you are ↑<u>not</u> a person ((gesture both hands open fingers pointing together)) who is good with building things or doing models >and things like that? ( ) then you shouldn't do that.

(Continued)

Table 4. (Continued)

75	J	[mmm]
76 77 78 79	G	Ja and kno:w (.) <u>knowing</u> yourself↑ is a very important thing. And obviously being reflective and seeing if (1.0) what you've <u>done</u> has worked and obviously then <u>working on yourself</u> 'cause yes (.) you must know yourself but you can also change yourself and >improve yourself for the <u>better</u><.
80	J	So how do you do your own ↓personal ↓professional) reflection↑?
81 82 83 84 85 86 87 88 89 90	G J G	Ahm:: (hhh) (1.0) A lot throu::gh >the learners' response< ((right hand gesture)) To what (.) to <u>what they say to me</u> or what they=especially with junior school kids ((gesture both hands)) you can <u>see</u> (.) They're not like high school children who are (0.2) very (.) rese::rved ((both hands horizontal with fingers pointing)) >and things like that<. ((laugh)) I can <u>see</u> it on their faces. And I can <u>see</u> ((left hand gesture)) if they're sitting and they're day dreaming ((left hand gesture)) ((scratching neck)) >I suppose in high school as well< if they're not listening at all and I can see the difference between if they're <u>engaged</u> with what I'm saying or not. And obviously through my assessments as well (.) uhm (.)=
91 92 93	J	((head resting on left hand)) =So would you say that (1.0) ((chin on right hand)) uhm (.) ill-discipline ((right hand pointing on table surface)) sometimes can be the result of the teacher not having↓ an engaging (.) lesson-
94	G	[mmm:: ↑definitely
95	J	(0.2) or involvement in the engaging pedagogics
96	G	Yes, definitely↓
97 98	J	Okay and do you feel that you can ↑<u>judge the success of your lesson planning</u> by the engagement↓ of the learners?
99	G	Mmmmm definitely (2.0)
100	J	I agree with you (2.0

In this episode the interaction is about teacher knowledge and what it means to be reflective as a teacher. The Mentor J starts in 52 by asking a question about the 'knowledges' needed by a teacher. Student G's response in 55 to 58 is approved in 59 and added to. In 60 to 65, G accounts and extends her views, which led J to summarise the points made in 67 to 70.

The utterance by J in 70 is an invitation to G to explain her understanding of what it means to be reflective. G informs J in 71 and 76 of her view that being reflective goes along with self-knowledge and 'working on yourself' to improve (77, 78). The question in 80 is J's way of focussing the interaction on reflection, and in 81 to 87 G claims her view that she does reflections based on observing and attending to learner responses. In this turn, G claims that in her experience teacher reflections should be based on actual observations.

In this learning episode the participation of both Mentor J and Mentee G reflect their status – J guiding the interaction and asking the questions, with G answering with confidence. Epistemic primacy on the part of the Mentor is observed in the continued reference to knowledge beliefs (59 and 67), while the Mentee's knowledge claims draw on practice experience (line 81 onwards).

The learning focus in this episode was introduced by the Mentor in 52 and includes the understanding of the 'kinds of knowledges' teachers should have. The Mentee's responses are accepted and extended by the Mentor, judging from lines 59 and 66. The Mentor pursued for a deeper understanding of what self-knowledge and reflection is about by inviting an extended account in 69 and 70. The Mentor accepts the account in 80 by asking how the Mentee does her reflection. The account given by the mentee in 81 onwards is agreed upon by the Mentor in 91 and 95, with the Mentee confirming her agreement in 96 and 99.

DISCUSSION

The finding that for the Mentors epistemic primacy involves confirming their status as mentors through the use of questions and specific conversational actions such as assessing, requesting, supporting etc., seems to be congruent with their institutional role as teacher educators. The epistemic status of the mentors is in the assessments of student utterances and the leading questions they asked. By soliciting views around the topic of learning, the mentors make eminent their stance of being more knowledgeable. This knowledge authority is made clear through the consistent questioning stance which, as has been argued by Heritage and Raymond (2005) often is a first speaker's way of indexing authority. Mentor authority has been exercised in terms of what Drew and Heritage (1992) described as the structuring of questions and the management of sequences. The Mentors used questions to create the learning episodes, explore, confirm and come back to a topic.

The mentees in this study confirmed their status by their response preferences of answering questions. They assert their knowledge by drawing on references to and reflections on practice experiences. This is the primary way in which mentees exercise their right to tell, drawing on own experiences and asserting their beliefs as their own "territory of knowledge" (Heritage, 2012). Mentee authority claims seem to be located in their own practice experiences. The questioning of mentor claims and assertions by the mentees is absent, which is probably an indication of status dominance. Heritage (2012) describes such social actions in conversations as epistemics in action, where participants do different things to form and maintain their knowledge territories.

The participation was clearly guided by the Mentor while Mentees were not inclined to request the Mentor to account for views. In all three episodes, learning seems to be mainly facilitated by the Mentors' conversational moves of assessing, asserting, requesting agreement and accounting for views. Learning was displayed interactionally by mentees agreeing and confirming the views of the mentor. In many ways, this is the process of 'talking knowledge into being' (Keoch, 2010:51).

Findings indicate that institutional norms seem to prioritise mentor access and inhibit stances of openness. Some evidence was found of questions which allow mentees their right to tell and explore their own depth of knowledge. These actions indicate how mentees assert themselves and claim authority of knowledge. The evidence of learning in these episodes indicate some achievement of knowledge congruence (see Heritage, 2010, 2012), which highlights Tillema and Orland-Barak (2006) notion that professional conversations involve forms of collaborative inquiry for the development of knowledge.

CONCLUSION

The intention with this study was to develop an understanding of the role of knowledge in mentoring interactions by zooming in on epistemic primacy – how both mentors and mentees participate in the interaction, and use their knowledge to contribute to learning. While the inquiry was limited in scope, the evidence suggests that mentors use specific conversational actions associated with their institutional role which included the ways in which they steer interactions by means of the questions, and that mentees use their knowledge to account for and make claims about their own experiences and learning.

This inquiry highlights the complexities of Koschman's (2013:1039) notion of "learning-in-and-as-interaction": interaction provides evidence of learning, and is at the same time the place where learning is to be found. This study showed how such learning may be identified in terms of Mentee utterances accepting what Mentors say, as an indication of change of state. It would be important however, to pursue studies of the interactional achievement of learning, considering the recommendation that CA studies need to also look at learning trajectories observed over time (Koschman, 2013).

The research reported here followed methods of conversation analysis to highlight the kinds of "primacy actions" in the mentoring of learning; actions which on one level confirm epistemic status and stance, and on another level ensuring progress towards learning by means of specific conversational actions. While the topic of this inquiry warrants further inquiry, some tentative implications for mentoring practice may be considered. Assuming that mentoring conversations involve processes of knowledge sharing /negotiating meaning (see Edwards, 2004), mentors may benefit from being reminded of the knowledge responsibility they have in mentoring. Such a responsibility would recognize the status and institutional role of the Mentor, while specific conversational actions can be used to create space for mentees to bring their own knowledge to the fore and inviting epistemic primacy.

Greater sensitivity to the dynamics and complex interplay of knowledge in mentoring would go a long way to ensure that the "the morality of knowledge"

Stivers et al. (2011) is taken seriously, in terms of both mentor and mentee carrying the responsibility to use their knowledge in the interaction for purpose of learning.

REFERENCES

Appel, J. (2010). Participation and instructed language learning. In P. Seedhouse, S. Walsh, & C. Jenks (Eds.), *Conceptualising learning in applied linguistics* (pp. 206–224). Basingstoke: Palgrave MacMillan.

Clark, H. H. (1996). *Using language*. New York, NY: Cambridge University Press.

Drew, P. (1991). Asymmetries of knowledge in conversational interactions. *Asymmetries in Dialogue*, 21–48.

Drew, P., & Heritage, J. (1992). *Talk at work: Interaction in institutional settings*. New York, NY: Cambridge University Press.

Drew, P., & Heritage J. (2006). *Conversation analysis*. London, England: Sage.

Edwards, D. (1996). *Discourse and cognition*. London, England: Sage Publications Limited.

Edwards, D. (1997). Toward a discursive psychology of classroom education. In C. Coll & D. Edwards (Eds.), *Teaching, learning and classroom discourse: Approaches to the study of educational discourse*. (pp. 33–48). Madrid: Fundacion Infancia y Aprendizaja.

Edwards, D. (2006). Discourse, cognition and social practices: The rich surface of language and social interaction. *Discourse Studies, 8*(1), 41–49.

Edwards, D., & Potter, J. (2005). Discursive psychology, mental states and descriptions. In H. TeMolder & J. Potter (Eds.), *Conversation and cognition* (pp. 241–259). Cambridge: Cambridge University Press.

Edwards, D., & Potter, J. (2012). *Pre-conference workshop: Discursive psychology: Psychology as an object in and for interaction*. DARG Conference, University of Loughborough, England.

Enfield, N. (2011). 12 Sources of asymmetry in human interaction: Enchrony, status, knowledge and agency. *The Morality of Knowledge in Conversation, 29*, 285.

Erickson, F. (1996). Going for the zone: The social and cognitive ecology of teacher-student interaction in classroom conversations. In D. Hicks (Ed.), *Discourse, learning, and schooling* (pp. 29–62). New York, NY: Cambridge University Press.

Goffman, E. (2005). *Interaction ritual: Essays in face-to-face behaviour*. Piscataway, NJ: Aldine Transaction.

Goodwin, C. (2007). Participation, stance and affect in the organization of activities. *Discourse & Society, 18*(1), 53–73.

Hayano, K. (2010). *Claiming knowledge and giving support to it: Epistemic stance, evaluation intensity and affiliation*. Paper presented at the annual meeting of the American Sociological Association Annual Meeting, Hilton Atlanta and Atlanta Marriott Marquis, Atlanta, GA.

Heritage, J. (1990). Intention, meaning and strategy: Observations on constraints on interaction analysis. *Research on Language & Social Interaction, 24*, 311–332.

Heritage, J. (2005). Conversation analysis and institutional talk. In K. L. Fitch & R. E. Sanders (Eds), *Handbook of language and social interaction* (pp. 103–147). Mahwah, NJ: Lawrence Eribaum Associates.

Heritage, J. (2010). Conversation analysis: Practices and methods. In D. Silverman (Ed.), *Qualitative research: Theory, method and practice* (pp. 208). Los Angeles, CA: Sage.

Heritage, J. (2012). The epistemic engine: Sequence organization and territories of knowledge. *Research on Language & Social Interaction, 45*, 30–52.

Heritage, J. (2013). Epistemics in conversation. In J. Sidnell & T. Stivers (Eds.), *The handbook of conversation analysis* (pp. 370–394). Hoboken, NJ: Wiley.

Heritage, J., & Raymond, G. (2005). The terms of agreement: Indexing epistemic authority and subordination in talk-in-interaction. *Social Psychology Quarterly, 68*(1), 15–38.

Heritage, J., & Sefi, S. (1992). Dilemmas of advice: Aspects of the delivery and reception of advice in interactions between health visitors and first-time mothers. In P. Drew & J. Heritage (Eds.), *Talk at work: Interaction in institutional settings* (pp. 359–417). Cambridge: Cambridge University Press.

Keogh, J. (2010). (In) forming formal evaluation: Analysis of a practicum mentoring conversation. *Journal of Applied Linguistics & Professional Practice, 7*(1), 51–73.

Koole, T. (2010). Displays of epistemic access: Student responses to teacher explanations. *Research on Language and Social Interaction, 43*(2), 183–209.

Koole, T. (2012). The epistemics of student problems: Explaining mathematics in a multi-lingual class. *Journal of Pragmatics, 44,* 1902–1916.

Koole, T. (2013). Conversation analysis and education. *The Encyclopedia of Applied Linguistics.*

Korver, B., & Tillema, H. (2014). Feedback provision in mentoring conversation-differing mentor and student perceptions. *Journal of Education and Training Studies, 2,* 167–175.

Koschmann, T. (2011). *Theories of learning and studies of instructional practice.* New York, NY: Springer.

Koschmann, T. (2013). Conversation analysis and learning in interaction. *The Encyclopedia of Applied Linguistics.* doi: 10.1002/9781405198431.wbeal0208

Kozulin, A. (2003). Psychological tools and mediated learning. *Vygotsky's educational theory in cultural context,* 15–38.

Magano, M. D., Mostert, P., & Van der Westhuizen, G. (2010). *Learning conversations: The value of interactive learning.* Johannesburg: Heinemann.

Maynard, D. W. (2006). Cognition on the ground. *Discourse Studies, 8*(1), 105–115.

Maynard, D. W., & Peräkylä, A. (2006). *Language and social interaction.* New York, NY: Springer.

Mercer, N. (2004). Sociocultural discourse analysis. *Journal of Applied Linguistics, 1,* 137–168.

Mondada, L. (2011). Understanding as an embodied, situated and sequential achievement in interaction. *Journal of Pragmatics, 43,* 542–552.

Orland-Barak, L. (2010). *Introduction: Learning to mentor-as-praxis foundations for a curriculum in teacher education. Learning to Mentor-as-Praxis.* New York, NY: Springer.

Orland-Barak, L., & Klein, S. (2005). The expressed and the realized: Mentors' representations of a mentoring conversation and its realization in practice. *Teaching and Teacher Education, 21*(4), 379–402.

Orland-Barak, L., & Yinon, H. (2007). When theory meets practice: What student teachers learn from guided reflection on their own classroom discourse. *Teaching and Teacher Education, 23*(6), 957–969.

Paulus, T. M., & Lester, J. N. (2013). Making learning ordinary: Ways undergraduates display learning in a CMC task. *Text & Talk, 33,* 53–70.

Raymond, G., & Heritage, J. (2006). The epistemics of social relations: Owning grandchildren. *Language in Society, 35,* 677–705.

Rintel, S., Reynolds, E., & Fitzgerald, R. (2013). Editorial: Knowledge and asymmetries in action: Proceedings of the 2012 Conference of the Australasian Institute of Ethnomethodology and Conversation Analysis. *Australian Journal of Communication, 40*(2).

Sacks, H. (1992). Lectures on conversation. *Volume I, II.* Edited by G. Jefferson with an introduction by EA Schegloff. Oxford: Blackwell.

Sacks, H., Schegloff, E. A., & Jefferson, G. (1974). A simplest systematics for the organization of turn-taking for conversation. *Language,* 696–735.

Schegloff, E. A. (2007). *Sequence organization in interaction: Volume 1: A primer in conversation analysis* (Vol. 1). Cambridge: Cambridge University Press.

Schegloff, E. A., Jefferson, G., & Sacks, H. (1977). The preference for self-correction in the organization of repair in conversation. *Language, 53,* 361–382.

Sert, O. (2013). 'Epistemic status check' as an interactional phenomenon in instructed learning settings. *Journal of Pragmatics, 45,* 13–28. doi: 10.1016/j.pragma.2012.10.005

Sidnell, J., & Enfield, N. J. (2012). Language diversity and social action. *Current Anthropology, 53,* 302–333.

Sidnell, J., & Stivers, T. (2012). *The handbook of conversation analysis.* Retrieved from Wiley.com.

Sidnell, J., & Stivers, T. (2012). *The handbook of conversation analysis* (Vol. 121). Blackwell: Wiley. Retrieved from Wiley.com.

Stivers, T., Mondada, L., & Steensig, J. (2011). *The morality of knowledge in conversation.* Cambridge: Cambridge University Press.

Tillema, H. H., & Orlaand-Barak, L. (2006). Constructing knowledge in professional conversations: The role of beliefs on knowledge and knowing. *Learning and Instruction, 16,* 592–608.

Tillema, H. H., & Van der Westhuizen, G. J. (2006). Knowledge construction in collaborative enquiry among teachers. *Teachers and Teaching: Theory and Practice, 12*(1), 51–67.

Van der Westhuizen, G. J. (2011). Leergesprekke in universiteitsklaskamers:'n Herwaardering (Learning conversations in Higher Education – a re-appreciation). *Litnet Academic, 8*(3), 392–410.

Van der Westhuizen, G. J. (2012). Reading comprehension interaction – A conversation analysis perspective. *Southern African Linguistics and Applied Language Studies, 30*(3), 361–375.

Gert J. van der Westhuizen
Department of Educational Psychology
University of Johannesburg, South Africa

ANNATJIE J. M. PRETORIUS

7. STRUCTURAL DIMENSIONS OF MENTORING CONVERSATIONS

INTRODUCTION

Mentoring without conversation between mentor and mentee is almost unthinkable. It is through conversation that mentoring and learning is facilitated. Tillema and Van der Westhuizen (2013:1308), refer to conversations as the main 'vehicle' through which learning takes place in mentoring, while Magano, Van der Westhuizen and Mostert (2010:1) refer to conversation as a 'place' in which learning takes place. Conversation is clearly a core dimension of mentoring. Baker, Jensen and Kolb (2002:53) refer to it as a meaning making process. This chapter is concerned with this core aspect of mentoring in, specifically, teacher education.

Given the centrality of conversation in mentoring, it becomes important to look at mentors' preparedness for such conversations. Professionals in education are expected to mentor novice teachers or student teachers, based on their knowledge and expertise. However, being an expert in a certain domain is not all the mentor needs to fulfil this role. Timperly (2001:121) highlights that expertise does not guarantee effective mentoring in teacher education. Research based mentoring strategies can be of great value in the light of Smith's (2014) apt reference to mentoring as 'a profession within a profession'. This implies that mentors should enter mentoring encounters well prepared and most importantly, as various researchers indicate, they should be guided by more than intuition and expertise (Hoover, 2010; Weiss & Weiss, 2001; cited in Keogh, 2005; Maynard & Furlong; cited in Quick & Siebörger, 2005; Timperley, 2001). In lieu of the above, this chapter explores structuring of mentoring conversations, as a conversational strategy to enhance learning.

Since the mentor is the party who determines the content and direction of the conversation, such as the format, the topics as well as when the conversation begins or ends Strong and Baron (2004:53), it makes sense to explore the structuring of a conversation through research. Further, when any two people engage in day-to-day conversation it is governed by certain social norms such as: Who has the right to know what?; Do the speaker have enough knowledge to make certain claims?, etc., as found in Stivers, Mondala and Steensig et al. (2011). They describe the social norms which guide 'epistemic authority', a notion of Heritage and Raymond (2005). In mentoring conversations, epistemic authority would be a natural position held by the mentor on the basis of his expertise and experience. In other words, mentoring conversations, just as any other conversations, are governed by social norms. It is

H. Tillema et al. (Eds.), Mentoring for Learning, 139–154.
© 2015 Sense Publishers. All rights reserved.

the authoritative position of the mentor which makes it necessary to equip him or her with research based strategies to optimize learning for the mentee.

Contributions in this chapter flows from a study performed by Pretorius (2013), which was concerned with the structure which mentors create for their conversations with mentees and how that relates to the learning outcomes for the mentees. In this study, the construction of 'conceptual artefacts' was considered to be indicators of learning in the mentoring conversation (Bereiter, 2002). Such conceptual artefacts include plans, approaches, schemes, outlines, recipes for practice, and so forth, which has potential to be used as 'tools' in the mentee's future professional practice (Bereiter, 2002; Tillema, 2005). The study was interested in finding conversational evidence of the production of such conceptual 'tools' for possible future use and considered such cognitive tools to be learning outcomes for the student teacher. The appropriation of these tools in teaching practice fell outside the scope of the study.

Underpinned by theoretical notions of the theorists Vygotsky (1896–1934) and Bakhtin (1895–1975),which will be explored later in the chapter, this study's hypothetical expectancy was that mentor intervention such as scaffolding and prescription, could be associated with significant and meaningful learning outcomes, as opposed to intervention which merely explores the current practice of the mentee. In other words, it was expected that learning would be more significant and meaningful when the mentee's practice was challenged when necessary, instead of just exploring the mentee's experiences. This chapter reports on the study's methodology, its findings and the implications for mentoring conversations with student teachers.

Tillema and Van der Westhuizen (2013) explains the process of learning through mentoring conversations via the metaphor of climbing a mountain, a conception which is inspired by Richard Dawkins's work on evolution (Dawkins, 1996). How mentoring conversations can be structured by the mentor, is explored through this metaphor within which Tillema and Van der Westhuizen (2013) suggest 'high road' – and 'low road' propositions. In Tillema and van der Westhuizen's (2013) work, high road propositions are related to 'climbing the mountain' of learning by prescribing to the mentee or by challenging and scaffolding the mentee's conceptions and practice. 'Low road' propositions relate to utterances in which the mentor simply explore the mentee's current practice. The main finding of the Pretorius (2013) study is that, although 'high road' propositions, in which the mentee's practice and ideas are challenged, do not guarantee significant learning, such learning seems unlikely without it. In other words, without 'high road' propositions, significant learning seems to be unlikely. It seems as though conversations are unlikely to be knowledge productive if the mentor only relies on 'low road' propositions, such as explorative propositions, or other propositions such as compliments, agreement, expression of empathy, etc.

This chapter contests for deliberate, research based structuring of mentoring conversations in order to facilitate significant and meaningful learning for mentees.

For the purposes of this chapter, mentoring conversations are defined, in line with Orland-Barak and Tillema (2006) and Hoover (2010), as conversational guidance of a novice teacher or student teacher by an experienced Educational professional in order to make a transition from theoretical knowledge to higher teaching proficiency.

CLIMBING THE MOUNTAIN TOWARDS HIGHER PROFESSIONAL PROFICIENCY –EXPECTATIONS THROUGH THE LENSES OF VYGOTSKY AND BAKHTIN

Evolution is described by Richard Dawkins (1996) as a gradual process in his book 'Climbing Mount Improbable'. He describes a process in which change happens gradually, over time. In mentoring conversations, this metaphor is strikingly relevant as the mentee is, ideally, gradually guided towards higher proficiency through many supportive steps which takes him or her to a higher level of proficiency (Gerretzen, 2012:7; Tillema & Van der Westhuizen, 2013). In a modern world in which change could be seen as a constant, it seems unlikely to ever reach a point of perfection in a profession such as teaching – thus, climbing a mountain of which one will probably never reach a summit or a point at which no more can be learnt. The implication is therefore interpreted, in my view, as continuous growth and evolvement for all educators, regardless their experience.

In mentoring conversations, the journey up the mountain is a collaborative effort (Tillema & Van der Westhuizen, 2006) between mentor and mentee. For the purpose of understanding this collaborative, conversational journey of growth, some theoretical notions of Lev Vygotsky (1896–1934) and Mikhail Bakhtin (1895–1975), will now be explored to frame the notion of learning through mentoring conversations: "*The word*" is central in the"*relation between the 'I' and the 'other'*"(Bakhtin, cited in Rule, 2006:80). This Bakhtinian notion highlights the centrality of conversation between mentor and mentee in the mentoring process. Further, the Bakhtinian notion of the "*process of becoming*" (Rule, 2006:79) is also seen to be facilitated by dialogic engagement in the mentoring conversation. In the case of preparing student teachers for practice, teaching proficiency develops out of the mentee's '*ideological becoming*' which is "*the process of selecting and assimilating the words of others*" (Bakhtin, 1981:341; cited in Rule, 2006:81). It is within mentoring conversations that mentees select and assimilate the words, i.e. ideas, of their mentors which subsequently contributes to the mentee's professional 'becoming.' This does not mean that the mentor is the only party who contributes knowledge. Collaboration, just as conversation, features at the centre of the mentoring process. Collaboration implies participation. Tillema, Van der Westhuizen and Van der Merwe (2012) imply that 'informed participation' (Edwards et al., 2002) is a pre-requisite for building new knowledge and knowing. It appears to be developed over time as the mentee participates in a community of practice, by which the mentee becomes aware of what is suitable and accepted in that particular community (Orland-Barak & Tillema, 2006:9).

One model which accommodates these Vygotskyan and Bakhtinian notions, is that of Tillema and Van der Westhuizen (2013), which provided a framework for the analysis of the structural characteristics of mentor conversations in this study. The model draws on Ericksson's (2002) concept of deliberate practice and the metaphor developed by Richard Dawkins (1996) as Tillema and Van der Westhuizen (2013) compares the road to higher teaching proficiency to 'climbing a mountain', as briefly mentioned earlier. This metaphor implies gradual professional growth. The notion of scaffolding (Wood, Bruner & Ross, 1976:90), which features as one of the 'high road' categories in Tillema and Van der Westhuizen's (2013) structural model for mentoring conversations, is associated with productive learning. Scaffolding is explained in Wood, Bruner and Ross (1976:90) as assistance which extends beyond the learner's current capabilities. It is within the Vygotskyan 'zone of proximal development' (ZPD) that the mentor can mediate and guide by scaffolding in order to take the learner, in this case the mentee, beyond what he would have learned on his own (Chaiklin, 2003:40).

Tillema and Van der Westhuizen's (2013) model describes three types of conversational activities in the 'climbing of the mountain' during mentoring conversations, which could affect the learning outcomes for student teachers. Firstly, they refer to exploratory statements as following the 'low road' which is aimed at exploring the student teacher's current practice. It is also here, where the mentor could find what Hoover (2010:20) refer to as 'critical entry points' into the mentee's practice. Utterances such as "Tell me about …", "What is your view on…", etcetera, are examples of exploratory or 'low road' statements. On this level, the mentee's practice is not challenged but simply explored. Secondly, Tillema and Van der Westhuizen (2013) refer to 'high road' mentor propositions which are made up of constructive-, or scaffolding propositions as well as prescriptive propositions. These statements have a perturbing- or challenging character and confronts the mentee or guides the mentee towards conceptual change and change of current practice. Examples of this could be, "Rather send him to his desk to reflect on ….", or "How could you approach this differently in future?". These 'high road' propositions facilitate the gradual growth which is implied by the collaborative journey up the mountain of professional development.

Tillema and Van der Westhuizen's (2013) model is further particularly demonstrative of the Vygotskyan notion of the zone of proximal development (ZPD), as described in Chaiklin (2003:39–59). When a mentor and mentee engage in a learning conversation, the mentor, as the more capable person, who guides the less capable mentee via scaffolding and prescription. Based on Vygotskyan theory, it is expected that such intervention should yield learning outcomes which are representative of movement towards higher professional proficiency. By interpretation,based on Vygotsky's theory of socio-cultural learning, with specific reference to the notions of scaffolding and mediation, it is expected that Tillema and Van der Westhuizen's (2013) model of taking the 'high road' approach in mentor conversations in order to 'climb mount improbable' should facilitate favourable

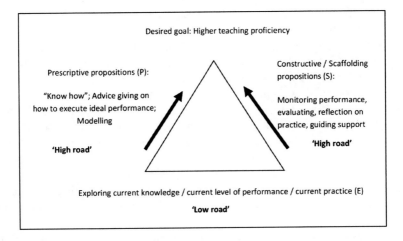

Figure 1. Tillema & Van der Westhuizen's (2013) model of 'climbing mount improbable' in the mentoring conversation, adapted to depict the hypothetical expectancy of this study (Pretorius, 2013:41)

learning outcomes. The reason is that Tillema and Van der Westhuizen's (2013) notion of constructive mentor propositions provide opportunity for collaborative knowledge construction. This could feature in form of the production of conceptual artefacts, an idea of Bereiter (2002), such as plans, approaches, schemes, outlines and recipes for better practice, as they are outcomes of deliberate thinking which is argued and shared between professionals (Tillema, 2005:82).

For this reason, the graphic depiction of Tillema & Van der Westhuizen's (2013) model is adapted to illustrate the hypothetical expectancy of the study.

Vygotsky further postulates that one first learns on a social plane and then on an individual plane (Kozulin, 2003; Offord, 2005; Wertsch, 2008). The mentoring conversation itself represents Vygotsky's social plane of learning. Kozulin (2003:19) reports on findings that activities are more complex when a learner is in an interactive situation with a human mediator, as opposed to individual learning. Vygotsky's notion that mediation is facilitated by adult guidance or a more capable peer (Chaiklin, 2003:40), is in line with Heritage and Raymond's (2005) *'epistemic authority'* in conversation. In mentoring this authority is gained through the mentor's expertise and experience, i.e., by being the more capable one who could mediate towards higher teaching proficiency.

RESEARCH PROBLEM

On the journey up 'mount improbable' (Dawkins, 1996), the mentor's position of authority makes him/her the expedition leader. This indeed implies mentoring to be a 'profession within a profession' (Smith, 2014). Professionals, with specific reference to teachers, who find themselves in a mentoring role in the training of student teachers or induction of novice teachers, need to enter mentoring encounters well prepared (Hoover, 2010; Weiss & Weiss, 2001, cited in Keogh, 2005; Maynard & Furlong, cited in Quick & Siebörger, 2005; Timperley, 2001). This means that, as mentioned earlier, they should be guided by more than intuition and expertise in their domain (Hoover, 2010; Keogh, 2005; Quick & Sieborger, 2005; Timperley, 2001) when they enter into mentoring conversations with their mentees. Foremost, Hoover (2010) and Keogh (2005) indicate the importance of careful selection and training of mentors and propose further that research based selection strategies and training programmes need to be developed. The problem is that literature remains unclear about exactly what the content of such training programmes should entail. An array of aspects could be included to prepare the mentor for his mentoring tasks taking into consideration the complexity of mentoring. One such aspect is the structuring of mentor conversations.

Having considered the centrality of conversation in mentoring encounters, the chapter pivots around the main question: In which way can mentoring conversations deliberately be structured to optimize conversational learning for student teachers? The following sub-questions facilitate an answer to the above mentioned core question: a) How does the structure of mentor conversations relate to knowledge production? b) Drawing from Tillema & Van der Westhuizen's (2013) structural model, how could prescriptive, scaffolding and exploring propositions be used in a conversation to promote optimal learning for the mentee?

METHOD OF STUDY

This qualitative study focused on the social construction of knowledge. The methodology involved deconstruction of text, textual analysis and conversation analysis (Terre Blance & Durrheim, 2006:6) which was done to describe how the structure of mentor utterances relates to student learning. Conversations between lecturers and student teachers, in the Faculty of Education of the University of Johannesburg, were targeted for convenience sampling. At the time of data analysis, three data sets were available and complete, which were broken up into sixteen smaller units for analysis, as will be explained below. These conversations provided a good range of variables and constants which was considered adequate for the study. The three mentors were all seasoned, accomplished academics in Education while all the mentees were students in Education. One student was in her final year of undergraduate studies. Her teaching experience was limited to a few weeks of teaching practicums, while the other two students' were post graduates who were already in teaching practice.

Firstly, verbatim transcriptions of these mentoring conversations were deconstructed into propositions and potential learning episodes (PLE's) were identified. These potential learning episodes served as units of analysis. Each PLE dealt with a specific topic or issue which flowed from the students' post-practicum reflection reports from the flow of the conversation. Each PLE was then analyzed in terms of structure and content in order to determine possible links between the structure of the mentor's utterances and learning outcomes for the student. Tillema and Van der Westhuizen's (2013) model provided four pre-determined categories of propositions, which served as the basis for the structural analysis of potential learning episodes, namely, a) prescriptive propositions, b) scaffolding- or constructive propositions, c) explorative propositions and d) 'other' propositions. Prescriptive propositions would be those in which the mentee is directly told how to practice and is considered 'high road' intervention. Constructive propositions, or scaffolding, would include invitations to collaborative reflection, questions to facilitate knowledge production, etc. and also resorts under 'high road' intervention. Explorative propositions would be attempts of the mentor to explore the current practice of the mentee and is seen as to remain on the 'low road'. These categories made up the primary layer of coding and analysis of the study. This level of analysis expressed the frequency of each of the four categories within each episode as a percentage of all the mentor propositions which occurred in the PLE.

Since one mentor conversation could include several topics of discussion, it was considered appropriate to compare PLE's instead of comparing entire conversations. It was noticed that the conversational structure was often adapted from one PLE to another. This depended on the nature of the topic under discussion, the mentor's perception of the topic, the needs of the mentee around the topic, or the mentor's ability to see the potential for learning in the conversational episode, etc. This approach, to identify and compare PLE's, yielded numerous units for analysis per conversation. It thus justified the use of a relatively small number of conversations. The three mentoring conversations yielded a total of sixteen PLE's for comparison. These PLE's were compared in terms of four elements, namely, structure, conversational evidence of conceptual artefacts, the complexity of these concepts or artefacts and finally, its significance or meaningfulness for the future practice of the student teacher.

Although initial expression of the frequency of each type of proposition in the PLE's provided an outline of the structure, it was soon apparent that it was simply not enough to compare the frequency of, say 'high road' propositions, to the number of conceptual artefacts produced in the conversation in order to draw a comparison between the structural characteristics and student learning. It was necessary to look at how and by whom the artefacts were constructed as well as how and when the various propositions were used in the conversation. This called for deeper analysis. In order to substantiate and understand the evidence of learning, in terms of the meaningfulness for the student teacher, a retrospective concept map was constructed for each potential learning episode by using the guidelines of Novak and Cañas (2008) and Kinchin et al. (2010). This shed light on how the concepts or artefacts were constructed and by whom. This step in the methodology reflected the construction of conceptual artefacts in a graphical format. It made it easier to substantiate an understanding of the quality of the learning, by means of the Index of Significance of Conceptual

Artefacts (ISCA), which was inductively compiled for this study, based on literature. It provided a guide to express the meaningfulness of learning on a scale of –1 to 4. Active and collaborative construction of conceptual artefacts received the highest score on the ISCA, which expressed the potential significance of the conceptual artefacts for the student's future practice, since the student's active involvement in the learning was considered to be a *"conscious"* and *"deliberate"* attempt towards meaningful learning (Novak, 1998; cited in Hay & Kinchin, 2008:174; Novak, 2011).

What Follows is a Brief Description of Each of the Categories:

Category 4 indicates the highest significance of a conceptual artefact and indicates that it was co-constructed by both the mentor and mentee and there is conversational evidence that the student was actively involved in its construction. *Category 3* indicates that either the mentor or the mentee offered the artefact and it was accepted by the other party. *Category 2* indicates that, in context of the conversation, there was an indication that the artefact was already used in the student's practice and that it was accepted or approved by the mentor. This would be an indication that existing mentee knowledge aligns with the mentor's. Although no conceptual change had taken place, existing knowledge was acknowledged by the mentor who is in a position of 'epistemic authority' (Heritage & Raymond, 2005). *Category 1* indicates that artefacts are proposed by one party but not confirmed or acknowledged by the other party. *Category 0* was assigned where no artefacts were proposed or constructed. *Category –1* (negative 1) indicates that the mentor offered an artefact but it is rejected by the mentee. Such an artefact would thus not be assimilated into the mentee's repertoire of knowledge.

The following conversation sample serves to illustrate what a conversational sequence looks like in a PLE which was classified as Category 4, i.e. a PLE in which significant, meaningful learning took place. The example illustrates the conversational co-construction of the notion that note taking in class could be much more than copying from the board (Key phrases are highlighted and printed bold so that the development of the artefact can be followed with ease):

Mentor: "So, what would be *better than* just sitting and *copying* notes from the board?"

Mentee: "I think that the teacher could be *more interactive*[1] with the children and get them involved."

Mentor: "I think you are right that the alternative is to be more interactive. The teacher could let the learning happen in the interaction. Where would note taking fit into such interactions, would you say?"

Mentee: "The teacher could *first explain* the work and then let *them write down the notes*[2], alternatively, they could *first write down the notes* and *then she could explain*[3] it."

Mentor: "But the notes could be used as a learning tool."

Mentee: "Yes."

Mentor: "Because note taking is a skill. How would it work if there is *no copying*[4] from the board but the notes are written while the lesson is going on? Which skill would you teach them?"

Mentee: "*To listen and to write at the same time*[5]."

Mentor: "Yes, it's listening and writing *but it's also identifying main ideas and distinguishing between what's good and what's not.*[6]"

Mentee: "It's *reasoning*[7]."

Mentor: "Yes."

Mentee: "*It's thinking about what you are writing* and *thinking about what you are hearing*[8] *instead of copying*[9]."

This sample shows conversational evidence of how conceptual change occurred and how a new artefact has been collaboratively constructed. It shows how the student's conception of note taking shifted from 'copying from the board' to 'reasoning':

[1] The student wants the teacher to be "more interactive" but her concept of the interaction is limited, as is seen in [2] and [3].

[2&3] The student remains with the idea that note taking is 'copying'. She only alternates the teacher's explaining of the notes to either before or after the copying.

[4] The mentor attempts to steer her away from the idea of note taking as 'copying'.

[5] Copying is now replaced by 'listening and writing at the same time'

[6] The mentor confirms this but scaffolds by contributing the notion that note taking can be a much more active process by letting the learners identify main ideas and distinguish what is relevant or not.

[7] The mentee now indicate a perspective shift from her previous idea of 'note taking as copying information' to 'note taking as reasoning'.

[8] She further elaborates on what she thinks the 'reasoning' is.

[9] The mentee's words 'instead of copying' serves as evidence of perspective shift.

WHAT DATA ANALYSIS REVEALED

The sixteen PLE's, or topics of reflective discussion, with its structural characteristics, as per Tillema & Van der Westhuizen's (2013) model, and learning outcomes, as per ISCA, are summarised in Table 1.

Table 1. Summary of data analysis. (Highest values are highlighted) (Pretorius, 2013:124)

Data set / PLE nr	Topic	Structure of mentor utterances			Index of significance of conceptual artefacts						
		High road	Low road	Other	Category 4	Category 3	Category 2	Category 1	Category 0	Category -1	Total artefacts
1/1	Copying notes from board without interaction	59%	36%	5%	3	0	0	2		0	5
1/2	Poor reading level of learners	70%	20%	10%	1	2	0	2		0	5
1/3	Discipline	33%	43%	24%	1	0	3	2		0	6
1/4	Methods for teaching spelling	63%	36%	0%	2	2	0	0		0	4
1/5	Poor class attendance	33%	17%	50%	0	0	2	0		0	2
2/1	Administrative tasks interfering with teaching time	0%	0%	100%	0	0	0	0	None	0	0
2/2	Poor parental involvement	0%	0%	100%	0	0	0	0	None	0	0
2/3	Discipline	0%	33%	67%	0	0	2	1		0	3
2/4	Professional reflection	0%	50%	50%	0	0	2	0		0	2
2/5	Teacher knowledge	20%	60%	20%	0	0	2	0		0	2
2/6	Engaging pedagogics	0%	38%	63%	0	0	3	0		0	3
2/7	Applying theory to practice	0%	67%	33%	0	0	1	1		0	2
3/1	Applying theory to practice	0%	83%	17%	0	0	1	0		0	1
3/2	Authentic learning in practice	50%	50%	0%	0	0	5	1		0	6
3/3	Adopting an engaging teaching style	27%	45%	27%	0	0	6	0		0	6
3/4	Incorporating technology into teaching practice	33%	67%	0%	0	0	2	0		0	2

Firstly, PLE's which yielded significant learning outcomes for the mentee, is of interest, since learning is the objective of the conversation. A closer look at these PLE's, reveal the following:

Possible learning episodes (PLE's) 1/1, 1/2, and 1/3, which contained more 'high road' utterances than 'low road' utterances, all yielded significant learning outcomes for the mentee, which is seen by Category 4 and 3 conceptual artefacts on the index of significance of conceptual artefacts. An exception is, however, noted in PLE 1/3, where the presence of more 'low road' utterances also yielded conceptual artefacts which were indexed as category 4 on the scale of significance. What these PLE's do have in common, though, is that, regardless of how many, they all contained high road utterances.

Secondly, the PLE's which did not yield any significant conceptual artefacts are of interest.

Note that PLE 1/5, 2/5, 3/2, 3/3 and 3/4 also contained 'high road' utterances but did not yield any artefacts of significance for the mentee.

The rest of the PLE's contained no 'high road' utterances an also no significant conceptual artefacts or no artefacts at all.

WHAT DOES THE DATA MEAN FOR MENTORS AS EXPEDITION LEADERS IN 'THE CLIMBING OF THE MOUNTAIN'?

What is the role of 'high road' propositions in a mentoring conversation? From the data analysis, it seems that high road intervention, which is constituted by prescriptive- and scaffolding propositions, is probably a requirement if significant learning is to take place. Looking at PLE's without any 'high road' intervention, it seems as though without it, significant learning is unlikely.

What, then, can be inferred regarding 'low road' propositions? Indications are that that 'low road' propositions, which are explorative in nature, and 'other' propositions, which in this study, included compliments, empathy, and agreement with mentee, are probably not enough to yield significant learning outcomes for mentees. The implication is that, if mentors want their conversations with mentees to lead to professional growth, they cannot only tread on the relatively safe side and merely enquire about the mentee's experiences and views. They have to dare to perturb by being prescriptive when needed or to respond critically and scaffold towards perception shifts and better practice. In short, mentors should be more than sound boards for their mentees if they want their mentoring conversations to be knowledge productive and thus meaningful for their mentees.

It is, however, important to note that all types of propositions have a role to play in the mentoring conversation, i.e. exploring, prescribing, scaffolding as well as other propositions which fall outside these categories. It is common sense that a mentor should not criticize, prescribe and scaffold towards a perception shift before there is a positive rapport between mentor and mentee. For this reason, it is very important to include 'low road'- and 'other' elements such as exploration, complimenting, reassuring, empathy, etc. into the conversation.

The PLE's which did yield evidence significant learning, have an interesting element in common – something that was also noticed by Tillema and Van der Westhuizen (2013:1319). They share a certain sequence in the various types of propositions. They all start off with low road propositions which seems to create a base line for the conversation from which the mentee could find 'critical entry points' (Hoover, 2010:20) into the mentee's practice. It is seen in the data sets of this study, that when the mentor found it necessary, he either moved straight onto prescriptive intervention or he first intervened by means of scaffolding propositions. In cases where the mentee did not arrive at the desired perception shift, after scaffolding attempts, the mentee would follow with prescriptive propositions. The pattern could repeat in cyclical manner until the topic is exhausted or until the mentor is satisfied with the mentee's perception shift. Figure 2 graphically illustrates this sequence.

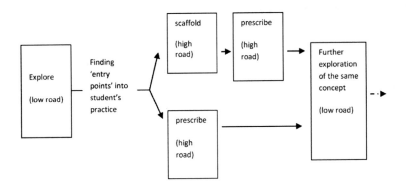

Figure 2. Sequential order of a combination of propositions for meaningful learning (Pretorius, 2013:128)

The discussion so far offered a possible answer to the main research question of the study, i.e. In which way can mentoring conversations deliberately be structured to optimize conversational learning outcomes for student teachers? From analysis of the sixteen possible learning episodes in this study, it seem that mentors could start the conversation by exploring the mentees current practice while actively being on the lookout for what Hoover (2010:20) refers to as 'critical entry points'. Whenever necessary and appropriate, the mentee should intervene by prescription, constructive critique and/or scaffolding in order to facilitate professional growth for the mentee. This structural pattern could be repeated within the same learning episode.

Additional insights into mentoring conversations also flowed from the qualitative data analysis in this study. It seems that the mentor's conversational awareness is of paramount importance in the learning process. His or her ability to find and seize 'critical entry points' (Hoover, 2010:20) into the practice of the mentee, hinges on this awareness. When 'learning readiness' (Kinchin et al., 2010) presents itself in the flow of a conversation, the mentor should be able to identify it as such and seize the learning opportunity. Without the conversational vigilance to identify the learning opportunities and student needs in the flow of a mentoring conversation, knowledge of contemporary theories on learning and conversation cannot be appropriately applied when the need arises. For this reason, mentors should be prepared for their role with specific reference to conversational aspects. The preparation of mentors could include educating them on the structural elements in mentoring conversations, the function of each element, sequencing of these elements for optimal learning development of conversational vigilance for learning opportunities.

Conversational vigilance would roughly refer to a focused, purposeful awareness of learning opportunities as it presents itself in the flow of a mentoring conversation. It would also include an awareness of one's own conceptual assumptions within one's domain of expertise. This should ensure that learning opportunities are not overseen because of one's own acceptance of the status quo in a particular field. For example, if mentors in Education accept that administrative duties are a necessary nuisance which will always be part of a day's work, it is unlikely that they will collaboratively seek better ways of incorporating it into a day's work. One data set in the study showed how a mentor expressed empathy when the student complained about administrative duties and said that it frustrates her that it interferes with her teaching. Conversational vigilance could have helped the mentor to identify the learning opportunity to collaboratively explore new solutions and options for old problems. Mentors should constantly challenge the general discourse in their field of expertise in order to be vigilant in their mentoring conversations.

On the other hand, it is noted that various factors could be at play when a mentor let a learning opportunity slip by. It could have nothing to do with a lack of conversational vigilance. There could be time constraints or fatigue of either the student or the mentor. The mentor might feel that he wants to build a stronger mentoring relationship with the student first, by explorative propositions which are followed by empathy, compliments, etc., where appropriate, before challenging the mentee's current practice. The mentor might use initial positive appraisals for emotional and interactional alliance (Tillema & Van der Westhuisen, 2013:1319) before he takes on high ground intervention. The exact reasons why mentors let learning opportunities slip by could be explored in further research, as it falls outside the scope of this study.

It is to be noted that where no evidence is found of significant knowledge construction in a learning episode, whether it was deliberate or not, it does not necessarily mean that the episode is 'knowledge-poor', a term borrowed from Bereiter (2009). The episode could be so rich in existing conceptual knowledge that, in the mentor's judgement, there is no immediate need for further knowledge construction or conceptual change. Where the mentee already displays a rich, integrated understanding of a concept, it could become frustrating if the mentor would attempt to turn the natural flow of the conversation into a superficial attempt to fit the conversation into a certain theoretical or structural mould. It would thus be unwise if a mentor would try and force an 'ideal' structure onto a conversation where there is no need for intervention.

Although this study contribute to what mentors should be aware of as they embark on mentoring conversations with their mentees, and what they should include in the structure of these conversations, the study had certain limitations. Due to the relatively small units of analysis (PLE's) which were compared, which facilitated a more refined and rigorous structural analysis, it often had to compare very low frequencies in utterance categories to learning outcomes. It resulted in expressing relatively low frequencies as percentages with the result that small variations in frequency had an effect on the percentages which are summarised in Figure 1. Since it is a qualitative study in essence, it refrains from claiming statistically significant relationships between variables. It is thus important to take note that any reference to significance in this study refers to 'practical significance' (University of New York, 2012) and not statistical significance.

The study also focused on the professional development of student teachers at a single tertiary institution, in one faculty. The only data available at the time of the study was once off conversations between lecturers and students. Longitudinal studies could explore the appropriation of conceptual artefacts in the practice of the mentee.

CONCLUSION

It is difficult to know exactly how much learning has taken place in a conversation or exactly how significant or meaningful the learning was or whether any learning truly took place at all. Asking the person directly might provide some answers to the question but it could be clouded by various influences and subjectivity. For this reason, this study used an evidence based approach in order to find a possible relation between structural dimensions of mentoring conversations and indicators of cognitive learning during the conversation. It looked for the construction of conceptual artefacts as indicators of learning and considered how these artefacts were constructed and by whom. These patterns were grouped and formed the categories of the ISCA instrument which is based on existing literature, and compiled for this study in order to determine the potential pragmatic significance the conceptual artefacts have for the mentee's future practice. Yet, although empirically based, it remains only an estimate of how significant the artefacts could be for the student teacher.

The findings of this study suggest guidelines for mentors in order to make mentoring conversations more knowledge productive. It outlines the value of the various types of propositions and the functional role of each in a mentoring conversation. It also offers a possible ideal for sequencing these propositions in a conversation and challenges the mentor to be aware of his/her own professional assumptions and it highlights the importance of conversational vigilance in order to seize learning opportunities as they present themselves within the flow of mentoring conversations.

This study found that the structural dimensions of mentoring conversations have an influence on the meaningfulness and significance of the learning outcomes of student teachers. High road propositions, (prescription and scaffolding) by the mentor do not guarantee significant and meaningful learning for the mentee. However, such learning outcomes seem to be unlikely without any 'high road' propositions. It was also found that 'low road' propositions (exploring) on its own, seem inadequate to lead to significant and meaningful learning. Propositions which fall outside these propositional categories, such as expression of empathy, paying of compliments, expression of agreement, etc., did not yield any evidence of learning. Possible learning episodes (PLE's) which yielded significant and meaningful learning were of particular interest. These episodes, with the exception of one, contained more high road propositions than low road propositions. Furthermore, these episodes included all the other propositional categories too, with the exception of one PLE. Evidence of a particular sequential pattern in the use of the various categories of propositions was found in all PLE's which yielded significant learning outcomes, as per ISCA.

Without deliberate, skilful application of structural elements when a learning opportunity presents itself in the flow of a mentoring conversation, the expertise and experience of the mentor could remain locked up within the mentor and of little value for the mentee. Conversational vigilance and knowledge of the structural dimensions of a mentoring conversation is invaluable if the mentor is to guide the mentee 'up the mountain' towards higher professional proficiency.

From this study it seems that at least two factors are of vital importance in mentoring conversations in order to yield significant learning for mentees, namely, research based knowledge of structural elements as well as the conversational vigilance to identify and seize potential learning opportunities as it features within the normal flow of conversation.

REFERENCES

Baker, A., Jensen, P. J., & Kolb, D. A. (2002). Conversation as experiential learning. In A. Baker, P. J. Jensen, & D. A. Kolb (Eds.), *Conversational learning: An experiential approach to knowledge creation*. Westport, CO: Quorum Books.

Bereiter, C. (2002). *Education and mind in the knowledge society/age*. Mahwah, NJ: Lawrence Erlbaum Associates.

Bereiter, C. (2009). Innovation in the absence of principled knowledge. *Creativity and Innovation Management, 18*(3), 234–241.

Chaiklin, S. (2003). The zone of proximal development in Vygotsky's analysis of learning and instruction. In A. Kozulin, B. Gindis, V. S. Ageyev, & S. M. Miller (Eds.), *Vygotsky's educational theory in cultural context*. New York, NY: Cambridge University Press.

City University of New York. (2012). *Statistical vs. practical significance*. Retrieved February 9, 2014 from http://gradnyc.com/wp-content/uploads/2012/08/GNYC_Academy_Workshop-4_Statistical-vs-Practical Significance.pdf

Dawkins, R. (1996). *Climbing mount improbable*. New York, NY: W. W. Norton & Company.

Edwards, A., Gilroy, P., & Hartley, D. (2002). *Rethinking teacher education: Collaborative responses to uncertainty*. London, England: Routledge Falmer.

Edwards, D. (1993). What do children really think?: Discourse analysis and conceptual content in children's talk. *Cognition and Instruction, 11*(3/4), 207–225.

Ericsson, K. A. (2002). The path to expert golf performance: Insights from the masters on how to improve performance by deliberate practice. In P. R. Thomas (Ed.), *Optimising performance in golf* (pp. 1–57). Brisbane, Australia: Australian Academic Press.

Gerretzen, F. (2012). *Effects of mentoring on student teacher's perceived learning outcomes: How mentor's approach and mentoring relationship influence perceived learning outcomes* (Unpublished dissertation). Leiden University, Educational Studies, Leiden.

Hay, D., & Kinchin, I. (2008). Using concept mapping to measure learning quality. *Education & Training, 50*(2), 167–182.

Heritage, J., & Raymond, G. (2005). The terms of agreement: Indexing epistemic authority and subordination in talk-in-interaction. *Social Psychology Quarterly, 68*(1),15–38.

Hoover, L. A. (2010). Comprehensive teacher induction: A vision towards transformative teacher learning. *Action in Teacher Education, 32*(4), 15–25.

Keogh, J. (2005). *Who's the expert and who's the novice? Mentoring tensions in the practicum experience*. Conference Paper (Paper code KEO05097). Australian Association for Research in Education (AARE), Deakin.

Kinchin, I. M., Streatfield, D., & Hay D. B. (2010). Using concept mapping to enhance the research interview. *International Journal of Qualitative Methods, 9*(1), 52–68.

Kozulin, A. (2003). Psychological tools and mediated learning. In A. Kozulin, B. Gindis, V. S. Ageyev, & S. M. Miller (Eds.), *Vygotsky's educational theory in cultural context*. New York, NY: Cambridge University Press.

Magano, M. D., Mostert, P., & Van der Westhuizen (2010). *Learning conversations – The value of interactive learning*. Cape Town: Heinemann Publishers.

Novak, J. D. (2011). A theory of education: Meaningful learning underlies the constructive integration of thinking, feeling and acting leading to empowerment for commitment and responsibility. *Meaningful Learning Review, 1*(2), 1–14.

Novak, J. D., & Cañas A. J. (2008). *The theory underlying concept maps and how to construct and use them* (Technical Report IHMC CmapTools 2006-01 Rev 01-2008). Pensacola, FL: Florida Institute for Human and Machine Cognition. Retrieved from http://cmap.ihmc.us/Publications/ResearchPapers/TheoryUnderlyingConceptMaps.pdf

Offord, L. (2005). The mozart of psychology. *Lev Semenovich Vygotsky*. Retrieved September 3, 2010, from http://vygotsky.afraid.org

Orland-Barak, L., & Tillema, H. (2006). The 'dark side of the moon': A critical look at teacher knowledge construction in collaborative settings. *Teachers and Teaching: Theory and Practice, 12*(1), 1–12.

153

Pretorius, A. J. M. (2013). *The structural dimensions of mentoring and how they relate to learning outcomes of student teachers* (Masters dissertation). University of Johannesburg Auckland Park, South Africa.

Quick, G., & Siebörger, R. (2005). What matters in practice teaching? The perceptions of schools and students. *South African Journal of Education, 25*(1), 1–4.

Rule, P. (2006). Bakhtin and the poetics of Pedagogy. *Journal of Education, 40*, 79–101.

Smith, K. (2014). Conference presentation – EASA 2014, Golden Gate National Park, South Africa.

Stivers, T., Mondala, L., & Steensig, J. (2011). Knowledge, morality and affiliation in social interaction. In T. Stivers, L. Mondala, & J. Steensig (Eds.), *The morality of knowledge in conversation.* Cambridge: University Press.

Strong, M., & Baron, W. (2004). An analysis of mentoring conversations with beginning teachers: Suggestions and responses. *Teaching and Teacher Education, 20*, 47–57.

Terre Blance, M., & Durrheim, K. (2006). Histories of the present: Social science research in context. In M. Terre Blanche, K. Durrheim, & D. Painter (Eds.), *Research in practice. Applied methods for the social sciences* (2nd ed.). Cape Town: UCT Press.

Tillema, H. (2005). Collaborative knowledge construction in study teams of professionals. *Human Resource Development International, 8*(1), 81–99.

Tillema, H., & Van der Westhuizen, G. J. (2006). Knowledge construction in collaborative enquiry among teachers. *Teachers and Teaching: Theory and Practice, 12*(1), 51–67.

Tillema, H., & Van der Westhuizen, G. J. (2013). Mentoring conversations in the professional preparation of teachers. *SAJHE, 27*(5),1305–1323.

Tillema, H. H., Van der Westhuizen, G. J., & van der Merwe, M. (2012). *Teacher knowledge building through conversation* (Unpublished draft article). Draft article related to Mentor Research Project, University of Johannesburg, Department of Education, Johannesburg.

Timperley, H. (2001). Mentoring conversations designed to promote student teacher learning. *Asia-Pacific Journal of Teacher Education, 29*(2), 111–123.

Wertsch, J. V. (2008). From social interaction to higher psychological processes: A clarification and application of Vygotsky's theory. *Human Development, 51*(1), 66–79.

Wood, D., Bruner, J. S., & Ross, G. (1976). The role of tutoring in problem solving. *Journal of Child Psychology & Psychiatry, 17*, 89–100.

Annatjie J. M. Pretorius
Department of Educational Psychology/Academic Development Centre
University of Johannesburg, South Africa

GUIDO VAN ESCH AND HARM TILLEMA

8. THE LEARNING POTENTIAL OF MENTORING CONVERSATIONS

INTRODUCTION

Mentor: "Yet I think that when you move on with this class you'll have to try to tackle a few things, because otherwise you'll get ... You'll bring a lot of work on to yourself. That is one. May be that is not the most important thing to you right now, but it means that you have to have to concentrate on how you conduct a conversation with everyone in the class. Then again, you do not have that on your mind ...."

Student: oh ...

Mentor: "When it becomes noisy in the classroom. What would you do to solve this in future?"

Student: "For example by...[EXPLANATION GIVEN]."

Mentor: "Can you do that, deal with all that happens around you?; what can you do?"

Student: "A number of things..."

This is an excerpt from a mentoring conversation. But do we understand what is occurring here and can we interpret the mentor's intentions from a learning perspective? This is the aim of the current chapter: to find ways to describe what we could call the "footprint" of a conversation.

Our main quest in this chapter is: Do students learn from mentoring conversations? Within the context of teacher education, the study we present explores different types of patterns in conversations from the perspective of student learning, asking: To what extent do patterned speech acts in mentoring conversations promote (professional) learning in students?

In an explorative, mixed method research design 12 mentoring conversations were analysed in depth with regard to the speech acts deployed in interactions in which the mentors tried to foster learning in their mentees. Our findings indicate a high variety of distinct patterns in mentoring conversations. A predominant preference was found for a reflection oriented pattern of mentoring which however was not positively related to student satisfaction or student learning outcomes. It is

H. Tillema et al. (Eds.), Mentoring for Learning, 155–179.

concluded that mentoring conversations can (and should) be critically analysed with regard to their potential for learning.

MENTORING AS IT RELATES TO (PROFESSIONAL) LEARNING

Mentoring is an important vehicle to make 'practical knowledge' explicit (Tillema & Van der Westhuizen, 2013) and is deployed widely as a major resource in professional learning (as is the case, for instance, in student teacher learning). Mentoring has been defined as the support an apprentice or less experienced practitioner (mentee) receives from a more experienced professional (mentor) (Hobson, Ashby, Malderez, & Tomlinson, 2009). Its aim is to raise the level of the mentee's expertise and to facilitate induction into the profession (Kwan & Lopez-Real (2005). Positive claims have been made about its impact on the capabilities of a beginning professional, such as improved skills and ability to manage workload (D'abate & Eddy, 2008). Tillema and Van der Westhuizen (2013) add that mentoring is important to educate apprentices professionally and promote further professional learning.

Within the apprentice relationship the mentor is expected to 'look after' a mentee (for instance in a practicum or internship). Depending on a mentor's goal, s(h)e will enact different roles; like: 'critical friend' to provide reflection on practice (Day, 1999), 'equal partner' to work together with the student, or 'observer' to give counsel and advise (Crasborn & Hennissen 2010). In their study on actual mentor roles Feiman and Carver (2009) identified mentors as local guides, educational companions, and as agents of change.

There are many studies to be found on mentoring (Edwards & Protheroe, 2003; Darling Hammond, 2003), but few of them are of an empirical nature. Despite the wide advocacy for mentoring, the critical issue still is the warranty of claims made; that is, in what way does mentoring lead to an apprentice's learning? Reviewing what has been said on the relation between mentor activity and learning points to the importance of a number of characteristics, for instance: addressing the willingness of a mentee to get the most out of a mentoring relationship (Hobson et al., 2009); being responsive to the needs of the mentee/learner (Alebregtse, 2008); identifying critically their conceptions of teaching (Lopez-Real & Kwan, 2005), using explicit reflection (Mena Marcos & Tillema, 2007); and seeking agreement on goals in the mentoring relationship, as well as periodically revisiting objectives (Shore, Toyokawa, & Anderson, 2008). Furthermore, several mentor skills have been stated to contribute to the student's learning such as: (1) the ability to develop a clear and consistent notion of good teaching, (2) the mentor's ability to model, analyse, and reflect on behaviour, and (3) the ability to help the apprentice with developing own ideas and approaches, as well as (4) the mentor's ability to define and redefine zones of the apprentice's proximal development (Wang & Odell, 2002; Edwards, 2010). Certain tactics in mentoring seem particularly effective for learning: i.e., supporting mentees emotionally; showing openness for discussion; allowing autonomy for making decisions (Kwan & Lopez-Real, 2005). Effective mentors ensure sufficient challenge and scaffold deeper levels of reflection.

Based on these studies recommendations have been made about mentoring practice, such as: (1) mentors need to know how questions should be posed and how apprentices have to be helped so that they pose relevant questions, (Núñez, Rosário, Vallejo & González-Pienda, 2013); (2) mentoring should engage apprentices in an ongoing dialogue about their teaching and learning (Baker, Jensen & Kolb, 2005); (3) mentors should provide opportunities for deep levels of understanding; and (4) approach learning from the perspective of students, (Hobson et al., 2009); as well as (5) mentors should help apprentices to construct their own conceptions of teaching and learning (Shore, Toyokawa, & Anderson, 2008).

In general: mentors have been advised to promote professional learning by: (a) engaging apprentices in reflective interactions, (b) challenging apprentices to re-examine crucial events to reconstruct meaning, (c) offering alternative interpretations for events, and (d) engage apprentices in analysing where they are in learning and where they need to go (Wang & Odell, 2002).

The platform on which these recommendations and advice become tangible and concrete is the mentoring conversation, i.e., the talk and exchange occurring between a student and a mentor. In order to promote and sustain the student's learning process a mentor can make use of a variety of approaches in conversation, such as determining the format, topics, start and finish of the conversation, choose certain roles, and adopt either directing or non-directing approaches in communication (Tillema & Van der Westhuizen, 2013). Conversational approaches contain ingredients, such as: questioning, support and challenge, reflective queries, and require relational and interpersonal skills, as well as meaning making and maintaining relevancy of conversation. From a study by Tillema and Van der Westhuizen (2013), it appeared, firstly, that there are different strategies related to the attainment of learning goals. Secondly, that the student teacher's perceived knowledge productivity, i.e., learning for professional action, was influenced by conversational moves of the mentor. Thirdly, that there was an overall positive effect of conversational moves on the learning outcomes of the student teachers. This pointed to the importance of 'explicating practical knowledge' in mentoring.

STUDYING MENTORING CONVERSATIONS

Of key concern then is whether mentoring conversations have a positive and direct influence on the learning of students as they prepare for practice (Tillema & Van der Westhuizen, 2013). Mentoring conversations are meant to be supportive in 'pushing' mentees forward in keeping (goal) direction while at the same time promote learners towards reflection on past performance as well scaffold the steps to explore or gain insights from their recent learning accomplishments (Núñez, Rosário, Vallejo & González-Pienda, 2013) (See also Sadler, 2010).

From previous studies (Ciga Tellechea, 2012; D'abate & Eddy, 2008) it can be argued that mentoring conversations that facilitate student's goal orientation during learning will result in enhanced levels of motivation and self-efficacy (Núñez et al., 2013). Other studies point to enhanced self-reflection as a result of participating in a mentoring conversation (Mena, Gonzalez & Tillema, 2012). Moreover, studies that focus on mentoring approaches (Crasborn & Hennissen, 2010) highlight the positive influence of mentor talk on professional growth, problem-solving capacities, and the development of professional capabilities (Hobson et al., 2009). It is therefore of interest to investigate in more detail in what way mentoring conversations result in changes in student's competence; that is: to explore types of patterns in conversations from the perspective of student learning, with the overall concern being: Do mentoring conversations have a positive influence on learning ?

Looking in greater depth at mentoring conversations may reveal how mentors scaffold learning in a concrete way; i.e., by using specific speech acts or moves that support student's understanding of past performance and promote further learning (Tillema & Van der Westhuizen, 2013) Typical examples of such conversational moves are: orienting probes, reflective questions, directing suggestions, regulative remarks, prescriptive advice giving, and constructive ideas. However, although many studies deal with the conversational analysis of mentoring few relate the analysis of talk to learning (or 'walk") of students as a result of conversation. Analysis of patterns in talk might reveal how mentors structure the conversation and 'organize' how to gain insight from past performance. Analysis of speech acts might help to ensure that students will learn from conversations, and may inform mentors about routes to take in a conversation. Mentors can use such information as feedback in order to improve learning in their students.

In literature from linguistics, several ways are described to analyse conversations. According to Clouston (2007), discourse analysis and conversation analysis are methods suited for analysing talk in a variety of settings. A conversation analysis is characterized by a levelled approach to talk: i.e., (1) identifying sequences of related talk, such as turns, overlaps, pauses and noting any 'remarkable phenomena', (2) examining how speakers take on certain roles or identities through their talk, and (3) the study of 'outcomes in the talk' (Clouston, 2007). Discourse analysis typically makes use of principles and methodology of linguistics to analyse discourse in structural-functional terms (in IRF/IRE cycles – Seedhouse, 2004). In analysing conversations in mentoring (Tillema & Van der Westhuizen, (2013), typically speech acts or moves are described in terms of styles and role-taking (Crasborn & Hennisen, 2010); often measured with self-developed coding instruments, which often involve a propositional analysis of transcribed video records of a conversation (Mena Marcos & Tillema, 2011). Conversational studies in mentoring portray mentoring most often as process. In this way Crasborn and Hennissen (2010) refer to the importance of effective guidance as an essential condition for learning of students. Key aspects of mentoring dialogues as process being studied are: content of dialogue, mentor teachers' style and supervisory skills, mentor teachers' input, time aspects of the dialogue, and phases in a dialogue. Findings from these process studies (Orland Barak, 2002) point to the relevancy of instructional and organisational aspects in the exchange. A repeated outcome of these studies is the predominant directing style and supervisory skill of the mentor (as the mentor usually decides about topics, gives active input, and does most of the talking). Furthermore, from these process studies it appears that there are three key aspects prominent in the analysis of dialogues: mentor style/supervisory skills, input provided by the mentor, and time, organisational aspects. Many of these process studies have identified a variety of roles taken on by the mentor, for instance: initiator, imperator, advisor and encourager (Crasborn & Hennissen, 2010) or Tillema and Smith (2007) who identify a relational, instructional and situational style in mentoring.

But, and this is a major drawback of these process studies, we do not learn how these mentor roles or manifestations of mentoring approaches relate to outcomes on learning, or gain in proficiency and understanding of the student/mentee. That is: how, by means of mentoring dialogues, mentors influence how and what student will learn.

MENTORING AS AID IN EXPERTISE BUILDING

In order to position mentoring in relation to learning a notion needs to be developed on how mentoring comes to aid in 'helping' the mentee to gain a higher understanding and improved proficiency in a domain. This notion we call "climbing the mountain" by which we mean that mentoring derives its purpose from the support it gives to the learner in achieving goals being set (either by the mentee, or by given standards; such as is the case in education). Mentoring, therefore, is concerned with developing expertise.

According to Ericsson's theory of expertise (Ericsson, 2002; Ericsson et al., 2007), developing expertise involves selecting a goal, drawing on an available or provided knowledge base, and checking or monitoring required behaviours to reach that goal. Schematically this theory can be represented as is shown in Figure 1.

From this perspective mentoring can be looked upon as reaching goals based on activating relevant knowledge and monitoring past performance or, in short what we call: "climbing the mountain". In this way we can interpret conversations as aiming for improved understanding and building of proficiency realised in interactions between a mentor and a mentee.

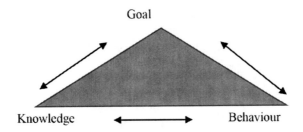

Figure 1. Schematic representation of Ericsson's theory on expertise

From the literature on meta-cognition (Zimmerman & Schunk, 2001), certain cognitive regulatory skills or abilities are identified that function to advance this process of attainment and would support a climbing of the mountain; and thus constitute a learning conversation. These are: a) (self)reviewing in terms of establishing a reflective looking back on past performance; b) goal orientation as looking forward to evaluate attainments or progress made, and c) planning steps for concrete action to attain the goals set. These three abilities can be rephrased in relation to Ericsson's model as: a) Knowing what has been done; b) Knowing where to go and c) Knowing how to get there (See also Sadler, 2010 who brought forward this distinction as typical for instruction and learning).

Figure 2 depicts these skills in mentoring conversation in a dynamical way:

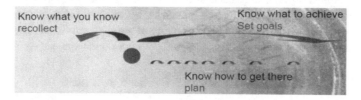

Figure 2. Taken from Ciga Tellechea, 2012

a. Reviewing or (self)monitoring of performance relative to standards or goals is important in a mentoring for learning conversation to reflect on and adjust performance. Detecting discrepancies between standards and actual performance may inform the learner to make efforts for improvements (i.e. recycling through the loop) so that these discrepancies are resolved.

b. Evaluating goal attainment is important in a mentoring conversation to determine the direction and relevance of efforts and link actions taken to the requirements of the task ("double loop learning"). In a conversation it is important for a mentor to highlight concrete, tangible goals, i.e., that are task-specific, proximal to possible attainment, and challenging to the learner to invest in improvements (i.e., slightly above his or her current performance level).

c. Action planning involves the determination or choice of concrete steps to achieve the goals relative to the past performance. It entails the (mentor supported) selection of effective strategies to cope with discrepancies and difficulties to improve performance.

ANALYSING MENTORING CONVERSATIONS

In this way mentoring conversations can be analysed in more detail, using the three key abilities to screen mentoring conversation on how the learner is supported "to climb the mountain".

Conversations as transcribed talk need therefore to be divided into meaningful units or episodes, that contain several mentor's speech acts or 'moves' which can be coded as: (1) know what you know – review or recollect, (2) know what to achieve - set goals, and (3) know how to get there – plan action. In the analysis of a conversation these smaller units or coded moves can be combined or merged into certain patterns that represent a typical arrangement of a mentor's intention to support the learner. By identifying beforehand possible combinations of moves (or patterns), mentor conversations can analysed in a meaningful way. The following patterns may represent the mentor's guiding intentions in a talk to climb the mountain:

- Review + goal + plan   = reviewing
- Goal + plan + review   = directing
- Plan + goal + review   = stimulating
- Review + plan + goal   = indicating
- Goal + plan + review   = orienting
- goal = >review => plan = constructive pattern

Looking at the conversation globally the analysis of moves and patterns could indicate a footprint of the conversation, i.e., give a total impression of the type of talk. (I.e., a footprint of a typical conversation could be: review – 50%; goal – 20%, and action – 30% of moves). Knowing a conversation's footprint can be informative to the mentor in assessing the talk afterwards.

The analysis of conversation into moves and patterns of a mentor's speech acts is meant to detect how student are supported to learn from conversations. In our study, a detailed analysis of individual speech acts is combined with a more global level of analysis on patterns to provide an overall account of about what happened in a mentoring conversation. In this way, it is scrutinized how advice is given on what was done, what was achieved, and which recommendations were given on how to get there.

THE STUDY

Participants

Twelve dyads of mentors (in teacher education) and their mentees (student teachers) participated in this study. Eight student teachers were enrolled in a teacher education program for secondary education (from one institute) and four student teachers were enrolled in a teacher education program for primary education (from another institute). Age range of these students was between 18 and 28 years. Four of these twelve student teachers were male. The students took courses in their third and fourth year of the four-year program. The participating mentors were practice teachers of schools affiliated to the program and had training as a mentor given by the teacher education institute. Their teaching experience ranged from 14–31 years. The length of mentorships in dyads varied, from a half year to close to a year. Data were collected in the 2nd half of the practice teaching period of one year.

Design of the Study

The design of study consisted of data collection on presage variables with regard to student beliefs on mentoring using questionnaires, as well as quality measures of the student's reflection on performance; and an in-depth analysis of the conversation between mentor and student. These measures were related to outcome variables regarding student's appreciation of mentoring conversation and learning results. Learning result consisted of an evaluation with regard to: student's problem understanding, student's willingness to change his or her perspective, and commitment to apply the recommendations given by the mentor. It was studied to what extent presage variables as well as conversational moves and patterns influence the outcome variables.

Procedure

As a first step, the dyads of student teachers and their mentors received an invitation by mail to participate in the study. The researcher randomly selected those who indicated their willingness to participate. After their consent, the presage questionnaires were distributed. For students it consisted of: the Student Beliefs questionnaire on professional learning and the evaluation questionnaire on Preferred Mentoring Behaviour. The belief questionnaire on Professional Learning was also administered to mentors. Furthermore student teachers were asked to write a Reflection Report on their past teaching performance; the researcher rated the reflection report using an instrument for quality of reflection (see *Instruments*). After the questionnaires were administered and analysed, an appointment was made for videotaping the mentors' and mentees' upcoming mentoring conversation. Before videotaping the conversation, the researcher first introduced the nature and the procedure of the study. Subsequently, the mentoring conversations were videotaped. With the camera installed, the researcher left the room in order not to disturb the process. The length of the conversation was on average 45 minutes (range 23–84 min). After the mentoring conversation, the researcher administered the learning outcomes questionnaire and the questionnaire on appreciation of conversation to the students Also a student interview was held, asking a written response to questions on memorable events happened during the conversation. The instrument was to gauge the students' perception on important learning outcomes that were taken from the conversation. The whole procedure, including conversation, was on average 2h;10 min.

The transcripts of the mentoring conversations were then coded and analysed by using the instrument for conversation analysis. The administered data from questionnaires and the reflection report were analysed and linked to the codes of the conversation analysis using SPSS and Excel.

Instruments

Conversation analysis. An instrument was developed to code and analyse transcripts of conversational propositions into episodes. An episode is defined as a smallest meaningful unit in a conversation (Tillema & Van der Westhuizen, 2013) and consists of topically connected (mostly 2–3) propositions. An episode has a clear beginning, middle and end. Each episode was coded into the following categories or "moves": know what you know (Review), know what to achieve (Goals), and know how to get there (Plan/Act). (In addition, there was a miscellaneous code). For correct coding each transcript was analysed by two raters. Inter-rater reliability (after a training session) was high – k = .90.

An example of an episode coded as Review is:

Mentor: "Let's pay attention to the lesson start: you start the instruction by giving homework. I think that is very good, because then you have all the attention. Not at the end of the lesson, great!".

Another example of an episode coded as Goals, is the following:

Mentor: "let's have a look at your lesson plan form"

Student: "Like this one?"

Mentor: "Yes, I would like you to include as a purpose in your lesson plan form: making compliments to pupils. Because what would that mean for next time?"

An example of code 3 – Plan is as follows:

Mentor 1: "There is a moment it becomes disrupted and loud in the classroom. What could you do to solve this in future?"

Student: "For example by…."

Mentor 1: "You can do that, but what else can you do?"

Subsequently, the coding of episodes was used for a topical analysis of patterns in the conversations. A topic consists of a combination of episodes subsumed under a common theme or subject, entailing mostly three to four episodes with a clear beginning and closure, (for instance with signal words like: OK, let's). A pattern analysis searches for combinations of episode codes that signify a mentor's intention or objective in the conversation. Several patterns were defined beforehand (See above)

For instance: an analysis of a transcript with a common theme/subject having high frequency codes for Goals (code 2) and low for 1 (Review) and 3 (Plan), would be coded as the pattern 0-1-0, and would receive as a label: stimulating. Alternatively, when a transcript was coded with high frequency on code 1 (Review) and but not on codes 2 and 3 it would be labelled as a reviewing pattern – for example the pattern

1-0-0. In the same way a pattern labelled as directing has a 1-1-0 code. A pattern was labelled as orienting would have 1-0-1. And one labelled as indicating having 0-0-1; and one labelled as constructive has as code 1-1-1.

Other Instruments

The Student Belief questionnaire on professional learning (Tillema, 2011, 2013) measures attitudes towards learning and professional development and is comprised of eighteen Likert type questions, having two subscales: the Rethinking one's Abilities scale (e.g. 'I regularly need to reflect on my way of teaching') and the Restructuring one's Performance scale (e.g. 'Mastery shows itself in my planning and organizing of teaching'). Reliability of the scale is. 85.

Student Mentoring Preference questionnaire measures attitudes of students regarding favoured mentoring behaviour and is based on the Ideal Mentoring Scale (IMS) by Rose (2000). The IMS entails the following subscales:

- Integrity, which consists of fourteen items (e.g., 'What I see in my mentor is that he values me as a person').
- Guidance, which consists of ten items (e.g. 'What I see in my mentor is that he helps me plan a timetable for my research').
- Relationship, which consists of ten items (e.g. 'What I see in my mentor is that he helps me realize my life vision') (Tillema & Van der Westhuizen, 2013).

The IMS consists of 34 closed questions, on a five point Likert scale (ranging from not true to very true). Internal consistency for the subscale integrity is. 87, for the subscale guidance is. 75 and the subscale relationship is. 78.

Afterwards the student's appreciation of the conversation was measured with a questionnaire using IMS items reformulated into 18 evaluative questions. It was determined: a) how the student valued the conversation (6 items), b) how well the mentor reacted to the student (7 items) and c) how positive a relationship was established during the conversation. This instrument is completed by the students and comprised of closed questions on a 4 point scale. An example of a reformulated item is: 'What I noticed during conversation is that my mentor treats me in a pleasant way.'

The Knowledge Productivity questionnaire on student learning (Tillema, 2007; Orland Barak & Tillema, 2006) measures evaluation of learning accomplishments by the student ('i.e., did the mentoring support your professional practice?') (Tillema & Van der Westhuizen, 2013). This questionnaire is comprised of twenty closed evaluation questions with respect to three categories on a five point Likert scale:

- Problem understanding: seven items on understanding of what was discussed during the mentoring conversation (e.g. 'I found the problems being discussed authentic and realistic')
- Perspective change: seven items on how the mentors, contributed to learning, (e.g. 'my thinking changed during the discussion')

- Commitment to apply: six items on the intention to actively follow up on recommendations after the mentoring conversation (e.g. 'I will take up ideas to practice further')

Internal consistency for the items of problem understanding was r = .71; perspective taking was r = .64, and the category commitment had r = .97.

The Interview questionnaire on Memorable Events is also completed afterwards by the student teachers and contains nine evaluative questions dealing with the knowledge gained from the conversation as a learning event (Tillema & Van der Westhuizen, 2013). In detail:

- Problem Understanding: three questions on whether the student teachers accepted and learned from the messages that were expressed in the discussions (e.g. 'what have you learned and gained from the examples your mentor expressed?').
- Perspective Change: two questions on whether the conversation led to insightful new knowledge (e.g. 'what the talk you had changed your way of approaching matters in teaching?').
- Commitment to Apply: four items on whether the student teachers participated actively in the process (e.g. 'what kind of consequences would you draw as a result of the mentoring conversation?') (Tillema & Van der Westhuizen, 2013).

The coding of each question was either positive, negative or neutral. The inter-rater reliability of this instrument was evaluated as 88% agreement

Furthermore the student teachers' reflection report was rated. It is an account of past performance, having a free format (i.e., open learner report). The quality of reflection (Mena Marcos, 2011; Winitzky, 2004)) was measured using a category coding instrument to assess the level of quality of the student's reflections by means of rating each kernel (full) sentence on a quality level ranging from 0 till 5. (Afterwards weighted by the amount of sentences, that is the number of lines of the reflection report). The assigned codes were used for further analyses.

Data Inspection

Questionnaire data were checked regarding their statistical properties. For these variables means and interquartile ranges were computed (Moore & McCabe, 2003). Furthermore histograms and Q plots were made in order to determine normality distribution of the data (De Vocht, 2009). No deviations were found. In order to determine linear relations between numeric variables, homogeneity of variances and outliers, scatterplots were made, as well computation of correlations between these variables (Moore & McCabe, 2003). Correlations are given in the Findings section.

Data Analysis

Firstly, a descriptive analysis was conducted on the data that resulted from the conversational analysis to determine frequencies of occurrence of moves (detailed level of conversations) and patterns (global level of conversations). Next, the (differential) impacts of the presage variables on the learning outcome variables were determined by t-tests and simple regression analyses. These findings provide a condition for findings related to the impact of patterns and moves of a conversation on the learning and appreciation outcome variables.

FINDINGS

Moves and Patterns in Conversation

The descriptive analysis of episodes showed a high variation in amount and type of mentor speech acts or 'moves' across conversations. The frequencies of episode occurrence in conversations are given in Table 1, together with the overall 'footprint'.

Table 1. Total frequencies of episodes in mentoring conversations

Mentoring conversation	Episode move	Total amount of episodes (n)	Footprint (percentage combination of three episode moves)
A	0^1	3	
	1^2	123	75-5-18
	2^3	8	
	3^4	30	
B	0^1	21	
	1^2	49	50-14-14
	2^3	14	
	3^4	14	
C	0^1	6	
	1^2	36	60-20-10
	2^3	12	
	3^4	6	
D	0^1	9	
	1^2	65	63-10-19
	2^3	10	
	3^4	20	
E	0^1	34	
	1^2	38	36-7-25
	2^3	7	
	3^4	26	

(*Continued*)

Table 1. (Continued)

Mentoring conversation	Episode move	Total amount of episodes (n)	Footprint (percentage combination of three episode moves)
F	0^1	13	
	1^2	12	35-15-15
	2^3	5	
	3^4	4	
G	0^1	43	
	1^2	64	44-5-21
	2^3	7	
	3^4	30	
H	0^1	22	
	1^2	42	43-20-14
	2^3	10	
	3^4	14	
I	0^1	11	
	1^2	32	64-2-12
	2^3	1	
	3^4	6	
J	0^1	3	
	1^2	31	54-16-25
	2^3	9	
	3^4	14	
K	0^1	15	
	1^2	47	44-4-39
	2^3	4	
	3^4	42	
L	0^1	16	
	1^2	27	46-2-25
	2^3	1	
	3^4	15	
Total averaged footprint			53^2-9^3-21^4

$^1 0 = miscellaneous$
$^2 1 = Know what you know – review$
$^3 2 = Know what to achieve – goal$
$^4 3 = Know how to get there – plan$

Each of the episode moves was present at some point in the conversation; episode move 1 (know what you know – review) being the dominant one. But there were marked differences between conversations (see Table 1), both in the occurrence of specific speech moves (the total averaged conversation's footprint being: 53% – for move 1; 9% for move 2 and 21% for move 3; miscellaneous having 18%); as well as within the course of a conversation with regard to the patterns of moves used (deployment of combinations of episode moves across the conversation). The patterned configurations of conversation (see Method) are shown for each mentoring conversation in Table 2.

Table 2. Frequencies of patterns in mentoring conversations

Mentoring conversation	Orienting	Reviewing	Directing	Stimulating	Indicating	Constructive	Not content oriented
A	0	18	2	1	8	5	0
B	3	17	4	4	4	5	2
C	2	7	0	1	2	1	0
D	1	3	0	0	0	4	2
E	1	8	4	2	7	6	11
F	1	7	1	0	0	2	3
G	0	17	5	1	5	3	6
H	0	4	0	2	3	3	4
I	0	8	0	1	3	0	0
J	0	1	0	0	1	6	0
K	0	1	0	0	2	3	1
L	1	2	0	0	5	0	12
Total percentage	.04	.43	.07	.06	.19	.11	

Table 2 shows marked differences in patterns between conversations as evidenced by the columns of the Table as well as differences in the overall use of patterns across each conversation as evidenced by the rows of the table. In most conversations we find a dominance of Reviewing pattern (notably in A, B and G) as well as for the Indicating pattern; both are reflective in nature. The Constructive pattern: E and J was next in frequency of use. In some conversations all patterns are present (B, E or G), but others have a specific and restricted use of patterns: e.g., L. Looking at the overall patterns in conversations, we find that most mentoring conversations could be typified as reflective; accounting for 62% of the speech acts.

In a more fine grain examination, the episode analysis of moves and patterns can be used to identify specific shifts in the flow of a conversation to identify at what point in a conversation specific patterns are being initiated. Such an analysis (however not fully described in this chapter) could reveal intentional redirections and 'meaning making' in the conversation (Clutterbuck, 2004). In this manner, a fine grain analysis of conversation A (with 164 episodes) would reveal, for instance, a flow of conversation that is characterized by: firstly, a lengthy period (67 episodes) of reviewing talk (footprint: 34-0-2), a short period (12 episode) of exploring action options (footprint: 3-0-9), followed by a short reflective period again (31-2-4) to finally wrapping up the talk (54 episodes) with: 7-3-3. This conversation would resemble more or less the GROW model of mentoring (Whitmore, 2001). In this way, a detailed account can be provided of the mentoring conversation as a whole as well as indicate at what points in a conversation actual shifts occur.

Mentoring Conversations and Learning

It was studied next to what extent student learning from mentoring and appreciation of conversation is influenced by student beliefs on professional learning, as well as to what extent conversational moves and patterns influence learning outcome variables.

In Table 3 t-tests results are shown with regard to the influence of student's Professional Learning Beliefs on appreciation of mentoring conversation, as well as on learning from mentoring (divided into: problem understanding, perspective taking, and commitment). The belief test consisted of two scales: importance of rethinking one's abilities and ability to restructure one's actions. High and low student beliefs on both tests were contrasted (split around the median) to test for differences on learning variables and appreciation of conversation.

From Table 3, it can be concluded that there are no significant differences between student with high or low scores on professional beliefs on learning or their appreciation of the conversation. Correlations between student beliefs and the dependent variables were small and slightly negative (Table 4).

It was further analyzed whether student Mentoring Preferences influenced outcome variables. Mentoring preferences were analyzed on two subscales: Integrity and Relationship. These scores were related to student learning (subdivided into: Problem Understanding, Perspective Taking and Commitment to Apply) and their Appreciation of conversation.

Table 5 shows a significant difference for Relationship on appreciation of conversations ($t(10) = -2.24, P \leq .05$); i.e., to value a conversation a personal mentoring relationship needs to be established. As far as student learning is concerned, a significant difference for integrity was found on perspective taking ($t=-2.66, p \leq .05$); i.e., in order to change one's ideas one has to trust one's mentor. Correlations between student beliefs regarding preferred mentoring and their learning, and appreciation of conversation are moderate and non-significant (Table 6).

Table 3. Results with regard to the influence of student beliefs of professional learning

| | Low on rethinking | | High on rethinking | | | | Low on restructuring | | High on restructuring | | | |
	M	sd	M	sd	t df=10	p	M	sd	M	sd	t df=10	p
Appreciation	4.15	0.25	4.13	0.28	0.13	0.90	4.10	0.20	4.17	0.29	-0.44	0.67
Problem underst.	4.32	0.45	4.39	0.43	-0.26	0.80	4.50	0.44	4.23	0.41	1.07	0.31
Persp. taking	3.91	0.42	4.07	0.64	-0.53	0.61	4.14	0.59	3.84	0.38	1.10	0.30
Commitment	4.29	0.42	4.13	0.39	0.63	0.55	4.23	0.43	4.22	0.40	0.04	0.97

Table 4. Correlations between student beliefs and their learning and appreciation

	Rethinking Φ	Restructuring Φ
Appreciation	-.12	-.03
Problem understanding	-.13	-.12
Perspective taking	-.21	-.24
Commitment	-.31	.10

Table 5. Results with regard to the influence of student mentoring preference on their learning

	Low scores on integrity		High scores on integrity				Low scores on relationship		High scores on relationship			
	M	SD	M	SD	t	p	M	SD	M	SD	t	p
Appreciation	4.06	0.27	4.24	0.19	-1.13	0.23	4.08	0.22	4.44	0.08	-2.24	0.05*
Problem understanding	4.20	0.38	4.54	0.44	-1.42	0.19	4.31	0.40	4.50	0.71	-0.55	0.60
Perspective taking	3.71	0.43	4.31	0.31	-2.66	0.02*	3.90	0.50	4.29	0.20	-1.04	0.32
Commitment	4.28	0.40	4.17	0.42	0.44	0.67	4.24	0.36	4.17	0.71	0.23	0.83

* $P < .05$ $df = 10$

Table 6. Correlations between the student mentoring beliefs on appreciation and learning

	integrity	relationship
Appreciation	0.38	0.43
Problem understanding	0.32	0.49
Perspective taking	0.46	n.c.
Commitment	0.43	0.15

After having established these associations between student beliefs and dependent variables, it was studied in a subsequent analysis whether there was a relation between specific conversational moves (i.e., Review, Goal, and Plan) and student appreciation, and student learning. No significant differences were found for type of conversational moves on dependent variables, with the exception for Review moves on commitment; i.e., reflective mentor speech acts increases student commitment. ($t(9)$ = -2.43, $P \leq .05$). Table 7 shows the results for conversation moves on dependent variables.

Correlations between conversational moves and appreciation, and learning (problem understanding, perspective taking and commitment) (see Table 8) are moderate but not significant.

This analysis on moves was also conducted for typical conversational patterns in relation to dependent variables: appreciation and student learning. In Table 9 results of the t-tests are shown for the different patterns.

As Table 9 shows, a significant difference was found for reflective patterns on appreciation of conversation ($t(10)$= -3.11, $P \leq .05$). Also directing patterns show a significant difference on problem understanding ($t(10)$ = -2.32, $P \leq .05$). Furthermore, the table shows significant differences for the orienting pattern on student appreciation ($t(10$ = -2.24, $P \leq .05$), problem understanding ($t(10)$ = -2.93, $P \leq .05$), and commitment ($t(9)$= -2.58, $P \leq .05$). There is also a significant difference found for the constructive pattern on problem understanding ($t(10)$ = -2.32, $P \leq .05$).

Furthermore, student's reflection reports were rated with regard to the quality of their reflection, having following levels: low (scores 7 to 29), middle (scores 30 to 52) and high (scores 53 to 75). This rating was related to their scores on Appreciation, Memorable Events based on the interview, and their learning scores: Problem Understanding, Perspective Taking and Commitment (see Table 10).

One-way analysis of variance revealed no differences between students levels of reflection and dependent variables except for memorable events (an inverse relation was found) and perspective taking (F(2;9)=4,23; p = .05). These results probably suggest that students high in quality of reflection learned more from the mentoring conversations.

Subsequently, it was examined whether the overall footprint of a conversation was related to quality of reflection (I,e whether a mentor's approach to conversation took into account the level of a student's reflection report). It appeared that footprints did not differ with regard to quality of reflection, except for memorable events and perspective taking (Table 11).

With regard to the overall conversation's footprint, it appeared that reflective talks had the highest score on appreciation, memorable events but not on the learning outcomes. A constructive footprint was more associated with positive learning outcomes. These results probably suggest that reflective footprints had a positive influence on the students' well-being but not on their learning.

Table 7. Results for t-tests with regard to the influence of type of moves on student appreciation, problem understanding, perspective taking, and commitment (df=10)

	Low in review		High in review				Low in goal		High in goal				Low in plan		High in plan			
	M	sd	M	sd	t	p	M	sd	M	sd	t	p	M	sd	M	sd	t	p
Appreciation	4.08	0.25	4.26	0.21	−1.28	0.23	4.06	0.23	4.22	0.25	−1.19	0.26	4.09	0.27	4.24	0.18	−0.96	0.36
Problem understanding	4.21	0.37	4.63	0.43	−1.76	0.11	4.26	0.43	4.43	0.44	−0.66	0.52	4.32	0.45	4.39	0.43	−0.26	0.80
Perspective taking	3.95	0.46	4.00	0.58	−0.17	0.87	3.86	0.62	4.07	0.31	−0.76	0.47	3.86	0.45	4.18	0.54	−1.10	0.30
Commitment	4.08	0.39	4.54	0.08	−2.43	0.04*	4.23	0.28	4.22	0.50	0.05	0.96	4.21	0.43	4.21	0.39	0.11	0.91

* P < .05

Table 8. Correlations between conversations moves and appreciation and student teachers 'learning

	review	goal	plan
Appreciation	.26	.14	.11
Problem understanding	.41	.35	.41
Perspective taking	.25		
Commitment	.29		

Table 9. Results of conversation patterns on learning and appreciation of conversation (df=10)

	Low in reflective pattern**		High in reflective pattern				Low in directing		High in directing				Low in stimulating		High in stimulating			
	M	sd	M	sd	t	p	M	sd	M	sd	t	p	M	sd	M	sd	t	p
Appreciation	4.04	0.20	4.43	0.06	-3.11	0.01*	4.07	0.23	4.33	0.20	-1.71	0.12	4.11	0.26	4.22	0.24	-0.66	0.53
Problem understanding	4.32	0.42	4.43	0.52	-0.38	0.71	4.21	0.35	4.76	0.41	-2.32	0.04*	4.21	0.35	4.74	0.45	-2.12	0.05*
Perspective taking	3.95	0.50	4.00	0.52	-0.14	0.89	3.90	0.45	4.14	0.62	-0.73	0.48	3.89	0.47	4.19	0.54	-0.94	0.37
Commitment	4.21	0.38	4.28	0.54	-0.25	0.81	4.10	0.40	4.56	0.10	-1.89	0.09	4.10	0.40	4.56	0.10	-2.09	0.05*

* P < .05 **reviewing and indicating pattern combined

Table 9 (Continued)

	Low in orienting		High in orienting				Low in constructive		High in constructive			
	M	sd	M	sd	t	p	M	sd	M	sd	t	p
Appreciation	4.08	0.22	4.44	0.08	-2.24	0.05*	4.07	0.23	4.33	0.20	-1.71	0.10
Problem understanding	4.22	0.34	4.96	0.05	-2.93	0.02*	4.21	0.35	4.76	0.41	-2.32	0.04*
Perspective taking	3.89	0.49	4.36	0.10	-1.31	0.22	3.90	0.45	4.14	0.62	-0.73	0.48
Commitment	4.11	0.33	4.75	0.12	-2.58	0.03*	4.10	0.40	4.56	0.10	-1.89	0.09

* P < .05

Table 10. Mean scores on dependent variables given rating of student's quality of reflection

	quality categories in reflection reports		
	Low N=4	Middle N=3	High N=5
Appreciation	4.09	4.15	4.25
Memorable events	3.17	3.75	2.01
Problem understanding	4.35	4.34	4.36
Perspective taking	3.90	3.93	4.22
Commitment	4.22	4.13	–

Table 11. Means of dependent variables for Quality of Reflection under typical patterns

	reflective	constructive	directing pattern
Appreciation	4.39	4.11	4.06
Memorable events	6	3	1
Problem understanding	4.00	5.00	4.29
Perspective taking	4.14	4.57	4.57
Commitment	3.67	4.50	4.17

DISCUSSION

Overall some interesting findings were noted in our study on conversational moves and student learning. From our analyses the following picture emerges:

Firstly, it appeared that the student teachers' (preference) beliefs on mentoring have a significant influence on their appreciation of conversation as well their learning. It showed that relationship influences appreciation and that mentor integrity influences perspective taking. These results suggest that student's evaluation of their mentor has a positive influence on their learning in that as they value their mentor more it will enhance their learning from mentoring conversations.

Secondly, it appeared that certain patterns in conversation have a significant relation with students' appreciation of conversation. A relation between appreciation and the reflective pattern was found as well as for the constructive pattern and student appreciation. These results probably suggest that the reflective and constructive moves are associated with the students' well-being.

Thirdly, it appeared that certain conversational patterns in mentoring have a relation with student learning. First, a relation was found between appreciation and the reflective pattern. Second, a positive relation was found for problem understanding and commitment with the directing pattern. Third, it appeared that this is the case

175

for the stimulating pattern as well. Fourth, the orienting pattern is associated with almost all outcome variables in a positive way, which is more or less the case also for the constructive pattern. These results suggest that typical conversational patterns may influence students' learning to different degree and suggest that conversational moves have a differential effect in the exchange between a mentor and a mentee. This is typically the case for the orienting, reflective and directing patterns (i.e, Table 2).

This study highlights the following outcomes on mentoring conversations: With regard to the influence of students' beliefs on professional learning, we found that student high on integrity prefer a constructive pattern, and that a positive valuing of a mentor is associated with students learning from conversations. Looking at the impact of conversational moves on learning we found, firstly, that frequency of conversational moves per se is not so much relevant, but instead the overall pattern used: all patterns have a positive impact on appreciation of the talk; mainly the reflective and directing patterns were most appreciated by students. Secondly, the orienting and constructive pattern have a (however, small) influence on learning of students. Student probably will learn more from conversations when their mentors use "climbing the mountain" moves during the conversation. Thirdly, the conversational move: review is dominant in a conversation's footprint; goal oriented speech acts are small in number, however (which actually speaks against a 'climbing the mountain" orientation).

This leads us to conclude that in the conversations we studied mentoring can be characterized as: oriented towards appreciated talk by mainly reviewing and reflecting upon past performance. Patterns in conversation that are related to learning were not often used. But there are marked differences between the conversations we studied, meaning that mentors can take different approaches to the talk they have with their mentees.

IMPLICATIONS

Analyzing mentoring conversations, such as in the approach we took, i.e., by gauging speech acts of the mentor and displaying them as moves and patterns of a conversation, has a number of benefits. A benefit related to learning of mentees is the awareness that a conversation can be analyzed and reconstructed with regard to the steps and directions taken during discourse, based on the assurance that a mentor may have selected question strategies with a deliberate choice in mind on the specific moves and patterns to be used. In this manner the level of quality of a conversation can be raised. This may work both ways: in evaluating as well as designing a talk. In as far as the mentee is concerned, raising the level of conversation may increase confidence and add to improved self-reflection (Hobson et al., 2009) in order to "climb the mountain' that is, to build further on current proficiency levels and change them for the better.

A main benefit of analyzing conversation lies directly on part of the mentor in that it may add to the mentor's professional development. Mentoring conversations can be carefully reviewed and planned as to its flow and process. As a review the tool provides feedback on successful or unproductive, (non-challenging) parts of the conversation; as a plan, it may help to select the relevant patterns of speech for the mentee (for instance based on reviewing a reflection report in advance). In our study we did examine the course of individual conversations at a specific level (i.e, the flow of moves) and revealed a detailed account of the mentor's actions – as such it is of importance to feedback to the mentor to see if intentions have been met.

A point of interest is the possibility of using a conversational analysis of mentoring talk for joint (peer based) assessment of a conversation to see how well it met expectations and, possibly, have another look at the talk from another person('s) perspective.

Based on the exit interviews we held, mentors' involvement in analysing mentoring talk (Hobson et al., 2009) may have enhanced their development of 'new ideas' and led to 'new perspectives' on their mentoring. More specifically, mentors indicated they became aware of improved mentoring styles and strategies as a result of analysing their talk, so as to improve their communication skills, and become more self-reflective in supporting mentees. Secondly, it appeared that our mentors felt reassured in having 'validated' ideas communicated to their learners (Franson, 2004). Furthermore, they felt less isolated in the approach they took during conversation because of knowing the footprint of their talk that could be communicated to and shared with other colleagues.

The attention given to mentoring conversation during the period of study and the mentors' collaboration with research was experienced as enjoyable, and increased confidence in their own mentoring. Mentors returned back afterwards that students judged their mentoring to be 'more demanding' and 'more tolerant'. The focus on conversation made the mentors take more pride in their mentoring, especially while noticing that their mentees succeeded and progressed in learning, which was made possible through the evidence mentors drew from the analyses. According to some mentors mentoring has achieved that 'their enthusiasm for teaching has been revitalised' they have become 're-energised' or 're-engaged' with the profession and are more committed to teaching. Finally, from our study it appears that involvement in mentoring has aided mentors in identifying their strengths and priorities.

REFERENCES

Alebregtse, M. (2008). *De invloed van persoonlijkheid en de aard van de mentorrelatie op effectiviteit van mentoring* (Master's thesis). Universiteit Utrecht, The Netherlands. Retrieved from http://dspace.library.uu.nl/handle/1874/30671

Baker, A. C., Jensen, P. J., & Kolb, D. A. (2005). *Conversational learning: An experiential approach to knowledge creation.* Los Angeles, CA: Sage Publishing

Ciga Tellechea, E. (2012, June). *Aprendizaje auto regulado y desarollo professional* {self regulated learning and professional development} (Doctoral dissertation). University of Salamanca, Spain.

Clouston, T. J. (2007). Exploring methods of analysing talk in problem-based learning tutorials. *Journal of Further and Higher Education, 31*(2), 183–193.

Clutterbuck, D., & Megginson, D. (2004). *Techniques for coaching and mentoring.* Amsterdam: Elsevier.

Crasborn, F. J. A. J., & Hennissen, P. P. M. (2010). *The skilled mentor. Mentor teachers' use and acquisition of supervisory skills* (Unpublished doctoral dissertation). Eindhoven, University of Technology Library, The Netherlands.

D'Abate, C. P., & Eddy, E. R. (2008). Mentoring as a learning tool: Enhancing the effectiveness of an undergraduate business mentoring program. *Mentoring & Tutoring: Partnership in Learning, 16*(4), 363–378.

Darling-Hammond, L. (2003). Keeping good teachers: Why it matters, what leaders can do. *Educational Leadership, 60*(8), 6–13

Day, C. (1999). *Developing teachers; the challenges if life long learning.* London: Falmer press.

Edwards, A. (2010). *Being an expert professional practitioner the relational turn in expertise professional and practice-based learning* (Vol. 3). New York, NY: Springer Publishers.

Edwards, A., & Protheroe, L (2003). Teaching by proxy: Understanding how mentors are positioned in partnerships. *Oxford Review of Education, 30*(2), 183–197

Ericsson, K. A. (2002). The path to expert golf performance: Insights from the masters on how to improve performance by deliberate practice. In P. R. Thomas (Ed.), *Optimising performance in golf* (pp. 1–57). Brisbane, Australia: Australian Academic Press.

Ericsson, K. A., Prietula, M. J., & Cokely, M. T. (2007). The making of an expert. *Harvard Business Review, 85*(7/8), 114–121.

Feiman Nemser, S., & Carver, C. (2009). *Creasting conditions for serious mentoring; implications for policy making.* Washington, DC: NSSE yearbook.

Franson, K. (2010). Mentors assessing mentees? An overview and analyses of the mentorship role concerning newly qualified teachers. *European Journal of Teacher Education, 33*(4), 375–390

Grossman, P. (2006). Research on pedagogical approaches in teacher Education. In M. Cochran Smith & K. Zeichner (Eds.), *Studying teacher education: Report of the AERA panel on research and teacher education* (pp. 425–477). Mahwah, NJ: Lawrence Erlbaum

Hobson, A. J., Ashby, P., Malderez, A., & Tomlinson, P. D. (2009). Mentoring beginning teachers: What we know and what we don't. *Teaching and Teacher Education, 25*, 207–216.

Instrumentenboek Mentorgesprekken, een onderzoek naar de rol van kennis in leraar-leerling interacties (n.d.). Onderwijskunde. Universiteit Leiden.

Johnson, S. M., Berg, J. H., & Donaldson, M. L. (2005). *Who stays in teaching and why: A review of the literature on teacher retention.* Cambridge, MA: Harvard Graduate School of Education. Retrieved June 4, 2013 from http://assets.aarp.org/www.aarp.org_/articles/NRTA/Harvard_report.pdf

Kwan, T., & Lopez-Real, F. (2005). Mentors' perceptions of their roles in mentoring student teachers. *Asia-Pacific Journal of Teacher Education, 33*(3), 275–287.

Lopez-Real, F., & Kwan, T. (2005). Mentors' perceptions of their own professional development during mentoring. *Journal of Education for Teaching: International Research and Pedagogy, 31*(1), 15–24.

Magano, M. D., Mostert P., & van der Westhuizen, G. (2010). *Learning conversations the value of interactive learning.* Johannesburg, South Africa: Heinemann Publishers.

Malderez, A., Hobson, A. J., Tracey, L., & Kerr, K. (2007). Becoming a student teacher: Core features of the experience. *European Journal of Teacher Education, 30*(3), 225–248.

Mena Marcos, G. I., & Tillema, H. (2012). Student teacher reflective writing, what does it reveal? *European Journal of Teacher Education, 4*, 1–17.

Mena Marcos, J., & Tillema, H. H. (2006). Studying studies on teacher reflection and action: An appraisal of research contributions. *Educational Research Review, 1*(2), 112–132.

Moore D. S., & McCabe, P. (2003). *Practice of business statistics: Using data for decisions.* Los Angeles, CA: Sage.

Moore, D. S., & McCabe, G. P. (2003). *Introduction to the practice of statistics* (4th ed.). New York, NY: WH Freeman & Co.

Núñez, J. C., Rosário, P., Vallejo, G., & González-Pienda, J. A. (2013). A longitudinal assessment of the effectiveness of a school-based mentoring program in middle school. *Contemporary Educational Psychology, 38*, 11–21.

Orland-Barak, L. (2002). What's in a case?: What mentors' cases reveal about the practice of mentoring. *Journal of Curriculum Studies, 34*(4), 451–468.

Orland-Barak, L., & Tillema H. H. (2006). Collaborative knowledge construction; the dark side of the moon. *Teachers & Teaching, 12*(1), 1–12.

Rose, G. L. (2003). Enhancement of mentor selection using the ideal mentor scale. *Research in Higher Education, 44*(4), 45–56.

Sadler, R. D. (2010). Indeterminacy in the use of preset criteria for assessment in grading in higher education. *Assessment and Evaluation in Higher Education, 34*, 159–79.

Seedhouse, P. (2004). Different perspectives on language classroom interaction. *A Journal of Research in Language Studies, 54*, 55–100.

Shore, W. J., Toyokawa, T., & Anderson, D. D. (2008). Context-specific effects on reciprocity in mentoring relationships: Ethical implications. *Mentoring*, (1), 17–29.

Shulman, L. S. (1999, July/August). Taking learning seriously. *Change, 31*(4), 10–17.

Tillema, H. H. (2007). Authenticity in knowledge productive learning of teams. In E. Munthe & M. Zellermayer (Eds.), *Teachers learning in communities, international perspectives* (pp. 27–45). Rotterdam: Sense Publishers. ISBN 978-90-8790-176-9

Tillema, H. H. (2011). Looking into mirrors: Teacher educators' dilemmas in constructing pedagogical understanding about their teaching. In J. Brownlee, G. Schraw, & D. Berthelsen (Eds.), *Personal epistemology and teacher education* (pp. 40–54). London: Routledge.

Tillema, H. (2013). Student involvement in assessment of their learning. In C. Wyatt Smith, V. Klenowski, & P. Collins (Eds.), *Designing assessment for quality learning* (pp. 37–52). London: Springer.

Tillema, H. H., & Smith, K. (2007). Portfolio assessment, in search of criteria. *Teaching & Teacher Education, 23*(4), 442–456

Tillema, H. H., & Van der Westhuizen, G. (2013). Mentoring conversations and student teacher learning. *South African Journal of Higher Education, 27*(5), 1305–1323.

Vocht, A. de (2009). *Basishandboek SPSS 17.* Utrecht: Bijleveld Press.

Wang, W., & Odell, S. J. (2002). Mentored learning to teach according to standards-based reform: A critical review. *Review of Educational Research, 72*(3), 481–546.

Whitmore, J. (2002). *Coaching for performance.* London: Brealy.

Zimmerman, B. J., & Schunk, D. H. (2001). *Self-regulated learning and academic achievement theoretical perspectives* (2nd ed.). Mahwah, NJ: Lawrence Erlbaum Associates.

Guido van Esch
Leiden University, The Netherlands

Harm Tillema
Leiden University, The Netherlands

ANNATJIE J. M. PRETORIUS AND GERT J. VAN DER WESTHUIZEN

9. SPACE MAKING IN MENTORING CONVERSATIONS

INTRODUCTION

Mentoring conversations involve differences in knowledge and expertise which are often significant. In their review of literature on the role of knowledge in conversations, Stivers, Mondala and Steensig (2011) noted how participants use their 'epistemic authority' (Heritage & Raymond, 2005), to guide a conversation. Because the mentor has epistemic authority in a conversation with a mentee,this epistemic status and epistemic authority could inhibit the co-construction of knowledge due to the social and institutional rules or norms which govern mentoring conversations.

This chapter is concerned with the issue of space for learning in mentoring interactions, i.e. the opportunity for the mentee to participate and contribute to knowledge construction. This would involve the mentor playing downplaying her role in offering knowledge ideas, and allowing the mentee to'take the chair', a phrase borrowed from Goffman (2007:221). This could disregard the social and institutional norms of mentoring and conversing. In pedagogical context, however, the mentor's holding back and refraining from expressing her knowledge views (i.e. epistemic authority), does not mean that she compromises her authority. It is merely a matter of allowing and making the conversational space in which the mentee could explore her own views. The argument here is that a professor of teacher education, for example, may, in a mentoring situation, keep quiet and/or do her talking in ways that, on a level of social interaction and conversation, be accepted as puzzling, while the pedagogical intention is to create space and invite the mentee to present her own thoughts. Because the mentor is assumed to be the knowledgeable person, with knowledge authority, the challenge lies with him/her to create space for learning and exploration (Baker, Jensen & Kolb, 2002).

This chapter is about mentoring interactions which are knowledge productive, i.e. interactions which involve the construction of meaningful conceptual artefacts in student teacher mentoring (Pretorius, 2013). The focus here is on *how* mentors create space for knowledge productive learning, i.e. learning aimed at knowledge on the topic of the interaction (Tillema & Van der Westhuizen, 2003). This study explored the notion of 'ostensible uncertainty' as a conversational strategy to create the mental freedom and space for mentees to enter into the knowledge construction process in conversations. It explores ostensible uncertainty in a mentoring conversation in terms of what Clark (1996:378) refer to as *'ostensible, communicative acts'*. Such

H. Tillema et al. (Eds.), Mentoring for Learning, 181–198.

acts are pretended and they conceal that the mentor is not really uncertain about the topic of discussion, but show uncertainty so as to invite the mentee to think more and respond.

The problem focus of this inquiry is the mediating role of the mentor, and the strategies that are involved in creating space for learning and the co-construction of knowledge between mentor and student teacher. The assumption is that learning is enhanced in what Baker, Jensen and Kolb (2002:62, 64) calls 'hospitable space' or 'receptive space'. Our purpose is to explore what is involved in space-making in mentoring, and how a mentor uses uncertainty as a strategy to allow the mentee to take part in knowledge construction. We assume that there could be various strategies which would contribute to the creation of a safe conversational space for mentees in interactional learning, such as justified compliments, but the scope of this study only covers the element of uncertainty as a space making agent.

The study considered questions about the differences/asymmetries in knowledge between mentor and mentee, and the creation of space for co-construction of knowledge. The main question asked: How can a mentor get a novice to co-construct knowledge despite vast differences in their current knowledge and experience? The inductive nature of the study allowed the following sub-question to contribute an answer: Can ostensible uncertainty be used to contribute to a 'hospitable space' for co-construction of knowledge?

It is important to note that before this study was conducted, the data set used here had already been identified by Pretorius (2013) in a parallel study (see Chapter... in this book), as a conversation in which meaningful learning had been achieved by co-construction of knowledge. This study thus took a conversation in which co-construction of knowledge had already been identified as a vantage point and explored ostensible uncertainty as a facilitating strategy.

THEORETICAL PERSPECTIVES

The mentoring interaction, as a face-to-face interaction between lecturers and student teachers may be conceived of, in Goffman's (2007:219) terms, as *'focussed interaction'* in which people effectively agree to sustain focus, such as learning about teaching, for a period of time.

In mentoring conversations, the mentor assumes 'epistemic authority', i.e. a stance of being more knowledgeable (Heritage & Raymond, 2005; Heritage, 2012; see also Stivers et al., 2011). The mentor usually determines the format and topics of the conversation (Strong & Baron, 2004:53, see Gerretzen, 2012:4). In the quest for collaborative knowledge construction, the mentor inevitably has to surrender some of his authority in order to make space for the mentee to contribute towards knowledge construction – an idea shared with Baker et al. (2002). In pedagogical terms, however, the mentor's refraining from expression of his epistemic authority does not mean that he compromises his role. It is, as mentioned earlier, merely a matter of allowing and making the conversational space in which the mentee could explore. In the process, the mentee finds her own 'voice' (Mkhize et al., 2004:5–14), which relates to the Bakhtinian idea of 'ideological becoming' (Rule, 2006). This notion will be explored in more detail in the next section.

Magano, Mostert & van der Westhuizen (2010:11) highlight the benefits of learning conversations in an idealistic way. They postulate that roles are not fixed in learning conversations. Where there is an atmosphere of trust, openness and collaboration facilitates learning in the conversation. Learning conversations provide a safe atmosphere for learners to make attempts to learn and to pursuit and investigate new ideas or meaning. Participants are made curious and challenged to reach higher levels of development (Magano et al., 2010). Their description of the benefits of interactional learning, as set out above, is without doubt the ideal, but Stivers et al. (2011) reveal complex dynamics, such as the social norms behind epistemic access and epistemic primacy shaping conversations in very specific ways. In this regard, Stivers et al. (2011:3, 8) refer to 'knowledge asymmetries' or 'epistemic asymmetries' (see also Pomerantz, 1980) in social interaction and mention that such asymmetries are transparent in lay-professional contexts. In interactional learning encounters, such as mentoring conversations, knowledge asymmetries form a significant part of the dynamics in the conversation (Pomerantz, 1980). Epistemic primacy, i.e., the authoritative stance or position of the speaker is governed by social norms, as summarised by Stivers et al. (2011:14), see also (Heritage & Raymond, 2005), as that a speaker may only make assertions if she has sufficient knowledge and if she has the right to do so. Further, a speaker with more in-depth knowledge has primary rights to make assertions and assessments in the relevant domain given her epistemic authority. This would for example be the situation in a case where a professor of teacher education uses what she knows to lead the conversation, assesses what the student knows, and shares her views about the topic of mentoring.

Stivers et al. (2011:10) also highlight asymmetries relating to epistemic access, which is about access to knowledge. In conversation, it is a social norm that a speaker should not make claims for which he/she does not have a sufficient degree of access (Heritage, 2005; Stivers et al., 2011). Given the epistemic asymmetries, i.e. differences in knowledge content in a mentor-mentee conversation, the interlocutors would have to disregard the social norms underlying epistemic access and primacy if the mentee is to take part in knowledge construction, despite her position of not having epistemic authority. When the mentor allows the mentee to 'take the chair' while he allows himself to play a minor role, (Goffman, 2007:22), it does not mean that the mentor compromises on his epistemic authority or -primacy. It is a matter of deliberately allowing some space in which the mentee could explore.

When space is created, 'short-sightedness' and 'tunnel vision' are prevented (Magano et al., 2010). This short-sightedness and tunnel vision could occur when the mentor abuses his epistemic authority as a position from which to dominate instead of leading by carefully and tactfully allowing the mentee to 'take the chair', as Goffman (2007:221) suggested, or in context of this discussion, one could say the mentee, at least temporarily, takes the epistemic chair. The mentee, after all, has epistemic access to her own experiences in teaching practice, as in the case study referred to in this paper. The mentee in this study, for example, experienced first-hand during her teaching practicum how discipline was handled and spelling was taught at a school in a community with certain social challenges. The mentor, who is a university professor with many years of teaching experience himself, did not experience the needs and challenges of this particular school on a day-to day basis. For this reason, in order to make the transition from theory to practice in a meaningful way, the mentee should be not only allowed, but invited to take part in the process of situated knowledge construction. The question is thus not *whether* it is necessary to create space for the mentee in the knowledge construction, but rather *how* this space could be created in a scenario where the epistemic asymmetries are so prominent that it is the very reason for the conversation, and not forgetting the social norms governing the conversation.

While Magano et al. (2010:26) touch on the idea that participants in learning conversations need 'room to move' mentally and physically, Baker et al. (2002:64) postulate that space making in learning conversations can be facilitated in many different dimensions, such as *temporal space*, in which time is set apart for the conversation, *physical space,* which refers to the physical placement of the participants and *emotional space* which is constructed through receptive listening. In their view the receptive space 'holds the conversation'. This chapter takes particular interest in the creation of *mental space* (Magano et al. 2010:26) in which the mentee has room to explore ideas and to find a 'voice' (Mkhize, 2004:5–14; 5–15; Rule, 2006:96).

Baker et al. (2002:53, 62–64) explore five dialectics, by which they say, conversational learning is guided and sustained. One of these dialectics is '*status*' and '*solidarity*' which '*shape the social realm of conversation*' (Baker et al., 2002:53). They cite Schwitzgabel and Kolb (1974), (see Baker et al., 2002:62) who worked with the notion of relationships among human beings as "*a two dimensional, interpersonal space of status and solidarity*". *Status* is explained to be an individual's positioning or ranking in a group (Baker et al., 2002), or in a conversation in this case. This relates to the already mentioned notion of 'epistemic authority' (Heritage & Raymond, 2005; Heritage, 2013) in a learning conversation. In this case study, status translates to the positioning of the mentor due to his vast knowledge and experience. *Solidarity,* on the other hand, refers to the extent of interpersonal linkage with others in a network of relationships (Baker et al., 2002). It is this interplay which will ultimately define and create a hospitable space which is conducive to conversational learning (Baker, 2002). Baker et al. (2002), postulate that both status and solidarity are necessary to sustain conversation. Further, status, which in this study relates to 'epistemic authority', is necessary because, without status or authority, which allow one participant to take initiative or lead, the conversation can 'lose direction' (Baker, 2002:62). They also caution that if any pole in this dialectic is dominating, it could impede or cease learning in the conversation (Baker et al., 2002:62). The mentor's position of status could thus be a guiding element in the learning interaction. On the other hand however, without solidarity, where mentor and mentee form linkages with each other, the conversation can lose the sense of connection and relevance, as explained by Baker et al. (2002:62), because the conversation will not benefit from the perspectives and diverse expertise of each person. Thus, the input of the mentee, who holds epistemic authority and access over her own experiences in teaching practice, contributes to keeping the knowledge which is constructed in the conversation, connected to her own practice, which ensures relevance.

In this study, tension is created by the discrepancy in knowledge and experience of the mentor and mentee. Considering that the mentee is expected to collaborate in knowledge construction, the tension lies within the unequal status which is socially very natural here. If the mentor is perceived to be the dominant and authoritative source of knowledge, this could result in traditional learning in which the mentee remains dependant on the mentor for one-way knowledge transfer. The focus of the study is to explore how space-making occurs in mentoring conversations in order for the mentee to contribute to knowledge construction, despite the dialectic tension. The mentor's conversational strategy of handling the boundaries of status is expected to facilitate the conceptual contributions of the mentee in the interactional learning.

The purpose of mentoring conversations with student teachers, as in this case study, is to guide the mentee towards *'higher teaching proficiency'* (Gerretzen, 2012; Tillema & Van der Westhuizen, 2013). From the work of Baker et al. (2002) it is inferred that successful mentoring conversations require a balance within the status-solidarity dialectic. In mentoring conversations, the *'temporary inequality'* (Miller, 1986, cited in Baker, 2002:63) should gradually be replaced by a balance in the status-solidarity dialectic between mentor and mentee. In a relationship where the in equality is seen as temporary, the mentor will assist the mentee to develop (Baker, 2002:63). The development, from unequal to equal status is the primary purpose of the mentoring interaction. The ultimate goal of this type of relationship is thus to even out the epistemic in equality (inferred from Miller, 1986, cited in Baker, 2002).

While acknowledging the in equality, it is to be noted too, that the mentee does not enter the learning conversation without any epistemic authority at all. The mentor cannot claim sovereign expertise. In this case study, where the mentee just completed an eight week teaching practicum, she is, to a certain extent at least, knowledgeable on the day-to-day running of the school she visited and on the specific issues and challenges which the school faces. The student thus has some contextual knowledge of the school and learners which she taught during her practicum. So, while the mentor might be in a position of status or epistemic authority on sound pedagogical practices in general, it is assumed that the student teacher is, to some degree, in a position of status or epistemic authority, as far as the appropriation of the knowledge in the specific socio-cultural setting in which she practiced is concerned.

It seems crucial for mentors to firstly understand and embrace the temporary nature of their authoritative status in the conversation and secondly, to be knowledgeable about strategies which they can adopt in order to allow and create the necessary space in which their mentees can find a '*voice*' (Mkhize, 2004:5–14 – 5–15; Rule, 2006:96) and co-construct knowledge. The creation of 'ostensible uncertainty' in the conversation is proposed to be one such strategy.

OSTENSIBLE UNCERTAINTY

In this study, the notion of 'ostensible uncertainty' is explored as a space making strategy in mentoring conversations. Clark (1996:378–383) postulates that '*ostensible communicative acts*' such as ostensible invitations, greetings, congratulations and apologies are not just rituals but instead, are '*subtle and effective tools*'. This study identified and explored the use of uncertainty as such a tool in mentoring conversations. We refer to uncertainty as displayed in this study as *ostensible* because the mentor, a professor in education, had, as implied by his curriculum vitae, more knowledge about the topics than he revealed and that his uncertainty was not authentic. Given the context of mentoring, we postulate that mentors can use this strategy in order to create what is noted in Baker et al. (2002) as 'hospitable space' in a learning conversation. The possibility will be explored in this chapter and illustrated by conversation samples of mentoring interactions.

The review thus far clarified the interactional nature of learning, outlined in terms of complex dynamics of epistemic primacy in a learning conversation and highlighting the importance of space making in mentoring.Our empirical inquiry is built around the question: How can hospitable mental space be created in a mentoring conversation which is marked by differences in epistemic status?

THE STUDY

Purpose and Design

This qualitative study is an analysis of space making in a mentoring conversation – how a mentor created space to enhance learning. The purpose is to explore how space is created and used as a strategy to balance the status-solidarity polarization, as indicated in the work of Baker et al. (2002), in an interactive learning conversation.

A video recorded mentoring conversation was transcribed. It was first noticed that the mentor's utterances in this conversation often displayed uncertainty. Conversation analysis followed in order to find what effect the expression of uncertainty had on the conversation.The analysis was done by looking at speech turns in pairs, which is explained in more detail later on. At first, the analysis was paper based, using a hard copy of the transcription. In order to better manage the analysis, a trial version of Atlas.ti was used and this proved to be a more effective tool in the analysis which could be used in subsequent studies with more data. The software proved to be of particular value when the expression of uncertainty was categorised into various types.

Participants in this single case study involved an experienced staff member (lecturer) in teacher education and final year student teacher.

Two factors rendered the conversation between these participants particularly suitable for this study: a) the significant difference in academic and professional background and experience of the two participants and b) the evidence of collaboration and co-construction of knowledge in their conversation despite the difference mentioned in (a).

Data and Analysis

The data collection involved the mentoring session being conducted in the office of the mentor. The office furniture in this particular office is arranged in such a way that there is a designated physical space for conversation. The mentor's personal work station faces the window while a round table and four chairs provide a practical space for meetings and discussions. The mentor's sensitivity to conversational dimensions is subtly but clearly depicted, not only in the physical arrangement of space, but also in various multi-cultural artefacts which are displayed in the office, such as a small hand-carved wooden ornament in the centre of the round table. The ornament depicts tribal figurines who are sitting in a circle, having a conversation. The office thus displays an element of openness on the mentor's side. However, like all the other office doors along the corridor, a name plate indicates the office number with the occupant's title and surname. The title of *Professor* on the name plate implies a substantial contribution to academia. With this contextual setting as backdrop for the conversation, it is to be considered that, even if the mentee would be unaware of the detail of her mentor's professional and academic achievements, and even if she feels welcomed by the physical arrangement of furniture and artefacts, his title indicates substantial knowledge and experience which could be an intimidating factor in her contribution to the conversation, given her relatively limited knowledge and experience as a student teacher. The very practical and essential office name plate further indicates the occupant's epistemic status in a covert way. It is a symbol of status that the mentee encountered before she entered his office. Thus, although the mentor created a very hospitable physical space for all his conversations by the furniture arrangement and cultural artefacts (physical space), the mentee cannot miss the clues which indicate that he is a seasoned and accomplished academic (epistemic authority). Without any dialogic display thereof, the mere physical surroundings display indications of the mentor's epistemic authority.

Data analysis included conversation analysis methods following the analytic principles mentioned in the studies of Edwards (1993), Nakamura (2008) and others. Conversation analysis (CA) was steered by the question: 'What does the talk do?' (based on Edwards, 1993).

For CA purposes, speech turns were paired by using a mentor's turn as the first half of the unit of analysis and the mentee's response as the second half of the unit.

Thus, each unit of analysis consisted of a mentor utterance, followed by a mentee response. Fifty one sequences of utterances were identified. Five of these units of analysis were coded as O, which means that it was not focused on the topic of the mentoring interaction. The remaining 46 identified sequences were coded in terms of the sequence patterns.

The units of analysis (paired speech turns) were categorised in terms of the mentor's expression of certainty or uncertainty and the mentee's subsequent responses.

Each sequences of paired speech turns was assigned to one of four categories, as inductively created from the data:

Sequence pattern A – Ostensible uncertainty appears in the mentor's utterance and it is followed by uncertainty in the mentee's response.

Sequence pattern B – No signs of uncertainty appear in the mentor's utterance which is followed by no uncertainty in the mentee's response.

Sequence pattern C– Exceptions to the patterns in categories A and B.

O sequences – These sequences was labelled 'other'. It contained talk which was not directly linked to the focus of the mentoring conversation and is thus not of relevance for this study.

In a parallel study (Pretorius, 2013), which also included this data set, it was found that this particular conversation has produced meaningful and significant learning. The analysis of the same data set in this study revealed the role of the spatial dimensions in the construction of knowledge. The mentee's response utterances suggest that a safe space or 'hospitable conversational space' (Baker et al., 2002) was created in which conversational learning took place, despite the potential polarization in the dialectic of status-solidarity, due to the vast difference in knowledge and experience between the two conversational partners. What the study revealed, was how the mentor facilitated the student's participation.

The data analysis was guided by the following leading questions:

• How can a mentor get a novice to co-construct knowledge despite vast differences in their current knowledge and experience?
• Can ostensible uncertainty be used to contribute to a 'hospitable space' for co-construction of knowledge?

Findings

What was of central interest in the analysis is the space the mentor's talk seemed to create for the mentee in which she could participate, explore and collaborate in knowledge construction. On single speech turn level, this seemed to be done by the following forms of expression of uncertainty which were evident in the data, as will be illustrated in conversation samples 1 to 5 below, and explained there after: (L= lecturer and S=student).

Conversation sample 1

37 38	S	=Sit and copy:: so:: that's why that (.) troubled <u>me::</u> feeling that (2) maybe she needed to interact with them <u>mo::re</u> (.) so. °ja.° -
39 40	L	So what would be ↑<u>be</u>↓tte::r than just sit and- eh- eh- sit and ah- ah-copying notes from the bo::ard?
41 42 43 44 45	S	°Uhm° (.) I feel that (1)<u>maybe</u>>↑even if she<↑<u>di::d</u> write all those notes↑(2) maybe be more inter<u>active</u> with the::m and trying to <u>teach</u> them what's going o::n >because< even when she <u>did</u> stand up it was "Oh this is what's on the ↓bo↑::a::rd, okay-" >you know< feeling that she should <u>interact</u> with them <u>mo::re</u>- try to get them invo::lved (.)>You know <it's more like a free (.) period
46	L	So it's not ha::rd wo::rk to sit an::: ah copy no::tes
47	S	No not at a::ll
48 49 50 51 52 53	L	Jah:::Its also::-its also::-ah(.)ahm:: (1) maybe ah establishing some kind of ah. relationship wher::e (.) you don't have to <u>work</u> hard, you can just come here and make ↑no::tes (.)Ah.and I think you're ri::ght ↑(.) the ah. the alternative is to be much more interactive a::h and ahm. to let the ↑learning happen ↑in the interaction (.)and then where would the ah. note taking ↓fit (1) into such interactions(2) ahm. would you say.?

Conversation sample 2

82 83	L	Okay. What about writing (.) ah.notes ↑<u>while</u> (.)ah.the lesson's going °↓on::?°

Conversation sample 3

136 137 138	S	I think what troubles me is the schoo::l where <u>I</u> came from:: reading was ↑never a problem but (2) the school experience <u>taught</u> me that (2) I ↑can't just assume (2) all grade tens can rea::d.
139 140	L	So what would you advi::se the:: teachers in that school:: (.) to do about reading- >the Life Orientation teachers<?
141 142 143 144 145 146	S	I think (1)ma::ybe::>especially what we were talking about<ahm (.)en↑couraging the learners to read 'cause it's not just something that (.) they did do(.) ahm- ↑asking them more <u>questions</u> about what it <u>is</u> that they read – Ahm what was ↑<u>difficult</u> while reading this for you? How can I <u>help</u> you:: to under↑stand it better? Ahm- >you know< asking them those kinds of questions that (.)they can think about (.) Why can't I read?
147 148	L	And also <u>teach</u> them the skill::s (.) to distinguish- to understand the main idea:: and to summari:::::ze and those kinds of things.
149	S	Yes that's very important.

Conversations sample 4

160	L	Was…was..<u>that</u> an opportunity where ah…ah…ah::m:: where you
161		had to do ↑discipline with the learners? Ah::that was interesting (.)
162		ah in your ↑notes her::e (.) tell me about that↑.

Conversation sample 5

192	L	Well::you're saying that there should be a more positive response
193		and I agree with that. I think ah::it is more <u>constructive</u>> you
194		know < (.) to work out the discipline (.) ahin class in a <u>different</u> way=
195	S	Ye::s
196	L	=ah-ah- ↑<u>rather</u> than being ah:: (1) punitive. Its better to ahm (.)
197		try to be more constructive and have other ways of establishing (1) ahthediscipline- yah:: yah::
198	S	°Yes°
199	L	Ahm.youahm ((clearing throat)) also ah.made one… you
200		referred in your notes to a method of spelling tests (.) ah:::::m ah:: let's ah:: talk about that please↑.
201	S	So that was mainly in the English class that they did the spelling
202		test was on a Friday. They'd look at what they di::d and then (.)
203		they'd also do spelling tests on (.)↑work that they did.
204	L	Yes
205	S	Ahm-
206	L	What were your thoughts about ↑tha::t(1) as a (.) ↑method?
207	S	So I ↑think I had mixed emotions >actually about it<ah::m…
208		because it's::there was a child particularly in the class- he'd
209		really get like ↑<u>one</u> out of twenty every time (1) and the boys would tease him about it.

Conversation sample 5

224	L	So but you're also saying it's ↑<u>not</u> just the ↑<u>spelling</u> its also
225		spelling words that you ↑kno:::w >or that you can <↑get to kno::w
226		and then <u>using</u> the words in- in different ah::settings::.
227	S	Yes
228	L	So you want to go <u>beyond</u> the spelling part (1)>and ah.I agree
229		with you I think< language learning is about <u>communication::</u> not so?
230	S	Ye::s

Expression of uncertainty:

- *Non-linguistic indicators of uncertainty*

This group includes non-linguistic utterances which indicate uncertainty. These could include non-words, for example, "Uhm" or "ah" which indicates thinking or wondering about something (For example, lines 48–53).

- *Broken speech*

This group indicates sentences which are self-interrupted. It is often interrupted by repetition of parts of the sentence, or a pause of one second or more in the flow of the utterance (For example, lines 160–162).

- *Words of uncertainty*

This includes words which relates directly to uncertainty, such as "maybe" or "kind of", etc. (For example, lines 48, 50, 192,193).

- *Pretended ignorance*

This is any utterance in which the mentor seems to withhold knowledge deliberately or pretend not to have the answer to the question, despite his knowledge status or his epistemic authority over the particular domain (For example, lines 39–40, 52–53).

- *Disguising knowledge as a question/suggestion*

Instead of prescribing to the mentee, the mentor turns the statement into a question or a suggestion in order to keep it open for discussion (For example, lines 82, 228–229).

- *Re-phrasing – acknowledging by apparent 'clarification'*

The re-phrasing seems to clarify uncertainty but instead, it seems from the context that he is actually acknowledging the mentee's contribution or seems to use it as a basis to subtly expand the mentee's conceptualization (For example, lines 224–228).

- *Asking for the student's opinion/advice/suggestions*

Talk in which the mentor openly encourages the mentee to express her own views. This is seen as a form of ostensible uncertainty because the mentor withholds his knowledge and creates the impression that there is more that he wants to learn from the mentee (Lines 39–40; 52–53; 139–140).

- *Pretending to think/explore*

Where the mentor or mentee indicates thinking before or during answering (Line 82).

The above forms of expression of uncertainty in itself indicates conversational strategies which the mentor used to create the hospitable conversational learning space on an utterance level.

On the level of utterance pairs or sequences, analysis yielded certain sequence patterns. Table 1 provides a description of each pattern as well as a summary of the data analysis.

Table 1. Frequency of sequences by sequence pattern

Sequence pattern A	Sequence pattern B	Sequence pattern C
Ostensible uncertainty appears in the mentor's utterance and it is followed by uncertainty in the mentee's response	No signs of uncertainty appears in the mentor's utterance which is followed by no uncertainty in the mentee's response	Exceptions to the patterns in types A and B
24 units	15 units	7 units
52%	33%	15%

Table 1 indicates that 52% of the identified sequences reflected a reciprocal pattern (Sequence pattern A) where the mentor's expression of what seemed to be ostensible uncertainty was followed by expression of uncertainty by the mentee (Lines 39–45 provide an example). By definition, these were the sequences which created conversational space for the student to test her ideas, as will be discussed later. The opposite pattern (B) made up 33% of the units of analysis, which indicate that when the mentor spoke in direct and to-the-point-sentences without creating ostensible uncertainty, the mentee's responses also followed with direct answers with no traces of uncertainty or further exploration (see lines 46–47 as an example).

Pattern A and B are two sides of the same coin: Pattern A (52%), which is supported by the opposite as pattern B (33%), thus totals 85% of the units of analysis which indicates that the notion that openness, created by the mentor's ostensible uncertainty, is reciprocal and is determined by the mentor's utterance. 15% of the units of analysis were exceptions to this notion of reciprocal openness. In other words, 85% of the sequences displayed the following: When the mentor uses uncertainty in his utterances, it is followed by uncertainty in the mentee's reply. When the mentor does not utter any form of uncertainty, it is followed by mentee utterances without signs of uncertainty. So, no uncertainty – no further exploration of knowledge which is offered as tentative.

The following conversation samples will illustrate the two main sequence patterns and explain it in terms of space making:

Sequence Pattern A

In conversation sample 6, ostensible uncertainty appears in the mentor's utterance in various forms, including exploration, speculating, wondering, thinking out loud and invitation. These are followed by uncertainty in the mentee's response, which include exploration or thinking out loud. The mentor's utterances in sample sequence 6, with reference to lines 48 and 52–53, are of particular interest: What it does, is to offer his knowledge as negotiable. This is followed by the mentee's indication of uncertainty in her opening in line 54. By replying with uncertainty, she offers a contribution of knowledge but keeps her contribution negotiable too. It is within this openness to negotiate the knowledge that the mentee has the freedom to try out her ideas. Apparently, if the professor uses utterances such as "ah.ahm:: maybe" and offer an invitation for the mentee's ideas by "Ahm. would you say.?", then the student could offer an answer about which she is not sure, and join in the exploration, speculating and wondering out loud. In the spirit of wondering about good teaching practice, the mentee is safe to offer her knowledge as tentative which could be confirmed by the mentor, or not. If the mentor does not confirm the mentee's knowledge offering, then there is no shame about her attempt because she was also just testing her current knowledge which is offered as tentative. '(L)oss of face' (Clark, 1996:379) is not a risk or at least a minimized risk because of the 'hospitable conversational space' (Baker, 2002).

Conversation sample 6

48	L	Jah:::Its also::- its also::- *ah(.)ahm::* (1) *may be ah* establishing
49		some kind of ah. relationship wher::e (.) you don't have to <u>work</u>
50		hard, you can just come here and make ↑no::tes (.) Ah.and I
51		think you're ri::ght ↑(.) the ah. the alternative is to be much more
52		interactive a::h and ahm. to let the ↑learning happen ↑<u>in</u> the
53		interaction (.) and then *where would the ah. note taking* ↓*fit (1)*
		into such interactions (2) ahm. would you say.?
54	S	*I think may be*firstly explaining (.) what it is that they're doing.
55		They can't take notes:: coming to cla::ss::. "This is what we're
56		↑doi::ng. This is what it's ab↑ou::t." Ahm<u>telling</u> (.) the students
57		what they're doing. <u>Then</u> they can write their notes, because
58		they know what it i::s and they know what they're doing or
59		alternatively let them write the notes and the ↑next day explaining
		everything to them.

Sequence Pattern B

It appears that where no uncertainty is created in the mentor's utterances, it is followed by responses from mentee with no display of uncertainty which marks exploration in the talk (See conversation sample 7). There is a distinct difference between the knowledge offered in the mentee's responses when conversation sample6 is compared conversation sample 7. What distinguishes the type A sequence, as in conversation sample 6, from the type B sequence in conversation sample 7, is that the mentee's responses to the mentor's utterances in sample 7 are, in essence, only paraphrasing of the knowledge offered by the mentor, in a way that does not invite negotiation. Line 91 – 93 shows how the mentor displays his conception about note taking during lessons. There is no invitation or indication that this knowledge is negotiable. The mentee's response does not bring anything new to the conversation, but simply summarise what the mentor already expressed.

Judging from the "yes" of the mentor in line 95, it seems that he accepts her summary. She repeats the mentor's conceptions in line 96–97 by means of paraphrasing.

Conversation sample 7

91	L	So its listen and wri::te but it's also identifying the main idea::
92		and to distinguish what's good and what's not goo::d; I should
93		write this and not tha::t and not- not copy everything.
94	S	It's like reasoning as well in a sense because=
95	L	Yes
96	S	=You're thinking about what you're writing and you're thinking
97		about what you're hearing instead of me::re (.) just copying.

DISCUSSION

The data, viewed in context of the participants' epistemic backgrounds, indicates that this mentor did not display his full range of knowledge or experience on the topics of discussion in his interaction with the mentee. This became clear within the dialogue in his withholding of knowledge only to fill in the conceptual gaps of the mentee at a point where he possibly realized that the mentees contribution to the topic is depleted. At a first glance, the mentor's contribution does not seem significant if it is viewed in context of the status he holds due to his expertise. However, from a CA point of view, it seems that he created ostensible uncertainty with the specific purpose of creating 'mental space' (Magano et al. 2010:26) in the conversation in which the mentee could test her views and ideas with her own future teaching practice in mind. Lines 52–53 in samples 3 and 6 serve as an example. Only later in this conversation, when the mentee could not depart from the idea of note taking being a form of copying from the board (see lines 54–59 in sample 6), despite her expressed feeling earlier that there should have been more interaction around the note taking, the mentor 'scaffolded' (Wood, Bruner, & Ross, 1976:90) with his own knowledge and expertise when he contributed the idea that the learners could be encouraged to decide what is important and what not before they write down notes, instead of copying everything. After this contribution by the mentor, the mentee came to the conclusion that *"It's like reasoning as well in a sense"* and *"You're thinking about what you're writing and you're thinking about what you're hearing instead of mere, just copying"* (see sample 7). What is of importance here is that space was created for the mentee's ideas before the mentor intervened by scaffolding.

Whether this strategy was deliberately implemented or whether it was followed intuitively, is irrelevant. Its functionality in the creation of 'hospitable conversational space' (Baker, 2002) is of interest. How it was achieved, is found among the codes that emerged from the data, such as a) indicating thinking (out loud) and indicating thinking by non-linguistic utterances such as "uhm... ahh..." or "m::" b) words of uncertainty such as "maybe" c) broken speech in which the flow of his thoughts is self-interrupted; d) asking for the mentee's opinion, advice or suggestions; e) pretended ignorance; f) apparent clarification by re-phrasing and g) disguising knowledge by posing it as a question or open suggestion.

Edwards' (1993) question, "What does the talk do?", guided the exploration of functionality of these conversational 'actions'.

Firstly, it seemed to create an atmosphere of openness in which no fixed answers were expected or pre-supposed. The mentee responded by working words of uncertainty into her replyso that she too kept her ideas open and flexible.

Secondly, Stivers et al. (2011:14) indicate that the phrases "I think" or "maybe" could be used as downgrading the claim of epistemic primacy as an attempt of 'epistemic mitigation'. This epistemic mitigation seems to be a pragmatic component of space creation in dialogic learning, viewed in the context of significant discrepancies in knowledge and expertise between interlocutors.

It is however possible that the student could be using words such as 'maybe' as some sort of an emergency exit in case the mentor would not agree with her contribution. Never the less, it kept her options open for further exploration, in case the mentor should disagree. The use of 'maybe' indicates the mentee's exploration of tentative ideas which is still open for change and can thus not be criticised on the same level as when she would present the view without 'maybe', and thus as a fixed belief. In this study, the use of uncertainty, expressed as 'maybe', seems to be an attempt to avoid 'loss of face', as Clark (2002:379) puts it.

The notion of reciprocal uncertainty which, in context of the conversation, indicates openness is highlighted by an opposite pattern in the data. Where the mentor's utterances did not contain any indication of uncertainty, the mentee's replies followed the same suit. As discussed earlier, it seems as though uncertainty creates a safe conversational space in which the knowledge is offered as tentative and open for negotiation. In this context, the mentee has the 'freedom to move mentally' (Magano et al., 2010:26) and to co-construct knowledge.

This study describes one possible strategy for creating a safe conversational space and, in particular, safe mental space between mentor and mentee. On a practical level, it indicates specific conversational actions with which this strategy can be executed. The point made by this study is that mentors could deliberately use the strategy of creating ostensible uncertainty to create hospitable mental space in which the mentee is invited to contribute to the knowledge construction.

LIMITATIONS AND SUGGESTIONS FOR FURTHER RESEARCH

This study was based on a single conversation which involved a single mentor-mentee pair, selected by convenience sampling. The scope of the study was narrowed down to exploration of a single strategy of space creation. Future studies which include multiple conversational pairs would give access to a wider variety of conversational mentoring strategies in general but also other ways in which the strategy of ostensible uncertainty could be executed in creating hospitable space. Other dialogic strategies in hospitable space making could also be explored across multiple mentoring conversations.

CONCLUSION

This study used, as a point of departure, a mentoring conversation which already proofed to be an example of meaningful learning (Pretorius, 2013). The meaningfulness of the learning in this conversation was established before this study commenced. What first sparked interest for further exploration was the observation that the mentor often expressed uncertainty in his utterances, despite being a professor in his field. This observation placed the focus on the differences in the knowledge and expertise of the mentor and mentee and more specifically the mentor's 'epistemic authority' (Heritage & Raymond, 2005). Because mentors have epistemic authority in conversations with a mentees, this status could potentially be an inhibiting factor in the co-construction of knowledge, due to the social and institutional rules or norms which govern mentoring conversations, as described by Stivers et al. (2011). This study took interest in the aspect of creating '*hospitable space*' (Baker et al., 2002) for collaborative knowledge conversation, given the position of epistemic authority of the mentor. The use of ostensible uncertainty in mentor utterances, as a strategy to create such space between mentoring speech pairs where there is a vast discrepancy in knowledge and expertise, was explored.

The study found that ostensible uncertainty as a space creating strategy could be executed in a variety of ways such as: indications of thinking out loud; indications of thinking by non-linguistic utterances; words of uncertainty;self-interrupted, broken speech; asking for the mentee's opinion, advice or suggestions; pretended ignorance; apparent clarification by re-phrasing and disguising knowledge by posing it as a question or open suggestion.

The study also found an interesting tendency in which uncertainty in mentor utterances was followed by expressions of uncertainty in the mentee's response. The mentee responses in this pattern consisted of contributions to knowledge construction where her reciprocal expression of uncertainty offered her contributions as tentative knowledge with a face saving element, which Clark (2002:379) refer to as 'loss of face', in case the mentor would not agree or approve. An opposite pattern, which complimented the first pattern,was also noticed in which no expression of uncertainty by the mentor was followed by brief responses without uncertainty from the mentee. These brief responses were not characterised by exploration of ideas.

It seems from the analysis that the use of ostensible uncertainty in mentor utterances created a safe conversational space in which contributions were offered as tentative and open for negotiation. This seemed to have facilitated the 'freedom to move mentally' (Magano et al., 2010:26) in the co-construction of knowledge.

This study explored only one possible strategy for creating '*hospitable space*' (Baker et al., 2002) in mentoring conversations, which are in essence, based on significant differences in knowledge and expertise. Being aware of the findings of this study, mentors could deliberately use ostensible uncertainty to create hospitable mental space in which their mentees are invited to knowledge construction.

REFERENCES

Baker, A., Jensen, P. J., & Kolb, D. A. (2002). Conversation as experiential learning. In A. Baker, P. J. Jensen, & D. A. Kolb (Eds.), *Conversational learning: An experiential approach to knowledge creation.* Westport, CO: Quorum Books.

Clark, H. H. (1996). *Using language.* Cambridge: Cambridge University Press.

Edwards, D. (1993). But what do children really think?: Discourse analysis and conceptual content in children's talk. *Cognition and Instruction, 11*(3/4), 207–225.

Gerretzen, F. (2012). *Effects of mentoring on student teacher's perceived learning outcomes: How mentor's approach and mentoring relationship influence perceived learning outcomes* (Unpublished dissertation), Educational Studies, Leiden University, Leiden.

Goffman, E. (2007). Encounters. In L. Monaghan & J. E. Goodman (Eds.), *A cultural approach to interpersonal communication.* Malden, MA: Blackwell Publishing.

Heritage, J. (2005). Conversation analysis and institutional talk. In K. Fitch & R. Sanders (Eds.), *Handbook of language and social interaction* (pp. 103–147). Mahwah, NJ: Erlbaum.

Heritage, J. (2012). The epistemic engine: Sequence organization and territories of knowledge. *Research on Language & Social Interaction, 45*, 30–52.

Heritage, J. (2013). Epistemics in conversation. In J. Sidnell & T. Stivers (Eds.), *The handbook of conversation analysis* (pp. 370–394). Boston, MA: Wiley-Blackwell

Heritage, J., & Raymond, G. (2005). The terms of agreement: Indexing epistemic authority and subordination in talk-in-interaction. *Social Psychology Quarterly, 68*(1),15–38.

Magano, M. D., Mostert, P., & Van der Westhuizen, G. (2010). *Learning conversations – The value of interactive learning.* Johannesburg: Heinemann.

Mkhize, N. (2004). Sociocultural approaches to psychology: Diologism and African conceptions of the self. In K. Ratele, N. Duncan, D. Hook, N. Mkhize, P. Kiguwa, & A. Collins (Eds.), *Self, community and psychology.* Cape Town, South Africa: UCT Press.

Nakamura, I. (2008). Understanding how teacher and student talk with each other: An exploration of how repair displays the co-management of talk in interaction. *Language Teaching Research, 12*(2), 265–283.

Pomerantz, A. (1980). Telling my side: "Limited access' as a "fishing" device. *Sociological Inquiry, 50*, 186–198.

Pretorius, A. J. M. (2013). *The structural dimensions of mentoring conversations and how they relate to learning outcomes of student teachers* (MEd dissertation). University of Johannesburg, Johannesburg.

Rule, P. (2006). Bakhtin and the poetics of pedagogy. *Journal of Education, 40,* 79–101.
Stivers, T., Mondala, L., & Steensig, J. (2011). Knowledge, morality and affiliation in social interaction. In T. Stivers, L. Mondala, & J. Steensig (Eds.), *The morality of knowledge in conversation.* Cambridge: Cambridge University Press.
Tillema, H., & Van der Westhuizen, G. (2003). Knowledge productive learning, a concept and tool for professional development. *Lifelong Learning in Europe, 3,* 18–26.
Tillema, H., & Van der Westhuizen, G. J. (2013). Mentoring conversations in the professional preparation of teachers. *SAJHE, 27*(5),1305–1323.
Wood, D., Bruner, J. S., & Ross, G. (1976). The role of tutoring in problem solving. *Journal of Child Psychology & Psychiatry, 17,* 89–100.

Annatjie J. M. Pretorius
Department of Educational Psychology/Academic Development Centre
University of Johannesburg, South Africa

Gert J. van der Westhuizen
Department of Educational Psychology
University of Johannesburg, South Africa

MARTIJN P. VAN DER MERWE AND
GERT J. VAN DER WESTHUIZEN

10. INVITATIONAL CONVERSATIONS
IN MENTORING

INTRODUCTION

This paper departs from the assumption that mentoring interactions are fundamentally human relationships between people. Mentors are regarded as people who are committed to developing others by supporting them through posing problems about current practice. Mentors are expected to assist mentees to uncover the underlying assumptions and beliefs that inform the mentee's practice. Mentors make use of guided critical reflection in this regard in an attempt to co-construct unique teaching practices for unique contexts (Wang & Odell, 2002:489). Mentoring of teachers should primarily focus on a deeper critical reflection and understanding of 'why' teachers actually teach the way they do, but also to assist them in developing a deeper understanding and knowledge of the subject matter they need to teach. In professional preparation, the understanding of learners is of great importance (Shulman, 1994). Views on knowledge and knowing of the participants in a professional collaborative learning situation such as the mentoring of pre-service teachers will in the view of Tillema and Orland-Barak (2006) influence how they understand the knowledge which is being shared, and how and when they will accept knowledge from others (see Elbaz-Luwisch & Orland-Barak, 2013).

The focus of this chapter is on the problematic of mentoring relations and the possibilities which 'invitational mentoring' may have for learning. We imagine a setting where a mentor looks at mentoring as a process of cordially inviting the mentee to learn – supported by a disposition of invitation, and the associated conversational actions, aligned at achieving the learning benefit of the mentee. Our study explores and describes the notion of an invitational style of mentoring, and clarifies the interactional nature of such a style, in order to consider the benefits for learning.

PROBLEM ISSUE AND ITS RELEVANCY

The study focuses on the issue of mentoring in an invitational style. The problem pertains specifically to the nature of such an Invitational Mentoring Style (IMS), and how this style is interactionally achieved. The theory of Invitational education has been described as 'a theory of practice' (Purkey & Novak 1996:3), and is typified as

H. Tillema et al. (Eds.), Mentoring for Learning, 199–223.

a 'developing theory of practice' which is 'incomplete, with questions unanswered and avenues unexplored' (Purkey & Novak, 1996:3), thus begging the question as to how this theory translates into mentoring and the interactions between mentors and mentees. Much research in Invitational education and learning have focused on whole school development (Steyn, 1993; Trent, 1997; Mahoney, 1998, Niemann, Swanepoel, & Marais, 2010), education management (Paxton, 1993; Stillion & Seagal, 1994; Asbill & Gonzalez, 2000; Egley, 2003; Thompson, 2004; Burns & Martin, 2010; Mboya Okaya, Horne, Laming, & Smith, 2013), teacher and learner perceptions (van der Merwe, 1984, 1985; Tung, 2002; Thompson, 2009), discipline and conflict (Davis, 1994; Reed & Shaw, 1997; Radd, 1997; Riner, 2003; Tanase, 2013), families and parental involvement (Briscall, 1993), teacher education (Rice, 2003; Steyn, 2005; Chant, Moes, & Ross, 2009; Kronenberg & Strahan, 2010; Kennedy, 2006), self-concept, self-esteem and self-efficacy (Pajares, 1994; Aspy & Aspy, 1994; Owens, 1997; Walker, 1998; White, 1999; Valiante & Pajares, 2002; Kitchens & Wenta, 2007; Ivers, Ivers, & Ivers, 2008) and counselling (Schmidt & Shields, 1998; Frakes, 1999; Cannon & Schimdt, 1999; Cowher, 2005; Zeeman, 2006; Haigh, 2008). However, a study relating to mentoring by Hofmeyer, Milliren and Eckstein (2005) developed the 'Hoffmeyer Mentoring Activity Checklist (HMAC). The development of the HMAC relates to studies about the mentoring of first-year school teachers. The focus of the Hofmeyer et al. study (2005) was the training of teachers/mentors to train first year teachers in predominantly Hispanic school communities in South Texas. The HMAC thus related more to the development of the mentoring process, and the activity checklist included activities related to qualities and activities of the mentors, and the institutional parameters of the process. Invitational education proposes that the kinds of 'messages' one needs to send, accept and negotiate about, are extremely important in human relationships. From the research cited here, it becomes clear that little has been written about how the actual interactions occur and progress in particularly mentoring interactions. The focus of this study therefore is about the interactional nature of mentoring interactions guided by invitational principles.

The relevance of this study alludes to the moral obligation of mentors to use their knowledge responsibly, and to encourage epistemic access and rights of mentees to know (see Stivers et al., 2011). The summary by Stivers (Stivers, Mondada, & Steensig, 2011) of the morality of knowledge and epistemics in social interactions help clarify aspects of access, primacy, and responsibility (see van der Westhuizen, this volume). In terms of this emphasis on the role of knowledge in mentoring, we want to argue in this chapter that mentoring in an Invitational style would be associated with associated talk actions, i.e. of the mentor inviting and making access to knowledge possible in unique ways associated with invitational principles.

The study of the interactional nature of IMS may best be pursued by means of conversation analysis. Advances in Conversation Analysis (CA) research over the last two decades since the original studies by Sacks Sacks (1992) and others, have opened up our understanding of the intersubjective and discursive nature of human interactions (Arminen, 2000; Edwards, 1997; Mondada, 2011). We have learned that institutional interactions such as mentoring are reciprocal (Mercer, 2008; Seedhouse, 2013), situational (Goffman, 2005) and particular to institutional norms (Drew & Heritage, 2006).

UNDERPINNINGS AND GROUNDED KNOWLEDGE

Mentoring is the 'concrete application of invitational theory (Hoffmeyer et al., 2005:54). Invitational mentoring can be defined as mentoring interactions that cordially summon mentees to realise their untapped potential (Novak, 2002) by intentionally inviting others, the mentees, personally and professionally toward 'epistemic congruence'. The latter, according to (Hayano, 2013) is about interactions where differences in knowledge are noted and considered in the interaction towards a shared understanding. Invitational mentoring is built on three foundations. These foundations are a belief that all people are important and have the ability to participate meaningfully and self-directed (a Democratic ethos), a belief that people's perceptions are vitally important (the Perceptual tradition), and the view that what people belief about the self is needed for maintaining internal motivation and the protection and enhancement of self (see self-concept theory; Novak, 2002:22). An important principle in Invitational education is that no interaction is ever neutral (Purkey & Novak, 1996). According to Purkey and Novak (1996) all social interactions carry meaning and messages relating to how we either call forth or shun human potential. The authors go on to propose that social interactions are either inviting or disinviting. Every inviting or disinviting interaction between people can then respectively be distinguished as being either intentional or unintentional behaviour. When others, in this case mentees, are invited on a personal level, the intention is to develop caring and trusting relationships by showing solidarity, by celebrating achievements and growth together, through sustaining civility and caring (Novak, 2002:29). When mentees are invited on a professional level, as is the case in this study on learning about teaching, mentors would intend developing the knowledge and behaviours associated with being a professional teacher.

When mentees are invited professionally, mentors relate to mentees by clearly indicating the levels of trust and appreciation in the mentees, by inviting them to become part of the larger 'we' that is being constructed in the interaction, to invite mentees into their 'inner circle' and not to feel 'marginalized'. Mentees should also experience assertion, particularly when attempting to meet their own needs while still respecting the needs of others. Asserting also implies a degree of control one has over a situation, allowing one to feel that learning possibilities are within reach. When assertion is allowed, democratic decision making, an own voice, and active participation follows. The view that people are valued, able and responsible and then are treated accordingly (Purkey & Novak, 1996) prevails. Inviting professionally also relies on creating opportunities for collaborative investing. Investing implies a willingness to try new things, to look at situations in different ways and to explore unexplored ways of thinking. Investing allows both parties to enjoy the activity itself. Investing in mentees is supported through the use of open-ended questions, brainstorming and participating in meaningful, unique enquiry. In these interactions mentees are allowed to search below the surface, to look at things in unique ways, and to go off the beaten path. An ethic of care is prevalent in most professional relationships. Mentors care and support mentees by ensuring that expectations are met and that mentees are not overwhelmed. Mentees are thus support to cope. Mentees need to experience a measure of success in their own ability and take pride in it. Mentors can support mentees by facilitating a clear perspective on past and present experiences, and by creating hope for the future through guided ideals collaboratively agreed on. A focus on attempting to understand what is happening and what the mentee might do to make things better is promoted by taking a long-range perspective and mistakes are seen as feedback on the way to improvement. Developing determination to continue is of importance in this interaction (Purkey & Novak, 1996:110–117; Novak, 2002:94–96).

Invitational mentoring is thus embedded in the so-called "Invitational stance". This stance is characterised by the elements care, trust, respect, intentionality and optimism. Care is the basis of an inviting stance in any interaction. Caring for the mentee involves "displaying full receptivity to the other and seeking to further the other person's educational purposes" (Novak, 2002:72). In practical terms this means that mentors should focus on the mentee to attend and listen to the mentee's interests, concerns, ideas and meanings. Trust, relates to the reciprocity and interdependence expected in mentoring interactions. Trust is established in practical terms by the competence (intelligent behaviour, expertness, and knowledge), genuineness (authenticity and congruence), reliability (consistency, dependability and predictability) and truthfulness (honesty, correctness of opinion, and validity of assertion) of the mentor in their interaction with mentees (Arceneaux 1994 as quoted in Purkey & Novak, 1996). Respect refers to the dialogical nature of invitational education. As each person's ability and uniqueness is recognized in the interaction, negotiation of acceptance and rejection of messages and meanings are expected. Intentionality, as Novak states, is "doing things on purpose for purposes that one can defend (2002:72). The implication is that in mentoring interactions the mentor would have a very specific direction in mind, and would persistently and resourcefully be pursuing it to the benefit of the mentee, the recipient. Having intentionality in one's stance relates to being able to take responsibility for your actions and not being averse to also correcting your own efforts in the interaction. It also implies being accurate in judgment and decisive in behaviour, but being able to allow for different opinions and choices. Lastly, optimism relates to approaching interactions with the hope that positive outcomes can be achieved. In mentoring interactions this implies openness, positive expectations and also continuous critical thought to better interactions. Optimistic mentors generally view mentees as valued, able and capable of self-direction in the mentoring process (Purkey & Novak, 1996:53).

In this paper we posit that an Invitational Mentoring Style is grounded and dependent on the ability to 'CARE'. Caring, according to Noddings (1999) provide the foundation for pedagogical activity. In listening with care, the mentor creates an opportunity for gaining the trust of the mentees. In this developing relationship of care and trust, a sense of mutual respect and optimism towards the development of untapped potential may be forthcoming. Mentoring of this nature will be identified by the four central components of ethical care (Noddings, 1992). These components form the core of IMS (Novak, 2002). Ethical care in mentoring is thus visible in how mentors model care in the relationship, and how mentors strive towards dialogue in the relationship. Modelling and practicing care involves genuine invitation to participate fully in the relationship in an attempt to create mutual understanding in the relationship, as well as confirmation where mentors are continually allowing possibilities for growth and own ideas in the relationship. The care (or core) of the IMS mentoring endeavour is encompassed within an intentional ring of collaborative decision making (see Diagram 1).

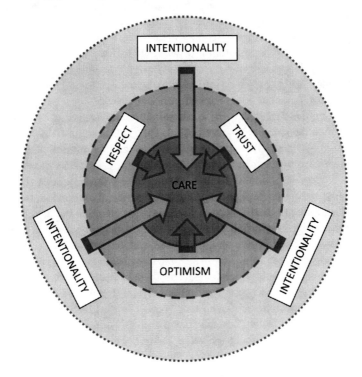

Diagram 1. Guiding beliefs of the Invitational Mentoring Style

We claim that every mentor probably has a unique mentoring style, which has been shaped by personal values, experiences, knowledge and relationships (Eckstein,

2005). In most cases these tendencies may allow us to favour a more "task-oriented" or "relationship oriented" approach to interactions with mentees. Mentors should attempt to balance these orientations and how we balance these styles become our preferred and unique style of mentoring. An Invitational Mentoring Style requires great flexibility as one's style should be adjusted continuously keeping the unique perceptual experiences of mentees in mind. From an IMS perspective, every mentor should develop the ability, and intentionality, to adapt their 'most natural response and style' when the situation requires. IMS requires very particular skills to enable the 'mentoring relationship'. Novak (1996:73) posits that taking an 'invitational' approach is an attempt to 'blend heart, head and hands". As we have seen earlier in this chapter, perceptions are the 'real' realities we deal with, while consistent, intentional behaviour needs to be carefully considered. Being able to handle many complex situations requires particular skills that are embedded in the five core values of the invitational stance. These skills are categorized into three interdependent phases, namely, being ready, doing with and following through.

Being ready requires the development of skills for preparing the environment and oneself. In terms of IMS the mentor ensures that the environment where the interaction takes place is comfortable, non-threatening, free from interruptions, and people-friendly. Thoughtful preparation of what the mentee should experience and what possible growth opportunities they should have is part of deep reflection before mentoring begins. Being ready also implies that the mentor should reflect deeply on own prejudices and personal needs for own personal growth.

Doing with implies that mentoring is essentially an interpersonal relationship in which communication and dialogue are central. The skills to support this relationship include developing goodwill, reading situations, sending attractive invitations, ensuring delivery, negotiating and handling rejection (Novak, 1996). Mentors should refrain from judgmental communication, should follow through consistently with agreements, non-verbal skills including tone of voice, facial expression, body stance and gestures; and the use of appropriate disclosure can all assist the development of a unique relationship. In addition probing for deeper meaning, making interaction very specifically intended for the unique mentee, and the opportunity to collaborate en initiate in the mentoring relationship are skills needed here.

Following through requires mentors, from an IMS perspective, to develop the skill of 'completing the invitation'. Initiations by the mentor or mentee in these interactions create expectations of achieving growth. Part of IMS involves therefore a deep reflection during and after the interaction as commitment to 'savouring' the experience and to developing the relationship, as has been argued by Novak, (1996:76). All of these characteristics of an invitational mentoring style would require mentoring education, through specific strategies such as those outlined by Smith (Chapter 13, this volume).

Mentor styles are generally depicted as being either Directive or Non-directive which includes styles such as the Persuasive, Participatory, and Transformational styles (Brouwer, Korthagen, & Bergen, 2008; Hennissen, Crasborn, Brouwer,

Korthagen, & Gergen, 2011). Mentors who are more 'directive' in their style, create structure and boundaries for mentees by explaining procedures, giving instructions, asking questions, pointing to possibilities, and setting rules in an effort to direct the attention and behaviour of the mentee. In theory, this style will be most appropriate when the mentees lack self-confidence and self-direction. They also use the assessing, instructing, appraising, confirming, expressing opinion, offering strategies and feedback predominantly in such interactions. Non-directive styles are more reflective, cooperative, and guiding in nature. The Persuasive style uses similar behaviours as those in the directive style, but attempts to gain the support of the mentee for these behaviours and opportunities. One could expect mentors using this style to explain the reasoning behind certain requests and activities more to allow the mentee to see a rational connection between the activities in the mentoring relationship and other tasks or functions. This style seems most appropriate when the focus is on developing skills and knowledge so that the mentee can function independently. The participatory style involves interacting on an interpersonal level by the mentor, where the relationship becomes vital. Such mentors will make use of much shared information, collaboration and shared decision making in the mentoring process. This style is most appropriate when the mentor wants to motivate the mentee and requires honesty and integrity. The transformational style is a style where the main outcome is the development of the mentee's ability to take control of the process and to manage it successfully. The mentor still asks questions, sets parameters, provides information and possibilities, but withdraws gradually from directing the process and even limiting regular interaction.

We posit that an Invitational Mentoring Style may be distinguished from the styles noted here, with some essential overlaps. IMS departs from the notion that the existing 'reality or perceptual world' of the mentee is crucial to fostering the mentoring relationship. As such, mentors who use the IMS may find that they will be required to move flexibly between directing, persuading and participating in the interaction. Flexibility in mentoring is supported by the Invitational skills of the 'Craft of Inviting' as stated earlier (Novak, 1996). Mentors who use the IMS will attempt to create conditions for the development of the 'untapped potential' which they believe every mentee has (Purkey & Novak, 1996:3). True Invitational mentors will attempt to allow mentees' self-directedness, self-confidence and self-worth to emerge, and to gradually invite growth in such a way that it becomes virtually 'invisible' to the untrained eye (Novak, 2002). What makes IMS unique though as mentoring style, is that it is based on the five value-based elements Care, Trust, Respect, Optimism and Intentionality that guide all mentoring activities (Novak, 2002). IMS can become the 'moral compass' for integrating all mentoring interactions towards one defendable aim, namely the emancipation of the mentee.

In mentoring interactions, knowledge plays a key role (Tillema, Van der Westhuizen & Van der Merwe, this volume; Van der Westhuizen, this volume). IMS adheres to the notion of knowledge as collaborative practice (Tillema & van der Westhuizen, this volume) as mentors who have this style attempt to engage in exploration and meaning making in the actual activity through intentional interaction. Such mentors may prepare an environment for the collaboration that is a 'safe' space for the mentee to engage with the mentor. Such spaces allow mentors to check their own prejudices and challenge them in an effort to unlearn and move beyond them, whilst creating trust by assuring confidentiality and reserving judgment through dependable, congruent verbal and non-verbal communication (Purkey & Novak, 1996:61–69). IMS is therefore an 'intentional' act (Novak, 2002) and aligns with Erickson's view that the mentoring conversation and interaction is systematic and deliberate (Tillema & Van der Westhuizen, this volume). IMS relies on the mentor's ability to 'read the situation' (Purkey & Novak, 1996) and to give feedback and create opportunities for the mentee to develop towards the desired goal.

An additional benefit of IMS relates to the level of interaction during the mentoring process. Initial views of mentoring regarded the process as straightforward and pragmatic, as it related to a 'virtually one-directional' development of the mentee. Tillema & van der Westhuizen (this volume) quote Strong and Baron (2004) when stating that mentors predominantly determine the mentoring interaction in planning what to discuss, when to discuss it and how to go about it. This alludes to the qualities of mentoring concerning the expected asymmetry in knowledge, skills and experience. Social interactions are characterised by knowledge asymmetries (Heritage, 2012), and knowledge asymmetry in mentoring interactions are functions of the setting and institutional nature of such interactions (van der Westhuizen, this volume). Such asymmetry is generally reflected in the cognitive state of the participants in the social process (Mercer, 2004). The asymmetry is further visible through the professional perspectives and personal theories that each participant in the interaction brings to the process of knowledge building (Pajares, 1992). Social interactions view eventual 'knowledge congruency' as the ideal (Heritage, 2012). Thus professional learning as social interaction is a process where participants in the learning immerse themselves in, and share in the knowledge building, but aim to develop personal agency in using, adapting and recreating knowledge (Edwards, 2013). IMS proposes that mentoring learning conversations should thus foster genuine collaborative relationships, where each participant is afforded the opportunity to develop knowledge and skills to unique levels, and concurs with Edwards's (2004) view that relational and interpersonal skills are of great importance in conversations. In this respect, we propose that IMS may lead to greater reciprocity and symmetry in the relationship between the mentor and mentee. Reciprocity in IMS develops based on beliefs inherent to this style that focus on the 'possibilities' of others, accountability and respect (Purkey & Novak, 1996). IMS is a 'doing-with' approach that builds on democratic and reciprocal principles to develop both mentor and mentee in an ethical and trusting relationship (Novak, 2002).

Tillema (Chapter 1 of this volume) posits a model for transformational professional mentoring based on a metaphor of "Climbing Mount improbable". This implies that the mentee is assisted and supported to reach a level of knowledge/performance the mentee 'perceived' to be difficult to reach. Tillema and van der Westhuizen also state that the mentor's approach is in line with the facilitative approach to assisting the mentee to climb "mount improbable". According to this metaphor, the mentor can assist the mentee in exploring what the mentees believe, know and can do. The mentor can also scaffold the mentee by monitoring and supporting by 'starting from the mentees beliefs' about self and performance. The mentor may also decide to be prescriptive by deliberately guiding the mentee towards the preferred goal. In IMS terms mentors attempt to take an 'insider perspective, and attempt to understand mentees belief systems as far as possible. Through collaboration and negotiation mentees are supported with 'invitations' that elicit positive notions of self and others. IMS is expected to have a stronger focus on exploring and scaffolding in conjunction with the fundamental beliefs and characteristics it represents, but may also be prescriptive, and intentionally so, due to its optimistic character.

Novak (2002) extends the view on an invitational stance with the metaphor of tennis. He maintains that in this dialogic interaction between mentors and mentees, mentors only have 'control' on their side of the net in terms of what they do, not about what the mentee does. This stance translates to specific conversational actions on the part of the mentor, and would include, 'when the communication is in your court', to make solid contact to allow the mentee to play his/her natural game (2001:70). Keeping in mind that an Invitational stance is founded on the perceptual tradition, communicative acts of the mentor should thus account for possible 'perceptual returns' that require particular values to be portrayed. We have chosen to center in on one element of an invitational mentoring style, namely an Invitational stance. In terms of invitational education theory, an invitational stance of the mentor would involve care, trust, respect, intentionality and optimism. We regard these attributes as typically the fundamental and guiding beliefs of the invitational mentor.

In terms of the theoretical perspective of interactional learning described above, specific conversational actions can be associated with an invitational style of mentoring. These would, in our interpretation, include specific ways in which sequences of interactions are organized, and specific response preferences of participants. In an invitational mentoring style, we would expect sequences consisting of assessments and questions, probing statements, and stance utterances, which invite learning responses. We would also expect mentor using conversational techniques to create space for personal views through questioning techniques, silences, and perhaps provocative statements. We would also expect response preferences to be more tentative.

EXPLORATION

The main question we attempted to answer in the empirical analysis is: How is invitation to learn interactionally achieved in mentoring interactions? This question relates to the 'talk moves' of mentors adopting the invitational style (IMS), which, in terms of Novak (2001:70), would entail the characteristics of an invitational stance.

The sub-question in this study relates to exploring and describing which 'talk moves' are associated with the guiding beliefs of mentor care, inclusive of mentor trust, mentor intentionality, mentor respect and mentor optimism, and how the talk moves the mentoring interaction towards these fundamental beliefs.

Approach and Design

This is an ethnomethodological study intending to contribute to the clarification of "members methods" (cf. Maynard & Clayman, 2003), in other words the methods used by mentors to achieve invitation to learn about teaching interactionally and invitationally. The empirical study formed part of a mentoring conversations research project at the University of Johannesburg. The larger project entailed analyzing mentoring interactions between lecturers and students in Teacher Education. Lecturers were invited to voluntarily take part in the project. Lecturers who indicated that they would participate were requested to invite one student that the lecturer had visited during the work-integrated learning experience at schools. Students' participation was also entirely voluntary. Each lecturer who participated in the research, held mentoring conversations with three different final year students who had completed a seven-week work-integrated learning experience at designated schools. Students, who indicated voluntary participation, were requested to submit a personal written reflection report on their experiences and observations during the work-integrated learning experience. Participating lecturers invited students individually for mentoring sessions of 30 to 45 minutes in duration with these reflections as the main point of discussion. Mentors selected the points of discussion from the student's reflection report with the aim to support developing classroom practice. The interaction took place in the mentor's office. All mentoring sessions were audio- and video-taped with student consent and on completion, transcribed verbatim.

The unit of analysis is the "talk moves", i.e. the utterances and response preferences and their social actions within the micro-context of episodes of learning. The latter is conceived of as segments in a conversation which work towards some learning outcome (see Van der Westhuizen, this volume).

For our analysis we used the data of one mentor/mentee pair, purposefully selected based on set criteria of the IMS, i.e. the core values of an invitational stance as outlined above. These criteria include the indicators of care, trust, respect, optimism making up an invitational stance. Based on these criteria we selected one mentoring session to explore in more depth the conversational patterns associated with invitational education.

Analysis

Our analysis of the videos and transcriptions [according to the Jefferson conventions] focused on identifiable learning episodes in which a clear question or topic was considered and where the interaction led to some indication of learning and point of conclusion. The analysis was guided by the main question: 'Which talk moves are associated with the guiding beliefs of mentor care, which include trust, intentionality, respect and optimism?' CA analytic principles associated with talk moves were used as the framework for analysis of the interactions. The CA analytic principles associated with talk moves include turn design (Sacks, Schegloff, & Jefferson, 1974), response preference, and sequence organization, among others (Edwards; see also (Koole, 2013)). Turn designs that one could expect in a IMS would for example take the form of open ended questions, using silences, incomplete sentences, requesting and soliciting information, confirming and rewarding etc. Principles of sequence organization associated with IMS would include question and answer (Q/A), extensions of Q/A sequences by means of pursuing other levels of understanding, and claims by mentors inviting responses or extensions. Response preferences in IMS would include extensions, accounting and claiming on the part of the mentee. Turn design on the part of the mentor in an IMs style is a crucial component. Turn-design alludes to a conscious decision on the part of the mentor. It refers to the social-sequential organization (Schegloff, 1991a, E992, as quoted by Lerner, 1995) of the talk and visible behaviour, which are produced in a very particular way. In terms of the IMS such turn-taking should be intentional, as the interactions are aimed at creating opportunities or possibilities for the mentee. In general, such turn-taking would 'invite' the mentee to participate in an interaction that would be beneficial to all involved.

Mentoring Learning Episodes Identified

We focused on two episodes in the analysis. The first was an episode where the topic of learning was learner performance in mathematical tests and the need of the mentee to learn about improving performance in class exercises and tests. The second episode was about the mentees perceived need to learn about assessment, i.e. marking and memoranda of assessments in the Mathematics classroom. The transcripts were scanned for the 'natural' talk that takes place in institutional settings, keeping in mind the 'assumed hierarchical rights, roles, responsibilities, rituals and uniform linguistic forms and patterns' (Keogh, 2010: 56). An analysis of turn-by-turn interaction was thus embarked on to attempt to show how the particular roles, values and relationships were constructed and how this influenced the talk (Keogh, 2010).

Data Analysis

Our analysis was aimed at identifying "talk moves", i.e. utterances by the mentor which in the micro-context of sequences of interaction would be doing invitational work, i.e. expressing trust, clarifying intentionality, communicating respect, and suggesting optimism.

Episode one commences with a directive questions from the mentor in line 196 (see Table 1) in which the issue of learner performance is introduced. The mentee reflects on own recent experience concerning learner performance in a recent test, and requests, rather covertly, clarity from the mentor about what to do to improve performance in lines 199–211. The mentor in turn, seeks clarity on this request in lines 212–214. This is followed by the mentee claiming that effort and dedication will improve performance in lines 215 to 224. The mentor uses assessment to ask for clarification in lines 225–226 upon which the mentee offers an account in lines 227–231 stating that more practice may lead to improved performance. The mentor agrees and offers alternative considerations in lines 232–243, which the mentee initially did not grasp (line 244), but was clarified in lines 245 to 246 as being about extra exercises of working slower. The mentee assesses these two options in lines 247–253, whereupon the mentor confirms and agrees with the mentee, but again offers alternatives in lines 254–258. The mentee then clarifies her own conviction that work overload is a probable factor in line 259–261, and that less work will possibly lead to better performance for weak learners. This is confirmed and agreed upon by both the mentor and mentee in lines 262 and 263. The mentor then elicits a personal reflection from the mentee in lines 264–265. The episode concludes with the mentor establishing a new point for discussion in line 266 to 267.

The majority of the talk is initiated by the mentor through the use of pauses, open-ended sentences and questions, and confirmations which act as 'continuers' (Keogh, 2010) in the conversation. Some mentor turn are longer (lines 232–243; lines 254–258), but the predominant structure in this episode is talk initiation by the mentor, followed by focused answers from the mentee. In accordance with research cited by Keogh, a typical pattern of 'initiate, respond, evaluate (IRE) is noticed. This may allude to the underlying discourse of the institutional talk in this conversation.

In terms of the conversational elements in episode one, the mentor utterances are predominantly proposals (line 232–235; 255), requests, clarification requests (lines 196; 245), soliciting of extended clarification (line 196; 212; 242), ethic of politeness (line 232), completion formulation (line 225), and confirmations (line 262; 263).

Mentee utterances in this episode predominantly indicated assessment (self-assessment) (line 215; 217; 220), giving account (line 247), confirmation (line 259), preference for agreement (line 227), realization and claiming insight (insight in line 250; certainty in line 252) as indicted in Table 1.

In this learning episode the following talk moves contribute and serve the purpose of emphasizing an invitational mentoring style:

In the first utterance of the first learning episode (line 196), the mentor introduces the focus of the talk, namely learner performance by using a pause to focus the attention of the mentee. In terms of IMS, this utterance alludes to an open invitation for the mentee to 'take' the conversation to where it feels safe at this point. The mentor thus indicates care for the mentee's accounts giving. The response preference

Table 1. Episode one – Invitational Style Mentoring

196	L	Have they <u>im↑pro::ved</u>(1) >in respect of< their:: their::
197		(.) >let's say< the the <u>perfo::r</u>mance – >their learning
198		performance<?
199	S	There's this ↑test they wrote (.) recently.
200	L	Yes::
201	S	They did <↑we::ll::> =
202	L	[Y↑es]
203	S	= but I ↑think they can ↑<u>do</u>°↓mo::re° (.)=
204	L	[more- better]
205	S	=if they <u>att↑end</u>classes (.)=
206	L	[mmm::]
207	S	= according to the way they- they are performing.
208	L	°Oh°
209	S	I need them to attend my classes >so that we can<(1)=
210	L	[mm-m::] [mm::]
211	S	= work things out (for them).
212	L	Are they- >are they<<u>weak</u> learners because
213		(.)>most of them don't actually< (care to do) their maths
214		exercises etcetera?
215	S	At ↑first I ↑<u>didn't↓kno:::w</u>(1) =
216	L	[Ah yes
217	S	= >about that< but <u>now</u> I can- I realise that they don't (.)
218		put <u>effort</u> =
219	L	Mmm
220	S	= on their work (.) That is why they ↑don't do well::
221	L	°Yes::°
222	S	I think if they can put more ↑<u>effort</u> (1.0)=
223	L	°Yes::°
224	S	=dedicate to their work, they can do– do (much better).
225	L	>So they might have the ability< but they are not (.) necessarily
226		…
227	S	[They might, they ↓might (.) they just need=
228	L	yes (.) yes
229	S	=more time to practi::ce. But if they run away from the
230	L	Yes
231	S	= practices, its not going to ↓help.

Table 1. (Continued)

232	L	Its ↑not gonna help (.) that's true. There is <u>nothing</u> else that you
233		can do (.) if you think ↑back now (.) >in respect
234		of the ↑weaker learners< (.) that >could have made a
235		↑difference<. Becau:se >in an average school< you will find this
236		group of weaker ↓learners >that you have to
237		deal ↓with<, and <u>I</u> found tha:t (.) ↑sometimes when you <u>go</u>
238		at a ↑slower ↑tempo (.) let's say::↑ if you <u>don't</u> stick to the
239		↑schoo::l's (.) curriculum, you know when they
240		do >this amount of maths in a week< they do just half of ↑that.
241		It might work, but then of ↑course they need
242		extra uh ↑exercises etcetera. Have you <u>tried</u> that↑ >or isn't it
243		allo:wed in the school at the moment<?
244	S	The::?
245	L	Sort of uh giving extra (.) exercises or >sort of< ah (.) a
246		following their own tempo?
247	S	I was <u>just</u> ↑worried about <u>that</u> sir (.) because if <u>they</u> (.) ↑say they
248		are ↓weak ↓learners (0.4) they don't have to (0.2) have >a lot of
249		work<. They just need to (0.2) ↑<u>get</u> maybe a piece of where they
250		need to ↓practice and >go back go back< and get used to (.) the
251		↑content. If we ↑<u>load</u> ↑them with a lot of work (.) they will
252		↑<u>never</u> cope, because they >are going to< (0.5)
253		
254	L	°yes° uh yes >I <u>hear</u> what you are saying< – so extra
255		work won't work. But if we ↑give them <u>perhaps</u> (.) just a slower
256		<u>tempo</u> (.) in other words >they do less than the others in respect
257		of of a weekly load< (.) <u>that</u> <u>might</u>
258		work ↑hey?=
259	S	=I think it's ah <u>more</u> work, >it's because< they they've
260		been loaded with a lot of work (.)°that's why they can't cope°
261		
262	L	((inaudible)) [>They can't cope with ↑that. They can't cope with
263		↑that< ja
264	S	[>Yes that is why they perform
265		↑low<
266	L	Yes (.) >I hear what you're saying< (0.2) Do you
267		↑<u>still</u> °feel personally responsible for ↑them°?

by the mentee in line 199 is an indication of the acceptance of the invitation. The mentor exhibits a number of such responses that show empathy, concern, and optimism in the mentee's abilities in episode one. Most utterances that indicate care, concern and respect were formulated in open questions, open-ended type questions and statements, which require completion formulation from the mentees for example in line 225. The utterance by the mentor in this line points to a gently guiding of the mentee towards a possible answer indicating a concern for the mentee. It may also indicate a cooperative stance (in invitational sense) of the mentor to engage the mentee in the conversation on as equal footing as possible, thereby depicting respect. The utterance in lines 232, 254 and 266 by the mentor supports the authority of the mentee, by agreeing with the mentee's view. A sense of 'doing-with' and acceptance is thus implicit which alludes to the IMS perspective. Through clear acknowledgment of the mentee's views and elaborations, the mentor defuses the 'ritual of asymmetry' characteristic of institutional teacher training contexts, indicating care, respect and trust.

Utterances in lines 235 onwards and in lines 255 onward that seem to indicate an invitational stance of 'intentionality' were formulated in more lengthy turns taken by the mentor, which attempted a rational and theoretical explanation of the requested behaviour of the mentee. Such utterances would again reflect the underlying care and positive belief in the mentees potential. These utterances ended in open questions in both cases, and with a rising tone of voice accentuation of the continuer 'hey'. Lines 235 onwards in particular relates to the implicit recognition that the mentee does have the ability, and the ability will develop if allowed. This implicit recognition is followed by the mentees response preference in line 247 that indicates deeper insight and understanding of how to assist weaker learners. The utterance in line 255 implies an expectation that the mentee is able to extend her understanding and invites the mentee to share her unique opinion.

In is interesting to note that the mentor's positive recognition of the mentee's ability is evident in her response preferences about the learners in the class as she focuses on external factors that influence the learners' performance, whilst their abilities are confirmed in line 249.

The optimistic and trusting characteristics found in the utterances of the mentee, appears to elicit a change in the structure of the talk. A more 'symmetrical' conversation ensue from line 247 onwards where statements allude to points of view now held by both participants, and are made without evaluation as for instance in line 254.

Optimism and trust relating to the belief that the mentee can co-produce knowledge and better understanding of the situation are created by the mentor talk in the form of questions or open-ended statements, which are particularly formulated to invite the mentee to respond in lines 197, 212 and 225. The mentor uses a slower tempo and pause particularly in line 226 to allow the mentee to enter into the collaboration. In these utterances, the mentor confirms the noticing of the previous utterance of the mentee, and allows the mentee to make clear statements in the context of the discussion in lines 215 onwards. This pattern is repeated in line 245 where the mentor allows similar opportunities for the mentee by simply using 'or sort of' to create an open-endedness that invites. Similar use of words such as 'perhaps' (line 251), 'in other words' (line 252), and 'hey' (line 253) indicates optimism in the mentees ability to extend the understanding, as well as allowing the mentee this opportunity.

Analysis of Episode 2:

Episode two follows a brief discussion by the mentor and the mentee on keeping a reflective journal from lines 451 onwards. The conversation in this episode starts with a confirmation report from the mentor in which the mentee is congratulated on having 'mastered' the art of reflection report writing in lines 459 to 462. The mentor then introduces a new topic on setting tests for assessment and the marking of in line 463. The mentor introduces this topic with multiple related questions; each with a particular focus (lines 463–468). The mentor thus initiates this interaction with the invitation to the mentee to share views about tests and memoranda. The mentee then reflects on own practice related to marking assessments and setting memoranda (lines 469–476). The problematic of marking assessments in general is extended in lines 478 to 492. The mentee extends her reflection on this professional activity by implying careful analysis of assessments and not only marking right or wrong answers (lines 478–484). The mentor confirms the difficulties in marking according to a memorandum in lines 485 to 488, and formulates an extended challenge about the use of an assessment framework in designing memoranda for a test in lines 493 to 496, and 498 to 500). The mentee proposes the importance of testing on different levels (lines 514–515; 517–518; 520), to which the mentor agrees and requests further clarification of the mentee about the use of memoranda and marking assessment in line 521. The mentee gives an explanation about the process followed in designing memoranda and marking tests (lines 5525–528; 532; 534–538) with an implicit open-ended affirmative statement in line 529 and a positive confirmation in line 533. The conversation then shifts to a discussion on taking the length of time in relation to the number of marks into consideration when setting a test from line 541. The mentee confirms that she was able to achieve this through an extended explanation from in line 548, to which the mentor replies with affirmations in line 569, 578 and 550 with which the episode concludes.

The talk in Episode 2 follows a similar patter as in Episode 1. The majority of the talk is again initiated by the mentor through the use of pauses, open-ended sentences and questions, and confirmations which act as continuers in the conversation.

In terms of the conversational elements in episode two, the mentor utterances are predominantly assessment of what the mentee says (line 533), soliciting explanations from the mentee (line 463, 521, 541, 556), requesting extension and clarification by the mentee (line 465), confirmation of mentee ideas and insights (line 461, 481, 493, 521, 533, 578, 580), and challenging and extending the mentee to engage with new ideas (line 501, 510, 512).

The Mentee utterances predominantly indicate account giving related to the mentor's challenges (line 469, 514, 534, 571), extending clarification solicited by the mentor (line 486, 562, 573) and self-assessment (line 525, 537).

The mentor makes various talk moves in support of his invitational style. The mentor indicates a sense of respect and acceptance by using positive comments relating to the mentee's achievement in lines 461, 481, 493, 498, 569, 578 and 580.

Table 2. Episode two – Invitational Style Mentoring

459	L	O:::h its like ↑reflective jou::rnal
460	S	Ye::s.
461	L	°Oh that's wonderful!° I think you >sort of< ↑got the
462		↑a::r::t >of writing a reflection report< ↑just ↓right. So
463		↑well ↓done. ↑Then (.) I want to now about the- the ↑tests,
464		the ↑ma::rking and the memora::n↓dums. Did
465		you pick up on tha::t? Was it ↑difficult for you to- >sort
466		of< (1) create the first memorandum- to mark the first
467		tests?. hh ahh Did you get used to- to what they
468		↓ex↑pected from you?
469	S	Marking:: was:: (.) >it was< fi:::::n::e >at first< b'cause
470		I ↑had to look at the ↑memorandum (.) bu- but my
471		mento::r came to me and said= "↓You ↑know (.) you
472		can't just (.) ma:::rk like that according to the
473		memorandu:::m (.) because you have to- (.) if I ha-
474		(.) >they give you a< ↑pro↓blem:: (1.0) you- (.) >there's
475		↑pro↓blem<= and they have to solve ↑it – if they answer
476		wro::ng (.)=
477	L	[Y↑es]
478	S	=you put (2) a ↑wro::ng but ↑if they continue- (1.0)
479	L	You must still give them a number of ↑ma::rks then
480	S	Ye:: you have to give them (2.0↑)=
481	L	>Oh I see< I ↑like↓ that
482	S	=a number of ↓marks= I ↑think ↓that's what makes- (.)
483	L	[Yes]
484		it makes it difficult=so it makes- yah it makes it difficult=
485		It- it(.) >it sort of< makes it a ↑te::di↓ous job hey
486	S	[Ye:::s 'cause]
487		you ↑have to make sure that you ↑pay attention=
488	L	[ye::s::]
489	S	=↑pay attention even though you ↑ that (.) they have (.)
490		answered (.)
491	L	[ye::s yes]
492	S	=↑incor↓rectly (.) They can ↑still do something (1) right.
493	L	[I ↑like that]
494		↑very ↓much b'cause in some cases they will say >you
495		know< if you've got the a↑rithmetic ↑wro::ng:: (.) >they
496		are not going to give you any marks< (further) on=
497	S	°yes°

Table 2. (Continued)

498	L	=>And I actually like-< because you can see if they've
499		had the ↑principles ↓the::re (.). hh and they can be
500		following the procedures and they've got something-
501		>they got< ↑something right at least (.). hhhh Do ↑you
502		u::se a certain a::h >let's call it a< ahm ↑frame↓work >to
503		sort of< (.) design a memor↑a::n↓dum for a test >in
504		other words< to test the level of ↑diffi↓culty:: (.) for
505		certain stuff= Let's say this is on a ↑knowledge
506		↓leve:::l:: and this is on an ↑inside ↓leve:::l:: >or
507		evaluation level< or ↑what↓ever (.) Do you ↑u::se that
508		↓no::w?
509	S	When ↑creating a memorandum?
510	L	Ye::s >and ↑also a ↑test< ↓actually.
511	S	[Oh when- (.) ↑°YES° yes]
512	L	When you design a test – and then >sort of< use a
513		memorandum
514	S	When designing a test it is ↓very important to test on
515		different levels=
516	L	Yes:yes
517	S	=because you can't >just maybe< create test based on
518		(.) ↓knowledge- you ↑ to test all the the=
519	L	Yes
520	S	=the knowledge levels.
521	L	I agree:::= So that memo↑ran↓dum, were they
522		↑satis↑fied when you actually >sort of< when you
523		drafted the first one and you got to the ↑ma::rkings,
524		etcetera?
525	S	↑It was fine (.) because when doing the
526		memora::n↑dum I started by (0.5) doing it >like
527		practically: solving the pro↑ble:ms< the:n typing it neatly
528		(.)
529	L	>You had written down all the steps< (.) ↑everything?
530	S	I wrote (1.0)=
531	L	=[Yes(.): yes
532	S	Yes then I go for a second op↑inio::n
533	L	That's good! (.) That's actually ↑wonderful!
534	S	[to my mentor and I
535		↑say:: >will you please check me< maybe there is a
536		mistake I've do::ne (.)°and without noticing it°. Then my

(Continued)

Table 2. (Continued)

537		mentor will che::ck (.) for me if I've do::ne mistakes (.)
538		she will say: here and here. But if its ok↓ (.) the::n
539	L	Then they >sort of leave it<
540	S	↓Ye::s.
541	L	[The most difficult thing for >teachers is actually to
542		determine how ↑long a test a should be< ↑how many
543		questions (.) you should have< (.) in other wo:rds (.)
544		let's say: a 45 minutes ↑test. Did you have any kinds of
545		problems related to ↑that?. hhh Did you have to set a
546		test for a certain ↑time period? (.) You said for one
547		period ↑hey?
548	S	Only for one period.
549	L	[is it (.) would they write the full ↑hour or
550		perhaps a little bit shorter?
551	S	Then they wri::te
552		(3.0)
553	S	I think an ↑hour it's an ↑hour and 15 minutes=
554	L	=↑Oh is ↑it?
555	S	((inaudible))
556	L	So its quite a ↑lengthy paper. Did you gain ↑any experience
557		in respect of ↑how to set the test so that
558		they actually write the full ↑time? >In other words< let's
559		say:: its 75 minutes uh 75 ↑marks (.) ah >did you gain
560		some experience in respect of setting it for that amount
561		of time as ↑well<?
562	S	Yes sir. In that case (.) you have to check (1.0) ↑how
563		long does it ta::ke in a normal basis to solve this
564		problem
565	L	[to solve this problem
566	S	((inaudible))
567	L	Did you do it on your ↑own?
568	S	Ye::s
569	L	Oh ↑excellent. Did you check it or >did you get
570		someone else to do tha:t<?
571	S	I ↑have to. I did it on my own.
572	L	((inaudible))
573	S	I checked to see on a normal basis (.) ↑how lo:ng can a
574		learner take

(Continued)

Table 2. (Continued)

575	L	[yes
576	S	to do this ↑one (.) and this one and this one and then I
577		added the problems together=
578	L	=That's excellent=
579	S	=Then you come up with the right time.
580	L	I think that's excellent! I think you've done well in that
581		sense.

Superlatives such as 'excellent', that's wonderful', 'well done', and I think that's excellent' are used to express this appreciation. These utterances are supported and emphasized by higher voice tone and volume. Approval of mentee utterances with talk such as 'I like that' (line 481), 'I like that very much' (line 493), 'And I actually like that' (line 498), and 'Oh is it? So it's quite a lengthy paper.' (line 556) indicate trust and optimism in the mentee's abilities.

Caring is displayed in terms of clear intentionality in line 464 onwards where the mentor supports the mentee in furthering the thinking about marking and designing assessment. The mentor intentionally moves the conversation to the underlying 'framework' (line 502) in the design of good assessment. The mentor uses a similar technique of pausing, repair and additional examples to assist the mentee in getting to grips with the issue (line 502-508) indicating an ethic of care, intentionality and underlying optimism. These particular aspects relating to IMS serves to scaffold the mentee in lines 464, 501, 510, 521, 529, 544, 556, 567 and 569.

In summary, the analysis found that the sequences of interaction were mostly in the form of question/answering. Questions seem to fulfill the functions of assessments, followed by accounts of views by the mentees. Q/A sequences were extended by means of additional questions and answers which include new information and 'upgrading' of prior accounts by the mentee. The analysis also showed turn designs and response preferences in the forms of open-ended questions and statements which invited extensions of views. Response preferences by the Mentor include the use of preliminaries followed by a variety of questions, the use of 'We', frequent time lapses, incomplete statements, voice intonations and body language displaying interest and support, constructive assessments, strong appreciation, etc. Response preferences on the part of the mentee include claims and assertions of views.

A brief discussion of these findings will now follow.

DISCUSSION

The findings from the analysis may be taken as evidence of the conversational actions associated with an invitational style of mentoring. The case example allows for an initial exploration and highlights the presence of different talk moves which may be further explored as characteristic of invitational mentoring.

The finding that sequences were mostly organized in terms of question/answer type, and extended to make space for the mentee to announce and claim own insights, may be taken as an indication of prolonged interest on the part of the mentor. Such organization seems to be in accordance with the expected institutional roles and rituals of mentoring in an academic learning context between a lecturer and a student (Gert Van der Westhuizen, 2011).

While mentoring relations are asymmetrical by design, evidence suggests that the mentor took many conversational actions to work towards a shared understanding (van Kruiningen, 2013) and knowledge symmetry (Sidnell, 2012). This preference facilitates epistemic primacy (Stivers et al., 2011), with the mentor allowing the student to state what she knows, and creating a space/possibility for reciprocity. This is strengthened by the use of 'we' to create a sense of solidarity, a respectful and trusting relationship, in which the mentor aligns himself with the mentee.

The frequency of time lapses by the mentor is an indication of the invitational style – allowing the mentee to gather thought concerning the discussion. These small 'periods' of silence allow some emotional security associated with care in the IMS. This is supported by the various incomplete statements which add to creating caring spaces for the mentee to respond. The body-gestures (facial and body movements) and voice-intonation, particularly in positive comments indicating optimism, and in questions that invite continuation and completion formulation was also noticeable.

The micro detail of the interaction clearly include the mentor rewarding and inviting the mentee to extend own accounts of views. These included subtle constructive assessments that assert student value, allowing student self-repair, and the use of preliminaries to pre-empt questions that follow.

The conversational actions in this case example go a long way towards supporting the invitational style in the sense that they display the guiding beliefs of mentor care, intentionality, trust, respect and optimism. The notion of intentionality for example, implies that the mentor has a particular purpose with the talk, and that the mentor can defend that talk in the context of professional learning such as this. In the case of the current analysis, the intentionality of certain talk moves was clearly evident.

CONCLUSION

This chapter offers a micro-level analysis of exchanges between a mentor and mentee on issues relating to a teaching practice reflection report.

The two identified 'learning episodes' clearly indicate a particular 'stance' by the mentor. The mentor in these two episodes seems genuinely interested in the experiences of the mentee. As IMS is proposed to be a collaborative interaction between mentors and mentees, it purports to allow the mentee the emotional and cognitive space to enter into the mentoring process without fear. The mentor's intentional focus on caring, trusting and respecting the mentee as a full partner in the process is thus of great importance. One would expect talk such as acceptance and confirmation of mentee's ideas to be visible from an IMS perspective, and this is indeed the case. 'Talk-moves' such as intentional turn design, through specifically requesting clarifications and extensions of the mentee's response and carefully constructed shifts in the conversations to bridge related concepts, highlight the invitational nature of the interaction. These talk moves allow the mentee the time and space to give clear account, but especially to come to deeper realisations, personal clarifications and self-assessment. Allowing the mentee to partake fully in his/her own learning, and to satisfy the need for emotional support, a sense of basic care and trust (Hennissen, et al., 2011), is regarded as essential ingredients for the mentee to move forward in the interaction. These 'talk moves' by the mentor in this case underscores Tillema and van der Westhuizen's (this volume) view that mentors, and in this case mentors who use the IMS, will engage in the exploration of collaborative meaning in their interactions, potentially leading to more 'reciprocal' than 'asymmetric' relationships.

It also became apparent in the analysis the mentor engaged in talk that continuously reflects, supports and extends the interaction. Tillema (2011) proposes that mentors can deliberately design their 'talk' to support mentees to achieve a higher level of efficiency. He proposes that the talk can be on three levels, namely on the levels of reflection, goal setting and planning. In the case in question, the mentor much of the talk in the interaction, intentionally or unintentionally, to allow the mentee ample opportunities to reflect through self-assessment, clarification, account giving. It also appears that from the analysis that the mentor requires the mentee to plan, all be it rather superficially in terms of own practice pertaining to the setting and marking of assessments. It is however, not quite clear from this analysis how the talk was designed to assist the mentee to goal-setting. Tillema's view hinges on a 'deliberate' design of the talk and interaction in mentoring. IMS has been defined as a deliberate and intentional act to support others to develop the relatively untapped potential they have. The analysis of the current case has not supplied adequate evidence to make a judgment as to the 'intentionality' of the discrete mentor talk and actions.

In conclusion, the evidence from the analysis of one case appear to indicate that particular micro-level conversational techniques/actions can be associated with an invitational style of mentoring. Although these findings are worth noting, further and more extensive exploration of the tendencies noted in this chapter are needed.

REFERENCES

Arminen, I. (2000). On the context sensitivity of institutional interaction. *Discourse & Society, 11*(4), 435–458.
Asbill, K., & Ginzalez, M. L. (2000). Inviting leadership: Teacher perceptions of inviting principal practices. *Journal of Invitational Theory and Practice, 7*(1), 16–29.
Aspy, C. B., & Aspy D. N. (1994). On rediscovering self-invitations to education. *Journal of Invitational Theory and Practice, 3*(2), 75–84.

Beach, S. (2001). Good falling: How one childcare professional invites positive self-talk in preschool children. *Journal of Invitational Theory and Practice*, 7(2), 66–71.

Briscall, M. A. (1993). Adapting the 5-P relay for inviting quality family time. *Journal of Invitational Theory and Practice*, 2(2), 87–97.

Bumann, M., & Younkin, S. (2012). Applying self efficacy theory to increase interpersonal effectiveness in teamwork. *Journal of Invitational Theory and Practice*, 184,11–18.

Burns, G., & Martin, B. N. (2010). Examination of the effectiveness of male and female educational leasers who made use of the invitational leadership style of leadership. *Journal of Invitational Theory and Practice*, 16, 30–56.

Cannon, W. C., & Schmidt, J. J. (1999). Invitational counseling: A fresh vernacular for marriage and family therapy. *Journal of Invitational Theory and Practice*, 6(2), 73–84.

Chant, R.H., Moes, R., & Ross, M. (2008). Enhancing teacher reflection and classroom creativity: Implementing a collaborative Problem-solving model. *Journal of Invitational Theory and Practice*, 15, 55–67.

Cheng, M. M., Tang, S. Y., & Cheng, A. Y. (2012). Practicalising theoretical knowledge in student teachers' professional learning in initial teacher education. *Teaching and Teacher Education*, 28(6), 781–790.

Cowher, S. J. (2005). Reflection upon the Invitational model and the 5 powerful P's in working with Post-Traumatic Stress Disorder (PTSD). *Journal of Invitational Theory and Practice*, 11, 63–70.

Davis, G. M. (1994). Don't fight, mediate. *Journal of Invitational Theory and Practice*, 3(2), 85–94.

Drew, P., & Heritage, J. (2006). *Conversation analysis: Institutional interactions* (Vol. 4). Thousand Oaks, CA: *Sage*.

Eckstein, D. (2005). *Encouragement, confrontation and reframing as a Capella University mentor*. Paper presented at Capella University, Altlanta, GA.

Edwards, D. (1997). Toward a discursive psychology of classroom education. In C. Coll & D. Edwards (Eds.), *Teaching, learning and classroom discourse: Approaches to the study of educational discourse*, (pp. 33–48). Madrid: Fundacion Infancia y Aprendizaje.

Edwards, D. (2005). Discursive psychology. In *K. L. Fitch & R. E. Sanders (Eds.), Handbook of language and social interaction*, (pp. 257–273). Hillsdale, NJ: Erlbaum.

Egley, R. (2003). Invitational leadership: Does it make a difference? *Journal of Invitational Theory and Practice*, 9, 57–70.

Elbaz-Luwisch, F., & Orland-Barak, L. (2013). From teacher knowledge to teacher learning in community: Transformations of theory and practice. *Advances in Research on Teaching*, 19, 97–113.

Frakes, D. L. (1999). Humor in counseling: A review and examination from an invitational perspective. *Journal of Invitational Theory and Practice*, 6(2), 85–92.

Goffman, E. (2005). *Interaction ritual: Essays in face-to-face behavior*. New Brunswick, NJ: Aldine Transaction.

Haigh, M. (2008). Cross-cultural instruction, consciousness raising, and inviting heightened Self-esteem. *Journal of Invitational Theory and Practice*, 14, 11–24.

Hayano, K. (2013). *Territories of knowledge in Japanese conversation*. Utrecht: LOT.

Hennissen, P., Crasborn, F., Brouwer, N., Korthagen, F., & Bergen, T. (2011). Clarifying pre-service teacher perceptions of mentor teachers' developing use of mentoring skills. *Teaching and Teacher Education*, 27, 1049–1058.

Heritage, J. (2012). The epistemic engine: Sequence organization and territories of knowledge. *Research on Language & Social Interaction*, 45(1), 30–52.

Heritage, J. (2013). Epistemics in conversation. In J. Sidnell & T. Stivers (Eds.), *The handbook of conversation analysis* (pp. 370–394). Hoboken, NJ:Wiley-Blackwell.

Hoffmeyer, C., Milliren, A., & Eckstein, D. (2005) The Hoffmeyer mentoring activity checklist: Invitations to professional growth. *Journal of Invitational Theory and Practice*, 11, 54–62.

Ivers, J. J., Ivers, J. J. (Jnr.), & Ivers, N. I. (2008). Cross-cultural instruction, consciousness raising, and inviting heightened Self-esteem. *Journal of Invitational Theory and Practice*, 14, 11–24.

Kennedy, J. (2006). *A study of learning environment in the extended practicum of a pre-service teacher education course at a catholic university*. Australian Catholic University, Banyo QLD.

Keogh, J. (2010). (In)forming formal evaluation: Analysis of a practicum mentoring conversation. *Journal of Applied Linguistics & Professional Practice, 7*(1).

Kitchens, A. N., & Wenta, R. G. (2007). Merging invitational education with mathematics education: A workshop for teachers. *Journal of Invitational Theory and Practice, 13,* 34–46.

Koole, T. (2010). Displays of epistemic access: Student responses to teacher explanations. *Research on Language and Social Interaction, 43*(2), 183–209.

Koole, T. (2013). Conversation analysis and education. *The encyclopedia of applied linguistics.*

Koole, T., & Elbers, E. (2014). Responsiveness in teacher explanations: A conversation analytical perspective on scaffolding. *Linguistics and Education, 26,* 57–69.

Kronenberg, J., & Strahan, D. B. (2010). Responsive teaching: A framework for inviting success with students who "Fly below the radar" in Middle school classrooms. *Journal of Invitational Theory and Practice, 14,* 11–24.

Magano, M. D., Mostert, P., & Van der Westhuizen, G. (2010). *Learning conversations: The value of interactive learning.* Johannesburg: Heinemann.

Mahoney, J. A. (1998). The inviting school superintendent. *Journal of Invitational Theory and Practice, 5*(2), 97–106.

Maynard, D. W., & Clayman, S. E. (2003). Ethnomethodology and conversation analysis. *The handbook of symbolic interactionism,* 173–202.

Mboya Okaya, T., Horne, M., Laming, M., & Smith, K. H. (2013). Measuring inviting school climate: A case study of a public primary school in an urban low socioeconomic setting in Kenya. *Journal of Invitational Theory and Practice, 19,* 15–29.

Mercer, N. (2008). Talk and the development of reasoning and understanding. *Human Development, 51*(1), 90–100.

Mondada, L. (2011). Understanding as an embodied, situated and sequential achievement in interaction. *Journal of Pragmatics, 43*(2), 542–552.

Niemann, R., Swanepoel, Z., & Marais, N. (2010). Challenging the 'Four Corner Press' as framework for invitational leadership in South African schools. *SA Journal of Industrial Psychology, 36*(1), 1–8. Retrieved June 23, 2014 from http://www.sajip.co.za/index.php/sajip/article/view/799/887

Orland-Barak, L., & Klein, S. (2005). The expressed and the realized: Mentors' representations of a mentoring conversation and its realization in practice. *Teaching and Teacher Education, 21*(4), 379–402.

Owens, K. (1997). Six myths about self-esteem. *Journal of Invitational Theory and Practice, 4*(2), 115–128

Paxton, P. (1993). Total quality management and invitational theory: Common ground. *Journal of Invitational Theory and Practice, 2*(1), 29–34.

Radd, T. R. (1998). Developing an inviting classroom climate through a comprehensive behavior-management plan. *Journal of Invitational Theory and Practice, 5*(1), 19–30.

Reed, C., & Shaw, D. (1997). Voices on schools without fear. *Journal of Invitational Theory and Practice, 4*(2), 101.

Rice, P. B. (2003). What are universities doing to help prospective teachers find positions? *Journal of Invitational Theory and Practice, 9,* 71–75.

Riner, P. S. (2003). The intimate correlation of invitational education and effective classroom management. *Journal of Invitational Theory and Practice, 9,* 41–56.

Sacks, H. (1992). *Lectures on conversation. Volume I, II.* Edited by G. Jefferson with an introduction by EA Schegloff. Oxford: Blackwell.

Sacks, H., Schegloff, E. A., & Jefferson, G. (1974). A simplest systematics for the organization of turn-taking for conversation. *Language,* 696–735.

Schmidt, J. J., & Shields, W. C. (1998). Integration of guidance lessons using invitational concepts in a friendship curriculum. *Journal of Invitational Theory and Practice, 5*(2),107

Seedhouse, P. (2013). Conversation analysis and classroom interaction. *The encyclopedia of applied linguistics.*

Shulman, L. S. (1994). Those who understand: Knowledge growth in teaching. In B. Moon & A. Mayes (Eds.), *Teaching and learning in the secondary school* (pp. 125–133). London, England: Routledge.

Sidnell, J. (2012). 'Who knows best?: Evidentiality and epistemic asymmetry in conversation. *Pragmatics & Society, 3*(2).

Stafford, W. B. (2003). To honor the net in invitational counseling. *Journal of Invitational Theory and Practice, 9,* 9–22.

Steyn, G. M. (2005). Exploring factors that influence the effective implementation of professional development programmes on invitational education. *Journal of Invitational Theory and Practice, 11,* 7–34.

Steyn, T. (1993). The manifestation of invitational theory in inviting schools. *Journal of Invitational Theory and Practice, 2*(1), 19–28.

Stillion, J. M., & Siegel, B. L. (1994). The transformational college teacher. *Journal of Invitational Theory and Practice, 3*(2), 55–74.

Stivers, T., Mondada, L., & Steensig, J. (2011). *The morality of knowledge in conversation* (Vol. 29). Cambridge: Cambridge University Press.

Tanase, M. (2013). Meeting student needs in the freedom writers movie: An activity in a classroom management course. *Journal of Invitational Theory and Practice, 19,* 4–14.

Thompson, D. R. (2004). Organizational learning in action: Becoming an inviting school. *Journal of Invitational Theory and Practice, 10,* 51–68.

Thompson, F. (2009). The instruction and assessment of multi-cultural dispositions in teacher and counsellor education. *Journal of Invitational Theory and Practice, 15,* 32–54.

Tillema, H. (2011). Mentor conversation research project at University of Johannesburg. Workshop notes and discussions [Study is still ongoing]. Unpublished research proposal.

Trent, L. M. Y. (1997). Enhancement of the school climate by reducing teacher burnout: Using an invitational approach. *Journal of Invitational Theory and Practice, 4*(2), 103–114.

Tung, E. (2002). Lifeskills for prospective teachers. *Journal of Invitational Theory and Practice, 8,* 27–41.

Valiante, G., & Pajares, F. (2002). Inviting one's self and inviting others: Influence of gender, grade level, and gender orientation. *Journal of Invitational Theory and Practice, 8,* 42–60.

Van der Westhuizen, G. (2011). Leergesprekke in universiteitsklaskamers: 'n herwaardering. *Litnet Akademies: 'n Joernaal vir die Geesteswetenskappe, 8*(3), 392–410.

Van der Westhuizen, G. (2012). Learning equity in a university classroom. *South African Journal of Higher Education, 26*(3), 623–637.

van Kruiningen, J. F. (2013). Educational design as conversation: A conversation analytical perspective on teacher dialogue. *Teaching and Teacher Education, 29,* 110–121.

Walker, D. C. (1998). Kaleidoscopic reflections: A story of self-concept and invitations. *Journal of Invitational Theory and Practice, 5*(2), 83–96.

White, S. D. (1999). Inviting self-efficacy in children: Taking competition out of the game. *Journal of Invitational Theory and Practice, 6*(2), 93.

Zeeman, R. D. (2006). Glasser's choice theory and Purkey's invitational education – Allied approaches to counselling and schooling. *Journal of Invitational Theory and Practice, 12,* 46–51.

Martijn P. van der Merwe
Department of Educational Psychology
University of Johannesburg, South Africa

Gert J. van der Westhuizen
Department of Educational Psychology
University of Johannesburg, South Africa

PART 3

MENTOR PROFESSIONAL DEVELOPMENT –
LEARNING TO BECOME A GOOD MENTOR

Mentors need to learn as well – but how?

A natural way for mentors to learn would be when mentors were confronted with the situations and dilemmas brought forward in the mentoring conversations they have; i.e., the cases presented to them by their mentees to which they are expected to have a solution. As authentic, case–based problems these situations or dilemmas call upon the professional knowledge and beliefs of mentors which would require them to further articulate their knowledge and help them to resolve problematic situation for their future practice.

While this may be regarded as "implicit learning" which provides "just' local knowledge for mentors, a more deliberate way of knowledge construction would be to, preferably, set up collaborative learning among mentors, that would be based on systematic inquiry and study of issues encountered in their practice. Such a joint shared learning could be highly profitable in the field of mentoring. How then can we set up a learning environment in mentoring as a continuing source of professional growth? Should it be largely bound to and within the individual opportunities encountered in the mentor's task environment or more educationally framed through professional programs? This part of the book explores this issue.

MAJOR ASSUMPTIONS ABOUT MENTOR LEARNING

We put forward three major key-points about the nature of professional learning that may guide a further reading of the chapters:

(i) Extended Professionalism:

We assume that mentors will be operating as 'extended professionals' (Hoyle, 1980), i.e.,.as amenable to improvement. Hoyle's view of extended professionalism is one which underpins an emphasis in professional development on the value of inquiry and continuous development. It lays emphasis on self-study, action-research and peer-assisted learning.

(ii) Developing by Resourcing:

For learning to occur explicated resources in the form of ideas and materials are needed, in order to support mentors' professional development. Following Huberman (1995) it is important to set up supportive networks to learn from each other. Such a support system could entail:

- Provision of off-site intensive workshops on professional strategies,.
- Requesting reflective journals, to include insights on the implementation of strategies in their own mentoring practice
- Asking mentors to involve other mentors to observe their mentoring
- Encouraging ongoing contact among mentors before, during and after mentoring, including contacts with supervision.
- Holding Focus Group meetings for all mentors to reflect as a group on their practices.

(iii) The Creation of Professional Knowledge:

Mentors need to make reference to external sources of knowledge, and connect them to their own meaning-making (Stoll & Louis, 2007). But also professional mentor development needs to take into account the mentor's personal response to professional knowledge-creation and at the same time acknowledge that practices and tools are needed to learn from each other

The current part of the book addressed these issues: that is, how would a possible "pedagogy for learning to become a good mentor" look like.

In chapter 11 Sanchez and Garcia provide a rich case about addressing learning needs of teachers in mentoring sessions and what kind of professional development would fit mentors' learning. Sanchez and colleagues provide more detail on formats of mentor learning in the subsequent chapter 12. In Chapter 13 Smith advocates mentoring as being a genuine profession and subsequently in chapter 14 Smith and Ulvik explore what makes up a mentor's professional pedagogical content knowledge that lies at the heart of professional action in mentoring. Chapter 14 closes this story line by giving examples and structure to a professional education of mentors.

REFERENCES

Hoyle, E. (1980). Professonalization and de-professionalization in education. In E. Hoyle & J. Megarry (Eds.), *World yearbook of education 1980. The professional development of teachters.* London: Kogan Page.

Huberman, M. Networks that alter teaching. *Teachers & Teaching; Theory and Practice, 1*(2), 193–221.

Stoll, L., & Louis, K. S. (2007). *Professional learning communities. Divergence, depth & dilemmas.* Maidenhead, Berkshire: Open University Press, McGraw Hill Education.

EMILIO SÁNCHEZ AND J. RICARDO GARCÍA

11. UNDERSTANDING TEACHERS AS LEARNERS IN READING COMPREHENSION MENTORING

Considering Teachers' Possibilities of Change as a Way of Bridging the Distance between Teachers' Practice and Research-Based Instructional Design Programs

OVERVIEW

Imagine a mentor working with a group of teachers. All of them were introduced to a reading comprehension program and learned about how important it is for teachers a) to assume an active role for students by means of setting them meaningful goals and b) showing the relevance of adopting a metacognitive approach to a learning task by encouraging learners to admit their own failures, and c) to seek ways of mending them. All teachers understood the relevancy of this research-based instructional program and all of them would have liked to develop their lessons according to it. However, they all felt that these programs are far away from their possibilities in practice. Even more so, some teachers indicate that they have already tried to help their students to assume an active role and/or had developed a metacognitive style of learning, but without success. All in all, these teachers do want to improve their practices but they cannot find ways to connect their current situation to these research based instructional programs. They do not feel confident enough to start such endeavour, and/or they do not perceive the essential difference between what they already do and what they are supposed to do. So, what can a mentor do in order to help teachers to improve their ways of teaching? In this chapter we propose some ideas to face this mentoring challenge in the field of reading comprehension.

INTRODUCTION

As a starting point, we claim that there is an *imbalance* in educational reform processes between what we know about student learning needs (to become competent) and what we know about teacher learning needs (to become responsive to student-learning-needs). Thus, in many domains (maths, science, social skills, self-regulated learning), we know a lot about:

H. Tillema et al. (Eds.), Mentoring for Learning, 227–255.

- What *resources* (skills) must be acquired by the students,
- What are the common students' *learning trajectories* in becoming competent, (including critical *steps*, *time* required, and *obstacles* to be overcome),
- What *aids* make their learning progress easier.

All of these issues (resources, learning trajectories, and aids) shape our knowledge on what students need in mastering a target domain. Nevertheless, the situation is not so clear when we move to teacher professional development. Here, most of the time we have determined what resources teachers *should deploy* in order to be responsive to students' needs, but we do not know to the same extent what teachers really do about it in their classrooms. Therefore, we cannot indicate either the teachers' learning trajectories -defined as overcoming the difference/s, gap/s or steps between teacher's habitual practice and research based practice- or determine what elements define teacher's learning needs (in time, obstacles, and aids).

This imbalance between our knowledge on students' and teachers' learning needs is a weakness in designing instructional programs. It becomes of special relevance when we accept that the more we know about students' learning needs, the more complex the teaching work becomes. Our central claim, then, is that in designing mentoring experiences (to overcome the imbalance), it is important to include both research on *student learning needs* and research on *teachers learning needs*. The purpose of this chapter is to provide evidence regarding this claim, taking reading comprehension as a grounding environment because this field has developed a considerable body of research and there have been many efforts in translating the knowledge generated on this topic to schools and teachers (Taylor, Pearson, Peterson, & Rodríguez, 2005).

This chapter is organized as follows. First at all, we go over research-based instructional design programs to document the abovementioned *imbalance problem* (between what we know about students learning needs and what we know about teacher learning needs).

Secondly, we present a fine-grained analysis of 32 whole-group reading lessons. The analysis will focus on three components that allow us to compare teaching practices with research-based instructional programs on: a) how the lessons were organized, b) how the teacher-student interactions unfolded throughout the lesson, and c) what kinds of aids teachers provided to deal with the reading comprehension task. This analysis reveals that there are important differences between teachers' practices and instructional design programs ranging from simple to the more complex ones.

Finally, we use findings from our analyses to show the different impact of possible trajectories on professional development; favouring one that helps teachers in a reflective and cyclical way and that leads them to identify their current practices and, subsequently, helps them to create attainable goals to change their practices.

CLARIFYING THE IMBALANCE BETWEEN WHAT WE KNOW
ABOUT STUDENTS' LEARNING NEEDS AND WHAT WE KNOW
ABOUT TEACHERS' LEARNING NEEDS.

How Instructional Design Programs Are Being Constructed

As represented in Figure 1, research-based instructional programs (at least in the field of reading comprehension) usually have been developed alongside three kinds of interrelated knowledge:

1. Knowledge about the cognitive *resources* and skills involved in reading comprehension (e.g. Kintsch, 1998; McNamara & Magliano, 2009). This knowledge specifies the target cognitive resources and skills needed to be mastered by the students.
2. Knowledge about *the learning trajectory* for each component and skill (e.g. Cain & Oakhill, 2007). That is: (a) what are the *steps* to become competent (e.g.: fluent reading, rhetorical competence (Sánchez & García, 2009)), (b) how much *time* is necessary to consolidate the different levels of achievement), and (c) what kind of *obstacles* must be overcome (deficits in individual differences as phonological awareness, inference skills, or students' cultural background*).*
3. Knowledge about *aids* that facilitate the reading comprehension process (e.g. McCrudden & Schraw, 2007) and reading skills acquisition (e.g. McNamara, 2007).

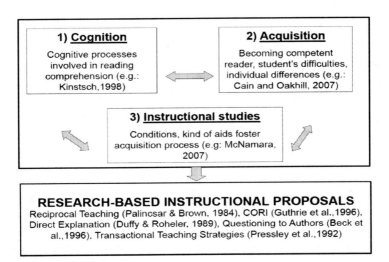

Figure 1. Interrelated knowledge grounding research-based instructional programs

The arrows in Figure 1 show how the knowledge summarized in boxes 1, 2 and 3 grounds reading comprehension instructional programs and justifies what must be taught, how and when. As examples of such an instructional design, we can refer to: transactional teaching strategies (Pressley et al., 1992), direct explanation (Roehler & Duffy, 1984), reciprocal teaching (Palincsar & Brown, 1984), or the concept-oriented reading instruction proposal (CORI Guthrie, McRae, & Klauda, 92007; Guthrie et al., 1996; Guthrie et al., 2004; Guthrie & Wigfield, 2000; Guthrie, Wigfield, & Perencevich, 2004).

Most of these programs teach specific reading comprehension strategies (summarizing, predicting, questioning) by explaining, modelling, and supervising teaching activities. The knowledge generated by this research based programs leads to more complex teaching in order to accommodate to students learning needs. Our point is: The teaching solutions and tools offered by these programs make up in fact a new problem that tends to be overlooked; i.e., teachers must master whole new ways of teaching activities in reading comprehension in their classroom. Consequently, teacher learning in this case must be carefully documented and better understood. The notion of *research-based practice*, often includes a great deal of research attention to students' needs. Our claim is, however, that we need research (and mentoring) attention to teachers' needs too.

Teacher learning challenge: what teachers should do according to research-based instructional design programs.

In order to clarify the teacher learning challenge posed by research-based instructional design, we have listed the main resources of an ideal reading lesson plan (Table 1).

Table 1. Elements of research-based instructional programs
in reading comprehension

Main elements taken from research-based instructional programs Teacher should create…
A meaningful learning environment.
A (more) symmetrical way to conduct teacher-student interactions.
Teacher's aids that holds active student participation and peer collaboration.

The three elements/indicators in Table 1 shape three layers of teaching activities:

a. A first element present in most of the instructional programs is that teachers are encouraged to create *rich learning environments* that promote engaged readers. That is to say: readers become involved in reaching specific and meaningful learning goals as a result of the program. It is assumed that experiencing the program (as an example consider CORI proposal by Duffy, 1993) will bring forward cognitive resources needed for achieving learning results.

b. Also promoted are *symmetrical ways of organizing teacher-student interaction* that will allow students to assume a more active role in making decisions about what to do in specific situations, in assessing the contribution of others (also those made by the teacher), and in participating in peer debates and discussions.

c. Finally, analysis of instructional programs suggests that *new ways of aiding* are required that will assure active student participation and peer collaboration. In fact, as Pressley et al. (1992) underscored, teacher prompts are (should be) "sensitive to the context of the particular story rather than pro forma (e.g., after title, after paragraph 1, etc.)" (p. 519). In other words, besides a rich global organization of the reading activity, specific prompts or aids must be provided during the reading and interpretation process.

No doubt, in all of the research-based instructional programs mentioned in Figure 1, teachers are expected to teach the new cognitive resources to their students. For instance, teachers have to explain what a prediction means and have to model how to carry it out. But, obviously, explaining and modelling cognitive strategies are often not part of common teaching activities.

In sum, the key elements these programs rely on are: creating learning contexts that provide reading comprehension strategies, developing more symmetrical teacher-students interactions, and supporting students with aids that maintain them as active learners. All of these characteristics pose a learning challenge to teachers, and we think that this challenge has not been well documented. This is what we consider to be the imbalance problem that needs us to revise what is known about real teaching practices and its professional development.

What We Know about Real Practices in Teaching Reading

We can differentiate between two sorts of evidence. The first one consists of studying implementation processes by means of describing what is achieved when teachers try to master a target instructional program as, for instance, in the transactional teaching program (Pressley et al., 1992). The second one consists of taking into account what the teachers tend to do during their classroom activities, examining the distances between what teachers usually do and what teachers should do according to research-based instructional designs.

Studying the implementation process As an example of this kind of studies, we take a citation from Pressley et al. (1992). After considering different reports about the implementation process of transactional strategies, he asserts that "training involves a week or so of intense instruction followed by a year of intermittent coaching, (plus an) additional instruction and support in subsequent years from supervisors and teaching peers" (p. 545). In fact, veteran teachers claim that it takes at least 2 years of in service training and support to feel comfortable with a new reading program. In more precise terms, "teachers required three years of practice before they emerge as expert" (Brown & Coy-Ogan, 1993, p. 232), and it is a demanding process that causes "confusion and rejection" at the beginning of the formative process (Duffy, 1993) and low rates of acceptability during the first training year (El-Dinary & Schuder, 1993). It is important to note that these results are taken from training processes that do not offer "pre-developed classroom materials" or scripts and, consequently, teachers have to create materials to meet their own needs (Duffy, 1993; El Denary & Schuder, 1993). In the same vein, Beck et al. (1996) points out, after studying a one-year long implementation process of Questioning the Author (QtA) that it was not easy for teachers due to the fact that "we asked these two teachers to break habits they had developed in their teaching" (p. 411). In fact, Andreassen and Bråten (2011) reached a similar conclusion. Their reading program addressed four different principles. Their findings show that 2 out of 4 principles remained underdeveloped (reading-group organization and reading motivation) whereas the other two principles (previous knowledge activation and teaching strategies) were implemented in a proper way by teachers. Interestingly, the two less developed principles correspond to the elements: "learning environment", and "teachers' helping/ teacher-student interactions".

The picture becomes slightly different when teachers are provided with specific guidelines and materials and when action is taken to determine whether programs have been administered with fidelity by checking different teaching activity indicators (see, for instance, van Keer, 2004; De Corte et al., 2001; McKeown, Beck, & Blake, 2009). Here, the results point to a higher level of implementation. Nevertheless, it is important to note that the main elements in instructional design programs described above (creating new learning contexts, developing symmetrical interactions, supporting students) are not pre-established in regular classroom teaching. Hence the difficulty of implementation reported by Pressley et al., or Brown, Coy-Ogan, Duffy or El-Dinary, and Schuder, 1911 remains.

In sum, implementation studies have reported on time needed, obstacles or difficulties that arise, and teachers' initial discomfort. These issues are documented in the literature as indications of an "imbalance" between research-based approaches and current teaching practice. We note, however, that such an imbalance is still documented in very general terms (See for examples next section). We claim that it is important to study specific imbalances in classroom reading comprehension teaching activities. Before undertaking such an analysis, we need to review what we know about reading comprehension classroom practices.

Classroom practice analysis. We have found few studies that describe what teachers actually do when they face typical teaching reading activities, such as whole-group reading lesson. The activity tends to follow a steady structure (Wolf, Crosson, & Resnick, 2005): 1) teachers select a text - mainly from the textbook, 2) teachers ask the students to read, perhaps in different turns, either aloud, either in silence, or in both ways, and 3) teachers raise different questions during reading and when finished, ask students to answer questions or solve tasks with help of specific aids the teacher provides them.

For instance, Smith et al. (2004) analyzed 35 literacy teachers from elementary school, half of the teachers were highly effective and the other half made average progress with their pupils. The whole group lessons were analyzed on specific teachers' moves (direction, explanation, open questions, closed questions, repeated questions, up-taking questions, probing questions, evaluate, refocus, general talk), students' moves (answering a question, choral response, presentation and spontaneous contribution), as well as the discourse pattern enacted. The results show clearly that a traditional approach was prevalent: teachers talk amounted to 75% of the whole talk, with closed questions, and explanations and directives in most of the moves, instead of using open questions. This approach was common (with small differences throughout the elementary school and between efficient and average teachers).

Wolf, Crosson, and Resnick (2005) analyzed 21 reading-comprehension lessons considering the relation between discourse specific moves and the quality of content elaborated from the text. The results showed that "teachers, in general, lead the conversation, and used more talk moves to obtain student responses" (p. 47).

More recently, McKeown, Beck, and Blake (2009), in analyzing a basal reading approach concluded that the more recitative teacher-led discourse was typical for four out of six teachers, whereas the other teachers adopted a more complex and open frame. In addition, the questions posed by five out of six teachers were far from eliciting students' experiences.

In short, studies that analyze what teachers actually do conclude that: a) teacher-centred teaching is the most common approach in classrooms; b) a traditional teacher-led discourse prevails; c) explicit teaching of reading strategies is not frequent, and de) low demanding teachers' aids (explanations, directions, closed questions moves) are more common than the more sophisticated ways of helping: open questions, revoicing or follow-up moves. This leads us to assert that in usual ways of teaching there is high variability in adopting guidelines from research based programs. Our intention is to capture what makes a difference between a reading lesson given in a traditional way of teaching from the one in a research-based instructional design program and, consequently, what can be done in mentoring to align with teacher learning needs.

EXPLORING TEACHER LEARNING NEEDS

In order to document what teachers do in reading comprehension lessons, we have collected a corpus of reading lessons and analyzed in a fine grained way.

Corpus

The corpus is composed of 32 whole-group reading lessons from 32 different primary school teachers. Each reading lesson was part of a curriculum unit in a variety of disciplines: literature (1 lesson), biology (10), geology (8), history (5), and geography (8). All of them were videotaped and transcribed. Each reading lesson adopts the typical structure mentioned by Wolff et al. (2005): 1) the teacher selects a text, 2) he/she asks students to read (aloud/in silence, in turns …), and 3) he/she raises different questions that the students have to answer.

System of Analysis

In order to offer a systematic comparison between what teachers should do according to instructional design programs and what teachers really do, we have established a comparative framework based on key elements of instructional design programs (See Table 1) and typical elements of teaching practice (see Table 2). In order to collect evidence from reading lessons, we segmented each reading lesson in our corpus into three units of analysis; thus narrowing our focus progressively: episodes, cycles and teacher's aids.

Table 2. Indicators and units of analysis of teacher's lessons

Main elements from the research-based instructional programs Teacher should provide …	Indicators in teachers' practice We need to know …	Unit of analysis We need to identify in teachers' reading lessons
A meaningful learning environment.	How the reading lessons are globally organized and, specially, planned or introduced.	Episodes
A (more) symmetrical way to conduct teacher-student interactions.	How teachers and students interact during the lessons.	Cycles
Teacher's aids that holds the active student participations and peer collaboration.	How teachers help students to face reading comprehension tasks.	Aids

In this way we could:

- Decompose each reading lesson into Episodes which reveals how the lessons were globally organized and establish distances with regard to the elements proposed by instructional design programs.
- Decompose each episode into communicative Cycles which allows us to identify the interaction pattern present in each cycle and how much it differs from the symmetrical pattern in the instructional programs.
- Identify the Aids delivered in each communicative cycle which provides us with the information we need to characterize the helping style of each teacher and how much it differs from the kind of assistance suggested in the instructional program.

Depending on how much each element in each reading lesson differs from instructional design proposals, the teacher's learning challenge will become more or less existent. At the same time, this triple analysis could be used as well in the conversations between mentors and teachers in order to promote awareness about teaching practice and to decide on accessible goals for change.

1) Episodes. The transcriptions from each reading lesson were segmented in *episodes*. This provides a map of each reading lesson showing all the activities and their sequence (see in Figure 2 some examples). An episode is defined as the main segment from a reading lesson that covers the set of exchanges gathered around a

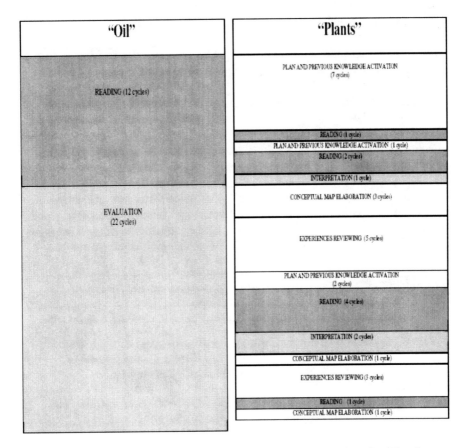

Figure 2. Two reading lessons segmented in episodes. Note that "Plants" reading lesson is composed of many episodes. Some of them are the most common (as the listed above: planning, interpretation, previous knowledge activation …) and others (as experience reviewing) are less frequent

specific goal. We have distinguished between the following main episodes (they are presented in a prototypical order according to how they appear in most lessons):

- *Previous knowledge activation*, what teacher and students "put on the table", i.e., the given information considered relevant to the reading activity.
- *Planning* or introductory episode that anticipates the reading activity. It can consist of mentioning the general topic of the text, and/or the specific issues, and/ or clarifying the instructional goals for the reading activity.
- *Reading* episode that comprises all exchanges devoted to reading the text. These episodes start when teachers ask students to read a text part and finish reading to develop questions-answers cycles about the ideas just read. The reading can be aloud or in silence, in turns (e.g. one student reads a paragraph and another student reads the next one) or individual, and by fragments or completed (the whole text is read in the same episode).
- *Interpretation* episode that includes comments or elaborates answers related to each specific text segment. This episode is used to create a round of questions-answers about the ideas just read.
- *Closing or closure* episode that encompasses the teacher-students exchanges to establish a kind of summary of the content just read (by means of conceptual map, a recapping, and underlining).
- *Evaluation* episode where students' understanding is assessed by different procedures (usually by specific questions).

2) Cycles. Each episode contains a string of teacher-students exchanges, and we segment each episode into grouping of exchanges labelled as teaching cycles (Bellack, Kliebard, Hyman, & Smith, 1966). Cycles are defined as turns necessary to reach a common ground about an issue involved in a joint reading activity.

EVALUATION EPISODE
Cycle 1
Cycle 2
Cycle 3
TURN 1. Teacher: You have to look now for information about the light. Why do plants need light? (...) Have you already found it, Elvira? (Elvira assents). So, tell my why.
TURN 2. Student: To live.
TURN 3. Teacher: All that plants need is to live. What is the most important idea? Antón, would you like to tell us?
TURN 4. Student: To make the food.
TURN 5. Teacher: Because they need to make the food taking the energy from...
TURN 6. Teacher and students: Light
Cycle 4

Figure 3. Example of the division in cycles

For example, in cycle 3 taken from Figure 3, the exchange starts with a teacher who poses a question to students that students try to solve in Turns 2 and 4, and, finally the teacher closes the exchange by formulating an answer. In the middle part, the teacher provides different aids (explained below) after the insufficient response from the first student. The presence of aids and the opportunity of giving more than one answer characterize an IRF structure (Wells, 1999). In determining the end of each cycle typically a statement occurs expressing an accepted and suitable response to the starting question. Sometimes, finding the end of a cycle is not so clear. For instance, after a student A's response, the teacher formulates a new question to student B instead of closing the current exchange. Here it is assumed that a new cycle starts in an implicit way.

Each cycle is categorized according to the type of discourse structure or pattern: – a cycle matching a simple and recitative Initiative-Response-Evaluation or IRE structure (Mehan, 1979); – a more complex structure, such as the IRF (Wells, 1999), – a scaffolding structure (Graesser, McNamara, & VanLehn, 2005), or some sort of symmetrical structure (Nystrand, Wu, Gamoran, Zeiser, & Long, 2003). Each episode and each lesson is analyzed cycle by cycle and represents a typical discourse pattern.

3) Teacher's aids. Once episodes are segmented into cycles, as is shown in Figure 3, each cycle is analyzed by considering the discourse moves or 'aids' provided by the teacher to reach a common ground. For example, an aid can be a close (or yes/no) question, a brief summary, a clue for an answer and so on. In this way we determine what sort of aids are given and how many of them are used in order to elaborate the shared idea from each cycle. For this purpose we use the taxonomy elaborated by Chi, Siler, Jeong, Yamauchi, and Hausmann (2001): before (in the Initiative part), during (in the Response part), and after the action/response (in the Evaluation or Feedback part).

The first step in identifying aids is to distinguish between the instructional content elaborated by students and the aids provided to generate them. For instance, from the previous excerpt of Figure 3, an idea/content is elaborated in turn 2, ("plants need to live") and another one in turn 4 ("plants need light to make food"). The other responses could be considered as support provided by the teacher. Thus, in turn 3 the teacher offers two aids: a corrective aid that hints the student in finding a more specific response and a prompting aid that pushes the student to try out again in a deeper way. Turn 5 extends the student's answer (see Sánchez, García, & Rosales, 2010 for details).

In short, in order to elaborate the idea "plants need to make the food taking the energy from the light" the teacher provides aids like: a hint, a corrective feedback, a prompt, and a reformulation. It is interesting to notice that depending on what kind of aid is provided, teachers provide more or less room to students to react to the questions raised.

RESULTS AND INTERPRETATION

We collected s of episodes, cycles and aids.

Analysis of episodes: how the teachers globally organize the whole-group reading lesson. The purpose of this analysis is to catch the global organization of the whole-group reading lessons to indicate the quality of the reading environment created by teachers. Basically quality depends on three variables: a) diversity or variability of episodes (as a correlate of the complex cognitive activities teachers want to foster in students), b) setting of a goal for the whole lesson, and c) arrangement of episodes around such a goal. Combining these quality indicators allows us track the progression of a lesson organization. The results of these analyses are shown in Figure 4.

a) Variability of episodes. We found that 10 from the 32 lessons are composed of only two episodes (see bar A of Figure 4): *reading aloud* the whole text and *evaluating* the students' understanding. We did not find a goal (episode) that organizes the lessons because there was not a planning episode. A different overall pattern is shown in the other 22 reading lessons. All of them involve a richer repertoire of episodes that includes prior knowledge activation (PKA), planning, and closure. This means that students are promoted to carry out a wider and more diverse number of cognitive processes than in the first group of 10 reading lessons. However, the point is to find out in which extent this set of episodes are articulated around the reading goal set up in the planning episode. Answering this depends on the next step in our analysis: whether episodes are articulated around a reading goal in the planning episode.

b) Setting goal process in the planning episodes. We could identify four different kinds of goal setting processes in the planning episode (plus a non-planning option) ordered as follows2:

- The more complex one (at the right of Figure 4) consists of revoicing/reflecting student's thoughts about the topic to prompt for relevant understanding (indicating they lack of an important piece of information, or there are inconsistencies with other student statements). Here, the students know in advance what they need to learn and why. We label this way of setting a plan as "*It's well known that ... BUT*".
- The second (named "*Before we saw.... AND now we will see...*") involves a recap of previous experiences related to the text AND to present a new theme without any relation to the previous recapitulation.
- The third kind of planning is called "*Theme plus topics list*", it requires a brief presentation of the theme ("it is about.") and forwarding of subtopics (or specific questions) covered by the text.

- The fourth way of planning includes an *"it is about."* statement that allows telling in advance the topic of the reading lesson without clarifying which sort of achievements are expected.
- Finally (as anticipated), any lack of planning (*"We are going to read this text. Please, read the first paragraph"*).

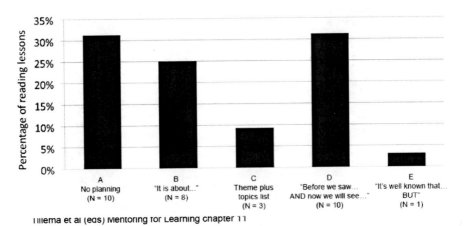

Figure 4. Types of planning episodes found in the 32 reading lessons

It has to be noticed that only in the three first planning episodes (the right part of Figure 4) students are guided in an explicit way on what to obtain by reading the text: only in these types of planning teachers allow students to perform reading in an active way. Among these three types of planning we can identify a trajectory to elaborate a goal from simple to most complex. On the left in Figure 4 there are the more simple ones and on the right, the most complex ones. For instance, in the most complex way (*"It is well known that..., BUT..."*) teachers must figure out and take on the student's perspective and rethinking its contents in a conscious way. However in *"theme presentation patterns"*, the teacher only need to engage in text reflection; while in the non-planning pattern both processes (assuming student's point of view, and rethinking text content) are lacking. This suggests how difficult it may be for a teacher who is used to enact pattern A (at the left of the Figure 4) to move directly to pattern E (at the right).

c) Global organization or articulation around a goal.   Interestingly, a sophisticated pattern such as E (or even D) does not ensure that the rest of episodes were in fact coherently developed according to planning. We could identify four different global patterns on the interconnectedness of the whole lesson (see Figure 5). In the first and simple one, there is no interconnection because there is not a plan guiding the lesson, or the plan is very unspecific ("It is about…" plan). Consequently, after reading the text, an evaluation episode starts with lots of questions that can cover the whole text content.

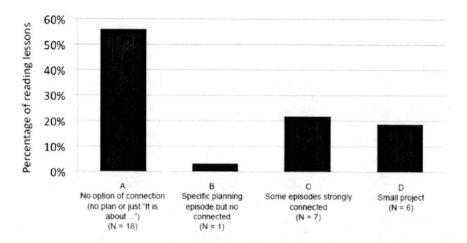

Figure 5. Global patterns of the reading lessons attending to the interconnection between episodes

Secondly, we have found one lesson that contains more differentiated episodes (prior knowledge activation, closure.) and a more specific plan, however the episodes were not interrelated (see pattern B from Figure 5). This is an interesting pattern due to the fact that students are engaged in expressing what they know about the topic. But the ideas activated are overlapping in a far-off way and the content addressed turns out to be disconnected from the rest of episodes.

A third structure (pattern C from Figure 5), requires, at least, that some episodes are strongly connected. For instance, there is a planning and evaluation connection which means that content related to goals is evaluated, while other episodes (e.g., previous knowledge activation and evaluation episodes) are less integrated. This is a complex partially integrated pattern.

At the end of this continuum, we have found a fourth and richer structure with a strong inter-connection ("small project": pattern D from Figure 5) that covers the main processes involved in reading comprehension (metacognitive, text-base, and situation model). We can speak of a project structure because the whole lesson is organized around a specific problem connected to the students' previous knowledge that justifies and organizes the rest of the episodes. The expression "small" means that the reading lesson as a whole is not well connected to other activities. In other words, we name it "small project" in order to emphasize that it is different from the Project Unit (see Polman's description, 2004), in which an overarching problem organizes a reading unit with different reading lessons, and in which each reading lesson has its own small project. Apparently, the CORI instructional design suggests such a kind of learning environment (also see Duffy's, 1993 comments).

What does global organization mean? Perhaps, the best way to clarify the results from our analysis is to reconsider the notion of participant structure (Cazden, 2001; Philips, 1979; Polman, 2004; Tabak & Baumgartnet, 2004). According to this notion, each pattern or structure elicits, in an implicit way, specific roles, responsibilities and cognitive activities: "Read carefully (now) because later I'm going to ask you about everything that has been read", – is the message from pattern A (Figure 5); "Try to work out (considering what you already know) these points by reading this part of the text that we're going to speak about them" is the message from the small project pattern.

In the same vein, we can consider the grade of interconnection. For instance, in a complex structure but poorly interconnected (option B from Figure 5), a potential guide is given for the students but it is one that loses power throughout the lesson. Implicit but powerful messages organize the mental and social student activity. In other words: each structure embodies values and conceptions, clearly different, about what the learning task is (Tabak & Baumgartnet, 2004). Therefore, a mentor equipped with this type of knowledge would be able to help teachers to take notice of these patterns and reflect on the implicit meanings teachers are transmitting to their students.

The imbalance problem and mentoring. The findings offered in Figures 4 and 5 provides further clarification to explain the lack of transfer between program and practice. The distance seems too large for teachers to cope with so that moving from current teaching to the instructional design program would be impossible for teachers (even if they felt motivated to do it). It would require participation in an extensive professional development process as documented by El-Dinary and Schuder (1993), Duffy (1993) and others. Our findings suggest that instead of advocating such a big step, it would be more suitable to plead for small changes. Perhaps, it is even better to help teachers to become aware of their current practice before conceiving these small changes, due to the probable implicit nature of these patterns. Moreover, it seems difficult that all teachers interpret a pedagogical prescription as CORI in the same way.

2) Analysis of Discourse Patterns

How teachers and students interact during reading lessons. Our analysis focused on cycles: the string of teacher-students exchanges needed to reach a shared knowledge on a validated answer. The categorization of cycles according to discourse patterns (IRE, IRF, symmetrical) allows us to recognise how the interaction between teachers and students flows and helps us to detect how far or close it is from the alignment with the research-based instructional design.

Variability of discourse patterns. In order to capture discourse pattern variability, the episodes were segmented into cycles, and each cycle is characterized by main discourse patterns according to the following criteria:

- IRE: the criteria for an IRE category, according to Mehan (1979), is: a) a testing purpose more than a teaching purpose, b) different ways or opportunities to answer, c) the E slot (the closure of the cycle) consists of a corrective feedback. In the analysis reported here, we decided that, at least, two of these indicators had to be present in order to assign this category to a specific cycle. For example, a cycle starting with a questions such as "Who is the president of the U.S.A.?" will be an IRE.
- IRF: according to Wells' (1999) definition, the criteria are: a) the purpose is teaching/learning more that testing, i.e., there is more than one acceptable answer, b) there are different opportunities to elaborate progressively on the answer, c) the F slot (the closure of the cycle) entails some aid to reformulate and re-appropriate activities. In the analysis reported here, we decided that, at least, two of these indicators had to be present in order to assign this category to a specific cycle. An example of IRF is the Cycle 3 from Figure 3.
- In Questioning, teachers pose an open question to the students, and teachers re-voice and recap each contribution before posing a new query that prompts the students to deepening the responses. This suggests that we had to distinguish between non-connected IRFs and complex *IRF sequence.*
- Symmetrical participant structure (Polman, 2004): this structure is present when the students have the right to speak in I and/or E/F slots, and when the IRF criteria already mentioned is also present: the purpose is learning, the answer can be progressively elaborated, and teacher can help students in searching for an answer.

Appendix provides examples of these discourse patterns. In short: we were able to distinguish four discourse patterns: IRE, simple and fragmentary set from non-connected IRFs, complex IRF sequence and symmetrical discourse patterns.

Each pattern could be interpreted as a (local) participant structure3. Thus, the IRE triadic structure expresses how knowledge is something "you can look up in your memory, and retrieve and express it in a sure and checkable form", while the IRF entails different assumptions: (1) there are various ways to word it, although, (2) at the end, there will be a canonical way accepted for everyone based on the teacher or textbook authority. Finally, in the symmetrical participant structure, it is assumed that the final understanding will hinge on a negotiation process in which all of the students should participate to make sure that the content is really shared and deeply understood.

In other words, each discourse pattern provides an implicit guide for action and enacts how the knowledge building process is deployed. Again, it is assumed that the more complex and symmetrical a participant structure is, the more enacted the instructional program will become. Now the question is how these structures are distributed in the different lessons we analyzed.

Tracking the discourse patterns progression. Our results are very clear: there is no variability in the 32 lessons studied. In all of them, the predominant local participant structure is the IRE. As Figure 6 shows, the presence of the IRE structure in the whole corpus (67,3%) is clearly larger than the presence of IRFs (non connected: 20,2%; or connected: 8,1%), and symmetrical patterns (4,4%). These results are compatible with Nystrand et al. (2003), Smith et al. (2004), Wolf et al. (2005), and McKeown et al. (2009).

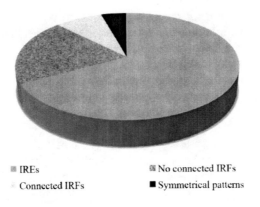

IREs	No connected IRFs
Connected IRFs	Symmetrical patterns

Total dialogic cycles: 911

Figure 6. Percentage of cycles from the total corpus for each participant structure

Consequences for mentoring. The lack of variability among the reading lessons is an interesting point to note because it means that we can find more styles among teachers in the global than in the local participant structure. In short, all of the reading lessons contain mainly IRE discourse patterns, but carry out different global formats.

3) From aids to teacher styles of helping

As cycles being small units inside episodes, aids are small units inside cycles (in fact, the smallest unit we have considered). Aids are discourse moves provided by the teachers in order to reach a common ground attained in each cycle. The point of this analysis is to determine how much teachers differ in helping their students from the kind of assistance suggested in instructional programs.

a) Kind of aids. Teachers' aids that were identified (see Figure 3) have been interpreted according to how much space they create to students in elaborating a response or solution to the questions or problems posed. We could distinguish three kinds of teachers' aids:

- *Regulatory* aids that consist of illuminating the problem space created by each question in order to foster the students to be active in elaborating the answer (e.g.: leading questions, recap, up to dating goals, highlighting the task, or offer a strategy). In the feedback slot, aids that consolidate the students' contributions have the same function (e.g. revoicing).
- *Pressing* aids that prompt the students to elaborate in a deeper way on their initial response by constraining or narrowing the path to reduce the problem space (e.g.: prompting and hint moves). In the feedback slot, aids that reformulate the students' contribution in a more sophisticated way.
- *Contributing aids* that are part of the solution (e.g.: filling in the blanks) invading students' space for elaborating the answer. In the feedback slot, it contains aids that enrich (adding new content) or redirect the students' contribution as well as teacher direct contribution to the solution.

b) Tracking ways of helping. Basically, only 271 out of the 1300 aids identified in the whole corpus (see Figure 7) are regulatory (in the sense of being an opportunity to prompt strategies), and only one teacher helped students by deploying this kind of aid which is compatible with intervention programmes (see option E from Figure 8).

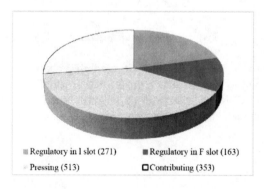

Regulatory in I slot (271)   Regulatory in F slot (163)
Pressing (513)   Contributing (353)

Total aids: 1300

Figure 7. Percentage of each kind of aid found in the total corpus

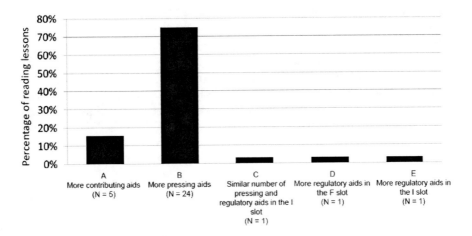

Figure 8. Type of reading lessons according to the predominant kind of aid

Each kind of aid can be related in a specific manner to the research based teaching programs from Figure 1. The aids that regulate students' activity are clearly directed towards specific strategies. This means that teachers accustomed to deploy this kind of aids will find it easy to implement instructional design strategies. Let us consider an example from the transactional instructional design program (Pressley et al., 1992):

(After the student's struggles with the reading of a large word)

Coy-Ogan [Teacher]: OK, we have some problem-solving strategies we can use. (Coy-Ogan points to the strategies bulletin board behind her as she thinks aloud about her options.) When we get to a word that we don't know, we can guess and substitute it; we can ignore it and read on; we can reread the sentence; we can look back in the story for clues; or we can use the picture clues.

Marie [Student]: Can I read this all over?

Coy-Ogan: You can decide. Marie says she wants to read it all over. I think that's a good decision.

Here, the teacher, adopting a traditional discourse pattern, offers a range of solutions instead of a specific directive that guides or illuminate how the problem space could be reduced. It is a regulatory aid. In the transactional approach, strategies must be elicited that consider what is going on at each moment and not merely at the beginning of the reading lesson. Therefore, teachers that use already regulatory aids in their reading lessons have a good starting point for adopting a program like the transactional approach. Also, the excerpt shows how much distance there is between this kind of help and contributing aids. Contributing aids are very distant from the transactional teaching program, in that the learning challenge for teachers who are used to provide such a kind of help will be larger, i.e., more than for teachers who prefer pressing or regulatory aids.

Interestingly, the pressing aids (preferred by 24 of 32 teachers) could be considered close to the kind of strategies suggested by Beck et al. (1996) to foster deep understanding. However, even in this case, the teacher learning challenge would be large for many of the teachers of our corpus.

The point we like to stress here is the different degrees to which teacher can and will (be able) to adhere to the various aids that are promoted by instructional programs.

DISCUSSION

The research-based instructional programs listed at the bottom of Figure 1 suggest that it is necessary (see Table 1):

- To create a rich learning environment where the different activities are interconnected and align with the students' previous knowledge and interests,
- That the students adopt an active role during the reading and interpretation.
- That the teachers offer aids to regulate the problems during the reading while guiding the student's interpretation process.

Our point is to understand why it is so difficult to transfer these research-based instructional design proposals to classroom activity. In order to understand this problem, we have collected three kinds of evidence from 32 regular teachers on: 1) how they create a global participant structure in their reading lessons and, especially, how the reading lesson is introduced or planned, 2) what kinds of discourse patterns or interactions are unfolded throughout the lesson, and 3) what kind of aids are provided by the teachers. In all of our cases we could lay out a continuum that unveils different degrees of congruency between research and practice that we have tried to interpret and understand.

The results offered by these sources of evidence suggest that:

- For many teachers, the distances between their current practice and the instructional programs are out of proportion, suggesting that new ways of mentoring to promote changes in classroom activities must be undertaken.
- The distances and variability in the three trajectories are different and this suggests that some aspects of needed change could be more accessible (e.g. planning episodes) than others (e.g. discourse patterns and aids).
- There is more distance between the current practices and the explicit teaching strategies, than between the current practices and the content covered by an instructional design approach (e.g. QtA).

The distances between what is required and what is practised are quite large in most cases we analyzed. Basically, the main result of our analysis is the huge difference between current teaching practices and research based instructional design programs. This is the case, especially, in connection with episodes, discourse patterns, and aids (but not so clear in case of planning episodes). In more detail, 59% of the global patterns, 67% of the discourse patterns, and 73% of the aids are very different from their respective elements outlined in instructional programs. These results gain special importance if we realize how teachers cope with the demands or requirements of research based reading programs; perhaps, teachers were not aware of what to do. It would involve realizing that different episodes are not connected, that usually contributing aids instead of regulatory aids are provided, that not always they express clearly what goals are expected to be met by the student after the reading lesson, and that the interaction is basically centred on teacher decisions.

We can imagine the effort and time necessary before teachers feel comfortable carrying out the strategies proposed in instructional design programs such as questioning closing, PKA, or planning episodes. The challenge could even become bigger if, at the same time, teachers need to change the local participant structure and the sorts of aids they provide. In fact, this provokes a new important question: Is it indeed possible to change everything at the same time? Related to this, one can predict the following issues: a) changing the global reading format could be more accessible than changing the local discourse pattern; b) enacting pressing aids could be easier than regulatory aids, c) explaining and modelling strategies could be easier than supporting the strategic enactment during the reading. Here, mentoring arise as a crucial tool in order to aid teachers to take acknowledge of what they do and in order to choose the best goals for change in every step of their professional development.

Some results from previous studies are compatible with our conclusions. For instance, Beck et al. (1996) reported that after one year of professional development, only 15% of questions were posed by the students although extended discussion took up 55% of the student/teacher exchanges (with only a 20% in the baseline). In the same vein, Andreassen and Bråten (2011) conclude that motivational and interactional dimensions of their program were hardly successful, whereas previous knowledge activation and teaching strategies were more enacted. El-Dinary and Schuder (1993) asserts that teachers felt comfortable with explaining and modelling strategies per se but found it difficult to coordinate them with their teaching practice. Duffy (1993) analysis suggests that a critical point for becoming expert teachers is to integrate reading into units where the focus is on "pursuit of an authentic goal, solving a genuine problem or producing a genuine product". Finally, it seems that content approach could be more closed to common teaching practice than strategic one.

CONSEQUENCES FOR MENTORING PROCESSES

The main consequences for the mentoring process from our data are the following:

1. Mentors can help teachers in examining their current performance and in detecting gaps with respect to other ways of teaching. I,e., focus on what do I really do?
2. Teachers can be guided to find on their own way of moving from current performance to other more complex ones.

These two important tasks can only be faced if mentors have substantial knowledge about teaching practices. To illustrate this, we summarize three studies in which we have tried out three different ways of promoting teacher change in the planning episode of reading lessons. In the first study, both components listed above (examining current performance, and establishing changes) were missing, which means that a traditional professional development experience was delivered: i.e., modeling and supervision. In the second one, only the first component is included. And, in the third one, teachers are helped in carrying out both.

1) Modeling Good Planning Practices + Supervision

This first mentoring study consisted of: (a) providing teachers with declarative descriptions about how to plan an activity, b) providing them with examples of good planning, and c) supervising how to set up a plan according to the model. Note that here supervision means that the mentor informs participants about their current performances (after trying out) and pushes them to adopt the better way of planning a lesson. Once this assessment is done, the participants are encouraged to enact the better way of planning in the sessions that followed.

This recursive process was carried out over a six months period and encompasses 33 teaching lessons and 11 supervision sessions. The results show that only two out of the ten participants (20%) acted in a coherent way with the proposals offered during the mentoring process. In analyzing, we were able to identify a certain number of distortions and simplifications teachers had with respect to what a good plan means. We assumed that these simplifications would hamper the changing of the target teaching practice as long as participants were not aware of them.

2) Modeling + Being Aware of Current Teaching Practices

In the second study, we preserved the same conditions of study 1 except that the 13 participants were informed about their main simplifications and about the scarce achievements attained in the previous study. Consequently, the participants were urged to overcome these low levels of achievement by assuming a very active role in detecting simplifications and distortions in their own practice. After each mentoring process, participants were encouraged to enact the best way to create a good plan. 11 out of 13 participants (85%) reached a very good level along the way, meaning that their reflective activity on their simplifications played a meaningful role in improving their teaching practices. Nevertheless, a year later we videotaped the teaching practices of the best five participants and this analysis showed that none of them sustained their level of achievement, despite the fact that three of them thought that they really were performing accordingly.

In short: mentoring in the second study led to changes that were quite substantial, but not sustained. This lack of sustainability could be explained by the distance between the participants' current practice and the new teaching requirement following the proposal. The research-based instructional design ended up being to much of a demand, pushing the participants to take up much effort in developing the best way of planning. Once the mentoring process finishes, the social support and the helping cues that guided the mentoring disappear. This would bring us to ask: What will happen if the distance between what is done and what it should be done is shortened in a more systematic and dynamic way?

3) A Study Lesson Based on Teacher Learning Trajectories

In order to answer this question, we conducted a new mentoring experience with 30 in-service teachers from 1st to 10th grades. Participants were meeting with a mentor once a month during three school years. Previously, they were informed about some of the lessons learned from our analysis of what teachers used to do: that there were different ways of planning a reading session, that is not possible to change many teaching aspects at the same time, and that it is difficult to change something if you are not aware of it.

The mentoring experience was based on a study lesson scheme that included complete cycles of assessment-planning-enacting-revising phases that take into account the actual teacher learning trajectories. This meant that each teacher was made aware of what he/she did (which pattern they usually enacted) and using this information as guidelines for determining and guiding his/her changes. Thus, each teacher decided what small change he/she wants to undertake (moving from their current pattern to another more complex and required one). In order to help teachers to analyze their practice and to choose what to change, mentor provided protocols that teachers had to fill out between one session and the next (see an example in Appendix). In this way, we could document the changes taken on by the teachers in each cycle, how much time was necessary to consolidate them, and some obstacles throughout this formative process.

Figure 9 shows how the planning episodes evolved throughout the 8 cycles. Two findings can be of interest at this point. Firstly, none of the teachers decided to undertake the best way of planning in the first cycles. This is an interesting result that can highlight the difficulties when teachers assume the best practice each time they try to improve their own teaching activity. The second finding is that teachers require a lot of opportunities before consolidating meaningful changes.

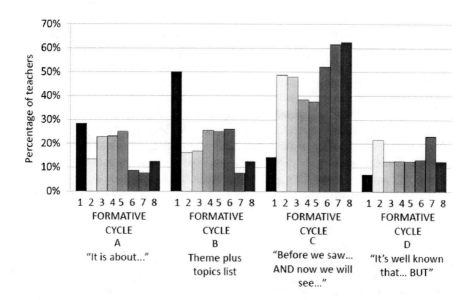

Figure 9. Evolution of the kind of planning episodes achieved
by teachers through 8 mentoring cycles

We grasped from this last study what difficulties teachers experience when implementing new practices. Apparently, what seems to be missing in formative (mentoring) processes is making reference to detailed knowledge about the teachers' learning needs. Knowing and reconciling in advance the actual teaching practices that needs to be changed allows mentors to involve teachers in a reflective process about what they really do and what they could try to do in pursuing what should be done. In short, the point we like to stress is to be able to consider four sources of information at the same time: what I really do, what it should be done, what would be possible to do (choices), and what I can try to do (now). The data shown in this chapter suggests that knowing teachers' learning trajectories facilitates efforts to change their practices.

NOTES

[1] On another level, the bidirectional arrows between boxes 1-3 and 2-3, mean that data from box 3 could support some predictions elaborated in 1 and 2.

[2] The name of the different types of planning episodes are based on the reading processes and reading strategies that a competence reader performs, according to several reading comprehension models (e.g., McNamara & Magliano, 2009: setting an specific reading goal, integrating text ideas with prior knowledge, etc.). Nevertheless, the final labels have been created taking into account the data we have collected and the work with many teachers through mentoring processes in order to build a sharing wording to think about their practice.

[3] Classroom discourse patterns and participant structures are used in an interchangeable way. However, if we track how these notions were originally proposed, the differences between both notions turn out well marked. Thus, if we compare Mehan's (discourse patterns) with Philips's (participant structures)

seminal works, we advise that Mehan (1979) was involved in capturing the co-occurrence relationships among different teacher and students acts (following the Sacks, Schegloff, and Jefferson's (1974) approach to study the conversational rules that funnel the everyday conversations). Consequently, Mehan offers a formal account in describing the teachers-student interactions that specify which is the most probable act given or known a previous one. In fact, the well-known IRE pattern is considered as containing "two coupled adjacency pairs" (p. 50). On the other hand, Philips's work (1979) is devoted to identify "the rights and responsibilities" that students must take in the different classroom activities. It is true that Phillips claims for describing different "structural arrangements of interactions" and this sounds as the Mehan's aims, but, in fact, her notions amalgam features such as the right to speak, the student role in instructional activity and the instructional purpose that go beyond the co-occurrence relations between communicative acts.

⁴ See end note 3.

REFERENCES

Andreassen, R., & Bråten, I. (2011). Implementation and effects of explicit reading comprehension instruction in fifth-grade classrooms. *Learning and Instruction, 21*, 520–537.

Beck, I. L., McKeown, M. G, Sandora, C., Kucan, L., & Worthy, J. (1996). Questioning the author: A yearlong classroom implementation to engage students with text. *The Elementary School Journal, 96*, 385–414.

Bellack, A. A., Kliebard, H. M., Hyman, R. T., & Smith, F. (1966). *The language of the classroom*. New York, NY: Teachers College Press.

Brown, R., & Coy-Ogan, L. (1993). The evolution of transactional strategies instruction in one teacher's classroom. *The Elementary School Journal, 94*, 221–233.

Cain, K., & Oakhill, J. (2007). *Children's comprehension problems in oral and written language: A cognitive perspective*. New York, NY: Guilford.

Cazden, C. B. (2001). *Classroom discourse: The language of teaching and learning* (2nd ed.). Portsmouth, NH: Heinemann.

Chi, M. T. H., Siler, S. A., Jeong, H., Yamauchi, T., & Hausmann, R. G. (2001). Learning from human tutoring. *Cognitive Science, 25*, 471–533.

De Corte, E. (2000). Marrying theory building and the improvement of school practice: A permanent challenge for instructional psychology. *Learning and Instruction, 10*, 249–266.

De Corte, E., Verschaffel, L., & van de Ven, A. (2001). Improving text comprehension strategies in upper primary school children: A design experiment. *British Journal of Educational Psychology, 71*, 531–559.

Duffy, G. G. (1993). Teachers' progress toward becoming expert strategy teachers. *The Elementary School Journal, 94*, 109–120.

El-Dinary, P. B., & Schuder T. (1993). Seven teachers' acceptance of transactional strategies instruction during their first year using. *The Elementary School Journal, 94*, 207–219.

Graesser, A. C., McNamara, D., & VanLehn, K. (2005). Scaffolding deep comprehension strategies through Point&Query, AutoTutor, and iSTART. *Educational Psychologist, 40*, 225–234.

Guthrie, J. T., & Wigfield, A. (2000). Engagement and motivation in reading. In M. L. Kamil, P. B. Mosenthal, P. D. Pearson, & R. Barr (Eds.), *Handbook of reading research* (Vol. 3, pp. 403–422). Mahwah, NJ: Erlbaum.

Guthrie, J. T., McRae, A., & Klauda, S. L. (2007). Contributions of concept- oriented reading instruction to knowledge about interventions for motivations in reading. *Educational Psychologist, 42*, 237–250.

Guthrie, J. T., Wigfield, A., & Perencevich, K. C. (Eds.). (2004). *Motivating reading comprehension: Concept-oriented reading instruction*. Mahwah, NJ: Erlbaum.

Guthrie, J. T., van Meter, P., McCann, A. D., Wigfield, A., Bennett, L., Poundstone, C. C., et al. (1996). Growth of literacy engagement: Changes in motivations and strategies during concept-oriented reading instruction. *Reading Research Quarterly, 31*, 306–332.

Guthrie, J. T., Wigfield, A., Barbosa, P., Perencevich, K. C., Taboada, A., Davis, M. H., et al. (2004). Increasing reading comprehension and engagement through concept-oriented reading instruction. *Journal of Educational Psychology, 96*, 403–423.

Kintsch, W. (1998). *Comprehension. A paradigm for cognition.* Cambridge: Cambridge University Press.
Lam, S., Law, Y., & Shum, M. S. (2009). Classroom discourse analysis and educational outcomes in the era of education reform. *British Journal of Educational Psychology, 79,* 617–641.
McCrudden, M. T., & Schraw, G. (2007). Relevance and goal-focusing in text processing. *Educational Psychology Review, 19,* 113–139.
McKeown, M. G., Beck, I. L., & Blake, R. G. K. (2009). Rethinking reading comprehension instruction: A comparison of instruction for strategies and content approaches. *Reading Research Quarterly, 44,* 218–253.
McNamara, D. S. (2007). *Reading comprehension strategies: Theories, interventions, and technologies.* Mahwah, NJ: Lawrence Erlbaum.
McNamara, D. S., & Magliano, J. P. (2009). Towards a comprehensive model of comprehension. In B. Ross (Ed.), *The psychology of learning and motivation* (Vol. *51,* pp. 297–284). New York, NY: Elsevier Science.
Mehan, H. (1979). *Learning lessons. Social organization in the classroom.* Cambridge, MA: Harvard University Press.
Nystrand, M., Wu, L. L., Gamoran, A., Zeiser, S., & Long, D. A. (2003). Questions in time: investigating the structure and dynamics of unfolding classroom discourse. *Discourse Processes, 35,* 135–198.
Olson, D. R., & Bruner, J. S. (1996). Folk psychology and folk pedagogy. In D. R. Olson & N. Torrance (Eds.), *The handbook of education and human development. New models of learning, teaching and schooling* (pp. 9–27). Cambridge: Blackwell.
Palincsar, A. S., & Brown, A. L. (1984). Reciprocal teaching of comprehensions fostering and comprehension monitoring activities. *Cognition and Instruction, 1,* 117–175.
Philips, S. (1979). Participant structures and communicative competence: Warm Springs children in community and classroom. In C. Cazden, V. John, & D. Hymes (Eds.), *Functions of language in the classroom* (pp. 370–394). Prospect Heights, IL: Waveland Press.
Polman, J. L. (2004). Dialogic activity structures for project-based learning environments. *Cognition and Instruction, 22,* 431–466.
Pressley, M., El-Dinary, P. B., Gaskins, I., Schuder, T., Bergman, J. L., Almasi, J., & Brown, R. (1992). Beyond direct explanation: Transactional instruction of reading comprehension strategies. *The Elementary School Journal, 92,* 513–555.
Pressley, M., Graham, S., & Harris, K. (2006). The state of educational intervention research as viewed through the lens of literacy intervention. *British Journal of Educational Psychology, 76,* 1–19.
Roehler, L. R., & Duffy, G. G. (1984). Direct explanation and comprehension processes. In G. C. Duffy, L. R. Roehler, & J. Mason (Eds.), *Comprehension instruction: Perspectives and suggestions* (pp. 265–280). New York, NY: Longman.
Sacks, H., Schegloff, E. A., & Jefferson, G. (1974). A simplest systematics for the organization of turn taking for conversation. *Language, 50,* 696–735.
Sánchez, E., García, J. R., & Rosales, J. (2010). *La lectura en el aula. Qué se hace, qué se debe hacer y qué se puede hacer.* Barcelona: Graó.
Smith, F., Hardman, F., Wall, K., & Mroz, M. (2004). Interactive whole class teaching in the national literacy and numeracy strategies. *British Educational Research Journal, 30,* 395–411.
Tabak, I., & Baumgartnet, E. (2004). The teacher as partner: Exploring participant structures, symmetry, and identity work in scaffolding. *Cognition and Instruction, 22,* 303–429.
Taylor, B. M., Pearson, P. D., Peterson, D. S., & Rodríguez, M. C. (2005). The CIERA School Change Framework: An evidences-based approach to professional development and school reading improvement. *Reading Research Quarterly, 40*(1), 40–69
Van Keer, H. (2004). Fostering reading comprehension in fifth grade by explicit instruction in reading strategies and peer tutoring. *British Journal of Educational Psychology, 74,* 37–70.
Wells, G. (1999). *Dialogic inquiry: Towards a sociocultural practice and theory of education.* Cambridge: Cambridge University Press.
Wolf, M. K., Crosson, A. C., & Resnick, L. B. (2005). Classroom talk for rigorous reading comprehension instruction. *Reading Psychology, 26,* 27–53.

Emilio Sanchez
Department of Education and Developmental Psychology
University of Salamanca, Spain

Ricardo Garcia
Department of Education and Developmental Psychology
University of Salamanca, Spain

APPENDIX: EXAMPLES OF DISCOURSE TYPE PATTERNS IN CONVERSATION

We provide some excerpts taken from Pressley et al., (1992). In the first one, a student proposes a solution for a problem detected by himself/herself, taking the initiative slot that opens a new cycle. This is an example of a symmetrical participant structure.

(1) Marie [Student]: (Reading) "And grew, until his..." (Pause) Can I skip it?
Coy-Ogan [Teacher]: OK, Marie's at a big word, and she wants to skip it. Fine.

This kind of interaction is not common in our corpus, where teachers usually deploy directives and take decisions. In the second excerpt, symmetrical too, different students express their thoughts on how a story can be interpreted, thereby breaking the rigid and traditional structure of a discourse led by the teacher. Here, each student assumes a different hypothesis claiming his/her own initiative without being questioned by the teacher (observe, however, how the teacher plays a critical role in extending the students' contributions).

(2) Marie [Student 1]: (Speaking about her prediction about the text after considering the title and some visual elements from the text) I just think he's dreaming, now.

Coy-Ogan [Teacher]: You think he's dreaming. What makes you think that, Marie?
Marie: Because there's no such thing as monsters, and he can't sail for a year.
Coy-Ogan: So Marie's validating her prediction by some facts that we know here's no such thing as monsters and, besides, you can't sail for that long.
Deborah [Student 2]: But he might have a fishing rod in the boat that we can't see because it's in the boat. And he might fish out fish and stuff to eat.
Coy-Ogan: Very good. You're bringing in a lot of background knowledge to give us some more understanding, OK.

A more detailed analysis suggest however that, in fact, interactions in many cases are more teacher-led talk ruled by IRF patterns, as in the following excerpt:

(3) Randall [Teacher]: Who would like to help us summarize what we've learned so far in his story? (Randall calls on Gina and waits for her to respond) What's the important part? What have we learned so far that's really important to remember?

Gina [Student 1]: To check the nose, ears, throat, and stuff, like that.

Randall: Yes, doctors have to do that. If we have to retell or summarize the important parts of what we've read so far in this story, could you think of a couple of sentences that might tell you what's important to know about being a doctor?

Paul [Student 2]: That they have to go to school to be a doctor.

Randall: And what else have we read that we want to add to our summary?

We want to summarize what's important about being a doctor.

Manuel [Student 3]: Younger doctors, well, the older doctors have to help them with their patients.

Randall: And at the beginning, what did we read about that some that you didn't know before?

Shari [Student 4]: There are different kinds of doctors.

Randall: Yes, there are lots of different kinds.

Here we see that all 9 turns shape a unique cycle due to the fact that only in the last turn the teacher indicates that an acceptable response has been attained. Different students contribute to this final statement but, apparently, Gina's, Paul's and Manuel's answers did not receive a complete positive feedback and, in a subtle way, teacher pushes the student to extend each tentative answer.

EXAMPLE OF PROTOCOL OFFERED TO TEACHERS TO HELP THEM TO ANALYZE THEIR PRACTICE AND TO CHOOSE ACCESIBLE GOALS OF CHANGE

AUTOINFORM ABOUT MY PLANNING EPISODE

1. I realized that what I used to do was4… □ No planning □ "It is about…" planning □ "Theme plus topic list" planning □ "Before we saw…. AND now we will see…" □ "It's well known that… BUT…"
2. After realizing what I used to do, I tried to do (think about what you wanted to do in a concrete lesson)… □ No planning □ "It is about…" planning □ "Theme plus topic list" planning □ "Before we saw…. AND now we will see…" □ "It's well known that… BUT…"
3. My planning episode was (please, transcribe what you told your students and attach to your inform a copy of the text read)…
4. The planning that I did was… □ No planning □ "It is about…" planning □ "Theme plus topic list" planning □ "Before we saw…. AND now we will see…" □ "It's well known that… BUT…"
5. What do you conclude? What will you try to do next? (write down any comment and reflection you want to discuss in the next session)

ELENA CIGA, EMMA GARCÍA, MERCEDES I. RUEDA,
HARM TILLEMA AND EMILIO SÁNCHEZ

12. SELF-REGULATED LEARNING AND PROFESSIONAL DEVELOPMENT

How to Help Student Teachers Encourage Pupils to
Use a Self-Regulated Goal-Setting Process

When a mentor met with a student teacher in order to review the reading problems of pupils in her classroom, the aim was to modify the student teacher's lesson practice according to a Self-Regulated Learning (SRL) approach. On that occasion, the student teacher addressed the issue in the following terms: "My pupil is not engaged enough with the tasks I organize and I am not sure about what I can do about it".

By what tactics can a mentor uncover the most common (mis)understandings when student teachers try to work according to an SRL teaching approach in their teaching practice? In this chapter, we cover the findings obtained from three studies on mentoring student teachers. In the first study, we identify the most common distortions and simplifications student teachers have after they took part in a training on SRL teaching. In the second study, we consider the consequences of informing mentors and student teachers about their distortions. Finally, in the third study, we conduct an in-depth analysis of the mentoring conversations from both studies in order to establish the nature of the scaffolding provided in each of them.

INTRODUCTION

One of the main goals in education today is to foster the SRL of learners (Zimmerman & Schunk, 2004). Given its importance, and thanks to several instructional design programs deploying SRL that have been studied (e.g. Zimmerman, 1998, 2000; Boekaerts, 1999; García & Pintrich, 1994; Schunk & Ertmer, 2000), we now have a broad body of knowledge on the nature and benefits of this type of learning; that is, on the promotion of self-regulatory skills in pupils. The large number of studies conducted on SRL (Boekaerts, 2011) has informed us of the cognitive phases and processes involved in SRL, its acquisition process, and the most common difficulties that tend to crop up during its implementation in classroom teaching, as well of the disparities between pupils who show adaptive self-regulatory skills and those who have less well-adjusted skills. As a result of this knowledge (on SRL in general, and on the needs pupils have in acquiring these self-regulatory skills), we are more

H. Tillema et al. (Eds.), Mentoring for Learning, 257–282.

aware of several teaching strategies and practices that can promote SRL in pupils. Meanwhile, there is a wide variety of teaching programs specifying in more detail how to proceed to instruct pupils (e.g. Butler, 1998; Schunk, 1998; Graham, Harris, & Troia, 1998).

As is clear from the many studies, SRL requires a new approach to teaching, whereby teachers have a keen awareness of pupils' needs, and understand the effective use of new SRL based teaching strategies (Perry, Hutchinson, & Thauberger, 2008). However, to date it is not very clear how teachers can be helped or mentored to implement this new teaching strategy in their classrooms. The literature on professional development with regard to SRL teaching (Brodeur et al., 2005) reports that prescriptive approaches prevail, with a lack of empirical research on the professional development programs that document effects on teachers' practices. Table 1 provides an overview of the more recent studies devoted to this issue.

The objective of this chapter is to present the results of three studies we have carried out on implementing SRL teaching in classroom practice by means of mentoring student teachers. On the one hand, we sought to understand the learning challenge involve for student teachers in mastering a specific teaching SRL tactic; in this case, we used goal setting by their pupils. On the other hand, we set out to show how the learning process is affected when mentors are informed about the typical difficulties student teachers experience in acquiring the SRL teaching tactic.

In an initial study, we aim to identify the difficulties student teachers experience after following a standard course on SRL. The second study seeks to discover the effects of deliberately informing mentors and student teachers about the nature of the most common difficulties. Finally, the third study documents how difficulties regarding teaching according to SRL can be modified during the mentoring process itself. Before presenting these studies, we provide an overview of the evidence gathered in professional development literature.

Our review analyses 12 studies that focus on the relation between the effect of the training program provided and the learning outcomes of (student) teachers and the performance of pupils as well. Our findings are presented in Table 1.

Firstly, not all the studies explored the learning attained by the teachers with regard to their teaching practices. This variable has been shown to have the strongest and most direct bearing on later pupils' performance (more than distal measures such as teaching beliefs or cognitions; Muijs & Reynolds, 2002; in Roehrig et al., 2008). Of the 12 studies reviewed, the last two (Perels et al., 2009; Delfino et al., 2010) focus on the cognitive aspects of teaching practices, and the first ten studies touch on 'teaching practices' as a measure for evaluating teacher learning.

Secondly, out of these last ten studies, the first seven use observational methods to record teaching practices by the teachers, whereas others use survey methods (questionnaires, self-reporting, interviews, etc.). It is our assumption that research findings and conclusions are highly dependent upon the way changes in teaching

Table 1. Overview of research studies on teaching SRL.

	RESEARCH FOCUS	LEARNING VARIABLE	METHOD	TYPES OF RESULTS
1) Perry, Phillips, & Dowler (2004); Perry, Phillips, & Hutchinson (2006); Perry, Hutchinson, & Thauberger (2007, 2008)[1]		Practices	Observation *(systematic, rigorous, not occasional)*	Empirical data (evidence)
2) Roehrig, Bohn, Turner, & Pressley (2008)[2]		Practices, self-reflections	Observation *(systematic, rigorous, not occasional)*	Empirical data (evidence)
3) Badia & Monereo (2004)[1]		Knowledge, practices	Questionnaire, observation	Empirical data (evidence)
4) Tillema (2000, 2004)[1]		Beliefs, reflective reasoning, practices	Questionnaire, test, observation	Empirical data (evidence)
5) Fishman, Marx, Best, & Tal (2003)[3]	LINK BETWEEN PROFESSIONAL DEVELOPMENT PROGRAM AND TEACHER LEARNING OUTCOMES	Pupil learning, practices, opinions (teachers)	Test, observation, questionnaires	Empirical data (pupil learning) Narrative-descriptions (practices)
6) Kramarski & Revach (2009)[4]		Knowledge, practices	Tests, observation	Empirical data (knowledge) Narrative-descriptions (practices)
7) Postholm (2010)[1]		Practices, self-perceptions of pupil learning	Observation, interviews	Narrative-descriptions
8) Duchnowski, Kutash, Sheffield, & Vaughn (2006); Kutash, Duchnowski, & Lynn (2009)[2]		Practices	Questionnaires (fidelity scales)	Empirical data
9) Bakkenes, Vermunt, & Wubbels (2010)[1]		Knowledge, beliefs, emotions, intentions, practices, learning activities	Self-reports	Empirical data
10) Butler, Novak, Jarvis, & Beckingham (2004)[1]		Reflections, knowledge, practices, self-perceptions of pupil learning	Interviews	Narrative-descriptions
11) Perels, Merget-Kullmann, Wende, Schmitz, & Buchbinder (2009)[1]		Knowledge, competence (teachers), pupil learning	Questionnaires, interviews	Empirical data
12) Delfino, Dettori, & Persico (2010)[1]		Own self-regulative competence	Online interaction analysis	Empirical data

259

are evaluated. Non observational methods tend to overestimate the presence of, or ability in, teaching skills (this seems to be the case especially when teachers in self assessments do not know much about new teaching strategies or have little opportunity to identify how they are doing when implementing new ones). As Kruger & Dunning note (1999; in Roehrig et al., 2008) it is more common for teachers to tend to overestimate their teaching abilities. We therefore strongly advocate the use of observational methods to evaluate teacher performance as a way of identifying the effects of a program designed to modify their practices (Duchnowski et al., 2006; Bakkenes et al., 2010; Butler et al., 2004). Based on the methods used in the review, we conclude that three studies are less reliable and less informative than the other seven (Perry et al., 2004, 2006, 2007; Roehrig et al., 2008; Badia & Monereo, 2004; Tillema, 2000, 2004; Fishman et al., 2003; Kramarski & Revach, 2009; Postholm, 2010).

Nevertheless, the seven studies that use observation as a methodology reported differences in overall outcomes, because not all of them conducted the observation (and analysis) process with the same systematic rigor, and with a sufficient number of teaching observations. In this respect, the first two studies (in Table 1) present us with a more meticulous methodology, with more observations extended over time than the other five. The fourth column in the Table shows the final results provided by each study. While the first four provided observational data (Perry et al., 2004, 2006, 2007; Roehrig et al., 2008; Badia & Monereo, 2004; Tillema, 2000, 2004), the other three provided narratives and descriptions (Fishman et al, 2003; Kramarski & Revach, 2009; Postholm, 2010).

Finally, it is worth mentioning that out of the 12 studies that focus on examining the relation between the training program and the learning of student teachers, only two studies (i.e., Perry et al., 2004 and Roehrig et al., 2008), together with the study by Bakkenes et al. (2010), concluded less satisfactory outcomes regarding the learning process (even though the courses they deployed were the longest- i.e., one year- and were also the ones that were well-established regarding the learning conditions provided). In contrast, the other studies documented only successful outcomes.

In view of the above rationale on the use of research methodology, we have found a possible explanation for this difference in results of training programs: the studies that recorded less successful results were those which a) evaluated the 'actual teaching practices', b) used systematic and rigorous observation, on more than one occasion during the course of an intervention, and c) provided empirical observation data. On the other hand, those studies which recorded most satisfactory outcomes were characterized by the following aspects:

- They did not evaluate 'practices', but instead evaluated other teacher characteristics (beliefs, knowledge, etc.)
- they did use questionnaire instruments;

- or they evaluated 'practices' but not by the observational method;
- or they evaluated 'practices' using observational methodology, albeit without a very systematic or rigorous approach (no category system, and few teachers and practices analyzed), and/or only in an incidental (occasional) way.

Furthermore, these studies did not present empirical data per se, but descriptions and narratives about what the teachers had done.

In short, out of the 12 studies reviewed, only two (Perry et al., 2004, 2006, 2007, 2008; Roehrig et al., 2008) systematically investigated (through rigorous observation methodology at several moments during the course of an intervention period) the effects of a training course provided on the teaching practices of student teachers, and were the only two studies to provide empirical data in this respect.

We therefore concentrated on the conclusions provided in these two studies for our own research, paying particular attention to their implications, which are as follows:

Perry et al. found a correlation of 0.57 ($p < 0.05$) between the empirical evidence on the SRL based training of student teachers (Perry et al., 2004; Perry et al., 2006) and the empirical evidence on the SRL-related teaching practices recorded in the post-observation teaching of the program (Perry et al., 2008). These data suggest that the amount of SRL related training offered in mentoring discussions was related to the amount of (successful) practices in SRL observed in the student teachers. Moreover, these researchers also found a small yet significant relation between the teaching practices of student teachers and the mentoring style (as more or less explicit) in these post-observation discussions. Student teachers provided with more explicit scaffolding (i.e., more explicit references to SRL and more explicit links between the practices observed and the 'model' practices to facilitate SRL) generally obtained higher ratings for their SRL teaching than those who were given less explicit scaffolding.

With regard to the possible reasoning behind this greater effectiveness, Roehrig et al. report the following: firstly, the importance of communication between the student teachers and their mentors, and secondly the build-up of meta-cognitive awareness in the student teachers themselves. In relation to the former, it is noted that not only is the number of discussions held with their mentors influential (in this respect, the most effective teachers were those who had the most meetings with their mentors), but also the content of the discussions. Accordingly, the more effective student teachers had more conversations about the ideal teaching practices targeted by the training course (instructional strategies, classroom management, etc.) than their less effective peers and, furthermore, they recorded better performance results.

With regard to the second factor (the meta-cognitive awareness of student teachers), it was found that by comparing the data from self-assessments (to gather their views on the use of SRL practices) with observations of student teachers´ practices, these researchers found that self-assessments of the most effective teachers about their achievements and difficulties (in relation to the use of the practices they had learnt) were more precise than those of their less effective peers. The latter group was less realistic and tended to overestimate their performance. The researchers suggest, therefore, that the precision of student teachers' self-assessments of their teaching practices (and hence of the difficulties they faced and the types of improvements they required) might play a role in the effectiveness and implementation of the program to change teachers' practices. Although the researchers are aware they could not determine a directional relation between the difference in meta-cognitive awareness and teaching performance, they assume that such a relation is plausible by arguing that the teachers who had more substantive discussions with their mentors were better at evaluating their skills and, consequently, proved to be better at implementing the intended teaching practices. This argument is also referred to in the study by Harrison et al. (2005) on the role of mentoring in helping teachers to develop critical reflection skills. Finally, Roehrig et al. conclude that teachers benefit most from mentoring conversations when they have sufficient meta-cognitive skills (to process, interpret and use the information provided) and, more importantly, these self-reflection skills interact with the skills of their mentors (see Chapter 5).

Nevertheless, we need to interpret the findings from these two investigations with caution, given that they do not reveal a causal relation, although they can still inform us with regard to the issue under study (how can we help student teachers to learn and develop their teaching strategies in SRL). As pointed out by several researchers, we still lack sufficient studies and further research is needed in this field. Our study raises the following questions: how important is it for mentoring to know in advance the difficulties student teachers experience when learning to deploy teaching strategies on SRL provided in a training course? Are learning outcomes affected by the mentoring process? Are mentor-student teacher interactions influenced during mentor meetings?[1]

OVERVIEW OF THE STUDIES

As mentioned above, and noted in Sánchez et al. in Chapter 11, a first step in order to help student teachers to develop new teaching skills (as involved in SRL) is to understand the learning challenge student teachers face when acquiring the skills. To do so, we conducted a systematic observational study of a typical training course (program) devoted to showing student teachers how to develop an SRL-based instructional intervention involving reading disabled pupils, paying particular attention to the tactic or process of joint goal-setting. This study was designed to collect evidence on how ten student teachers modified their teaching practice over 32 mentoring sessions, as well as on the difficulties they experienced throughout the process. Subsequently, we conducted a second observational study on the same

SRL teaching tactic in which both student teachers and mentors were informed about the learning outcomes obtained in Study 1 and about the difficulties experienced by the student teachers. Our aim was to determine whether awareness of difficulties helps to improve the learning outcomes. Finally, in the third study, we analyzed interactions between the student teachers and their mentors in both previous studies, and compared the nature of the (reflection) scaffolding provided in each one of them. Our specific goal was to discover the impact of the awareness of difficulties in teaching according to SRL with respect to:

- The participation structures that emerge in both mentoring experiences.
- The content of the interactions between student teachers and mentors.
- Student teachers' level of participation in these meetings and analysing their actual practices and limitations with regard to joint goal-setting in teaching.

Our general objective is to provide empirical support on how to help student teachers learn and develop a teaching skill in SRL and, in our particular case, how to help them encourage pupils in the classroom to adopt self-regulatory goal-setting behavior.

TEACHING GOAL-SETTING AS AN SRL SKILL

The topic of training and mentoring in studies 1 and 2 was an intervention in teaching reading from an SRL perspective with particular focus on the process of joint goal-setting by pupils and the difficulties experienced by student teachers to teach according to the SRL perspective. The reading task was situated in the case of teaching disabled pupils. The goal of the study was to analyse how student teachers aided their pupils by comparing their current performance (in the case of spelling words) with the teaching standards they had to achieve, to be accomplished by setting short-term goals for pupils that will regulate their subsequent learning episodes. This is considered to be a recursive process, in which each learning episode requires creating specific teaching goals for the task. Table 2 depicts the specific moves student teachers needed to master to ensure pupils visualize specific goals when they face a task.

Not surprisingly, working according to this teaching format in a consistent way requires considerable time and effort, and mentor supervision throughout the student teacher's acquisition process. The actual teaching process with pupils is constantly calling for new tasks and posing fresh challenges. Student teachers need to learn how to convert general goals into specific ones, compare current performance with standards, and establish new short-term sub-goals. As a result, student teachers must develop a broad and detailed meta-cognitive understanding of the whole intervention process, and adopt a sophisticated decision-making process that allows them to assess when a goal has been achieved by the pupils and how to select a subsequent

Table 2. Teaching goal-setting: student teachers' tactics or moves

	SRL teaching tactics in goal-setting
Current state scanning	*Activity reminder:* picking up on the activities undertaken over the previous days: which tasks were done, what exercises were done, etc. In this category, we can differentiate between two versions, depending on whether the task is done in a complete way or incomplete. In this sense, we can talk about complete activity reminder (in which important content is rehearsed), and diffuse activity reminder (in which only the intention and the activity steps appears). Example:*"the other day we were reading the syllables lists. First we were reading the list with syllables with "r" and after that, the list with syllables with "l". Finally we read the mixed syllables list".* *Achievements reminder:* recalling how the task was carried out in the previous sessions, which outcomes were achieved, mistakes made, etc. In this section, like the one before, depending on whether the reminder is made in a complete or diffuse way, we distinguish between a general achievements reminder and a specific achievements reminder. Example:*"Well, each time we have reduced the mistakes, up until now we made only one, do you remember?, this one".*
Comparison to standards	*Problem definition:* a joint formulating or explanation of the pupil's problem (difficulties) according to the results observed in a reading and writing pre-test. This defines the problematic situation to work jointly. Example: *"Well, looking at these mistakes, we realize now what the problem is because you were writing an "n" instead of "m", right? You're confusing these letters, what do you think? Shall we start to work on this?".* *General goal-setting (objective of the intervention):* this step involves explicitly stating the general goal that is going to be guiding the whole intervention period. It constitutes the main objective why the pupil (together with the student teacher) is going to work during that time. Examples: *"to improve my reading" "avoid mistakes when writing" "to enjoy and learn with reading".* *Specific goal-setting:* this involves itemizing or operationalizing the general goal into operative sub-goals to work on in a progressive way. Example: *"Let us see if we can (achieve) read the words that have "l" and "r" in complex syllables (i.e., gir, bru, blu, gri, bro, gla...) correctly during the following sessions".*
Task goal-setting	*Task goal:* the concrete and immediate objective (challenge) that the student teacher and pupil agree on to reach with the teaching activity. For Example: *"today: do not commit more than 5 mistakes –omission of the phoneme "l"– when reading" "write 10 words correctly out of the 20 that we are going to write today" "read three paragraphs without interruptions".*

Task:
The teaching activity or exercise explanation (what is the task going to involve, steps or order to follow, what strategies or procedure the pupil has to use, with what resources...)

one. Once a new goal has been set, student teachers have to create specific tasks and undertake the recursive process anew, as shown in Figure 1.

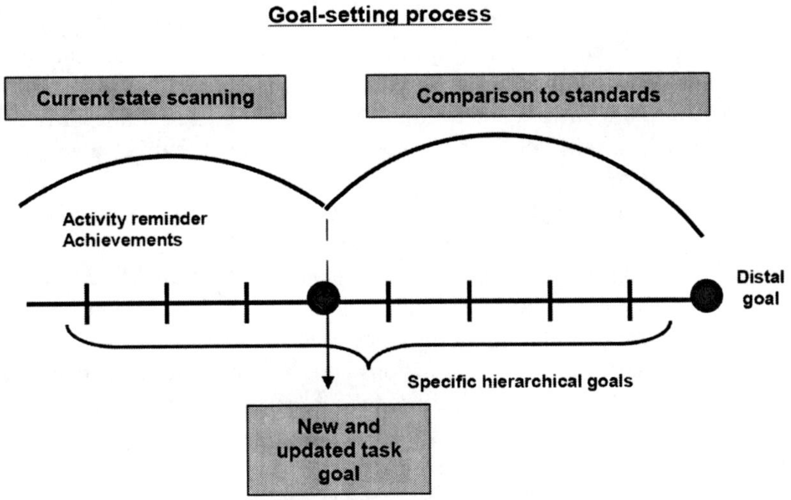

Goal-setting process

Figure 1. Visualizing the goal-setting process

The components for the SRL teaching model of the goal-setting process were extracted from the theory on self-regulation (Zimmerman, 1998, 2000; Schunk & Ertmer, 2000; Schunk, 2003).

STUDY 1: DOCUMENTING STUDENT TEACHERS' DIFFICULTIES

The objective of the first study was to document the learning outcomes obtained in a training course for student teachers, paying special attention to their performance, and whether they were showing simplifications and distortions regarding to the SRL teaching model proposed (see Figure 1).

Method

Ten student teachers took part in the course (which lasted for six months) comprised of the following sections:

Instruction. Initially, the student teachers attended a training seminar of around 20 hours given by two of the authors of this chapter. This seminar mainly covered the SRL teaching model and worked with student teachers on the teaching model they would subsequently use in the intervention period with their pupils. Its objective was to ensure that the student teachers were provided with an in-depth understanding of

265

the teaching model (in terms of both the theory and its procedures). The training involved various activities: theory sessions, in-depth readings and analyses of articles, case analyses, role-playing, and a joint design (each student teacher with his or her assigned mentor) of the first intervention session (lesson) with a pupil.

Intervention + reflection on teaching practices. Following the seminar, the student teachers followed a five-month intervention period (mentored teaching practice). Each student teacher was assigned a pupil with reading and writing difficulties. During this period the student teacher worked with the pupil individually applying the SRL teaching model given in the seminar (two 30–45 minute sessions per week; a total of approximately 30 sessions). In addition, throughout this period (approximately every two weeks), the student teachers had individual mentoring sessions with their assigned mentor. These sessions involved joint troubleshooting of the problems that arose during the intervention and, in general, joint reflection on the teaching practices. The aim of these sessions was to help the student teachers as follows: 1) become aware of their actions and the difficulties encountered and, building awareness, 2) establish guidelines for subsequent action.

An observational method was used for collecting and analysing data; all intervention sessions (student teacher-pupil and student teacher-mentor) were recorded. For this particular study, only the student teacher-pupil sessions were used. After the intervention period, a sample of sessions was transcribed (between four and nine sessions for each student teacher, at different times during the intervention: start, middle and end). For coding purpose, a teaching practice analysis system was developed by the research team itself (Sánchez et al., 2008; Sánchez, García, Rosales, De Sixte, & Castellano, 2008). The written sessions were coded from start to finish, but only the planning episodes were analyzed in-depth in order to study the goal-setting components of interest for this study; i.e., to what extent the student teachers guided their pupils in the self-regulatory process of goal-setting. The components for an analysis system of categories the SRL teaching model of the goal-setting process were extracted from the theory on self-regulation (Zimmerman, 1998).

Results and Conclusions

1. The findings from this 1th study show that- at some point in the teaching with pupils- most of the student teachers apply appropriate teaching tactics in accordance with the SRL model of joint goal-setting, especially in the first sessions, which were co-designed with the mentor and, consequently, reflect all the critical teaching tactics (see Graph 1). However, after the first period, difficulties were encountered by eight of the student teachers in terms of sustaining the SRL model of teaching throughout all the sessions with their pupils.

2. Student teachers seem to use different patterns or combinations of tactics throughout the process: Graph 1 shows five patterns and three types of progressions

throughout the teaching process: The sustained progression (steady line) reflects two student teachers who keep using all the critical components in almost all the sessions (i.e., current state scanning, comparing it with specific standards, and creating a goal for the task to be developed). The oscillating progression reflects changes in the patterns of four student teachers, indicating a selective use of teaching tactics. And the downward line shows a decrease in, or even non-use of, tactics by a group of four student teachers, who end up making a simple scan of the pupil's difficulties before presenting the teaching task.

3. A detailed analysis of the patterns allowed us to identify typical simplifications and distortions of the SRL teaching model in student teachers' teaching. These are:

- Current state scanning is being simplified, and contains 'recall activities' rather than 'achievements'.
- Teaching is simplified in comparison with standards by contrasting the current state with the general objective only.
- The task goal is omitted even when having a specific goal in mind. A typical finding is the low proportion of tasks with a specific goal and a task goal.
- In addition, we found certain distortions that conflict with the model:
- The pupil's current state is scanned routinely.
- Excessive time is spent on planning.

We can conclude by saying that if teaching tactics according to the model of joint goal-setting, they are not well developed and, in consequence, the effects of SRL teaching activity on pupils become almost negligible or even lead- after several instances of incorrect application- to misuse (which may explain the drop in required SRL teaching patterns over time). The oscillating pattern obviously reflects the momentary and temporary effect of mentoring meetings.

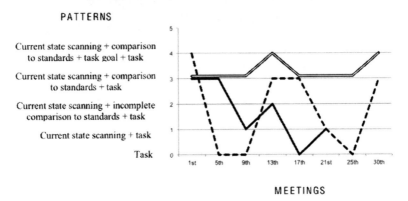

Graph 1. Kinds of learning progressions followed by student teachers

In short, the teaching practices associated with the adoption of goal-setting were difficult for student teachers to implement and, above all, sustain throughout the whole intervention period. As shown, despite considerable time for training (instruction and intervention + reflection on teaching practice), only two student teachers uphold the SRL teaching model pattern.

As found in other studies (Wilson, 1990, in Randi & Corno, 1997; Roehrig et al., 2008), the student teachers still believed they were implementing the "model" practices appropriately. However, most of the student teachers in our case seemed no to adhere to the spirit of the framework (as in Perry et al., 2004; Wilson, 1990).

An important question arises as to why the student teachers had difficulties implementing the teaching practices associated with the joint goal-setting process despite an intensive training program. The possible reasons we encountered in the professional development literature were:

> Mere access to a mentor does not ensure that mentees became better teachers. Mentors have been found to not always be effective teachers themselves, and even if they are effective teachers, they are not necessarily qualified to teach teachers. (Roehrig et al., 2008, p. 685)

Another reason mentioned in this chapter is that in order to help student teachers (successfully, the mentors not only need to know about the specific innovation and teaching practices associated with it, but also about the associated learning difficulties student teachers encounter when acquiring these new practices; in other words, about their learning needs (see Chapter 11).

As Roehrig et al. (2008) suggest, we believe that a lack of meta-cognitive awareness on the part of student teachers about their real performance could influence (interfere with) their learning. Furthermore, the mentors (since they did not observe the student teachers' practices during the program) were not aware of actual practices, but had to refer to the student teachers' (positive) beliefs about them and, therefore, they could only promote a superficial (not in-depth) reflection on practices at the mentoring meetings.

In order to overcome these obstacles, the next study was designed to take a closer look at the learning processes of student teachers.

STUDY 2: MENTOR AND STUDENT TEACHERS: KNOWLEDGE ABOUT LEARNING PROGRESSION

Our aim here was to refine the conditions of the training program (especially the design of mentoring meetings) in order to study the learning trajectories of student teachers. Basically, we introduced two modifications with respect to Study 1: informing student teachers and mentors about learning trajectories as depicted in Graph 1 (thereby treating the most commonly found distortions and simplifications), and discuss with them the problem of the positive awareness of performance. We used the same method of observation and a detailed analysis of the student teachers' teaching practices.

Method

Thirteen student teachers (a different group) took part in a training program similar to that involved in the previous study. The program covered the same topic (intervention in reading and writing difficulties from an SRL perspective); it lasted the same period of time (six months), and included the same sections (instruction and intervention + reflection on practices); but with certain new features added as a result of what was learned from the previous study.

Instruction. The content and materials in the training were exactly the same as the one in the previous study. Two members of the research team conducted this seminar, with a new feature being: the last session reserved time with the student teachers for discussing the difficulties identified during teaching practices related to joint goal-setting. It was meant to raise awareness in advance regarding potential problems that might be encountered, so student teachers would be vigilant during their intervention with pupils. The idea was to forewarn them, and trigger a more in-depth exploration and consideration of these problems.

The list of problems treated was as follows:

- Failure to establish the correct goal hierarchy, hence working towards a single goal (normally with the general objective of the intervention).
- The specific goals and task goals were left out, and therefore the explanation and execution of the tasks were tackled head on.
- Too much dialogue due to an overly long focus on the regulatory aspect.
- The planning episodes turned into a repetitive routine.
- There was no sense of progress. No new challenges were introduced in the tasks, and for this reason the work became deadlocked.[2]

Intervention + reflection on teaching practices. The intervention section with the pupils was not changed, having the same characteristics and conditions as the Study 1; however, the individual mentoring meetings were changed as follows:

The mentors who guided the meetings (who were also the instructors of the training seminar) were the same as the ones in the Study 1, and took part in the process of discussing and interpreting the data from that study. They therefore had in-depth knowledge about the process and learning difficulties facing the student teachers when dealing with pupils in the joint goal-setting process. It is important to note that this time the mentors were also familiar with the difficulties in student teachers' meta-cognitive awareness.

The mentors followed a pre-established script similar to the one used in the Study 1, but also devoted part of the mentoring session (preferably the final part) to explicitly reflecting upon the list of difficulties mentioned above, as well as upon each individual student teacher's teaching problems.

As regards data collection and analysis, the same procedures were used as in the previous study: once again, all the sessions were recorded, with the same coding procedure. A sample of the intervention sessions was chosen for analysis (this time between seven and eight sessions for each student teacher) and transcription, and the same category system was used to analyze the teaching practices (Sánchez et al., 2008; Sánchez, García, Rosales, De Sixte, & Castellano, 2008). Likewise, the planning episodes of the sessions in particular were taken for in-depth analysis in order to examine how the student teachers encouraged pupils to set self-regulatory goals.

Results and Conclusions

Graph 2 shows the three kinds of learning trajectories: one that remained stable in the application of the SRL teaching tactics from start to finish throughout the intervention; this applied to five student teachers (sustained line); a second one characterized by first ascending and then levelling out; this applied to four student teachers (upward and sustained line); finally, one that ascended first, remained stable afterwards and then descended. This applied to three student teachers (upward, sustained and downward line). It is worth pointing out that a drop occurred in all three trajectories, approximately around the third session, coinciding with the fact that at that time the student teachers had not attended any mentoring meetings due to course requirements.

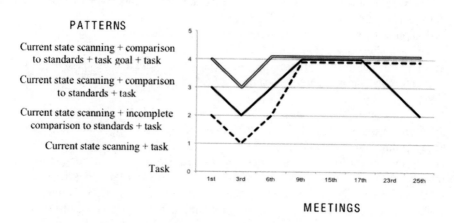

Graph 2. Kinds of learning trajectories followed by the student teachers

To sum up, the teaching practices of student teachers clearly improved compared to those recorded from the Study 1. The practices of student teachers in this study fell much more in line with the 'model' practices derived from goal-setting theory, and the student teachers also performed in a much more sustained way over the course of their intervention with pupils.

Knowing what difficulties occur in setting goals with pupils, and being able to overlook their limitations (one of the factors that might have contributed to the low effectiveness of the meetings in the Study 1), helped student teachers to keep closer to the intended model of SRL teaching tactics. Our impression from the findings is that the mentors in this study were particularly sensitive to these issues. We believe that in the mentoring meetings and means of scaffolding, the mentors raised the student teachers' awareness on their actions and limitations instead of insisting on ideal practices or prescribing behavioural changes or advocating new teaching guidelines for interventions with pupils. We also believe that this could have led to the more satisfactory learning outcomes in this study.

In addition, we decided to undertake a follow-up analysis to study the level of sustainability and transfer by student teachers (from this Study 2) one year after they had completed their training. We were interested in examining whether (and to what extent) the student teachers were still implementing the SRL teaching practices in joint goal-setting one year later, without any mentoring support; that is, in different classroom contexts and with different pupils.

Bearing in mind the importance of 'meta-cognitive awareness of one's own practices', as a possible influential variable in the student teachers' learning process, we were also interested in recording their perceptions about their practices after twelve months in order to corroborate how these perceptions matched their actions. We were able to work with five of the thirteen student teachers. At that time, they were in their third and final year of the teacher education program and involved in teaching practicums, where we could observe them for the purpose of this follow-up analysis. Even though they were fewer than half of the original student teachers who participated in Study 2: four of them had a learning trajectory that consisted of the ideal pattern during the whole intervention period, and the fifth student teacher's trajectory ascended halfway through the intervention and then remained at the ideal level.

Exactly one year after completing the training, the five student teachers were recorded (by audio or video) in their new interventions contexts; observations were made between one and three times each. The teaching sessions were recorded (with a special focus on their planning episodes) and then analyzed to check the level of sustainability and transfer of the SRL teaching practices they had learnt the previous year. In other words, we verified whether (and to what extent) the student teachers were still implementing the self-regulatory teaching tactics in goal-setting and planning with their new pupils. We used the same coding categories as in the previous studies (current state scanning, comparison to standards, and task goal-setting) with their respective associated teaching tactics. Although the student teachers worked in different intervention contexts from those of the training, the challenges pupils faced were similar. In these contexts, too, the teaching skills the student teachers needed to help their pupils in goal-setting remained the same. This provided the research setting to analyze how student teachers were managing with setting goals and sub-goals. After the audio recording of the interventions, semi-structured individual meetings were held with each student teacher. The first six questions in the interview were aimed at measuring the student teachers' self-perception with regard to factors that influence the use of the self-regulatory teaching skills learnt (knowledge, value, capacity to adapt, and opportunity for action; Pressley et al., 1990); the other questions were aimed at measuring their self-perception regarding the level of transfer per se (present/ or not, applied in which areas of their teaching, etc.). These questions informed the subsequent analyses of interviews.

In our follow up study, only two student teachers showed some sustainability and transfer of the SRL teaching model they had learnt, but to a very low level: in only one of the three sessions observed we found student teachers used a simple version of the model (the 'activity reminder' and 'achievements reminder' tactics, see Table 3). These findings did not align with the student teachers' self-perceptions (which were more optimistic), as they claimed they were using practically all the elements of the SRL teaching model (see Table 4).

Table 3. Level of sustainability and transfer by the ST (student teachers) of the teaching tactics associated with joint goal-setting process

	Goal-Setting		
	Current State Scanning (activity and achievement reminder)	*Comparison To Standards (problem definition, distal goal setting, specific goal)*	*Task Goal-Setting (task goal-setting)*
ST1	–	–	–
ST2	–	–	–
ST3	x	–	–
ST4	x	–	–
ST5	–	–	–

Table 4. Self-perception of the ST (student teachers) with regard the level of transfer and of the influential factors

	Self-Perception Transfer			Self-Perception Influential Factors			
	Yes/ No	*Where (teaching areas)*	*How much (model parts)*	*Knowledge*	*Value*	*Capacity adapt*	*Opportunity action*
ST1	no	–	–	low	low	high	high
ST2	yes	2 of 3	current	high	high	medium	high
ST3	yes	2 of 3	all	high	high	high	high
ST4	yes	2 of 3	all	high	high	high	high
ST5	no	–	–	high	high	medium	high

STUDY 3: ANALYSIS OF MENTORING MEETINGS

Since the data from Study 2 did not allow us to make assertions on what happened in the mentoring meetings, or compare them with the mentoring meetings in Study 1, we decided to examine the mentoring meetings in each study in more detail (on the type of reflection on teaching practices); i.e., what type of (reflection) scaffolding took place in the mentoring meetings in each study?

Three specific questions guided the analyses:

- Conversation structures: What kind of conversation guidelines and structures were used by the mentor and student teacher to reflect upon practices and limitations?
- Content of the interactions: To what extent, and how, did the mentor and student teacher discuss the practices and limitations associated with joint goal-setting; in other words, what meta-cognitive dialogue took place with pupils about establishing goals? What evidence was forthcoming in the meetings on content relating to joint goal-setting?
- Student teachers' participation: What was the student teachers' level of participation in these meetings when considering their practices and limitations associated with joint goal-setting?

Method

A sample of 20 mentoring meetings was selected (10 from each study), transcribed, and subsequently analyzed in line with the three questions above. The same coding analysis system was used as in the other studies (Sánchez et al., 2008; Sánchez, García, Rosales, De Sixte, & Castellano, 2008), except that this time we focused on both the student teacher and the mentor in the dialogues.

Which conversation guidelines and structures were used by the mentor and student teacher to reflect upon practices and limitations? We analyzed the student teacher-mentor conversation, segmenting these interactions into episodes that occur during mentoring on joint problem-solving:

- reviewing (exploration) the current situation
- identifying the problem (first inter-subjective definition)
- analyzing the current situation
- identifying the problem (final inter-subjective definition)
- establishing future solutions and/or interventions
- summing up and/or final reflection

We subsequently identified the sequence or time order during the session. Finally, we compared the 20 meetings under analysis to obtain different formats or types in the sequences of episodes. These formats were interpreted as conversation structures, and from them we derived the implicit guidelines given for action, i.e., different reflections that were exchanged at the mentoring meetings.

The extent to which, and how, the mentor and student teacher discuss the practices and limitations associated with joint goal-setting.   In this analysis, we look at the meta-cognitive dialogues with student teachers on goal-setting. What evidence did the meetings provide on content relating to joint goal-setting? We were interested in recording the joint goal-setting that was discussed between the mentor and student teacher, with a view to examining the following: frequency (in which episodes it was discussed), the level of explicitness used (using the 'examples' indicator of the meta-cognitive dialogues on goals with pupils) and, finally, whether the difficulties in this self-regulatory process were discussed or not.

We analyzed the following issues:

- In how many sessions was goal-setting discussed?
- In how many sessions were goals discussed in the episode: reviewing the current situation?
- In how many sessions were goals discussed in the episode: establishing future interventions?
- In how many sessions were examples of formulating goals put forward?
- In how many sessions were examples given in the episode: reviewing the current situation? How many per session? How many in total?
- In how many sessions were examples given in the episode: establishing future interventions? How many per session? How many in total?
- In how many sessions were the problems associated with goal-setting identified?

What was the student teachers' level of participation in these meetings when discussing joint goal-setting?.   We analyzed the following five issues:

- What was the student teachers' average level of participation in the episode: reviewing the current situation?
- What was the student teachers' average level of participation in the episode: establishing future solutions and/or interventions?
- What was the student teachers' average level of participation when providing examples (for goal-setting) in the episode: reviewing the current situation?
- What was the student teachers' average level of participation when providing examples (for goal-setting) in the episode: establishing future solutions and/or interventions?
- 'What was the student teachers' average level of participation when identifying the problems related to joint goal-setting?

For this purpose, we used the analysis system by (Sánchez et al., 2008; Sánchez, García, Rosales, De Sixte, & Castellano, 2008), and coded the interaction between student teacher and mentor.

We used the following indicator of participation: "assistance rendered during the interaction" to code the conversation; in this instance, the assistance or advice offered by the mentor to the student teacher. The criterion was as follows: the more assistance offered to the student teachers, the lower their engagement in establishing attachment to the topic; on the other hand, the less assistance provided by the mentor, the higher the participation or involvement in establishing a personal knowledge base or understanding by the student teachers. This criterion is in line with SRL theory (Boekaerts, 2011).

Results and Conclusions

The conversation guidelines and structures used. As shown in Table 5, most of the mentoring meetings in Study 1 (80%) featured a simple format of reflection. In other words, only the following two episodes were promoted: a review of teaching practices (i.e., actions undertaken and results achieved), and the establishment of guidelines for future action. This format implies, on the one hand, traditional (and simplified) guidance for reflection based on confirmatory feedback from the mentor, and on the other, a directed (prescriptive) conversation structure equal to a "telling" style of mentoring (Harrison, Lawson, & Wortley, 2005).

In Study 2, however, most of the mentoring meetings (80%) featured a more complex reflection format. In addition to these two mentioned episodes, the sessions also, and prevalently, featured the episode of jointly identifying problems. This meant that the guidance was different: it was no longer only about (a) reviewing what had been done, (b) receiving feedback (in most cases confirmatory) from the mentor, and (c) planning future interventions, but in this instance reflection involved also questioning the practice, subjecting it to a critical process in order to raise awareness on what was done and, most importantly, addressing the difficulties that arose. From here, it was possible to move on to establishing future goals and guidelines for action.

The mentoring model proposed by (Daloz, 1986; in Harrison et al., 2005) is similar, in which two key ingredients for making the mentoring process effective stand out: "support" and "challenge".

> If a new teacher is to progress and develop fully, then high levels of both support and challenge need providing through the mentoring activities. Support without challenge may lead to confirmation of the new teacher's competence, a replication of what already exists, but with little or no growth. (Harrison et al., 2005, p. 274)

Moreover, we found that more complex conversation structures were established for Study 2 meetings as compared to the simpler format of Study 1. Depending on the identification or explanation of problems (whether they were more or less 'directed' by the mentor, with or without input from the student teacher.), several conversation structures followed. See Table 5 for an overview of the different structures found.

Table 5. Types of sequences of episodes identified in the 20 meetings under analysis

Type of format	Formal structure (episodes)	Meetings		
		Study 1	Study 2	Total
Simple	• Episode reviewing (exploration) the current situation • Episode establishing future solutions and/or interventions	8	2	10
Complex	Type A: • Episode reviewing (exploration) the current situation • Episode identifying the problem • Episode establishing future solutions and/or interventions • Episode summing up and/or final reflection	2	2	
	Type B: • Episode reviewing (exploration) the current situation • Episode analyzing the current situation (and comparing with ideal situation) • Episode identifying the problem • Episode establishing future solutions and/or interventions • Episode summing up and/or final reflection	0	2	10
	Type C: • Episode reviewing (exploration) the current situation • Episode identifying the problem (first inter-subjective definition) • Episode analyzing the current situation • (Episode identifying the problem (final inter-subjective definition)) • Episode establishing future solutions and/or interventions • Episode summing up and/or final reflection	0	4	

Although in all of these Study 2 meetings the mentor was still primarily responsible for the conversation (continuing to control the process), more joint conversations were observed, with a more equitable division of roles than in Study 1 meetings. A particular example of this (see Table 5) involved the complex formats of B and C, in which the student teachers adopted a clearly active role.

The extent to which, and how, the mentor and student teacher discuss the practices and limitations associated with joint goal-setting. In this analysis, the meta-cognitive dialogues with student teachers about establishing goals are scrutinized. As we can see in Table 6 above, the meetings in both studies provided evidence of goal-setting in the conversations between the mentor and the student teacher. In other words, in both Study 1 and Study 2, the topic was discussed at all the meetings (no meeting failed to mention this subject).

Nonetheless, there *were* some differences. Firstly, the degree of explicitness used when discussing SRL teaching tactics related to goal-setting differed (see Table 6). When exemplifying the meta-cognitive dialogues on the subject of goals, the meetings in Study 2 recorded twice the number of examples given (in terms of both the review episodes and the establishment of new practices). Secondly, when it came to explaining the problems associated with goal-setting, in Study 2 it occurred in 70% of the meetings.

Table 6. Evidence of content relating to joint goal-setting
in the meetings in both studies

	Study 1		Study 2	
	Frequency	Proportion	Frequency	Proportion
1. In how many sessions was goal-setting discussed?	10	100%	10	100%
1.1. In how many sessions were goals discussed in the episode on reviewing the current situation?	8	80%	9	90%
1.2. In how many sessions were goals discussed in the episode on establishing future interventions?	10	100%	10	100%
2. In how many sessions were examples of formulating goals put forward?	7	70%	10	100%
2.1. In how many sessions were examples given in the episode on reviewing the current situation? How many per session? How many in total?	6 1 6	60%	9 1'8 16	90%
2.2. In how many sessions were examples given in the episode on establishing future interventions? How many per session? How many in total?	4 1'5 6	40%	8 1'6 13	80%
3. In how many sessions were the problems associated with goal-setting identified?	2	20%	7	70%

What was the student teachers' level of participation in these meetings when considering their practices and limitations associated with joint goal-setting? As shown in Table 7: Student teachers in Study 2 participated more in the meetings than those in Study 1. This increase in participations was most noticeable on the following episodes: establishing future solutions (at the time of putting together new practices), and identifying problems. While student teachers in Study 1 barely participated (actively) in the processes of identifying problems and building new goal-related practices, and were very dependent on the explanations and proposals provided by the mentors, their participation in Study 2 was much greater. While it is true that the mentors continued to play a predominant role (which is quite common in these episodes), there was also clearly more participation and independence observed among the student teachers as well.

This greater participation is probably related to the change in the conversation structure recorded: from a more 'steering' approach typical of a 'telling' style of mentoring to a more equally distributed and more joint style of mentoring (encouraging complex reflection formats).

Table 7. Average level of participation of the ST (student teachers) in the meetings in both studies

	Study 1	Study 2
1. What was the STs' average level of participation in the episodes on reviewing the current situation when discussing joint goal-setting?	$\overline{X} = 2'2$	$\overline{X} = 2'5$
2. What was the STs' average level of participation in the episodes on establishing future solutions and/or interventions when discussing joint goal-setting?	$\overline{X} = 0'5$	$\overline{X} = 1'4$
3. What was the STs' average level of participation when providing examples (for goal-setting) in the episodes on reviewing the current situation?	$\overline{X} = 2'3$	$\overline{X} = 3'3$
4. What was the STs' average level of participation when providing examples (for goal-setting) in the episodes on establishing future solutions and/or interventions?	$\overline{X} = 0$	$\overline{X} = 1'8$
5. What was the STs' average level of participation when identifying the problems related to joint goal-setting (in the episodes on identifying problems)?	$\overline{X} = 0'5$	$\overline{X} = 1'3$

Discussion

Although no conclusive data can be drawn from these three studies (and therefore discretion is called for our interpretations), we *can* establish a relationship between our evidence from the mentoring meetings (Study 3) and the data from the practices observed (from Study 1 and Study 2): The student teachers who received a mentoring approach dominant in Study 2, in other words, who were immersed in the following: a) contexts of *critical* reflection on practices, b) more explicit discussions of the meta-cognitive dialogues with pupils regarding goals and the problems encountered with SRL teaching tactics related to goal-setting, and c) interactions with high levels of participation, were found to have a learning trajectory that was more in line with the proposed teaching model, than among the student teachers who were immersed in a mentoring approach characterized by the following: a) simple reflection, b) less explicit discussions of meta-cognitive dialogues and less discussion of the difficulties encountered, and c) interactions with little participation. These are the three main characteristics that seem to differ between both studies.

CONCLUSIONS

Referring to the goals stated at the beginning of this chapter, we may conclude that the effects of student teacher learning under a mentor's supervision are quite different. In both studies, we observed that student teachers' practices vary greatly in performance according to the SRL teaching model proposed.

Most student teachers in Study 1 (with a highly "telling" type of mentoring and training) adopted a simplified version of the teaching model. Apparently, the mentoring meetings had not been a critical experience for acquiring the skills needed to adopt SRL teaching tactics. Only two out of the ten student teachers were able to adopt them. Furthermore, the findings from Study 1 provide information about the common simplifications and distortions that were uncovered during the student teachers' teaching practice. We noted that the misunderstandings were not recognized by mentors, at least not explicitly. Even the student teachers themselves were unaware of them and rarely mentioned them at the mentoring meetings.

Data from Studies 2 and 3 allow us to draw a second conclusion, namely, the importance of mentors and student teachers becoming aware of the most common difficulties encountered during the teaching process. On the one hand, sharing this knowledge with student teachers – before the teaching process starts- facilitates their practice and identifies what exactly they are doing wrong. The more active role by student teachers in Study 2 can be considered as evidence in this respect. On the other hand, mentors being informed about the student teachers' learning trajectory and difficulties may deploy specific episodes (i.e., conversations) to identify what exactly is happening during the intervention sessions with pupils that cause difficulties for a student teacher, as our analysis of episodes in Study 3 shows. In other words, without such knowledge, the mentors are unaware of the existence of the problems encountered in the student teachers' teaching practice, and tend to focus merely on what the student teachers must do in subsequent sessions. Not surprisingly, we found the learning outcomes to be clearly better in Study 2.

Generally taken, the studies presented here would seem to indicate that, as is also maintained by other researchers, the adoption of SRL in teaching is extremely complex and difficult for novice teachers to implement. Even when student teachers have undergone intensive training and mentoring, and even after having successfully demonstrated the attainment of tactics, and used them in their teaching practices (Study 2), we found that one year later, once the mentoring support was no longer available, the result was that only two out of the five student teachers were using the model they had learnt, and then only a fraction of it. This result was recorded despite the positive finding that all student teachers (except for one) valued the proposed teaching model, and despite their high level of recollection of knowledge about the model, and even despite their high self-perceptions of their capacity to adapt it to new contexts. With regard to this last finding, it is of interest to note that it turned out not to be a very reliable indicator. As we have seen (in Study 1), our data on meta-cognitive awareness indicate low precision when student teachers evaluated their own practices. This leads us to question the accuracy of the level of precision in the self-perception of the development of teaching skills by student teachers.

This result of our analyses adds significance when considering that student teachers in Study 2 were immersed in substantial levels of mentoring about their practices, whereby the mentors fostered a process characteristic of phase 3 of (Fuller & Bown, 1975; in Perry et al., 2007); that is, focusing on the pupils' needs, assessing whether goals were achievable, and adapting them to their needs. Such a mentoring could help student teachers to develop (and maintain throughout the program) targeted practices on joint goal-setting. However, we found that such mentoring was not enough since once that mentoring support was withdrawn, the student teachers were unable to practice on their own. In addition, we might argue that deliberately promoting the model of joint goal-setting (as depicted in Figure 1) could have helped student teachers to become aware of the fact that their practice needs adjustments. Based on what we saw, student teachers tend to simplify the goal-setting model. Taking these findings, it might be more appropriate to accept these simplifications as an intermediate step in mastering the targeted teaching model. Such a position is claimed in Sánchez et al. (in this volume), who advocates a more practical mentoring approach that could involve proposing a diversity of "models", not only the best one, and let student teachers decide which one of them they will deploy in subsequent intervention sessions. Only when they feel comfortable in developing a teaching model they consider appropriate to their needs, they can assume proficiency and engage in more challenges to performance (similar to the learning trajectories we identified). Perhaps this has to do with the professional development in mentoring.

REFERENCES

Badia, A., & Monereo, C. (2004). La construcción de conocimiento profesional docente. Análisis de un curso de formación sobre la enseñanza estratégica. *Anuario de Psicología, 35*(1), 47–70.
Bakkenes, I., Vermunt, J. D., & Wubbels, T. (2010). Teacher learning in the context of educational innovation: Learning activities and learning outcomes of experienced teachers. *Learning and Instruction, 20*, 533–348.
Boekaerts, M. (1999). Self-regulated learning: Where we are today. *International Journal of Educational Research, 31*, 445–457.
Boekaerts, M. (2002). Bringing about change in the classroom, strength and weaknesses of SRI. *Learning & Instruction, 12*(6), 589–604.
Brodeur, M., Deaudelin, C., & Bru, M. (2005). Le developpement professionale des enseignants, apprendre a enseigner pour soutenir lápprentissasage des eleves. *Revue des sciences de léducation, XXXI*, 1, 5–16.
Butler, D. (1998). A strategic content learning approach to promoting self-regulated learning by students with learning disabilities. In D. H. Schunk & B. J. Zimmerman (Eds.), *Self-regulated learning: From teaching to self-reflective practice* (pp.160–172). New York, NY: Guilford Press.
Butler, D. L., Novak Lauscher, H., Jarvis-Selinger, S., & Beckingham, B. (2004). Collaboration and self-regulation in teachers' professional development. *Teaching and Teacher Education, 20*, 435–455.
Delfino, M., Dettori, G., & Persico, D. (2010). An online course fostering self-regulation of trainee teachers. *Psicothema, 22*(2), 299–305.

Duchnowski, A., Kutash, K., Sheffield, S., & Vaughn, B. (2006). Increasing the use of evidence-based strategies by special education teachers: A collaborative approach. *Teaching and Teacher Education, 22*, 838–847.

Fishman, B. J., Marx, R. W., Best, S., & Tal, R. T. (2003). Linking teacher and student learning to improve professional development in systemic reform. *Teaching and Teacher Education, 19*, 643–658.

García, T., & Pintrich, P. R. (1994). Regulating motivation and cognition in the classroom: The role of self-schemas and self-regulatory strategies. In D. H. Schunk & B. J. Zimmerman (Eds.), *Self-regulation of learning and performance: Issues and educational applications* (pp. 127–153). Hillsdale, NJ: Erlbaum.

Graham, S., Harris, K. R., & Troia, G. A. (1998). Writing and self-regulation: Cases from the self-regulated strategy development model. In D. H. Schunk & B. J. Zimmerman (Eds.), *Self-regulated learning: From teaching to self-reflective practice* (pp. 20–41). New York, NY: Guilford Press.

Harrison, J., Lawson, T., & Wortley, A. (2005). Facilitating the professional learning of new teachers through critical reflection on practice during mentoring meetings. *European Journal of Teacher Education, 28*(3), 267–292.

Kramarski, B., & Revach, T. (2009). The challenge of self-regulated learning in mathematics teachers' professional training. *Educ Stud Math, 72*, 379–399.

Kutash, K., Duchnowski, A. J., & Lynn, N. (2009). The use of evidence-based instructional strategies in special education settings in secondary schools: Development, implementation and outcomes. *Teaching and Teacher Education, 25*, 917–923.

Perels, F., Merget-Kullmann, M., Wende, M., Schmitz, B., & Buchbinder, C. (2009). Improving self-regulated learning of preschool children: Evaluation of training for kindergarten teachers. *British Journal of Educational Psychology, 79*, 311–327.

Perry, N. E., Hutchinson, L., & Thauberger, C. (2007). Mentoring student teachers to design and implement literacy tasks that support self-regulated reading and writing. *Reading & Writing Quarterly, 23*, 27–50.

Perry, N. E., Hutchinson, L., & Thauberger, C. (2008). Talking about teaching self-regulated learning: Scaffolding student teachers' development and use of practices that promote self-regulated learning. *International Journal of Educational Research, 47*, 97–108.

Perry, N. E., Phillips, L., & Dowler, J. (2004). Examining features of tasks and their potential to promote self-regulated learning. *Teachers College Record, 106*(9), 1854–1878.

Perry, N. E., Phillips, L., & Hutchinson, L. (2006). Mentoring student teachers to support self-regulated learning. *The Elementary School Journal, 106*(3), 237–254.

Postholm, M. B. (2010). Self-regulated pupils in teaching: Teachers' experiences. *Teachers and Teaching, 16*(4), 491–505.

Pressley, M., Woloshyn, V., Lysynchuk, L. M., Martín, V., Wood, E., & Willoughby, T. (1990). A primer of research on cognitive strategy instruction: The important issues and how to address them. *Educational Psychology, 2*, 1–58.

Randi, J., & Corno, L. (1997). Teachers as innovators. In B. Biddle, T. Good, & I. Goodson (Eds.), *International handbook of teachers and teaching* (pp. 1163–1221). New York, NY: Kluwer.

Roehrig, A. D., Bohn, C. M., Turner, J. E., & Pressley, M. (2008). Mentoring beginning primary teachers for exemplary teaching practices. *Teaching and Teacher Education, 24*, 684–702.

Sánchez, E., García, J. R., Castellano, N., De Sixte, R., Bustos, A., & García-Rodicio, H. (2008). Qué, cómo y quién: Tres dimensiones para analizar la práctica educativa. *Cultura y Educación, 20*(1), 95–118.

Sánchez, E., García, J. R., Rosales, J., De Sixte, R., & Castellano, N. (2008). Elementos para analizar la interacción entre estudiantes y profesores: ¿Qué ocurre cuando se consideran diferentes dimensiones y unidades de análisis? *Revista de Educación, 346*, 105–136.

Schunk, D. H. (1998). Teaching elementary students to self-regulate practice of mathematical skills with modeling. In D. H. Schunk & B. J. Zimmerman (Eds.), *Self-regulated learning: From teaching to self-reflective practice* (pp. 137–159). New York, NY: Guilford Press.

Schunk, D. H. (2003). Self-efficacy for reading and writing: Influence of modelling, goal setting, and self-evaluation. *Reading & Writing Quarterly, 19*, 159–172.

Schunk, D. H., & Ertmer, P. (2000). Self-regulation and academic learning. Self-efficacy enhancing interventions. In M. Boekaerts, P. R. Pintrich, & M. Zeidner (Eds.), *Handbook of self-regulation* (pp. 631–649). San Diego, CA: Academic Press.

Tillema, H. H. (2000). Belief change towards self-directed learning in student teachers: Immersion in practice or reflection on action. *Teaching and Teacher Education, 16*, 575–591.

Tillema, H. H. (2004). Embedding and immersion as key strategies in learning to teach. In H. P. A. Boshuizen, R. Bromme, & H. Gruber (Eds.), *Professional learning: Gaps and transitions on the way from novice to expert* (pp. 141–155). Dordrecht: Kluwer Academic Publishers.

Zimmerman, B. J. (1998). Developing self-fulfilling cycles of academic regulation: An analysis of exemplary instructional models. In D. H. Schunk & B. J. Zimmerman (Eds.), *Self-regulated learning: From teaching to self-reflective practice* (pp. 1–17). New York, NY: Guilford Press.

Zimmerman, B. J. (2000). Attaining self-regulation: A social cognitive perspective. In M. Boekaerts, P. R. Pintrich, & M. Zeidner (Eds.), *Handbook of self-regulation* (pp. 13–39). San Diego, CA: Academic Press.

Zimmerman B. J., & Schunk D. H. (Eds.). (2001). *Self-regulated learning and academic achievement* (2nd ed.). New York, NY: Springer-Verlag.

Elena Ciga
University of Salamanca, Spain

Emma Garcia
University of Salamanca, Spain

Mercedes Rueda
University of Salamanca, Spain

Harm Tillema
Leiden University, The Netherlands

Emilio Sanchez
Department of Education and
Developmental Psychology
University of Salamanca, Spain

KARI SMITH

13. MENTORING

A Profession within a Profession

INTRODUCTION

The Principal had informed me (not asked) that a new teacher would be under my responsibility for the next year. I was given a web site where I could read about my responsibilities as mentor. I was scared to learn that I was, more or less, the one who decided if the candidate would become a good teacher or not. I know how to teach children, I know my subjects, but being a mentor for an adult colleague, was far beyond what I had ever studied or wanted. I like to do a good job, and for this, I felt totally unprepared. I was worried I would not be of help to the new colleague, and most of all, I really felt this added responsibility would come in the way of doing what my real job was, teaching children.

The education of professionals is recently seen in a career wide perspective, consisting of three stages, initial, induction, and in-service education. In all three stages, mentoring activities are given a central role. During the preparation for the profession, initial education, mentors have the responsibility of introducing the practice field to professionals-to-be. During induction, mentors become supporters and guides for the novice, whereas in the phase of in-service education, formal mentoring by appointed mentors and informal collegial mentoring within communities of practice are found to promote professional learning. In this chapter mentoring is mainly discussed in relation to initial teacher education and the induction phase of newly qualified teachers.

In most cases mentors are chosen based on their reputation of being experienced and successful professionals, in our case, teachers, or they are practitioners towards the end of their professional career whose work load is reduced, and mentoring is seen as a suitable activity towards the end of a long career.

The question raised in this article is if all experienced teachers can be mentors or is mentoring a different experience than practicing the profession? The claim I make is that mentoring is not the same as teachers' first order professional practice, it is a profession within the profession in which mentoring takes place. Teaching children is a different practice from mentoring adults prior to or at the entrance of their professional career, and in this chapter the main differences will be discussed in support of the claim, that mentoring is a profession within a profession.

H. Tillema et al. (Eds.), Mentoring for Learning, 283–298.

The story in the beginning of this chapter was told to me by a mentor, and it is a typical example of the increasing importance of work-based learning for teachers (Zeichner, 2010). The learner is, perhaps, at first sight, the mentee (the student teacher or novice teacher), however in the above situation the mentor, the more experienced teacher sees herself as a novice in the mentoring role and feels she needs to learn the new job for which she has not been educated. Recent views on teacher education have given the concept a wider meaning. Teacher education does not only relate to initial teacher education, but to a career long teacher education. The Irish Teaching Council (2010) defines teacher education as a broad concept that "encompasses initial teacher education, induction, early and continuing professional development and, indeed, late career support" (The Teaching Council, 2011, p. 5). European Commission and OECD state that "The education and professional development of every teacher needs to be seen as a lifelong task and be structured and resourced accordingly" (European Commission & OECD, 2010, p. 12). Concepts such as continuous professional development (CPD), career long teacher learning, and life-long learning (Richter, Kunter, Klusman, Lüdtke, & Baumert, 2011) have been part of the language of teaching and teacher education for quite some time now, yet it is only recently that we see it becoming part of the political discourse as well. Such developments imply that teachers are being educated throughout their careers, yet the form, the venue and the formality of the education vary. Teacher education is often considered to be the main responsibility of academic teacher education institutions, however, today it has to a larger extent become a shared responsibility of various actors, and in particular, the practice field. In many places student teachers spend more time in schools than at the university during their initial education (Ellis, 2010). During the induction phase the main responsibility for teacher learning is placed with the school, whereas both work based and formal learning at universities contribute to in-service teacher learning. Thus, the school, its leadership and teachers hold multiple responsibilities, in addition to teaching children, at different phases of teacher learning. An additional responsibility for experienced teachers is often the task of mentoring student teachers or novice teachers employed by the school. It is usually taken for granted that teaching experience is enough to qualify for mentoring, without taking into consideration that the purpose of mentoring differs from the purpose of teaching. The goal of this chapter is, however, to argue that mentoring is a different practice which takes place in school, the context of teaching, but it has a completely different purpose. Mentoring is about supporting the search for professional self-understanding and professional growth of new professionals. The target audience of mentoring are adults at the starting point of a professional career. Thus mentoring becomes a separate profession within the teaching profession.

TEACHERS' PROFESSIONAL CAREER DEVELOPMENT

A challenge for many systems is that career long teacher learning and added responsibilities do not necessarily lead to a different position in school. Teachers often remain classroom teachers without possibilities for earning a more acknowledged professional status if their heart still lies with the teaching of children. Career development in teaching usually means taking on a leadership role which to a large extent removes the teacher from the classroom. Thus, teaching is often seen as a flat career (Lortie, 1975; Darling-Hammond, 2012), and motivation for professional learning rests on personal interests and is not sufficiently supported by external incentives. Some countries, Lithuania and Poland, for example, which have experienced a positive development in terms of educational achievements, have at the system level created a staged career route for teachers built around continuous professional development, increase in salary, and in professional status (Mourshed, Chijioke, & Barber, 2012). In the Lithuanian example teachers start out as junior teachers having an *apprentice* role, before becoming fully *qualified* teachers after a full year teaching. The next step in a teacher's career in Lithuania is a *senior* teacher, and at this level, there are added responsibilities, including mentoring other teachers in school. It is the principal and the municipality who decide on the designation. After five years as a senior teacher, including mentoring other teachers in school and in the district, the municipality can upgrade the professional level to a *methodist*. The last level in a teachers' career is the *expert*, which means that the teacher has been a methodist for at least seven years, and a teacher for a minimum of 15 years. Mentoring at the national level, as well as contributing to curriculum writing are added responsibilities for those who want to achieve the expert status. The designation is granted by the Lithuanian Teacher Qualification Institute, a national council under the Ministry of Education, and after nomination by the principal as well as endorsement by the municipality. Not every teacher reaches the advanced levels, for example in 2005 only 20% of teachers reached the methodist level (Mourshed, Chijioke, & Barber, 2012, pp. 78–79). Likewise, Scotland already in the nineties introduced the Chartered Teacher Scheme, which in 2009 was replaced by The Standards for Career Long Professional Learning and includes informal work place learning, added responsibilities as well as formal academic education at a master level (General Teaching Council, Scotland, 2012).

Supported by the above examples, the claim in this paper is that becoming a mentor should be seen as a stage in the career development of teachers who want to increase their professional knowledge, skills, and responsibilities by sharing their professionalism with the coming generations of teachers. Teachers, who are still in the classroom, add to their professional activities and become school based teacher educators by taking on added responsibilities and engaging in further formal mentor education. Subsequently, they need to acquire new unique professional knowledge.

The model for teachers' professional career development developed by Smith (2012) is similar to the Lithuanian model, however, in Smith's model the role of mentoring in the various career phases of teachers is being emphasized. Jointly the two models will serve as background for supporting the statement that mentoring is, in fact, a profession within the teaching profession.

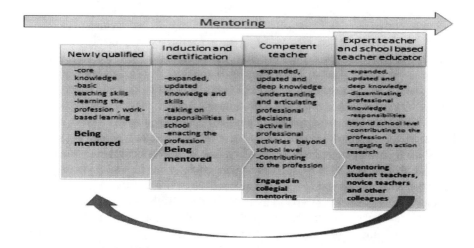

Figure 1. The role of mentoring in a staged career development model

The need for school based teacher educators (mentors) is a closely related to the fact that we are currently witnessing that the practice component of initial teacher education is expanded, at the same time as induction of newly qualified teachers becomes a built-in phase of teachers' professional careers in many countries (McNamara, Murray, & Jones, 2014; Smith & Ulvik, 2014; Hulme & Menter, 2014).

In initial teacher education mentoring of student teachers by experienced teachers in school during the practicum is a well-known phenomenon internationally. The mentors are often chosen based on their reputation as being good teachers, role models, or teachers whose teaching schedule is not filled (Cox, 2005). Research shows that the practicum during teacher education is, by many students, found to be the highest valued component of their education (Smith & Lev-Ari, 2005), even though most mentors have not been educated do undertake the responsibility of acting as school based teacher educators. The increased practicum component in teacher education puts more emphasis on work based learning. Professional learning takes place within the school, when practicing teaching and it is supported by mentors. The challenge is, however, that there has not yet been given sufficient attention to the infrastructure of an expanded practical component of teacher education, and in many cases the assigned mentors lack the knowledge and the skills to act as school based teacher educators. So mentoring is needed in the very beginning of a teacher's professional career.

During the induction and certification phase novice teachers are in many countries, such as Scotland and Israel (among others), given a mentor whose task it is to support and guide them during the important induction phase (Hulme & Menter,

2014; Lazovzky & Reichenberg, 2006). In this context mentoring is still central to the mentee's professional development, yet the mentor takes on a different role, it is about mentoring a colleague. The novice teacher is still the one thought of being in need of support from a more experienced colleague. The mentor plays a central role in the way novice teachers experience the crucial induction phase, and if they decide to stay in the profession or not (Rots, Kelchtermans, & Aelterman, 2012).

In the next phase, where the teacher aspires to be accredited as a competent teacher, collegial mentoring within communities of practice (Wenger, 1998) is conducive to teacher learning which aims at deepening professional theoretical and practical knowledge. Through collegial discussions and support lie possibilities for teachers to develop the skill of articulating their tacit knowledge, which has been found to be a challenge for teachers (Bertram & Loughran, 2012). At this phase the role of mentoring is intentionally planned to serve the purpose of the whole school development, and not only the professional growth of individual teachers. It is, however, a must in any mentoring activities in which teachers' personal practice theory has to be made accessible to other teachers and to the coming generation of teachers (Smith, 2005).

In the last phase of the teacher career model presented here, teachers still remain in the classroom with the main responsibility of teaching children, but they are also acting at mentors for others. Only teachers in the last phase of the model are allowed to take on the role of being school based teacher educators serving as mentors for student teachers in phase one, as well as appointed mentors for novice teachers during the induction phase (phase 2), and being involved with school development (phase 3). Moving from one career level to the next does not necessarily reflect years of teaching experiences beyond the induction phase. The model reflects teacher learning and development, and not years of teaching. This means that a teacher cannot become a competent teacher without documentation of continuous learning which is acknowledged by the profession such as The General Teaching Council Scotland, or by other bodies with an authorisation power. Similarly, a teacher cannot become a mentor just because she has accumulated years of experiences. In order to become a mentor (school-based teacher educator), the teacher has to be educated for the role through formal mentor education. In this respect, being a mentor means taking on additional and different responsibilities from those of a teacher.

In the above discussion it has been argued that mentoring plays a central role in the professional development of teachers throughout the various phases of their professional career. Moreover, the claim has been made that to take on the role of mentors, unique knowledge and skills have to be acquired (which will be explained later in this chapter), thus making mentoring a profession within a profession. To clarify the position taken in this paper, the next section will briefly discuss what makes a profession, and the extent to which mentoring can be said to fulfil the requirements of a profession.

WHAT MAKES A PROFESSION?

Preceding the discussion about what makes a profession it is useful to define what is meant by acting as a professional within the context of the current paper. The Merriam-Webster on-line dictionary defines professionalism as "the skill, good judgement, and polite behaviour from a person who is trained to do a job well". There are some inherent features in the Merriam-Webster definition, such as 'good judgment' meaning that there is no clear-cut right or wrong way of acting, but the 'good judgement' has to be exercised within a given context. Moreover, 'polite behaviour' implies that the professionalism is practised in relation to other people. Finally, the professional is 'trained to do the job well', implying that judgment is based on specialised professional knowledge and skills. The professional acts out of theoretical and practical professional knowledge, jointly with extended situational knowledge and experience, all of which are essential ingredients of a person's professional wisdom (Brunstad, 2007). A model for illustrating the meaning of professional wisdom is presented below.

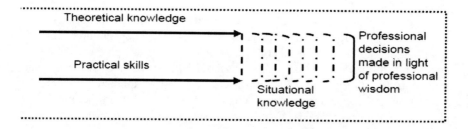

Figure 2. professional wisdom, Smith, 2013
(Adapted from Brunstad, 2007)

Professionals will constantly experience unexpected situations, and the way they react to this situation is grounded in their professional wisdom, which against relies on formal education, on job experience, and knowledge of the situation. Thus it is difficult to make a recipe list of correct professional actions. A simplistic definition of acting professionally could therefore be "Doing the right (optimal) things at the right time in specific situations, and being able to explain why it was right" (Smith, 2013). The last part of this definition is the ability to articulate tacit knowledge discussed above.

So, what makes a profession? A profession consists of a group of people who have undergone specialised education to provide services to others (adaption from Merriam Webster on line dictionary). The classic examples of professions are medical doctors and lawyers. Both professions meet the criteria for a profession, as presented in the literature. The core characteristics of the traditional trait model for a profession are:

- Clearly defined practical and theoretical knowledge base
- Systematic education
- Certification of professional practitioners
- Professional autonomy
- Explicit ethical code
- Priorities serving others to personal economical gains (Burbules & Densmore, 1991; Runtè, 1995; MacBeath, 2012)

For an occupation to be called a profession there has to be a clearly defined knowledgebase which is unique to the profession and which is acquired through systematic education, in other words, a formal education. Practitioners of the profession are required to be certified at the end of the education to engage in professional practice characterised by a large extent of autonomy which allows for making optimal professional decisions when encountering unexpected situations. In addition to being guided by the professional knowledgebase, practitioners are also guided by an ethical code known to all members of the profession out of awareness of and concern for 'the other' who is the receiving part of the professional practice.

A different view on what constitutes a profession is presented by Runte (1995). In his paper he discusses the structural-functional definition for a profession which says that all occupations will, little by little, develop a unique knowledge base that only practitioners of that profession holds. As this knowledgebase is being developed, the occupation will eventually become a profession. If we take mentoring as an example, the understanding and the articulation of the knowledge and the skills required to practice mentoring are little by little being developed and known (see Smith & Ulvik's Chapter 14 in this book on The Professional Knowledge of Mentoring). The practice of mentoring can therefore, according to the structural-functional model, be called a profession.

In spite of the fact that the two models differ greatly, they both share, however, the perception that a profession is defined by a genuine knowledgebase owned by practitioners of the profession. When the profession is within education, the professional knowledge can be seen in relation to Shulman's (1986) concept, pedagogical content knowledge (PCK). The elaboration of mentors' pedagogical content knowledge is discussed elsewhere in this book, whereas in the next section the extent to which mentoring can be called a profession or not will be raised. The first issue to discuss is how the mentoring profession can be distinguished from the teaching profession.

MENTORING – DIFFERENT FROM TEACHING

Having established the claim that mentoring plays a central role in the various phases of teacher education, and that professional practice is guided by theoretical and practical knowledge applied in an optimal manner in light of the analysis of specific situations, there is a need to explain why mentoring is a profession in itself, and that it is quite different from teaching children in school. Mentoring can rightfully be said to be a profession within the teaching profession. It is practiced at the various phases of teacher education, but the responsibility, the purpose, and the methods are distinctively different from those of a school teacher. In this section some of the main differences will be illuminated before moving on to discussing various roles the mentor takes on, and examining mentoring in relation to the traits which characterizes a profession as discussed above.

A major difference between mentoring as discussed in the current paper and teaching children is that mentoring takes place within the profession. Teachers teach a subject, math, history, English, physical education, etc. Mentoring is about teaching, an activity practiced by both the mentee and the mentor. So it is not teaching a subject, it is providing support and guidance within the profession they both practice.

Another difference is the age of the recipient of teaching/mentoring. School teachers teach children, and their education is built around children's learning and development, in addition to the subject matter taught. A mentor within the framework of teacher education works with adults, either these are student teachers, novice or more experienced colleagues. Adult learning differs from children's learning, and instead of discussing the pedagogy of mentoring, perhaps we should start discussing the andragogy of mentoring? Related to this is the challenge inherent in mentoring a colleague, either it is a colleague-to-be, a novice or a more experienced colleague. The hierarchy that is found in a teacher-pupil relationship is minimized, and if there is a hierarchy, it is grounded in accumulated experience and seniority, and not necessarily in formality. Giving constructive criticism to a colleague might, for many, be more difficult than to do the same with pupils in class.

Mentoring includes a great deal of assessment, and assessing the practice of a colleague is for many one of the most difficult parts of mentoring. Formal, summative assessment is mainly found when mentoring takes place in initial teacher education context, where at the end the mentor might be involved in deciding if the mentored student teacher has passed the practicum or not. Even in the mentoring of novice teachers during the induction phase summative assessment takes place when the mentor is involved in deciding if the novice is to be certified as a teacher or not. The double role of acting as an assessor versus guide and supporter, has been found to be a difficult challenge in mentoring situations (Bray & Nettleton, 2007).

It is, however, the informal formative assessment of mentoring which is at the heart of the activity. Mentoring is about providing feedback, support and guidance, all of which is based on observation of performance, often preceded, as well as followed by mentoring activity. Observation includes assessment by the mentee as well as by the mentor, deciding what should be discussed during the mentoring activity is assessment, and providing support, ideas, guidance, is all about feedback and feed forward, in other words, assessment for learning. So mentoring is, to a large extent an assessment activity when looking at assessment in a broad perspective with a main focus on assessment for learning, yet, mentoring also includes assessment for judgmental purposes. Assessing a colleague's practice is a challenge as there are personal, social, and contextual factors to be considered. This is the case also in teacher-pupil relationships, yet not to the same extent.

The main differences between mentoring and teaching are summarised in the following table:

Table 1. Differences between mentoring and teaching

	Teaching	Mentoring
content	subjects (math, history, etc.)	Teaching about teaching
age	children	adults
theoretical foundation	pedagogy	andragogy
hierarchy	explicit, accepted	Implicit, problematic
relationship	teacher-student	collegial
assessment	explicit formative and summative	explicit formative, implicit summative

MENTOR ROLES

As illustrated by the above table, there are clear distinguishes between teaching and mentoring, and the difference becomes more salient when taking a closer look at the roles of the mentor, as presented in the literature. The mentor takes on multiple roles in mentoring situations which makes mentoring a complex activity.

Teacher. Part of the mentor's responsibility is to teach the mentee about teaching, either it is contributing with new understandings about teaching or providing practical ideas for teaching. The teacher role is complicated because the mentor herself is acting out the role when teaching about it.

Guide. The mentee is entering a new world, the professional world of teaching. When encountering a new world, a new culture, it might be overwhelming and confusing, and the newcomer is likely to feel lost, not knowing the way(s) (Sabar, 2004). The mentor becomes the guide who leads the way, as we say in Norwegian (veileder = mentor), through the demanding socialisation process the novice goes through. The guide shares her knowledge and experience with the mentee when points of interest are met, or the road becomes demanding with scary curves and tough hills.

Counsellor. Mentoring is not, however, just to show the way. At times the curves have been too sharp and the hills too steep, and the mentee is most of all in need of somebody who can listen and show empathy. It is not necessarily the cognitive sides of teaching that are experienced as most difficult, but there are affective sides related to relationships with students, colleagues, leadership, and just to find time for oneself when things get tough (Smith, Ulvik, & Helleve, 2013). In these situations the mentor becomes foremost a counsellor.

Motivator. Many students teachers decide to become teachers out of intrinsic and altruistic motifs (Watt & Richardson, 2008; Roness & Smith, 2009). When they are faced with the reality of school, such as discipline problems, extensive documentation requirements, temporary employments (Smith, Ulvik, & Helleve, 2013), their motifs for being teachers are challenged, and teacher attrition rates are worrying in many countries, including Norway (Roness, 2011) and USA (Ingersoll, 2012). The mentor plays a central role as a motivator to continue in the profession, by providing support and being herself an enthusiastic member of perhaps, a society's most important profession (MacBeath, 2012).

Sponsor. When the mentor takes on a sponsor role, she speaks in favour of the mentee and recommends her for job openings, various responsibilities in school, and in-service learning opportunities. It is not always easy to speak in favour of oneself, but the mentor, who is working in close relationship with the mentee, can act as a sponsor and recommend the mentee for suitable responsibilities in school. This is also a way of supporting the mentee in the socialisation process into the new culture.

Role model. The last mentor role presented in this paper, yet not the last in a long list, and certainly not the least, is the mentor acting as a role model for the mentee. The mentor should be, in addition to being formally educated as a mentor, also be an exemplary role model for the mentee as a teacher, communicator, and I would also add, as a human being. Teaching is basically a moral practice (Murrell, Diez, Feiman-Nemser, & Schussler, 2010). Mentoring is an important part of the identity formation of teachers, especially during initial teacher education and the induction phase. The relationship established between the mentor and the mentee will affect not only the teaching skills and understanding of the complexity of teaching hold by the mentee, but the whole person, including professional attitudes and values, what Hansèn (2008) calls teachership. The mentor should be alert to the influence she might have on the mentee's perception of the teaching profession and act with this in mind.

"The roles you undertake as a mentor depend on the needs of the candidate, and of the relations you have established with the candidate. Sometimes you will act in one role, other times you will take on different roles" (United States Department of Health and Human Services, quoted by Smith, 2010, p. 23). Mentoring is a complex activity in any context, and in a school setting the differences between mentoring a student teacher, novice teacher or experienced colleagues and teaching children are, as discussed above, two very different practices taking place in the same context. But is it a profession in itself? In the next section I will be revisiting the traits of a practice which makes it into a profession (see p. 289).

MENTORING AS A PROFESSION

When taking a second look at the traits that characterise a profession presented above, the first impression is that mentoring does not align with the suggested list of traits. What is, for example, the knowledge base of mentoring? Moreover, there are probably more mentors without systematic education than those who are qualified as mentors. However, I would like to challenge such a first impression by relating to our own work at the University of Bergen, Norway. We are able to, as a result of five years of research on mentoring (observing activities, interviewing mentors and mentees, collecting data on mentor education, and by diving into relevant literature) present a framework of a possible professional knowledge of mentors, or its pedagogical content knowledge (Shulman, 1986). A more complete presentation of the proposed knowledge base for mentoring is presented elsewhere in this book, and a framework of this knowledge base can be presented. So, when revisiting the first characteristic of what makes an occupation a profession, it seems that mentoring is moving in the direction of fulfilling this 'requirement'.

When a knowledge base has been established, it is also possible to develop systematic mentor education for the profession. Such an education has taken place at our University since 2007, and it has all the ingredients of a formal academic education. From 2009 the mentor education has been a two years course consisting of two levels. Level one focuses on mentoring student teachers in initial teacher education. The year-long course allows for 15 European Credit Transfer and Accumulation System (ECTS), whereas the second level addresses mentoring novice teachers and collegial mentoring. This course also runs over one year with an additional 15 ECTS value. The first level (mentoring student teachers) is a prerequisite for the second level (mentoring qualified colleagues). The courses have to meet the academic criteria of all academic courses offered by the University, including involving external examiners for the summative assessment assignments (portfolio for level one and action research project for level two). The mentor students are practicing teachers with at least three years of experience, and they have to be recommended for the course by their school principal. Similar courses are offered by all Norwegian teacher education institutions in Norway with national funding. So, in the Norwegian context today there is a systematic education for the mentoring profession.

Regarding the certification of its professional practitioners, the mentor profession is only at the very beginning of the process. There are still more mentors without formal mentor education than with in Norwegian schools. The political steering documents and the professional opinions suggest that in a long term perspective all mentors should be certified as mentors, and that is also the reason why the Government has decided to support mentor education programmes. Yet, there is still a long way to go. However, when looking at the international literature on mentoring, required systematic education leading to certification is still rare (Smith & Ulvik, 2010), and Norway seems to be in the forefront towards accepting mentoring as a profession by having initiated a process of systematic education leading to certification of practicing mentors.

Professional autonomy, another trait in Burbules' and Densmore's list (1991), is to a large extent met, at least in the mentoring context with which I am familiar. There is a framework for mentoring, but there are few directives regarding how mentoring should be practiced, and explicit standards have not been set in Norway. This means, there is much room for the mentor to act out of professional knowledge and wisdom (Brunstad, 2007), enacting her professional competence. The question is, will the autonomy be more restricted as the profession becomes more strongly established, and will the profession itself, in dialogue with policy makers be able to find an optimal balance by defining professional standards without letting them have a reductive impact on professionalism? When looking at the teaching profession, there are worrying signs in Norway and internationally of the restriction of teachers' professional autonomy. It is worthwhile noticing, however, that in the most successful educational systems teachers' professional autonomy is strategically being extended (Darling-Hammond & Rothman, 2011; Mourshed, Chijioke, & Barber, 2012). In the process of establishing mentoring as a new profession, it wise to keep this in mind.

The next trait to be discussed is if the practice of mentoring is enacted in accordance with an explicit ethical code. In the Norwegian context this is not yet the case, however, our mentor students are introduced to the European Mentoring and Coaching Council's ethical code (http://www.emccouncil.org/) which covers five areas; competence, context, boundary management, integrity, and professionalism. Each area has a number of points which are meant to serve as guidelines for both mentor and mentee. The competence of the mentor has to be ensured alongside continuous professional learning and development. Mentoring should take place within a context of shared expectations and goals, and which is conducive to learning, and in full awareness of the limitations of responsibilities and personal competence of the mentor. Integrity of the mentor and the mentee should be maintained, especially as regards to confidentiality and with alertness to rules and culture of the context in which mentoring takes place. Professionalism in mentoring is first of all to act in the best interest of the mentee, and safeguard the mentee's privacy. It is therefore possible to say that the profession of mentoring has an explicit ethical code, and it is left to the actors in the various mentoring contexts to become familiar with it and adhere to it.

The last trait of a profession discussed is that the main priority of the practitioner is to serve others, especially over personal economic gains (Burbules & Densmore, 1991). In most mentoring situations within the educational system the mentoring practice is done voluntarily or as part of the job of the mentors. In Norway the school receives a small fee per student teacher they host during the practicum, and it is up to the school principal to decide how the money is to be spent. When the mentee is a novice teacher or other colleagues, at best the mentor's teaching hours is reduced to give space for the second profession, mentoring. But it is hard to say that mentoring in schools is a financial profitable activity. The profits are more in the form of mutual learning for mentor and mentee and gaining a deeper understanding of the teaching profession.

CONCLUSION

The conviction that has guided the writing of this article has been that mentoring should be accepted as an independent profession within the teaching profession. The perception is that teacher education is a career long education consisting of various phases, initial, induction and in-service teacher education. Mentoring plays a central role in each of these phases, however there is a lack of clarity as regards who the mentors are and what qualifications are requested. The argument put forward is that to be able to practice mentoring formal and informal professional learning has to take place, which suggests that mentoring offers, for those who engage in the required professional learning programmes, a staged career development which opens up for different professional responsibilities, status and salary.

The second part of the paper has discussed the extent to which mentoring meets the criteria for being called a profession, first by discussing the complexity of the mentor role, and then by addressing the various traits of a profession suggested in the literature (Burbules & Densmore, 1991; Runtè, 1995; MacBeath, 2012). To be a mentor, experience is not enough, formal education for qualification is required. The aspiration of this author is that in order to practice mentoring, the practitioner must be qualified and certified to practice the profession. Mentor education leads to qualification, and the mentoring profession itself, in cooperation with the school leadership and the authorities, should be the certifying authorities. In order to continue practising mentoring after certification, the quality of the mentor's work has to be subject to quality assurance examinations, for example every five years. Again it becomes the school leadership and the mentoring profession which have the authority to renew a mentor's licence, yet the documentation of sustained and improved quality is at the responsibility of the mentors themselves. A dynamic mentor portfolio which also includes feedback from mentees, is a possible means to document professional practice.

As a summary we can say that the practice of mentoring in the educational system, and more specifically as enacted in Norway, is in the process of establishing itself as a distinct profession within the teaching profession. Such a view places heavy responsibilities on the various stakeholders; the politicians, school leaders, mentors and not least, the mentees. The politicians' responsibility is to provide resources for creating a solid infrastructure for the rising profession to grow and develop and avoid restricting the practice of mentoring through top down regulations. The school leaders need to accept that teacher education is a career long activity and provide space and protected time for professional learning at all levels to ensure sustained school development. Mentors are requested to develop a second professional identity as school-based teacher educators, which means undertaking further formal and informal education in order to accumulate theoretical and practical knowledge and understandings to be certified as mentors. Finally, mentoring in itself does not lead to professional learning and development. It depends on the quality of the mentoring process, and in addition to the mentor's profession competence, the mentee must be open to mentoring at all levels of her professional career. There is, however, still a long way to go, and in Norway it is exiting to be involved with the professionalization process of mentoring in full awareness that the process has started!

REFERENCES

Bertram, A., & Loughran, J. (2012). Science teachers' views on CoRes and PaP-eRs as a framework for articulating and developing pedagogical content knowledge. *Research in Science Education, 42*(6), 1027–1047.

Bray, L., & Nettleton, P. (2007). Assessor or mentor? Role confusion in professional education. *Nurse Education Today, 27*(8), 848–855.

Brunstad, P. (2007). Faglig klokskap (Professional wisdom). *PACEM, 10*(2), 59–70.

Burbules, N. C., & Densmore, K. (1991). The limits of making teaching a profession. *Educational Policy, 5*(1), 44–63.

Cochran-Smith, M. (2012). A longitudinal study of teaching practice and early career decisions. A cautionary tale. *American Educational Research Journal, 49*(5), 844–880.

Cox, E. (2005). For better, for worse: The matching process in formal mentoring schemes. *Mentoring and Tutoring, 13*(3), 403–414.

Darling-Hammond, L. (2012). The right start: Creating a strong foundation for the teaching career. *Phi Delta Kappan, 94*(3), 8–13.

Darling-Hammond, L., & Rothman, R. (Eds.). (2011). *Teacher and leader effectiveness in high-performing education systems*. Washington, DC: Alliance for Excellent Education and Stanford, CA: Stanford Center for Opportunity, Policy in Education.

Ellis, V. (2010). Impoverishing experience: The problem of teacher education in England. *Journal of Education for Teaching: International Research and Pedagogy, 36*(1), 105–120.

Hanssèn, S. E. (2008, December). *Rapport från den koordinerande programsensorn för lärarutbildningen vid Universitetet i Bergen* (Report from external evaluator of the Teacher Education Program at the University of Bergen). University of Bergen.

Hulme, M., & Menter, I. (2014). New professionalism in austere times: The employment experiences of early career teachers in Scotland. *Teachers and Teaching: Theory and Practice, 20*(6), 672–687. doi:10.1080/13540602.2014.885707

Ingersoll, R. M. (2012, January 5). *Beginning teacher induction: What the data tell us*. Philadelphia, PA: University of Pennsylvania Scholarly Commons.

Lazovsky, R., & Reichenberg, R. (2006). The new mandatory induction programme for all beginning teachers in Israel: Perceptions of inductees in five study tracks. *Journal of Education for Teaching, 32*(1), 53–70.

Lortie, D. C. (1975). *Schoolteacher: A sociological study*. Chicago, IL: University of Chicago Press.

MacBeath, J. (2012). *Future of the teaching profession*. Cambridge: University of Cambridge, Educational International Research Institute.

McNamara, O., Murray, J., & Jones, M. (Eds.). (2014). *Workplace learning in teacher education. International practice and policy*. London, England: Springer.

Merriam-Webster on line dictionary. Retrieved from http://www.merriam-webster.com/

Mourshed, M., Chijioke, C., & Barber, B. (2012). *How the world's most improved systems keep getting better.* Chicago, IL: McKinsey & Company.

Murrell, P. C. Jr., Diez, M., Feiman-Nemser, S., & Schussler, D. L. (2010). *Teaching as a moral practice: Defining, developing, and assessing professional dispositions in teacher education.* Cambridge, MA: Harvard University Press.

OECD. (2010). *Teachers' professional development Europe in international comparison. An analysis of teachers' professional development based on the OECD's Teaching and Learning International Survey (TALIS).* Belgium: European Union.

Richter, D., Kunter, M., Klusmann, U., Lüdtke, O., & Baumert, J. (2011). Professional development across the teaching career: Teachers' uptake of formal and informal learning opportunities. *Teaching and Teacher Education, 27,* 116–126.

Roness, D. (2011). Still motivated: The motivation for teaching during the second year in the profession. *Teaching and Teacher Education, 27,* 628–638.

Roness, D., & Smith, K. (2009). Postgraduate Certificate in Education (PGCE) and student motivation. *European Journal of Teacher Education, 32*(2), 111–135.

Rots, I., Kelchtermans, G., & Aelterman, A. (2012). Learning (not) to become a teacher: A qualitative analysis of the job entrance issue. *Teaching and Teacher Education, 28*(1), 1–10.

Runté, R. (1995). Is teaching a profession? In T. Gerald & R. Runté (Eds.), *Thinking about teaching: An introduction.* Toronto: Harcourt Brace.

Sabar, N. (2004). From heaven to reality through crisis: Novice teachers as migrants. *Teaching and Teacher Education, 20*(2), 145–161.

Shulman, L. S. (1986). Those who understand: Knowledge growth in teaching. *Educational Researcher, 15*(2), 4–14.

Smith, K. (2005). Teacher educators' professional knowledge- How does it differ from teachers' professional knowledge? *Teaching and Teacher Education, 21,* 177–192.

Smith, K. (2010). Mentorrollen – norske og internasjonale stemmer. (Mentor role- Norwegian and International Voices). In K. Smith & M. Ulvik (Eds.), *Veiledning av nye lærere- nasjonale og internasjonale perspektiver* (Mentoring Newly Qualified Teachers – National and International Perspectives). Oslo: Universitetsforlaget.

Smith, K. (2012). Utvikling av profesjonskompetanse (Developing professional competence). In *Utdanningsforbundet. Profesjon og politikk* (Profession and Politics) (pp. 61–66). Oslo: Utdanningsforbundet (Union of Education Norway).

Smith, K. (2013, February). *Teacher education–A profession or not?* Keynote presented at the EU Precidency Conference 'Integration, Innovation and Improvement – The Professional Identity of Teacher Educators', Dublin.

Smith, K., & Lev-Ari, L. (2005). The place of practicum in pre-service teacher education. *Asian Pacific Journal of Teacher Education, 33*(3), 289–302.

Smith, K., & Ulvik, M. (Eds.). (2010). *Veiledning av nye lærere- nasjonale og internasjonale perspektiver.* (Mentoring newly qualified teachers- National and international perspectives). Oslo: Universitetsforlaget.

Smith, K., & Ulvik, M. (2014). Learning to teach in Norway: A shared responsibility. In O. McNamara, J. Murray, & M. Jones (Eds.), *Workplace learning in teacher education. International practice and policy* (pp. 261–279). London, England: Springer.

Smith, K., Ulvik, M., & Helleve, I. (2013). *Førstereisen – Lærdom hentet fra nye læreres fortellinger.* (The first journey. Lessons learned from newly qualified teachers). Oslo: Gyldendal Akademisk.

Taylor, Y., & Meyer, K, (2011). Teacher professional leadership in support of teacher professional development. *Teaching and Teacher Education, 27*(1), 85–94.

The General Teaching Council Scotland. (2012). Retrieved from http://www.gtcs.org.uk/standards/standard-for-career-long-professional-learning.aspx

The Teaching Council, Ireland. (2011). *Policy on the continuum of teacher education.* Dublin: The Teaching Council.

Watt, M. G., & Richardson, P. W. (2008). Motivations, perceptions, and aspirations concerning teaching as a career for different types of beginning teachers. *Learning and Instruction, 18*(5), 408–428.

Wenger, E. (1998). *Communities of practice: Learning, meaning, and identity.* Cambridge: Cambridge University Press.

Zeichner, K. (2010). Rethinking the connections between campus courses and field experiences in college- and university-based teacher education. *Journal of Teacher Education, 61*(1–2), 89–99.

Kari Smith
Department of Education
University of Bergen, Norway

KARI SMITH AND MARIT ULVIK

14. AN EMERGING UNDERSTANDING OF MENTORS' KNOWLEDGE BASE

INTRODUCTION

Sara had just observed a lesson taught by May, one of the student teachers she had been given the responsibility of mentoring during their practicum. May had planned the lesson without conferring with Sara, and the lesson was planned far beyond the level and the competence of the class. When May put the pupils to work, they all sat quietly staring at the assignment they had been given and seemed to work on it. May sat next to her desk, she did not walk around in class to guide the pupils in their work with the assignment. Neither did she go over the assignment at the end of the class, she 'would do it in the next lesson, the pupils were so busy working'. At the end of the lesson May expressed her satisfaction with how successful the lesson had been, 'the pupils were busy working quietly all the time so they had really enjoyed the activity.

Sara was unsure of how and when she should tell May that she and the class were not interacting during the lesson, and that little or no pupil learning had taken place. If May is an unexperienced student teacher in her first practicum, she may need time to discover how her teaching works for students and to be supported and become more secure in her teaching role before being challenged. Furthermore, to nurture critical capacity and reflection by asking questions that make May think through her teaching from a new perspective and find out how to improve by herself, could be a better strategy than to tell her what to do. The dilemma for the mentor, however, is that she is both responsible for the student teacher and the class, and the class should be her main priority.

Another case is the following:

Per was a second career student teacher who had worked with young people for years. He was an experienced lecturer and had arranged conferences and had traveled around and talked to school classes about substance misuse. Additionally he worked in a project related to young people that hang around in the city center in their spare time.

H. Tillema et al. (Eds.), Mentoring for Learning, 299–312.

At first in his practicum he seemed reserved and not especially engaged. During mentoring sessions he brought pen and paper and made notes, but he had no suggestions for topics to discuss. Initially he had made it clear that the one year post graduate teacher education was something he participated in only because he had to if he wanted to work as a teacher. He had no questions about the mentors teaching and thought everything worked okay.

Eventually Per took over more and more of the teaching and as if by magic he changed the personality the mentor had learned to know. He encountered the students with a cheerfulness and enthusiasm that they knew to appreciate. He entered into an agreement with students about behaviour and had a lot of creative suggestions for alternative teaching. He got on very well with the students and the topic he should cover was very well taken care of.

However, during mentoring sessions, the seemingly careless and disengaged Per was back.

Per has quite different needs than May. In his case emotional and practical advice does not work. His experiences from teaching young people make him more like a colleague than an unexperienced novice. The school could benefit from his experiences, but at the same time, he could learn from his mentor about the framework a teacher has to consider and how it is to teach a school subject. The mentor is supposed to mentor in the profession, and even if Per has a great deal to offer students, he does not fully know what it means to be a teacher. However, it is not easy to mentor someone who is not willing to be mentored. The mentor needs to know something about adult learning and learning more like equals. Per seems to go on well with the students. However, as a teacher he also needs to go on well with and cooperate with colleagues, and in his practicum he gets an opportunity to work together with an experienced teacher. The mentor and the mentee can learn from and challenge each other, but they both have to be open minded and not appear as the one who knows all the answers.

The above situations were recently presented to the students in our mentor course at the University of Bergen. They are all experienced teachers, mostly with some mentoring experience, but without mentoring education leading to mentoring qualifications. The cases initiated a lively discussion around the tables as many of them recognized the situation from their own experience as mentors or as student teachers, and also teachers. To focus the discussion, the task they were given was to discuss what kind of knowledge the two mentors needed to provide May and Per with realistic critical feedback which would not discourage them, but help them reflect on the lessons and their attitudes so May would understand her misjudgements and avoid similar situations in the future, and Per understands that it is enough for a professional teacher to go well on with his students. He is also supposed to cooperate with his colleagues. In other words, the mentor students were asked to discuss what pedagogical content knowledge (PCK) (Shulman, 1987) mentors need to have.

In this chapter we will discuss the concept of PCK in relation to the scholarship of mentors' practice arguing that the concept in itself is transferable. Before going into mentoring, we will start with how Lee Shulman in his work discusses the concept pedagogical content knowledge in relation to teaching and the professional knowledge of teachers. He calls it 'the most powerful analogies, illustrations, examples, explanations, and demonstrations—in a word, the ways of representing and formulating the subject that makes it comprehensible for others' (1986, p. 9). Shulman includes in the PCK concept the expertise of the content specialist integrated with pedagogical knowledge and skills, which blends into each other in what is called teachers' pedagogical content knowledge. In other words, Shulman makes an attempt to define the professional knowledge of teachers by simply saying it is all about how to best teach their content to their students (Shulman, 1987). In an interview with Amanda Berry, John Loughran and Jan van Driel, the authors of an editorial which revisits the concept PCK, Shulman says that the understanding of teachers' PCK was developed in the search of finding the answer to the semantically simple, but conceptually very complex question' How does somebody that really knows something, teach it to somebody who doesn't?' (Berry, Loughran, & van Driel, 2008, p. 1274). In the same interview Shulman discloses that through research with colleagues at that time, a growing understanding for the interplay between the way teachers' understood their subject and how the subject was taught emerged. Accordingly, the concept PCK, integrating content knowledge with pedagogical practical and theoretical knowledge, was introduced in 1987 (Berry et al., 2008).

Pedagogical content knowledge is situated within the scholarship of practice, and it is related to theoretical content knowledge and the practice of supporting students to get access to and personalise that knowledge. In a way a teacher's PCK represents a comprehensive view on teaching, the scholarship of teaching. However, whereas the scholarship of teachers' practice is widely discussed in the literature, the scholarship of mentors' practice is less known. In the next section we will therefore discuss the scholarship of mentoring in relation to relevant literature.

SCHOLARSHIP OF MENTORING

Orland-Barak (2010) claims that today mentoring has taken on an extended understanding referring to Zanting, Verloop, Vermunt, and van Driel's work (1998). Recent understanding of the scholarship of mentoring is grounded in the work of mentors which ranges from 'modelling and instructing to information sources, co-thinkers, and inquirers, evaluators, supervisors, and learning companions' (Orland-Barak, 2010, p. 2). Smith (2010) presents a similar view when discussing the many roles the mentor takes on, and which illustrate the complexity of mentoring (see previous chapter in this book).

Anderson and Shannon (1988) explain how a mentor is perceived by referring to Homer's Odyssey. The mentor is somebody with expertise who guides and instructs, as well as protects and challenges the mentee, the novice. Odysseys gave Mentor

K. SMITH & M. ULVIK

the responsibility for Telemakos, his son, when he himself was busy fighting wars. Another perspective of examining the scholarship of mentoring is to look at how the word 'mentor' is translated into the culture of practice in various contexts. In Norwegian the most common understanding is that a mentor is usually a more experienced colleague who functions as somebody who shows the way (*veileder*) for somebody with less experience with a focus on activity and reflection (Smith, 2010; Ulvik, & Smith, 2011). In the Norwegian context the practice of mentoring is understood as somebody who is showing the way, which to a certain extent also implies that mentoring is not just showing and telling the mentee what to do. It also implies the understanding that the mentee has to walk the way herself, with the support of somebody who is familiar with similar roads. In Swedish the mentor is somebody who' takes you by the hand' (handleder), whereas in Hebrew the mentor is a person who accompanies the novice and provides professional, cultural and emotional support (Israeli Ministry of Education). These brief glimpses into the understanding of mentoring in a few cultural contexts suggest that the practice of mentoring is to a large extent influenced by the culture in which it takes place, something that is also suggested by Orland-Barak (2010).

Brunstad (2010) compares the mentor to a nomad when presenting his view of the mentoring practice. He suggests that mentoring is largely an ethical enterprise and that mentors need to examine their power position in relation to the mentee when engaging in mentoring practice. He warns about misusing the inherent power in mentoring situations, and suggests that the mentor should see herself as a nomad who is a visitor to the world of knowledge and skills of the mentee. The language in which mentoring practice takes place is of utmost importance, according to Brunstad, who claims that when the mentor sees herself as a temporary visitor in the mentee's practice, the power position is slightly changed, and the mentor becomes the one who is seeking information from the mentee about her understandings of own practice. It is not only the mentee who is engaged in learning in mentoring situations, the learning dialogue opens for mutual learning. This awareness will form the communication and the language used in mentoring conversations (Brunstad, 2010).

The above discussion points first of all at the complexity of understanding the scholarship of mentoring, and that the practice of mentoring is not uniform, but influenced by the context in which it takes place. The practice of mentoring is coloured by the mentor's understanding of the scholarship of mentoring, as in Shulman's explanation of the concept pedagogical content knowledge. Therefore, it is now time to look at the pedagogical content knowledge of mentors.

MENTORS' PEDAGOGICAL CONTENT KNOWLEDGE (PCK)

As already mentioned, we know little about the mentors' PCK, what is the theoretical content of mentoring, and what skills are needed to impart that knowledge and make it accessible and useful to the mentees? In our work through a number of small studies we are trying to create an understanding of mentors' PCK. Being aware that to a large extent this was a phenomenological project, we wanted to get insight into the mentors perceptions of what knowledge they drew on when practicing mentoring. So we have asked mentors to discuss the types of knowledge mentors need to have to solve dilemmas in mentoring situations, we have collected data by the help of questionnaires, and we have examined the curricula of mentor education programs offered by in Norwegian teacher education institutions. In the following a brief presentation of some of the studies is given.

KNOWLEDGE ESSENTIAL TO SOLVE MENTORING DILEMMAS

On the very first day of the mentoring course January, 2014, the mentor students were (n=14) were presented with various authentic dilemmas from other mentors' experiences. The situation presented in the beginning of the chapter was one of them. The mentor students discussed the dilemmas in groups, not necessarily to find a solution to the dilemmas, but by addressing the knowledge needed to solve the situation in a professional way.

The initial situation with Sara and Per can be used to exemplify the PCK of mentors as discussed by mentor students. The data collection was done through note taking by the two course leaders during the group discussions, thus this small, informal study is a qualitative study using observation and note taking as the main. The notes were compared and we learned that in this group of mentor students there was strong agreement that *content knowledge* was needed, in other words, Sara needed to know the subject taught in the lesson (the teaching subject was not given) in order to help May plan the lesson and to help her adjust the subject teaching to the pupils' level. Per would benefit from developing better his communicative competence. In our research on novice teachers' experiences the first year of teaching, we found that a number of novices preferred the mentor to have the same subject expertise, as they often needed guidance in how to teach the subject (Smith, Ulvik, & Helleve, 2013).

Another type of knowledge that was frequently mentioned by the mentor students was *communicative knowledge*, how to develop a learning dialogue in a situation where Sara's and May's perceptions of the situation are miles apart. Within the umbrella title, communicative knowledge, or more exactly communicative skills, various central knowledge areas were mentioned, such as: understanding how adults learn from critical feedback, how to give critical feedback, and how to maintain motivation when things are getting difficult. When translating this into academic knowledge areas, *adult learning, assessment for learning, and motivation* are by mentor students viewed as essential to mentoring.

An interesting issue that came up in the discussions was that perhaps the mentoring session should not take place immediately after the observed lesson, to give May some time to reflect on what had taken place. However, to make the reflection focused and useful, Sara should give May some guiding questions to help her analyse the lesson in a critical perspective. So, knowledge about how to promote critical *reflection* is, perhaps, one of the most important knowledge areas of mentors.

Summarising the PCK of mentors as suggested by mentor students in the beginning of their mentor education the following knowledge areas came up:

- Content *"The mentor should help the student teachers planning good lessons, and this can they do only if they know the subject".*
- Communication *"It is not always easy to tell students they did not do very well without demotivating them. How should the mentor create an atmosphere in the meeting which allows for that?"*
- Adult learning *"I know how to teach children, but I am not quite sure of how to teach adults. I need to think of how I learn, so I can better understand how to help the mentee".*
- Assessment/feedback *"It is so much easier to praise the student teacher. I really have to think twice before I criticise. I don't want to be negative, and I have to know how to direct the mentee so the lesson will be better next time".*
- Motivation *"Not all mentees are equally motivated, like Per, for example. He was not very motivated to start teacher education, and I have to help him understand it is important for him. Other mentees sometimes become demotivated when listening to some of the negative discussions about teaching in the staff room".*
- Reflection *"It would not help much if I just told May what was wrong in the lesson, or that Per had to see the importance of learning to be a teacher. In a way the mentor must make the mentees understand it themselves, to help them look at themselves and their teaching from an outside perspective. This is, probably, what reflection is about".*

PERCEPTIONS OF MENTOR ROLES

In another study we wanted to learn how mentors perceive their role as mentors and how they prepare for that role (Smith, Hansèn, Skagen, Aspfors, Helleve, & Danielsen, 2012). Data was collected in Norway (n=34) and Finland (N=12) with the purpose of getting a broader understanding of mentoring also across the two cultures, and to look for trends which might be more contextual dependent. A more formal data collection process than in the previous study was used as data were collected by the help of an open ended questionnaire. The study does not look at the PCK of mentors specifically, but some of the questions in the open-ended questionnaire provide information about how practising mentors perceive their role and the knowledge needed for that role.

The analysis of the data was first done by the Norwegian and the Finnish research teams separately, before the data were cross referenced in a joint meeting. The findings suggest that there are similarities in the Norwegian and Finnish data material. For example, mentors have to be capable of *handling the day-to-day pragmatics of school* and adjust mentoring to the current situation in which mentoring takes place.

This means that *improvisation* seems to be core characteristics of mentoring, as also discussed by Orland-Barak (2010). The ability to handle unexpected situations is an inherent part of any professional practice, and this issue has been elaborated in the previous chapter, where Brunstad's definition of acting out of professional wisdom is a characteristic of professionalism. Beneficial improvisation is only possible when the practitioner acts out of knowledge, skills, experience, and creativity (Barker & Borko, 2011). The Norwegian- Finnish data uses the term *day-to-day pragmatics of school* which is understood by the researchers as knowledge about the school and the organisation of the school in which mentoring takes place, so mentoring practice is in rhythm with school life in general.

Knowledge about *reflection* and how to support the mentee develop reflective skills was also in this data material found to be a salient aspect of the mentor's professionalism. The danger is that reflection has become a buzzword in teacher education with multiple local and even personal interpretations. When reflection and how to develop reflective praxis is introduced as a knowledge area within mentors' PCK and taught in formal mentor education, an approach which elaborates the concept theoretically, as well as how to engage in reflective practice, must be chosen.

Assessment was another knowledge area which was detected in the Norwegian as well as in the Finnish data. The respondents pointed at assessment as a core activity in mentoring and it was the informal aspects of assessment such as giving feedback, developing learning dialogues and encourage mentees to engage in self-assessment, critical analysis of own practice.

A final similarity to be discussed in the current chapter is, perhaps, the most challenging construct to define and translate into a teachable knowledge area, how to help mentees developing *teachership* (Hansèn, 2008). Teachership is a comprehensive view on teachers' job, which goes beyond teaching the subject matter. It is about cognitive, practical and affective aspects of teaching, and beyond all, to connect to and develop relationships with children, colleagues and parents. In a way, it is possible to say that teachership is another word for teachers' PCK. Mentors do not only need to have an understanding of what teachership is, but also the ability to articulate it, break it down into handable parts, to make it accessible to the mentees. The findings do not lead to a clear definition of *teachership* and how to help mentees develop their own understanding, but it became clear that mentoring goes beyond mentoring how to teach a certain subject or how to write tests, it is about acting out the many different roles teachers have from being knowledge broker to social worker and caretaker.

There are several similarities in what mentor students at the onset of their mentor education and what experienced mentors think the PCK of mentoring consists of. Mentors' PCK seems to relate to disciplinary and pedagogical theoretical knowledge as well as practical knowledge, especially related to interpersonal communication.

Still, mentors' PCK is still, as we see it, a rather defuse concept, but in spite of that, nearly all teacher education institutions in Norway offer formal mentor education. The next step in the search for a clear understanding of mentors PCK, we undertook a study which examined how higher education institutions offering mentor formal mentor education translate the mentor's PCK into course curricula.

CURRICULA FOR MENTOR EDUCATION

The data from this study is comprehensive as it is collected from 9 Norwegian teacher education institutions, 5 universities and 4 colleges, which offer mentor education (Smith, Krüger, & Sagvaag, 2013). The University of Bergen (UoB) was not included in the data collection as the researchers were involved with mentor education at UoB. The examined institutions were selected based on geographical criteria as we wanted to have representation from all over Norway. The data was collected in the autumn of 2012 and spring 2013 and online curricula and reading lists were examined. The findings were presented at the Nordic Educational Research Conference (NERA) in Iceland, March, 2013. We looked at the level (undergraduate or graduate level), European Credit Transfer and Accumulation System (ECTS), duration of the course, required reading, content, and examination forms. For the purpose of this chapter, discussing the PCK of mentoring, the focus of inquiry was the content of the courses, however, it is also useful to take a look at the reading lists and the examination forms. The below table presents a summary of the data in relation to the above domains:

Table 1. Overview of formal mentor education in Norway

	Universities	*University Colleges*
Academic Level	4 Master, 1 Bachelor	1 Master, 1 Bachelor, 2 'specialization'
ECTS	30, 15 ETCS per phase	30, 15 ETCS per phase
Duration	Partime, 4 semesters, 2 semesters per phase	Partime, 4 semesters, 2 semesters per phase
Required Reading	Norwegian, Nordic, some English	Norwegian only
Content differences	Internationally oriented, transmission from student to teacher, planning mentoring programs, group/individual mentoring, research	Mentoring in preschool/ vocational teacher education, didactics of mentoring
Examination form	Oral and written assignment in phase 1, action research on mentoring in phase 2	Take home exam in phase 1, take home exam and oral presentation of this in phase 2.

When taking a brief look at the differences between the curricula of the universities (mainly secondary school teacher education) and the university colleges (mainly pre-school, primary school and vocational teacher education) we learn that the required reading is to a large extent Norwegian literature with a few other Scandinavian references. At the university programs we find some English literature with a broader international perspective. The national literature, with some exemptions, deals more with the practical aspects of mentoring than with more theoretical aspects and research based information.

The examinations forms are multiple, and the demands are increased at level 2. Some of the examination forms are traditional exams, but portfolios, oral group examinations, and written home exams are most frequently used at level 1, whereas project work, e.g. action research projects, are the most common examination form at level 2. This indicates that part of the PCK of mentors is conducting practice oriented research, especially as reflected in the universities' mentor education programs.

By examining the content of the courses a long list came up and there is to a large extent similarities across the institutions. Some of the differences, which seem to reflect the type of teacher education in the institution, are presented in the above table. Later in this paper a synthesis will be discussed in relation to the other two data sources described above. But first, the list from the curricula will be presented in full:

- Communication, interaction
- Professional knowledge and development
- Learning and teaching
- Organisation, culture and innovation
- Mentoring roles/ traditions
- Didactical perspectives in mentoring
- Ethics in mentoring
- Mentoring language/definition of concepts
- Mentoring student teachers/novice teachers
- Systematic reflection, models of reflection
- Action learning/research
- Communities of learning
- Organisation of Mentoring in school / preschool
- Mentoring in vocational education

Courses offered by the big universities seem to be more academically oriented with a stronger emphasis on theoretical aspects related to professional learning, reflection, and learning communities, for example. The research element is more salient, both in the course content, in the reading lists, and in the final assignment. Most university-based mentor courses have action research as the final examination form. In institutions which offer vocational teacher education and/or pre-school teacher education, aspects of mentoring in professional education stand central in the curricula. Common to all are areas such as communication and ethics in mentoring, as well as discussions and literature about the mentor role, often in a national (Norwegian) perspective. Ulvik and Sunde (2013) found that becoming familiar with theory related to mentoring during mentor education was found useful by the participating teachers (students of mentoring).

SYNTHESIS OF FINDINGS IN THE VARIOUS STUDIES

The data collected from the varied studies described above indicate that there is an emerging understanding of mentors' PCK. In this section we will try to make a synthesis of the data.

We have grouped the findings from the various studies into three main dimensions of knowledge which might give as a framework of what represents the PCK of mentors. To be more specific the emerging dimensions are: structural/practical, theoretical, and inter-personal knowledge and skills. Each knowledge dimension is presented below:

1) Structural/Practical Knowledge

Mentoring takes place in a specific context, nationally, regionally and in a given school. Each of these systems functions within a structural/practical framework, such as national steering documents and regional structures of schools. The mentees, either they are student teachers of novice teachers, must be induced in to the educational system at large, including regional applications of the national framework. In Norway, for example, there is a national framework for assessment, however each region has developed different ways in the application of the rules. The mentor should be well informed about both systems and guide the mentee through the often confusing territory of rules to follow. In addition to the broader frameworks, the individual school's culture and micro-politics (Kelchtermans & Ballet, 2002), are, perhaps, the most challenging aspects to become familiar with. Much of the school culture is tacit, and there is often a local language which newcomers have to become familiar with. Expressions such as 'the Friday meetings', 'coffee making-duty', and 'our special student' alongside rules about turn taking during breaks, mean little to the outsider who is in the process of becoming an insider. In addition each school has its own power struggle of which the new colleague is unaware, yet it might have a crucial impact on the way the mentee experiences and perceives the new work place. A trusted mentor who is well acquainted with the local context is likely to be valuable to the mentee searching for her own position and identity within the school.

2) Theoretical Knowledge

In addition to theoretical knowledge about the content of mentoring, knowledge about adult learning, and more specifically work-place learning, is central. Adult learning differs from children learning, there are different types of social and motivational aspects that have to be taken into consideration, in addition to knowing how to use previous experiences the adult learner brings into the learning situation when supporting in understanding new experiences. Work-place learning differs from formal learning, and experiences, positive and negative, become the textbook that initiates the learning process. The mentor's task is to exploit the mentee's as well as own experiences, and make them relevant to the mentee's learning processes. Thus theoretical knowledge about motivation, feedback and self-efficacy are all knowledge areas the mentor will draw upon during mentoring. Knowing how to detect and exploit moments of contingency (Black & Wiliam, 2009) becomes a central aspect of the mentor's work in supporting the mentees to construct meaning from their experiences (Brodie & Irving, 2007).

3) Interpersonal Knowledge and Skills

In mentoring situations which is essentially situated in practice, theoretical knowledge by itself is not sufficient to create useful mentoring activities. The theoretical knowledge must be implemented in practicing mentoring, both in the language used in mentoring conversation as well as in understanding the mentee and her situation, showing empathy. The mentoring discourse is thoroughly discussed elsewhere in this book, and other aspects of interpersonal skills are discussed in this section.

There is often a delicate balance between pushing through critical constructive feedback and being open and empathetic to the mentee's challenging learning processes. The first step is, perhaps, to establish a relationship characterised by trust with the mentee. People are more open to accept and use feedback when the receiver of the feedback trusts the provider's professional competence as well as believing that the intention is to support development and learning (Hattie & Timperley, 2007). A central aspect of interpersonal skills is to be able to develop a mutual learning dialogue in the mentoring relationship. The understanding of dialogue here is the process of understanding each other, not necessarily to agree and develop a shared understanding, but to be able to draw on each other's perceptions, experiences and knowledge to develop personal as well as shared knowledge about the complexity of teaching, and the many roles and responsibilities a teacher holds (Besley & Peters, 2012).

TRANSLATION OF MENTORS PCK INTO MENTOR EDUCATION

In the final section of this chapter the translation of the emerging understanding of the PCK of mentoring into a mentor education program is presented.

The University of Bergen has offered mentor courses to mentors to our partner-schools for nearly a decade, and five years ago the course was developed into a

30 ECTSs course consisting of two phases running over two years. The course syllabus is under constant revision, as we use our experiences with the course in the ongoing work of improving the education. The syllabus represents the three knowledge areas which emerged from our studies and which have been presented above.

During the first year emphasis is put on the articulation of tacit knowledge, a skill which Smith (2005) found to be a major difference between teachers and teacher educators. As discussed in the previous chapter of this book, mentors act as school-based teacher educators and a central part of mentoring is to make the mentor's tacit knowledge accessible to the mentee. In the course ample time is given to sharing experiences and to practice mentoring each other, influenced by Wenger's (2006) work on communities of practice, especially for experienced professionals such as the mentor students. The course teachers' job is to present new information and to support the participants in developing a sense of ownership to the knowledge in the process of forming their own professional identity as mentors. In the first year topics such as theories and traditions of mentoring, research on the transition process from student to teacher, from education to the profession, mentoring in various school subjects, the ethics of mentoring, the mentor role, and interpersonal communication are discussed. At the completion of the first phase (15ECTS) the mentor students are asked to collect their various reflective assignments and mentor plans in an presentation portfolio which is assessed by an internal and an external (from another institution) examiner.

In the second phase of the course there is a stronger emphasis on mentoring novice teachers and collegial mentoring. The participants are first introduced to action research, as they are required to engage in action research of their own mentoring activity for the final assignment of the course. Other topics dealt with are research on novice teachers and their challenges, professional learning and critical reflection from a theoretical as well as practical perspective, and the role of mentoring in school development activities. In this second year the mentor students become familiar with international literature and the mentoring practice in other countries. Much time is spent on the participants' presentations of their action research projects, within which feedback and assessment in collegial situations is discussed. The final examination is an internal and external assessment of the candidate's action research project.

An explicit goal of the mentor education at our university is to educate mentors who are not only consumers of research on mentoring of NQTs, but also producers of research. Good practitioner research is an essential part in the work of continuously developing a knowledge base on mentoring, which is a central goal in our work. With this vision in mind, our next goal is to develop a full program at a master level in mentoring based on the emerging understanding of the PCK of mentors within the frame work of structural/practical, theoretical, and inter-personal knowledge and skills.

310

CONCLUSION

In this chapter we have shown that it is possible to claim an emerging understanding of the pedagogical content knowledge (PCK) (Shulman, 1987) of mentoring by referring to various local, national and international studies. Mentor students, experienced teachers, educated mentors, student teachers, as well as course curricula, have been used as resources in our ongoing work to understand 'How mentors, who really know about the complexity of teaching, teach it to student teachers, novice and experienced teachers' (Adaption from Berry, Loughran, & van Driel, 2008, p. 1274). At the current stage of our work, we argue that mentors' PCK is framed within three main areas, the structural/practical aspects of teaching, theoretical knowledge, and inter-personal knowledge and skills. The more specific content of the three main areas will, to a large extent, depend on the context in which mentoring takes place. The University of Bergen has developed a mentor education program of 30 ECTSs which reflects the Norwegian and the local context. The detailed content of the mentor education program is under constant revision as we are continuously in dialogue with the work and practice of international colleagues, our own research, national steering papers, and not least, with student teachers, teachers and mentors. A stronger focus on mentored practice of mentoring is one of the things we want to change in the future, as well as gaining more knowledge about and practice in group mentoring versus individual mentoring. The overall conclusion is, however, that mentors' PCK can be presented in general terms, such as the above framework, across contexts. The specifics, however, will always be context dependent, as good mentoring should, the same way as good teaching should, be adapted to the specific context.

REFERENCES

Anderson, E. A., & Shannon, A. L. (1988). Toward a conceptualisation of mentoring. *Journal of Teacher Education*, 38–42.

Barker, L., & Borko, H. (2011). Presence and the art of improvisational teaching. In K. Sawyer (Ed.), *Structure and improvisation in creative teaching* (pp. 279–298). New York, NY: Cambridge University Press.

Berry, A., Loughran, J., & van Driel, J. H. (2008). Revisiting the roots of pedagogical content knowledge. *International Journal of Science Education, 30*(10), 1271–1279. doi:10.1080/09500690801998885

Besley, T., & Peters, M. A. (2012). Introduction: Interculturalism, education and dialogue. In I. T. Besley & M. A. Peters (Eds.), *Interculturalsim, education and dialogue* (pp. 1–25). New York, NY: Peter Lang.

Black, P., & Wiliam, D. (2009). Developing the theory of formative assessment. *Educational Assessment, Evaluation and Accountability, 21*(1), 5–31.

Brodie, P., & Irving, K. (2007). Assessment in work-based learning: Investigating a pedagogical approach to enhance student learning. *Assessment & Evaluation in Higher Education, 32*(1), 11–19.

Brunstad, P. O. (2007). Faglig klokskap (Professional wisdom). *PACEM, 10*(2), 59–70.

Brunstad, P. O. (2010). Mentoren som nomade (Mentor as nomad). In K. Smith & M. Ulvik (Eds.), *Veiledning av nye lærere- nasjonale og internasjonale perspektiver* (Mentoring newly qualified teachers- National and international perspectives) (pp. 191–201). Oslo: Universitetsforlaget.

Hansèn, S. E. (2008, December). *Rapport från den koordinerande programsensorn för lärarutbildningen vid Universitetet i Bergen* (Report from external evaluator of the Teacher Education Program at the University of Bergen). University of Bergen, Bergen, Norway.

Hattie, J., & Timperley, H. (2007). The power of feedback. *Review of Educational Research, 77*(1), 81–112.

Kelchtermans, G., & Ballet, K. (2002). The micropolitics of teacher induction. A narrative-biographical study on teacher socialization. *Teaching and Teacher Education, 18,* 105–120.

Orland-Barak, L. (2010). *Learning-to-mentor-as-praxix.* New York, NY: Springer.

Shulman, L. S. (1986). Those who understand: Knowledge growth in teaching. *Educational Researcher, 15*(2), 4–14.

Shulman, L. S. (1987). Knowledge and teaching: Foundations of the new reform. *Harvard Educational Review, 57*(1), 1–22.

Smith, K. (2005). Teacher Educators' professional knowledge- How does it differ from teachers' professional knowledge? *Teaching and Teacher Education, 21,* 177–192.

Smith, K. (2010). Mentorrollen – norske og internasjonale stemmer (Mentor role- Norwegian and International Voices). In K. Smith & M. Ulvik (Eds.), *Veiledning av nye lærere- nasjonale og internasjonale perspektiver* (Mentoring newly qualified teachers – National and international perspectives). Oslo: Universitetsforlaget.

Smith, K., Krüger, K. R., & Sagvaag, I. (2013, March). Mentoring in Norway. Paper presented at the Nordic Educational Research Association (NERA) Conference in Reykjavik, Iceland.

Smith, K., Ulvik, M., & Helleve, I. (2013). *Førstereisen – Lærdom hentet fra nye læreres fortellinger* (The first journey. Lessons learned from newly qualified teachers). Oslo: Gyldendal Akademisk.

Smith, K., Hansèn, S.E., Skagen, K., Jaspfors, J., Helleve, I., & Danielsen A. G. (2012, December). *Mentorship and mentor education – Finnish and Norwegian perspectives.* Paper presented at the World Educational Research Association (WERA) conference, Sydney.

Tillema, H., Smith, K., & Leshem, S. (2011). Dual roles – conflicting purposes: A comparative study on perceptions on assessment in mentoring relations during practicum. *European Journal of Teacher Education, 34*(2), 139–159.

Ulvik, M., & Smith, K. (2011). What characterise a good practice situation in teacher education? *Education Inquiry, 2*(3), 517–536.

Ulvik, M., & Sunde, E. (2013). The impact of mentor education: Does mentor education matter? *Professional Development in Education, 39*(5), 754–770.

Wenger. (2006). *Communities of practice. Learning, meaning and identity* (14th printing). Cambridge, USA: Cambridge University Press.

Zanting, A., Verloop, J. D., Vermunt, J. D., & van Driel, J. H. (1998). Explicating practical knowledge: An extension of mentor teachers' roles. *European Journal of Teacher Education, 21*(1), 11–28.

Kari Smith
Department of Education
University of Bergen, Norway

Marit Ulvik
Department of Education
University of Bergen, Norway

INGRID HELLEVE, A. G. DANIELSEN AND KARI SMITH

15. DOES MENTOR-EDUCATION MAKE A DIFFERENCE?

INTRODUCTION

It gives me a lot to see a student teacher or a newly qualified colleague become confident. It helps to make tacit knowledge visible. Actually it leads to more reflection; not only on the newcomer's way of teaching, but also on my own.

The aim of this chapter is to focus on differences between formally educated and not educated mentors. However, as an introduction we have chosen a quote that illustrates the similarities we found rather than the differences. The core value of mentorship according to our informants in the current study seems to be two-fold. First, the satisfaction they experience when they realize that their support to the newcomer contributes to increased confidence. Second, that mentoring helps themselves to increased self-awareness and self-reflection.

The last thirty years school-based mentoring has come to play an important role in the induction period of newly qualified teachers. Considerable resources have been spent on developing induction programs and on the process of mentoring (Hobson et al., 2009). Mostly experienced teachers are asked to be mentors (Jones, 2010). Teachers are educated to facilitate pupils' and not colleagues' learning. How to guide, support and challenge equal partners is something quite different. However, teachers are educated to facilitate pupils' and not colleagues' learning, and their expertise is related to teaching in the classroom. How to guide, support and challenge equal partners is something quite different. Internationally formal academic education for mentors is an unusual enterprise (OECD, 2005). More common are short courses connected to induction programs for newly qualified teachers. Research shows that programs intended to prepare mentors for their tasks vary in nature and quality and often focus more on administrative precautions than on developing mentors' abilities to facilitate mentees' professional learning (Hobson et al., 2009). In Norway formal education for mentors has been established and offered to experienced teachers throughout the country the last few years. Almost all teacher education institutions provide formal studies in mentoring for experienced teachers (Kroksmark & Aaberg, 2007; Smith, Kruger, & Sagvåg, 2013). Norwegian authorities have developed a proposal for a framework of competence-aims for education of mentors. Learning

H. Tillema et al. (Eds.), Mentoring for Learning, 313–332.

outcome is articulated based on the qualification framework (Knowledge Department, 2010, p. 4; KD, 2011). According to this document educated mentors should have developed proficiency in communication and mentoring. They should also gain knowledge about professional development for teachers. Their main task should be to support newly qualified teachers in their professional development, but the document also states that mentors should develop a more general competence in how to contribute to school development. Thus Norwegian authorities want to contribute to mentor education of teachers who are able to support professional development as a support to organizational development through the new profession of mentors that is emerging inside the profession.

Concerning induction in Norway little is said in political documents about the formal framework mentors meet in schools and how mentoring should be understood and practiced. Summing up, on the one hand teacher education institutions in Norway are encouraged to formally educate mentors who can guide and support, not only newly qualified teachers, but also the rest of the staff. On the other hand there is no formal induction period for newly qualified teachers in Norway. Once they have passed the examination from the teacher education institutions Norwegian teachers are certified for the rest of their lives. Schools are encouraged by the authorities to give newly qualified teachers a mentor (formally educated or not), but there is no demand of it (MER, 2008–2009).

The aim of the study is to examine how mentors with and without mentor education perceive and practice their role, and if there are any differences in the way these two groups understand their missions. The study is conducted in a county in the western part of Norway.

BACKGROUND

Why Mentoring?

According to Jones (2006a), structural, social and cultural changes make the understanding and interpretation of the concept of mentoring change over time. Mentoring is often viewed as a solution to different national goals and challenges (Wang et al., 2008).

There are different reasons and justifications for mentoring. Mentoring has occurred informally as a supportive activity between teachers for years. Relatively recently it has been recognized as a distinct, integral component of professional teacher education and development programs (Jones, 2006b). Referring to the English educational context Jones points to the fact that from the 1950's the mentor had the role of a master who applied rules and values to the mentee. Further she shows how the conceptual framework of teacher education dramatically changed in 1992 from an academic into a vocational domain (DFE, 1992). Teacher education in England is no longer planned and delivered by tutors in higher education, but through partnerships between schools and teacher education institutions. Emphasis is on training more than education, and practicing teachers play a key role in professional development for novice teachers. Experienced teachers are no longer supposed to be just models; they are also expected to be assessors and gate-keepers for newly qualified teachers in order to fill the required standards; and are to decide if the novice teacher is qualified according to the standards for induction. Hargreaves and Fullan (2000) claim that mentoring programs should be designed to prepare mentors for becoming *change agents* for the whole school community. In what they call "the fourth professional age" they argue that:

> We are on the edge of postmodern professionalism where teachers deal with diverse clientele and increasing moral uncertainty where many approaches are possible and more and more groups have an influence. (Hargreaves & Fullan, 2000, p. 52)

In times when teaching is embedded in uncertainty and there are few "correct" answers, mentors should learn how to provide strong emotional support to the school community (Zemblyas, 2003; Kelchtermans, 2009). Experienced as well as novice teachers are constantly being challenged by new demands and reforms, diverse pupil population, and increased demands for accountability. Mentoring should be seen as a devise to build strong professional structures in schools dedicated to improving, learning and caring.

Langdon (2007) argues that the aim and purpose of mentoring differs internationally. The fact that political *justifications* seem to go in two different directions is supported by the OECD report (OECD, 2005). The aim of the first approach is to focus on adjustment and adaption. In this approach, the novice teacher is looked upon as helpless and in need of support (Langdon, 2007). The aim is to help the novice teacher to fill the standards and adapt to the existing organization. Based on a study from 25 countries Langdon claims that politicians in these countries want to fix problems, increase recruiting and avoid retention. The main task for the mentor is to give advice to the newcomer on how to act in order to be accepted. The second approach values the newly qualified teachers' personal abilities and possibilities as a contribution to the school as a learning community. The purpose of mentoring is to encourage newly qualified teachers in exercising self-assessment and reflection in collaboration with other teachers. Novice teachers contribute with new perspectives on learning. Consequently they are seen as recourses that can challenge the existing school culture in line with the view of Hargreaves and Goodson (2000). The literature suggests that to avoid unnecessary frustration and to support and fully benefit from the new teachers' updated knowledge, a mentored induction period for novices is recommended. Per day, Norway has no systematic induction program for novice teachers, and it is therefore useful to take a closer look at what the literature says about mentoring models during the induction phase.

Maynyard and Furlong (1993) refer to three different mentoring models; the apprentice model, the competence model, and the reflection model. In the *apprentice* perspective the mentor is looked upon as a model for the novice teacher in line with the first, above mentioned, period in England. The *competence* model refers to standards and how the mentor can support the newly qualified teacher in reaching required goals. According to the *reflection* model the mentor is a critical friend; a person who asks provocative questions, provides data to be examined through another lens, and offers critique of a person's work as a friend (Schuck & Russell, 2005). Mentors in England following the competence model are required not only to nurture capacity facilitating personal and professional growth, but also to assess the novice teachers' competence as future teachers. To be the gatekeeper who decides if the novice teacher should be given a license to the profession or not makes the role even more complicated.

In Norway mentoring newly qualified teachers is suggested as an important enterprise in Whitepaper 11 (MER, 2008-2009), but no formal political legislation is made. As a result, we see today that the Government's recommendation to provide newly qualified teachers with mentoring is still to a large extent dependent on the value local authorities and school leaders find in establishing mentor programs. Thus, we find that the practice of mentoring differs from county to county.

Currently two national political initiatives related to mentoring are taking place at the same time, and they do not seem to acting in full harmony with each other yet. One initiative is the governmental support to mentor education as briefly described in the beginning of the paper, and the second initiative is the governmental recommendation to provide mentoring to novice teachers during the first year of teaching. However, it is up to the school to allocate a mentor and to establish a mentored induction program. Consequently, some educated mentors who have taken formal mentor education are unable to practice mentoring because the schools and local communities where they teach do not offer any kind of mentoring.

MENTORING FOR PROFESSIONAL DEVELOPMENT OF NOVICE COLLEAGUES

There is a lot of research on why mentoring is important and on the effects of mentoring for newly qualified teachers (Rippon & Martin, 2006; Hobson et al., 2009; Roths et al., 2012). There is less research on how the role as a mentor should be performed and how mentors should learn to practice their role (Hobson et al., 2009). The answer to the question of how to act as a mentor is not clear. Wang and Odell (2002) argue that what mentors look upon as their main mission is to provide emotional support and technical guidance to the mentees.

In the reflection model novice teachers are looked upon as colleagues and equal partners. In Norway teachers get their everlasting certificate and license for teaching upon graduating from teacher education. As newly qualified teachers they are equal peers to their mentors. Consequently mentors may hesitate to influence the way the novice teacher performs teaching and may not see it as part of their role to help the newly qualified teacher to understand the relationship between theoretical knowledge and classroom practice. The result is that mentoring tends to help to stop retention, because of the support the teachers receive from their mentors, but not to change traditional teaching and learning practices (Jones, 2010), because the mentors may be reluctant to challenge these practices. In order to support learning processes mentors have to find a balance between challenge and support rather than primarily making teaching manageable for novice teachers (Ulvik & Sunde, 2013). Loughran (2006) asserts that mentors should stimulate to reflection and challenging taken-for-granted ideas by reframing and questioning underlying personal theories. Theories about teaching are often deeply rooted after many years of observation as pupils. In learning about teaching student teachers and newly qualified teachers need to question the taken for granted in their learning about teaching through metacognition. One aspect of the mentor's role is to challenge novice teachers in their self-reflection and metacognition. Kelchtermans and Ballet (2002) remind us that more attention in research has been paid to novice teachers' role as teachers in the classroom than to their role as new colleagues. In what the researchers call the micro-political reality teachers negotiate their positions. To understand and move in this terrain may be just as challenging as class management for novice teachers. Mentors' role as guides in the micro-political terrain is important. According to Jones (2010) the role of effective mentoring requires developing an awareness of the multi-faceted and conflicting role, understanding of adult learners' needs and workplace learning, a critical capacity in the analysis and reflection of classroom and mentoring practice, mediating skills, and emotional intelligence. The list of requirements is long and demanding. Jones (2010) further argues that in England mentors are selected on the basis of their expertise as teachers based on the assumption that they can be good role-models and evaluators. She challenges the belief that a good teacher necessarily becomes a good mentor and claims that mentor education is needed. In order to facilitate novice teachers' professional learning, mentors need to have access to relevant and focused training and development, be provided with professional and personal support and be allocated adequate resources (Jones, 2010, p. 127). Referring to a research project conducted in twelve European countries Jones claims that the majority of mentors in these countries had undergone minimal training. The literature discusses widely the complexity of mentoring by describing the many roles the mentor has, yet there seems to be little knowledge about how mentors are prepared to take on the complex responsibilities of mentoring., addressed.

EDUCATED INTO A PROFESSION?

Many countries i.e. the UK and USA have long traditions for mentoring newly qualified teachers, often linked to an induction program. More uncommon is an organized mentor education that gives a formalized competence (Hobson et al., 2009). Within the OECD-region mentor education is regarded desirable but not widespread (OECD, 2005). An important question is what should be the curriculum in mentor education? What should mentors know and why? The aims of mentor education will differ with the aims of induction. If newly qualified teachers are supposed to learn how to adjust to the existing school culture and to fill the national standards, in line with the competence model (Maynyard & Furlong, 1993) mentors should be trained to assess colleagues' work and to assess the results. If the aim is to support and challenge (Langdon, 2007) experienced as well as newly qualified teachers the curriculum should be different. Hargreaves and Fullan (2000) claim that mentoring programs should have three main aims; first mentoring should be seen as an instrument for building strong professional cultures dedicated to improving teaching, learning and caring. Second, mentoring should aim at addressing all teachers, not just novices, and third those who are involved in mentoring programs should realize that they are contributing to recreation of the profession. Mentors should learn not just to support others but also how to transform and challenge the teaching profession (ibid.).

In order to understand more of how the teachers experienced their formal mentor education a study was conducted in the same local context as the one described in the current chapter (Helleve & Langørgen, 2012). 25 students participated in the study which was conducted by two of the teacher educators. By the end of education the students were asked how the study had influenced the way they perceived their role as mentors. Four central concepts were selected from the analysis of the data-material; increased *consciousness, reflection, awareness*, and *confidence*. The possibility to discuss their own experiences with peers seems to the most important activity. The mentors brought their own cases into the discussion in different ways, and report two main reasons why the formal mentor study has contributed to increased consciousness, reflection, awareness, and confidence. The first was that the mentor-students have had the possibility to discuss recognizable situations from practice. The second reason was the communicative skills they have developed through the study.

In spite of the fact that every situation is unique in education the situations are recognizable. As teachers the mentor-students had experienced different ethical dilemmas with no correct answers. The possibilities for discussing these situations, highlighted by theory gave the students possibilities to see the situations from different angles. One of the students said:

> Where earlier I used to react through intuition, without reflection I now ask more questions. I often ask myself why I act like I do. The consequence is not necessarily that I act differently. Rather that I am more conscious on the decisions I take.

Through formal education the mentors have adopted new perspectives on well-known situations. Distance to practice and different theoretical perspectives have contributed to increased consciousness.

Development of communicative skills is the second field the mentor-students acknowledge as an important contribution to development of increased consciousness, reflection, awareness, and confidence. One student said:

Through this study I have reached my own goal: to be able to give theoretical reasons for my practice and to develop strategies and methods for mentoring.

The students were regularly in groups of three where they practiced as mentors for each other based on authentic cases from their own practice. They changed the roles as mentor, mentee, and observer and after the session was finished the "mentors" got feedback on their mentoring skills from the two other peers. According to the students the practical training and feedback made the students more confident on their role as mentors in authentic situations.

Another study among educated mentors shows that the Norwegian formal mentor education provided the mentors with a new knowledge base that was different from what they had gained as teachers (Ulvik & Sunde, 2013). When the teachers started their mentor education they had focus on themselves as mentors and how they should act. By the beginning of their mentor education they expressed that through development of personality and attitudes they wanted to become good mentors. During the program their focus changed from the individual perspective to focus on how to facilitate others' development. The researchers claim that this process might be compared to the process newly qualified teachers go through. Further they maintain that mentors' experiences and consciousness made it easier to support others' development. Based on the fact that a new knowledge base emerges, the question is raised: Is mentoring a new profession within the profession (Smith & Ulvik, 2010).

What We Wanted to Investigate

The aim of this study described in this chapter is to examine how mentors with and without mentor education perceive and practice their role as mentors. We have focused on the following research questions: 1. How do mentors with and without formal education perceive and practice their role? 2. Are there any differences in the way the two groups understand their mission? As researchers we were interested to know if the mentors had a formal education or not, and what the educated mentors thought they had learned. We were also curious to know how the mentors understood their own role. Further we asked about their goals for mentoring. We also wanted the mentors to give descriptions of how they actually practiced their role. We wanted to find out if and why they practiced mutual class-room observations and how they organized the mentor-sessions. We were also interested to know if and eventually why they enjoyed their role as mentors.

THE APPROACH WE TOOK

The current study we describe as a pilot study which examines how mentors perceive their role as mentors, and if there is a difference between the perceptions of mentors with and without mentor education. As already mentioned previously in this chapter, formal mentor education as practiced in Norway is a relatively new initiative nationally as well as internationally. Consequently, there is a strong need for research in order to get a deeper understanding of the value of mentor education, and specifically by examining if mentor education leads to change in how the practice of mentoring is perceived.

Context and Sample of the Study

The data was collected from a convenient sample of secondary school-teachers who were all mentoring newly qualified teachers (NQT). The participants (n–23), who were related to a network of mentors established by the university in case, voluntarily participated in the study, and they were assured of the anonymity of their responses. Their teaching experience was varied, ranging from 4– to 30+ years, whereas their experience as mentors was less (range of 1–10 years). Most of the teachers were without a formal mentor education, yet the majority reported that they had participated in short workshops of half a day or so. The teachers represented a variety of content subjects, and most of the subjects taught in secondary school were represented. Data were collected in the autumn term 2012.

Tools We Used

We chose to use an open ended questionnaire which had first been developed in English jointly by Finnish and Norwegian researchers for the purpose of a larger comparative study. This project is still in progress and therefore we do not relate to it further in this paper. The questionnaire was translated into Norwegian for the purpose of this study. In order to ensure the validity of the Norwegian version of the questionnaire, small group of mentors who did not take part in the study, agreed to read through it and respond to the questions. Only minor revision (wording) were found necessary.

The first part of the questionnaire asked for demographic data, some of which have been presented above in the description of the participants. The open ended part of the questionnaire inquired how the mentors valued the preparation and education they had taken as mentors, how they perceive their role as mentor, and the goals they have for their mentoring activities. Furthermore they were asked how they plan to achieve the goals by planning the content of the mentor meetings. We were also interested in learning about what expectations they had of the mentees, the novice teachers, based on the assumption that mentoring is a two way communication and dialogue. Therefore we pursued to inquire about how the mentors felt they personally benefitted from being a mentor (see English version in the appendix).

It turned out that the data collection was far from being a simple process, and we needed to use two different procedures to gather data. First an electronic version sent to 84 mentors, however only 12 responded. To increase the number of respondents, the same questionnaire was handed out in paper form in a workshop for mentors, and

11 new responses were collected, making a total of n=23 respondents. This was still not a large sample, but big enough to start data analyzing which would add to our knowledge about mentor roles and practices.

How We Analysed the Data

We did not use a priori system of codes and categories for the analysis besides those which were related to the questions asked. The three authors first interpreted the qualitative statements individually. Next, each of the authors categorized the statements using a grounded theory approach. The authors compared and discussed the categories. There was a high level of reciprocal understanding. With minor adjustments, the authors arrived at the categories for the open-ended questions as presented in the findings. The first category tells who the mentors are. If they define themselves as educated or not, how long they have practiced as mentors and if they are mentoring student teachers, novice teachers or both groups. The participants were divided into two groups; formally educated and not educated mentors. The second category is concentrated on educated mentors and their experiences from mentor education. How did they perceive their education and what did they learn from it? In order to answer the research questions the next categories are divided in two columns; educated and not educated. The following categories are selected: How do the mentors perceive their role? What are their goals for mentoring? Do they practice observation in their own and their mentees' classrooms? Do they practice individual or group-mentoring? The last category was first divided into two sub-categories: Do the mentors enjoy their job as mentors or not? The next sub-categories were why or why not? If the answer was positive, the reasons were categorized into support and self-reflection. The first refers to the satisfaction it gave the mentors to see that their support was a contribution to novice teachers' growth. The answers in the second category told that the mentors themselves were stimulated to self-reflection through the mentoring process. In the following the categories are presented. Quotes are selected to illustrate the different categories.

FINDINGS

The findings address the research questions of how mentors with and without mentor education perceive and practice their role, and if there are any differences in the way these two groups understand their mission.

Who Are the Mentors?

The results show that from the total group of respondents (N = 23) as many as 17 report that they are not educated as mentors. Education in this context means courses including level 1 with 15 EJTC's or level 2 with 30.

> I attended mentor education at the University and took my exams there. Altogether 30 EJCT's

Some mentors who have announced that they either have a one-day course, a mini-course or that they have practiced as mentors are not counted in the group of those with mentor education (N=3). What it means to be an educated mentor is obviously perceived differently as illustrated by the following quote:

> I once attended a course during an afternoon.

Few mentors are given time for mentoring. To a large extent mentoring newly qualified teachers is a task that comes on top of their ordinary job as teachers (N =15). Two mentors are part of the school's leader-team and mentoring novice teachers is one of the tasks they have to take because they are responsible for the welfare of a whole group of teachers. The numbers are almost the same for newly qualified teachers, but slightly different. 10 mentors claim that novice teachers in their school have protected time for mentoring while 13 take it as part of their ordinary job. In some cases it does not help if time for mentoring is said to be protected. One mentor writes that the novice teacher she is mentoring thinks that one hour every week is more than she is willing to spend because she has so much else to do.

Who Are the Mentors?

Few of the teachers who are practicing mentors have mentor education (N=6). The main essence of what the six educated mentors claim to have learned is that it is important to stimulate the novice teachers to self-reflection. They have learned why and how communicative abilities like listening and asking questions can help "the other" to find answers. These are abilities they have developed during mentor education. The mentee should not be told what to do. The point for the mentor is to find out where he or she actually is, and through a dialogic approach learn together with the novice teacher in a relationship characterized by equality. The mentors have learned that their task is not to give answers or advice but to listen to the novice teacher and support and stimulate to independence like this mentor says:

> The social aspect is important, to be present and to listen. The mentee needs to talk to somebody. My job as a mentor is not to come with the solution, but to support the novice teacher's way of thinking, to ask questions and not necessarily answer all of them, but to make the other person reflect.

Another mentor says that action research was important for him and made him understand more of his own professional development:

> Action research was an activity that helped me understand my own development.

Learning about oneself as a teacher and mentor was another comment. Apparently mentor education has been a personal profit for the mentor, not only as a future mentor for novice teachers but as a human being and a teacher.

HOW DO MENTORS PERCEIVE THEIR ROLE?

In the analysis of this question we chose to use two categories; support or reflect. This means that the mentor either sees it as her mission to be a model and to contribute to adaption for the newly qualified teacher or to stimulate to reflection. An example of the role as a supporter is the mentor who writes: *The essence of the role as a mentor is to support, mentor and give advice.* Another quotation is: *My role is to help newcomers into different subjects and school as an organization.* The personal aspect is important. What the mentor looks upon as his or her most important mission is to help the novice teacher s to become part of the school community. The newly qualified teacher should adapt to the role as a teacher as it is understood in this specific school context and as it is required by the authorities. The second category is the mentor who sees herself as a catalyst for the mentee to become reflective. An example is: *Listen, make the other person reflect and discuss different challenges as for example assessment.*

Altogether 18 mentors answered the question of how they perceive their role as mentors. Their opinions of how they look upon themselves seem to differ a lot. Within the first category with the mentor as a supporter we find altogether 12 mentors. In the second category where the mentor perceives herself as a mediator for reflection there are 6. When we split up between educated and non-educated mentors we find the pattern shown in Table 1.

Table 1. How educated and non-educated mentors perceive their role

	Not educated		Educated	
Role	Support	Reflect	Support	Reflect
N	11	1	1	5

Note: N=Number of participants

The majority of not educated mentors perceive themselves as being of support, while the majority of educated mentors want to stimulate reflection.

How Do Mentors Practice Their Role?

Our next question was what the mentors looked upon as their goals for mentoring (Table 2). 20 mentors answered the question. Based on the answers the two categories support and challenge/reflect were chosen (N=11). One quotation is selected to illustrate each of these categories:

My goal is to strengthen the novice teacher's knowledge about how school works on different levels, to give support and strengthen self-confidence. Help the newly qualified teacher to become a better leader in the class-room.

The other group wanted to challenge the novice teacher and to stimulate to reflection and independency (N=9). One mentor says:

I want to contribute to change of practice.

Another quote is:

I want to discuss authentic situations. We know well that we can teach each other something we know well and discuss challenges, like assessment for learning.

This mentor compares the outcome of mentoring to assessment for learning. The experienced as well as the newly qualified teacher learns from discussing their experiences.

Table 2. Goals for mentoring

	Not educated		Educated	
Role	Support	Reflect/challenge	Support	Reflect/challenge
N	9	5	2	4

Note: N=Number

The mentors were asked to what extent they used classroom observation as a support for mentoring (Table 3). Altogether 21 answered the questions.

Table 3. Classroom observation

	Not educated		Educated	
Observe mentor	No: 11	Yes: 4	No: 1	Yes: 5
Observe NQT	No: 7	Yes: 8	No: 1	Yes: 5

The main impression is that observation is not much used as an activity for learning among not educated mentors. To a larger extent newly qualified teachers are given the opportunity to observe their mentors than the other way round. On the other hand most of the educated mentors seem to observe and be observed.

When it comes to individual versus group-mentoring there are small differences between educated and not educated mentors.

Table 4. Individual or group-mentoring

	Not educated		Educated	
Individual	Group	Individual	Group
11	6	5	1

The main impression is that individual mentoring is the main pattern of mentoring. Not educated mentors tend to use group-mentoring more than educated mentors.

Do Mentors Enjoy Their Role?

The final question was if the mentors enjoyed their job. This question was combined with a follow-up question of why or eventually why not (N=19). In spite of the fact that two respondents mention that it is time-consuming, all the mentors agree to the question and argue that they enjoy their role as mentors for newly qualified teachers. We have divided their explanations of why they enjoy their job into two categories (Table 5). One group claim that it gives them a lot to see that the novice teachers become confident and that they have contributed to growth and safety (N=7). The second group is concerned with the fact that they as mentors have learned a lot (N=12).

From the first category the following quotation is selected to illustrate:

I am interested in education, didactics and pedagogy. I want to support other teachers to become as good teachers as possible so that as many pupils as possible can have a good education.

Mentors in the second category are occupied with the personal gain they have from mentoring. One says:

Yes, I learn a lot. I have to be updated and sharpened all the time.

Others in the same group claim that when they are mentors they always have to reflect on what they are doing themselves. Another mentor says:

I learn a lot because I can use my competence differently.

In spite of the fact that few teachers have protected time for mentoring all of them enjoy their role as mentors. The majority claim that they learn a lot from being mentors. When summing up the findings we find that most of the teachers in this study are not educated as mentors and the majority does not have protected time for mentoring. Mentors who are not formally educated as mentors tend to perceive and practice their role as support for newly qualified teachers, while educated mentors are concerned with challenge and reflection. Individual mentoring tend to be more used than individual. All mentors (with and without education) enjoy their role as mentors.

Table 5. Why do mentors enjoy their job?

	Not educated		Educated	
	Support competence	Self-reflection Learning	Support competence	Self-reflection Learning
N	5	8	2	4

Note: N=Number

DISCUSSION

The aim of the study was to gain a deeper understanding of how educated and non-educated mentors understood and practiced their role and mandate. The discussion first deals with the framework of mentoring practice, the mentors' perception of their roles, further the personal benefits of mentoring

Framework of Mentoring

Norwegian authorities have so far not formalized an induction period for newly qualified teachers, yet they have advised school owners to appoint mentors and granted economic support to mentor education. The only political document that says anything about aims and goals for mentor education says that mentors should gain competence in mentoring to support not only newly qualified teachers, but the whole school as a community (KD, 2010). Nothing is said about the framework, like e.g. protected time for mentoring. This means that the political signals are vague and difficult to interpret for principals. Compared to teachers who mentor student teachers relatively few mentors responded to the questionnaire. From the population who report that they mentor novice teachers a large majority claim that they have no mentor education. There may be different reasons for the fact that educated mentors are not used for mentoring as one of the respondents insinuates. This may indicate that mentoring newly qualified teachers still is uncommon in schools. The request from political authorities of appointing mentors is still only two years old (MER, 2008–2009) but research so far shows that formal mentor education is not prioritized in Norway (Harsvik & Norgård, 2011; Ulvik & Sunde, 2013). The role as mentor for newly qualified teachers is new within the organization, and it is not merely a role; it has some features of a profession inside the profession. One reason why educated mentors are not preferred may be that it takes time to recognize the new profession. Unlike many other organizations where educating mentors would be seen as an investment in future, school leaders tend to look at mentor education as a personal gain for the individual teacher and not as a support for the whole organization. They may be unaware of the fact that they have educated mentors in their staff's professional development (Helleve & Langørgen, 2012). Another reason linked to this may be that a new profession within the profession is perceived as threatening to the hierarchical system in schools. Schools can be understood as bureaucratic environments exerting professional and social pressure on newcomers towards existing norms and behavior (Lortie, 1975; Jones, 2006b). Kelchtermans (2002) is concerned with the micro-political reality; strategies and tactics used by individuals and groups in school organizations to further their interests. A new role with a competence characterized as a profession inside the profession may be a threat to some of the members of the existing school society.

Still another reason may be that if team-leaders are appointed as mentors they have to take it as part of their job as leaders and no discussion concerning extra time and money for mentoring is needed. In this is the case, the challenge of being mentored by a leader should be discussed. The study also shows that relatively few teachers have appointed time for mentoring. According to Roberts' (2000) definition of the role as mentor it should be part of a process that is formalized. If mentoring is something teachers do on top of their ordinary jobs without a defined mandate, can it then to be perceived as formalized mentoring? Norwegian authorities have been vague in their formulations of why mentoring is necessary. Norway differs from i.e. England where the apprentice and competence model is dominant and New Zealand where learning for the whole schools' professional development is the aim. Norwegian authorities have also been careful not to promise anything concerning conditions for mentoring. This may be the reason why there are relatively few mentors, why the majority is not educated, and why mentoring is something that comes in addition to other important tasks for teachers.

Understanding and Experiences as Mentors

This study, which is too small for generalization, suggests that teachers who are educated as mentors are satisfied with the outcome of their education. They are concerned with reflection and how to challenge mentees to engage in reflective dialogues. Through the combination of theoretical input and practical exercises based on their own experienced they see mentoring as a process of reflective dialogues between equal partners. This corresponds to other studies within the same context (Helleve & Langørgen, 2012). Mentors claim that they have gained competence in how to mentor students, newly qualified and experienced teachers. They also realize that they are able to contribute to school development and to their school as a learning organization. The education gives them a competence that seems to support what is earlier referred to as the reflection model (Maynyard & Furlong, 1993; Jones, 2006b). Increased consciousness and insight have contributed to professional development for teachers who have become mentors.

So How Do Mentors Perceive Their Role?

According to Hargreaves and Fullan (2000) mentoring in "the forth professional age" should be to challenge existing beliefs about teaching, not just sustain the existing school culture. They assert that mentor education should prepare mentors to become change agents.

The results from our study show that the majority of the mentors claim that providing support to novice teachers is most important. When the answers are divided into mentors with and without mentor education, the picture is changed. Non-educated mentors mainly look upon their role as supporters, while the majority of the educated mentors are concerned with stimulating reflection. When it comes to what mentors value as important goals for education, the tendency is less clear, but still the majority of educated mentors rank challenges through reflection highest, whereas mentors without education believe providing support is most important. If the mentor serves as a supporter he or she will act as a model for the novice teacher in hierarchical pairs where one part knows more than the other. The role of the mentor is to teach the newcomer how to adjust in order to become a member of the community of practice (Lave, 1992). In "the forth professional age" nobody is an expert, according to Hargreaves and Fullan (2000), because there are no correct answers. Learning takes place when novices as well as experienced teachers are challenged to engage in reflection. According to Wang and Odell (2002) a critical constructive perspective on mentoring means that mentors and novices can develop new knowledge in collaboration.

Reports from respondents in this study show that educated mentors use observation as a support for mentoring more than those who are not educated. Educated mentors observe and are observed, while a few more of the mentors without mentor education observe newly qualified teachers instead of being observed themselves. According to Hobson et al. (2009) numerous studies have found that one of the most valued aspects of the work done by mentors is lesson observation. There seems to be several aspects that are important in order to make observations valuable. First that the observation is conducted in a sensitive, non-threatening way, second that focus is on specific aspects of the observed teachers' teaching and third that it provides an opportunity for genuine and constructive dialogue between mentor and mentee. The fourth and final point is that effective mentors ensure their mentees are sufficiently challenged. If mentoring is understood as newly qualified teachers' personal abilities and possibilities for contribution to the school as a learning community in line with Langdon (2007) then classroom observation should be used by mentors as well as mentees. For educated mentors this is part of their knowledge base from their formal education. They have practiced peer-mentoring and in some cases also classroom observation. They have become aware of the benefits of mutual observation from a theoretical and practical perspective.

When it comes to individual versus group mentoring, there are small differences between mentors with and without mentor education. The main tradition in Norway is individual mentoring (Handal & Lauvås, 2000). This differs from mentoring practice of newly qualified teachers in Finland where group mentoring is the normal practice (Heikkinen et al., 2012). According to Hargreaves and Goodson (2000) mentoring should be moved from pairs to an integral part of the school society, from hierarchical approach to shared inquiries and from isolation to integration. Traditions that favor group-mentoring versus individual may easier pave the way for the change that these researchers advertise for.

Benefits from Mentoring

A clear finding in the study is that all the mentors enjoy their role. The majority appreciate it because it provides opportunities for self-reflection. As mentors they also have to look at their own way of teaching. Dialogues with mentees forces them to stop and reflect which they seldom do. Another reason for enjoyment is to notice the positive development of the newly qualified teacher. This experience is in line with the satisfaction teachers have when their pupils learn and develop (Skovholt, 2001). Professional development should be sustained, ongoing and include participant-driven inquiry, reflection and experimentation, according to Darling-Hammond and McLaughlin (2011). Research shows that mentoring has a positive impact on professional and personal development of teachers who act as mentors (Hoban, 2009; Hudson, 2007). There are different aspects of mentoring that seem to impact mentors' learning; self-reflection and learning from mentees. The third main effect is the pride mentors experience when they see that the mentees become self-sufficient due to their contribution as mentors. According to Hudson (2007) mentoring professional development should be a priority for education departments. Investment in experienced teachers to become mentors can build system capacity in two ways; first because mentors can educate their mentees, and second because mentors can develop and evolve their pedagogical knowledge by engaging in mentoring activities. This means that mentoring itself is a way of promoting professional development for teachers. But is it then necessary to educate mentors? This study shows that there are differences in the ways educated and non-educated mentors perceive and practice their role. Formal education tends to have prepared the mentors way of mentoring for "the fourth professional age" (Hargreaves & Fullan, 2000); mentors that can serve as change agents for school communities. The educated mentors are prepared through education to take responsibility for their colleagues' professional development because they know how and why it is important to challenge to self-reflection. However, mentoring in itself tends to stimulate to self-reflection among mentors with and without education.

Implications

Norway is at a cross-road when it comes to mentoring and induction programs for newly qualified teachers. The political intentions are good, yet they are not yet fully coordinated. So far there is no established national program for induction of newly qualified teachers and no steering documents prescribing how mentors should perform their role as mentors. This is a positive development, especially in relation to the understanding that mentoring is highly contextualized. On the other hand schools are gradually provided with teachers with additional education, mentor education, and this group carries certain characteristics of a new profession inside the profession. In addition to the responsibility of teaching pupils, they are also educated for and have the responsibility of supporting the professional growth of their colleagues through mentoring. Our study shows that so far the mentors' education and additional competence are used mainly to support newly qualified teachers in the induction phase. None of the informants report that they are mentors for individual or groups of experienced teachers, thus engaging in mentoring activities aiming at whole school development. Mentors who have formal mentor education, as it is developed in Norway (30 ECTS), are educated to take responsibility for adult learners. They share a common knowledge based on theory and science, and their motivation seems to be based on public service and personal engagement making them able to support teachers' professional development (Darling-Hammond & McLaughlin, 2011). We do not, however, per today know enough about how to best develop curricula for mentor education, and we still need to learn more about how mentor education contributes to improved mentoring practice in Norway as well as internationally. Therefore, further qualitative as well as quantitative research on the conditions, understanding and practice of mentors, and how to prepare mentors for the complexities of mentoring, is much needed.

REFERENCES

Darling-Hammond, L., & McLaughlin, M. W. (2011). Policies that support professional development in an era of reform: policies must keep pace with new ideas about what, when, and how teachers learn and must focus on developing schools' and teachers' capacities to be responsible for student learning. *Phi Delta Kappan, 92*(6), 81–93.

Department of Education (DFE). (1992). *The initial training of teachers (Secondary phase) standards for the award of qualified teachers' status* (Circular 9/92). London: Author.

Handal, G., & Lauvås, P. (2000). *Mentoring and practice theory (Veiledning og praktsik yrkesteori; in Norwegian)*. Oslo: Cappelen.

Hargreaves, A., & Fullan, M. (2000). Mentoring in the new millennium. *Theory into practice, 39*(1), 50–56.

Harsvik, T., & Nordgård, J. D. (2011). *The best intentions. About introducing mentoring arrangements for newly qualified teachers. Report from enquiry 2.* Oslo: Union of Education.

Heikkinen, H. L. T., Jokinen, H., & Tynjälä, P. (2012). *Peer group mentoring for teacher development.* Hoboken, NJ: Taylor & Francis.

Helleve, I., & Langørgen, K. (2012). Educated as mentor-educated for what? *Uniped, 35*(4), 67–68.

Hobson, A. J., Ashby, P., & Malderez, A., & Tomlinson, P. D. (2009). Mentoring beginning teachers. What we know and what we don't. *Teaching and Teacher Education, 25*(1), 207–216.

Hudson, P. (2007). Mentoring as professional development. Growth for both mentor and mentee. *Mentoring & Tutoring, 15*(2), 201–217.

Jones, M. (2006a). The balancing act of mentoring: Mediating between newcomers and communities of practice. In C. Cullingford (Ed.), *Mentoring in education: An international perspective* (pp. 57–86). Aldershot: Ashjate.

Jones, M. (2006b). Mentoring in the initial training and professional development of teachers in England: Conceptual, epistemological and methodological issues. In M. Mataboa, K. A. Crawford, & R. S. A. Mohammed (Eds.), *Lesson study: International perspective on policy and practice* (pp. 158–188). Beijing: Educational Science Publishing House.

Jones, M. (2010). The needs of mentors. In K. Smith & M. Ulvik (Eds.), *Mentoring newly qualified teachers Veiledning av nye lærere; in Norwegian* (pp. 115–130). Oslo: Universitetsforlaget.

Kelchtermans, G. (2009). Who I am in how I teach is the message: Self-understanding, vulnerability and reflection. *Teachers and Teaching, Theory and Practice, 15*(2), 257–272.

Kelchtermans, G., & Ballet, K. (2002). The micropolitics of teacher education. *A narrative-biographical study on teacher socialization, Teaching and Teacher Education, 18*, 105–120.

Knowledge Department. (2010). *Mentoring newly educated teachers* (Veiledning av nyutdannede lærere og veilederutdanning; in Norwegian). Brev fra Kunnskapsdepartementet. Retrieved June 22, 2010 from http://www.regjeringen.no/nb/dep/kd/dok/andre/brev/utvalgte_brev/2010/Veiledning-av-nyutdannede-larere-og-veilederutdanning-.html?id=609178

Knowledge Department. (2011). *Mentoring new teachers is on the track* (Veiledning av nye lærere er godt i gang; in Norwegian). Pressemelding fra Kunnskapsdepartementet. Retrieved February 4, 2011 from http://www.regjeringen.no/nb/dep/kd/pressesenter/pressemeldinger/2011/veiledning-av-nye-larere-godt-i-gang.html?id=632942

Kroksmark, T., & Åberg, K. (2007). *Mentoring in education (Veiledning i pedagogisk arbeid; in Norwegian).* Oslo: Fagbokforlaget.

Lave, J. (1992). *Learning as participation in communities of practice.* Paper presented at the Annual Meeting of the American Educational Research Association. San Fransisco. University of California, Berkerley, CA.

Langdon, F. J. (2007). *Beginning teacher learning and professional development: An analysis of induction programmes* (The degree doctor philosophiae). The University of Waikato, New Zealand.

Lortie, D. (1975). *Schoolteacher: A sociological study.* Chicago, IL: University of Chicago Press.

Loughran, J. (2006). *Developing a pedagogy of teacher education.* New York, NY: Routledge.

Maynyard, T., & Furlong, J. (1993) Learning to teach and models of mentoring. In I D. McIntyre, H. Hagger & M. Wilkin (Eds.), *Mentoring: Perspectives on school-based teacher education* (pp. 10–24). London, England: Kogan Page.

MER. (2008–2009). Whitepaper 11, [Undervisnings- og forskningsdepartementet] [UFD]. *The Teacher. Role and Education* [Læreren Rollen og utdanningen]. Retrieved March 18, 2009 from http://www.regjeringen.no/nb/dep/kd/dok/regpubl/ stmeld/2008-2009/stmeld-nr-11-2008- 2009-.html?id=544920

OECD. (2005). *Teachers matter: Attracting, developing and retaining effective teachers.* Retrieved October 9, 2007 from http://www.oecd.org/document/52/0,3343,en_2649_201185_34991988_1_1_1_1, 00.html

Rippon, J. H., & Martin, M. (2006). What makes a good induction supporter? *Teaching and Teacher Education, 22*(1), 84–99.

Roberts, A. (2000). Mentoring revisited: A phenomenological reading of the literature. *Mentoring & Tutoring: Partnership in Learning, 8*(2), 145–170.

Roths, I., Kelchtermans, G., & Aelterman, A. (2012). Learning (not) to become a teacher: A qualitative analysis of the job entrance issue. *Teaching and Teacher Education, 28,* 1–10.

Schleicher, A. (2012). *Education at Glance: OECD indicators.* Retrieved from http://www.oecd.org/edu/skills-beyond-school/eag2012.htm

Schuck, S., & Russell, T. (2005). Self-study. Critical friendship, and the complexities of teacher education. *Studying Teacher Education, 1*(2), 107–121.

Skovholt, T. (2001). *The recilient practitioner.* Boston, MA: Allyn & Bacon.

Smith, K., & Ulvik, M. (Eds.) *Veiledning av nye lærere- nasjonale og internasjonale perspektiver* (Mentoring Newly Qualified Teachers – National and International Perspectives). Oslo: Universitetsforlaget.

Smith, K., Krüger, K. R., & Sagvaag, I. (2013, March). *Mentoring in Norway.* Paper presented at the Nordic Educational Research Association (NERA) Conference in Reykjavik, Iceland.

Ulvik, M., & Sunde, E. (2013). The impact of mentor education: Does mentor education matter? *Professional Development in Education, 39*(5), 754–770.

Wang, J., & Odell, S. (2002). Mentored learning to teach according to standard-based reform. A critical review. *Review of Educational Research, 72*(3), 48.

Wang, J., Odell, S. J., & Schwille, S. A. (2008). Effects of teacher induction on beginning teachers' teaching: A critical review of the literature. *Journal of Teacher Education, 59*(2), 132–152.

Zemblyas, M. (2003). Emotions and teacher identity: A poststructural perspective. *Teachers and Teaching: Theory and Practice, 9*(3), 213–238.

I. HELLEVE ET AL.

Ingrid Helleve
Department of Education
University of Bergen, Norway

A.G. Danielsen
Department of Education
University of Bergen, Norway

Kari Smith
Department of Education
University of Bergen, Norway

MAUREEN ROBINSON

16. SO HOW HIGH HAS THE MOUNTAIN BEEN CLIMBED?

A Reflective Overview of the Book

The first thought I had when asked to write a concluding chapter to this book was – *So much has been written about mentoring. It is going to be a challenge to find something new or different here. I hope there are some unique or special insights and observations that would encourage somebody to read this particular book, otherwise I will not be sure how to write this chapter!*

A concluding chapter can of course enter a book from many angles and through many lenses. And particularly, in a case like this, when the book sets out to cross a number of discourses and domains, the potential entry points multiply. At the most obvious level, there is the *conceptual* entry point. For this one would need to ask – is this book adding anything to our understanding of the theory of mentoring? What new ideas and concepts are being introduced? Then there is the *practice* entry point, for which one would need to ask – Will this book help practitioners to implement better mentor programmes? What helpful tips and advice are included here? Will this book contribute to improving educational outcomes? A third angle could be that of a *research* lens. For that one would ask – What new insights are generated from the empirical studies? Does the research take us beyond what we already know about mentoring?

And with these daunting thoughts, I set about reading the chapters.

An overview chapter like this one is not there to repeat or to summarise what all the previous chapters have already said. Rather, this overview will highlight some key concepts that stand out in the different sections of the book, and link these to some central debates around mentoring. These debates have been partly drawn from the literature, but are also based on my own experience in the field. Of course, other readers might – and must – pick up other key concepts and debates, and this in itself should generate further discussion.

Before proceeding further, let me declare my own starting point for thinking about the contribution of this book. I do this not to draw attention to myself (after all this concluding chapter is the only chapter which does not have to face the rigour of working from an empirical study) but rather to motivate what I, as one reader among many, would like to get from a book like this. I have worked in initial and continuing teacher education for twenty-five years. For my doctoral research, I

H. Tillema et al. (Eds.), Mentoring for Learning, 333–341.

studied the implementation of a mentor programme at the university where I was working at the time. As a South African whose professional life has spanned the transition years from apartheid to democracy, I know that education is a fundamental aspect of social change. I have argued that mentoring by experienced teachers not only offers a vehicle for classroom support, but also has the potential to transform schools into sites of active and critical engagement, where deep questions can be asked about the purpose of schooling and the nature of learning (Robinson, 2001). At the time of writing this chapter, I was coordinating a national policy research project into the school and university conditions required to optimally support the practicum in initial teacher education. My interest in mentoring, therefore, is mainly at a systems level, and I am always particularly keen to learn more about the personal, institutional and contextual conditions that support mentoring as a tool for the greater public good.

So what does the book contribute to this interest?

My interest was immediately piqued by the introductory overview of the book which declared that mentoring conversations are not intended to be ends in themselves. As the authors point out, it is about process *and outcome*, conversation *and learning*, knowledge for professional *action* (all my italics), captured in the concept of knowledge productivity. The extremely useful notion of knowledge productivity is broken up into three helpful steps, namely problem understanding, perspective shift, and commitment to apply. These steps, as the authors argue "ensure the productivity of conversations that will surpass the basic needs for guidance, integrity and relatedness in conversations". So right from the start the book makes an important contribution, as the intertwining of the learning element with the action element locates mentoring directly as a tool for improving (and transforming) education.

The introduction to the book clarifies from the start that mentoring is understood as being about *learning in conversations.* This definition is deceptively simple for it immediately stimulates a number of complex questions that a reader might want to pursue. We might, for example, want to know: What is meant by learning? Is the learning of a mentor or a mentee different from any other kind of learning? Is there a particular theory of learning that is more appropriate to understand or to implement mentoring? And to go further – Does this learning only happen through conversations? Do some kinds of conversation support learning better than others? Is learning through mentoring different from other kinds of professional learning in which the participants are involved?

In *Knowledge building through conversations,* Tillema, van der Westhuizen and van der Merwe emphasise the action potential of mentoring by asserting that "in our view, being a professional is to use knowledge to produce solutions for practice". While one might quibble as whether a complex field like education can ever find "solutions", the intention is to be lauded, particularly as this orientation is based on knowledge building that is interactional and collaborative, and aimed at situational understanding. Of particular interest is the link here to the moral domain of knowledge building, that includes epistemic access, epistemic primacy and epistemic responsibility – in other words, who owns knowledge, and who decides on the goals and the relevance of talk. By asserting this moral domain, the action element of mentoring moves out of a so-called neutral space into the realm of values, thus becoming, one hopes, a strategy for finding those solutions that advance the greater good.

Parts 1 and 2 of the book develop the theme of *conversations for learning* in a variety of innovative ways. Knowledge is seen as being actively constructed in and from contexts, and understandings as situational. The complexity and depth of the mentor-mentee interaction is vividly expressed, as the different chapters collectively explore forms of feedback and conversation. A variety of powerful concepts, all of which have pragmatic use value are introduced, like conversational strategies, modes and content of feedback, feedback utilization, conversational vigilance, space creation, invitational style, emotional security, perspective, reciprocal relations, etc. The overall message here is that conversations aimed at mentoring do not just happen; we need to pay close attention to the content, structure and context of such conversations if they are to provide the type of powerful learning experiences at which mentoring is aimed.

The message of Parts 1 and 2 is very relevant for Part 3 of the book, where mentor training and professional development are discussed in more detail. It is my hunch (and not empirically tested) that there could be many mentor programmes out there that have not considered the nature of mentor conversations in sufficient detail, relying rather on a common-sense approach to such interactions. If we are to work from the premise that a knowledge base for mentoring does exist (see the chapter by Smith and Ulvik in Part 3), then it is essential that we unpack in detail the dimensions of this knowledge base. Such a knowledge base includes not only *what* mentors and mentees do together, but also, as these chapters show, *how* they do what they do. By analysing their own talk, mentors can become aware of their own mentoring styles and strategies, and so "improve their communication skills and become more self-reflective in supporting mentees" (see van Esch and Tillema in *Patterns in mentoring conversations*).

Against this background, and in the light of the authors' emphasis on knowledge for professional learning, it is fascinating to read a study that found that almost 60% of conversational talk between mentors and student teachers consisted of non-learning goal related relational remarks (*Mentoring conversations and student teacher learning* – Tillema and van der Westhuizen). The authors acknowledge that a considerable amount of time is needed to provide for "emotional and interactional alliance", but remind us that this should not be at the expense of 'high road' feedback, information and advice. Student teachers differ though in their need for emotional security and/or prescriptive advice, often linked to their experience and relative proficiency. This once again is a call to carefully consider the particular context and parameters of a mentoring relationship.

In general, all the chapters challenge an often taken-for-granted assumption that feedback automatically produces learning, and remind us that it is the *nature of feedback* that is important. As Siv Gamlem (*Feedback in mentoring – teachers' perceptions of useful feedback*) indicates, feedback is essential in mentoring, "but not all kinds of feedback have the power to support learning". Conversations that are both supportive and challenging are argued to be most productive. Years ago Daloz (1986) wrote about the relationship between different levels of support and challenge. Working within a quadrant of high and low support and challenge, high support/ high challenge is argued to be most effective for learning. If we do not support student teachers, they can flounder in the harsh reality of practice, but if we do not challenge them, their learning is not mediated to a higher level of insight and proficiency.

The complex relationship between support and challenge is developed in the chapter by Korver and Tillema (*Feedback provision in mentoring conversations*). This chapter reminds us that mentoring normally has two purposes, namely assessment/evaluation/monitoring, as well as scaffolding/enhancement/guidance. The fact that these purposes need to be carried out simultaneously can create a complex, and sometimes contradictory, set of relations and expectations in the feedback process. In student teaching, for example, this potentially contradictory set of purposes can undermine each purpose in its own right. This relates back to the support and challenge nexus. A teacher who wants to support a student relationally, might choose to do so by providing little challenge pedagogically and by inflating the students' grades. A teacher who wishes to challenge student teachers might choose to grade their performance poorly, arguing that 'the student must understand that there is always room to learn more'. It seems to me that the notion of scaffolding is the most crucial here, as it advances the basic premise that a mentor is there to build and develop the student teacher's knowledge and expertise. The introduction to Part 2 puts this well, in its argument that we need to favour both a "more explicit and informed professional language", as well as "reflection on personal knowledge".

The book draws on the experiences of authors from a number of different countries, including the Netherlands, South Africa, Norway, Spain, Canada. Such a varied set of locations immediately begs the question of the extent to which *context* affects and is affected by mentoring conversations. Context in itself can be viewed from a number of different angles, each with its own set of considerations. National context creates (or does not create) the conditions for mentoring through the particular policies and resources of the country, state or province. Institutional context frames the possibilities and constraints for mentors in their own sites of work, through, for example, institutional ethos and culture, support from leadership, time, etc. My own research in South Africa many years ago showed how particular conditions can enable or constrain even the most active and committed mentors, for a mentor who works very enthusiastically under difficult conditions runs the risk of becoming burnt out, with little sustained benefit for the system as a whole.

These issues can potentially play themselves out in a conversational settings as well, as power relations, or cultural norms, or language barriers. Against this background, it is somewhat surprising that few chapters in the book deal directly with issues of context. The chapter by van der Westhuizen (*The role of knowledge in mentoring conversations for learning*) works from the premise that contexts can include a diversity of social and cultural norms. The chapter explores the ways in which institutional and language cultural norms play out in mentoring relationships, and points out that various dynamics of diversity can exist in learning interactions. Conversation analysis is used to explore "how diverse students exercise their relative rights to tell, inform, assert or assess something, given the asymmetries in the depth, specificity, or completeness of their knowledge." Knowledge authority, status dominance and knowledge territories are useful concepts to alert us, as van der Westhuizen does, that mentors need to be sensitive to the extent to which their status and institutional role might inhibit the contributions of mentees to the conversation.

Part 3 moves to more systemic issues, in particular that of professional development for mentors, or more specifically – how collaborative learning can be set up among mentors, based on systematic inquiry and study of issues encountered in practice. A fundamental question here – and one that is reflected in the professional development literature more generally – is whether such training should occur in an individual mentor's own task environment, or whether it should be more purposively structured and educationally framed through professional programmes.

In my own research into the conditions required for effective mentoring, the question of mentor training has taken centre stage, for it is no use implementing (and funding) a national programme to support student teachers if the teachers involved are not able to add full value to the learning process. The notion that an experienced teacher can in fact be seen as a novice mentor opens up interesting questions around adult learning. This can lead to a fascinatingly cyclical (and linguistically tongue-twisting) challenge as we ask – What does it take to teach teachers to teach student teachers to teach?

A further important consideration is the relationship between discipline-specific and generic professional training. Sanchez and Garcia (*Understanding teachers as learners in reading comprehension mentoring*) locate their research on mentoring within the specific subject domain of reading comprehension, while a number of other chapters in the volume talk more generically. In my view this is a fundamental issue to consider as different subject areas might lend themselves to different approaches. While there are clearly many areas of overlap in approach and process (eg to promote self-regulated learning), perhaps a next step for the editors of this book might be to analyse approaches to mentoring within particular schooling subjects?

Smith (*Mentoring – a profession within a profession*) asks if all experienced teachers can be mentors or if mentoring is a different experience from practicing the profession. She claims that mentoring is not the same as first order teaching, but is a profession within a profession, for teaching children is very different from supporting and challenging novice teachers. She makes the case for mentor training to be formal and certified, with ongoing quality assurance of the practice of the mentor. Having made this case, though, she acknowledges the responsibility that this places on stakeholders, for with formal certification comes requirements of resourcing, infrastructure, career pathing and time, many of which are challenging requirements in pressurised educational systems. As mentioned at the beginning of this concluding chapter, I am part of a research team investigating the conditions to support mentoring in South African schools. Smith's chapter on the challenges of formalising mentoring in a well-resourced country like Norway is certainly informative for our country as well.

Smith and Ulvik pursue the interest in mentor training by exploring the nature of the knowledge base for mentors (*Mentor pedagogical content knowledge*). These authors argue that mentors' pedagogical content knowledge is framed within three areas: structural/ practical aspects of teaching, theoretical knowledge, and inter-personal knowledge and skills. Drawing on a real case, the authors illustrate why it is important to ask what kind of knowledge mentors need in order to be able to provide student teachers with realistic critical feedback which does not discourage them. Examples are given from a mentor training syllabus, including making tacit knowledge about teaching visible, action research, critical reflection, school development, and mentoring in other countries. From my own experience from an entirely different context, it is useful to see some basic principles being articulated, namely that good practitioner research forms the basis of a programme, and that mentors' PCK, even if presented in general terms, needs to be context-specific.

In the end, of course, we do need to answer the question as to whether mentor education makes a difference. Helleve, Danielsen and Smith cite Hobson et al. who have pointed out that programmes intended to prepare mentors for their task often focus more on adminstrative precautions that on developing mentors' abilities to facilitate mentees' professional learning. True to my own heart, they argue that mentoring should be seen as a device to build strong professional structures in schools dedicated to improving, learning and caring. To this I would add – to build strong professional *cultures,* for without an enabling culture, structures can become another form of bureaucracy. Their account of the Norwegian situation shows that formal mentor training can promote self-reflection and pride, important components of teacher motivation and efficacy. However, these authors are still cautious about what exactly a curriculum for mentor education should like look – suggesting perhaps a potential follow-up topic for this book!

I started this chapter by asking what was significant about this book. More particularly, I wanted to know what it would say to someone who was interested in the personal, institutional and contextual conditions that support mentoring as a tool for the greater public good.

It seems to me, by way of conclusion, that the focus on *mentoring for learning* is very important. By emphasising learning, we focus by implication on *why* we would want to engage in mentoring. This is not an administrative exercise, it is an exercise that aims to improve teaching, both for the individual in his or her classroom, and for the system as a whole. No educational system can improve if each of its teachers is not offering his or her best, and individual teachers will not improve if the system does not support them. And by emphasising mentoring for learning, we emphasise the ongoing lifelong journey of being a teacher across a whole career span.

The focus on practice and action is fundamental to the book. However luckily this is not practice without a theoretical or research-base. Conceptual issues are included and all chapters are research-based. Through sharing the work of those who have been involved, the book helps readers to better understand and apply the practice of mentoring. While much of the focus is on classroom-oriented practice, the final section of the book takes us into the domain of policy, and a consideration of how to systematise, institutionalise and sustain good mentoring practices. In general, the case studies can provide illustrative value to those who are designing their own programmes.

Having said that, though, there is a niggling concern with the methodological base of many of the chapters. Fine-grained analyses lend themselves methodologically to working with small samples. The challenge for all of us is how to extrapolate to bigger samples, across sites, and perhaps across contexts. The importance of mentioning this is in part to address a concern (Sleeter, 2014) that a very slim proportion of published research articles in teacher education examine the impact of teacher education on teaching practice and/or student learning, with most of this research being conducted within rather than across silos. An international book like this one lends itself to comparative and impact data across sites; perhaps a next step in the literature on mentoring.

The authors of the book would probably also be interested to read Dawson (2014), who argues that there is a false consensus that we all know what a mentor programme looks like. To assist us, Dawson has offered a common framework for specifying mentoring models. This framework contains sixteen elements to distinguish the design of different mentor programmes. I list these in full, as they are very useful: objectives, roles, cardinality, tie strength, relative seniority, time, selection, matching, activities, resources and tools, role of technology, training, rewards, policy, monitoring and termination. It is beyond the scope of this book, but I can imagine that those involved in mentor programmes might benefit from sharing across sites how their different programmes are designed, so that close comparisons can be made of the relative strengths and weaknesses of particular design elements.

When I was writing my doctoral dissertation, I recall my promoters asking me to stop assuming that mentoring was in itself a "good thing" but to be more reflective about potential pitfalls and tensions. Important in this book is the fact that it does not preach, but also offers a sober reflection on constraints of mentoring. Mentoring, it is argued, does not necessarily lead to improved action, but needs to be carefully constructed. Mentors need to be trained, and different contexts can yield different outcomes. This awareness of constraints is important to action, for we need to be realistic about the conditions under which any programme is initiated and implemented

As mentioned at the beginning of this overview, the book approaches mentoring from a conceptual, practical and research entry point. I would thus like to offer some over-arching research directions within each of these domains, bearing in mind that the topic of professional learning for improved educational outcomes can generate many more areas of research than those mentioned here

- Conceptually, one could ask: Could a framework of critical reflection and action stand in tension with a framework of support and care, especially for novice teachers?
- Practically, one could ask: What, if any, are the minimum enabling conditions (eg policies, resources, school culture, etc) for good mentoring to be sustained over time? What are the enabling and constraining conditions within different educational contexts?
- Research-wise, one could ask: What common insights can we draw from case studies of school-university partnerships for initial teacher education in different countries of the world?

To these questions I can add those research challenges already alluded to earlier in this overview chapter

- What is the relationship between strategies for mentoring and a mentor's personal and professional values?
- What are the significant differences between a curriculum based on subject-focused or generic mentor training?
- Does teacher involvement in mentoring make a difference to student learning outcomes?

Finally, a comment on the title of the book, *Climbing the Mountain.* In his note to authors, one of the editors explained that this is meant as a concise metaphor to indicate that mentoring for learning is to help and guide the beginning professional in the attainment of higher levels of proficiency. One appreciates the suggestion that (like climbing a mountain) mentoring requires motivation, hard work, organisation, planning, and clear goals and procedures. However, I am sure the editors would not like us to read into this metaphor that mentoring (like climbing a mountain) has a point of arrival and a moment when one descends back to where one began the journey. I therefore (tongue-in-cheek) challenge the editors of the next book to find a metaphor that contains all the climbing mountain imagery, but also captures mentoring as a tool for ongoing personal and professional learning, and a strategy for system-wide social and educational improvement.

REFERENCES

Daloz, L. A. (1986). *Effective teaching and mentoring: Realizing the transformational power of adult learning experiences.* San Francisco, CA: Wiley.

Dawson, P. (2014). Beyond a definition: Toward a framework for designing and specifying mentoring models. *Educational Researcher, 43*(3), 137–145.

Robinson, M. (2001). Teachers as mentors: A critical view of teacher development in South African schools. *Perspectives in Education, 19*(2), 99–115.

Sleeter, C. (2014). Toward teacher education research that informs policy. *Educational Researcher, 43*(3), 146–153.

Maureen Robinson
University of Stellenbosch, South Africa

HARM TILLEMA, GERT J. VAN DER WESTHUIZEN
AND KARI SMITH

17. "IT IS NOT JUST THE TALK...." – A REJOINDER

Maureen Robinson, who is an eminent scholar in the field of mentoring and learning was asked to offer an overview perspective, and a critical reading of our work We, as authors, were very interested to learn what messages our first reader took from our work. We were curious to learn if our intended central claims and aims coincide with the readers' understanding of the text.

To recapitulate our main message throughout the book we could state the following:

It is not just the talk that matters in mentoring, but really whether the conversation mounts up to learning. Talk is, as we see it, the main vehicle to bring about learning on part of the mentee. Learning is being viewed from the perspective of 'knowledge productivity', that is, has the mentee become more able to cope with the demands of practice. Mentoring, therefore, is primarily for learning for the mentee as well as for the mentor.

Our basic claim is that mentoring matters, provided that mentors become aware about how they conduct conversations and we strongly argue for mentor professional development in this respect.

The summing up of our work can be positioned against messages or highlights taken from the review of our book:

- "Mentoring is to be understood as learning conversations; – it stimulates to questions"

What follows in the review are a set of intriguing questions on the nature of learning in mentoring. Indeed this relation between mentoring and learning lies at the heart of our work. Some readers might assert we overstate the relation since mentoring is primarily about relationship and "helping". Certainly the relation between mentoring and learning is different from the one between instruction and learning in the sense that the setting, mode of communication, intention, structure of relationship differ. But, nevertheless, mentoring is about learning, which is: bringing the "learner" to understand, shift perspective, and accept the recommendations given by a helping agent. Learning in mentoring in our view is governed by 'knowledge productivity", i.e., bringing about change in practices. This does not in any way discard or denounce the importance of relationship in mentoring. Typical for learning

H. Tillema et al. (Eds.), Mentoring for Learning. 343–346.

in mentoring is: trust in guidance based on integrity (Garvey, 2008). These principles should govern the learning conversations between mentor and mentee.

- "Conversations that are both supportive and challenging are argued to be most productive".

In short, mentoring is at its best when learning conversations occur. The conversational analysis described in the book point to two important ingredients: monitoring of past performance and scaffolding of future action. The speech moves which are shepherding a learning conversation are (Chapter 2 & 8): exploring, monitoring, and directing. Several modes of challenging learning conversation have been identified (Mostert & Vander Westhuizen, 2004); such as: open disclosure; inviting other viewpoints, detecting assumptions, exploring possibilities, planning for action, questioning to remove barriers (Barnes, 2008).

A more or less implicit assumption in the book is that many mentoring conversations stay well within the comfort zone of partakers. We noted in our studies (as did our reviewer) that most of the speech acts in a conversation were of a relational kind, i.e., avoid silences, small talk, and paying attention to relationships, which, no doubt, are part and parcel of a normal conversation, but do not suffice in a knowledge productive environment.

- "Mentoring is not an end in itself"

The notion of mentoring displayed in this book regards mentoring as a vehicle, a process in hand of the mentor and mentee to attain learning goals. These learning goals are set mutually by both partakers and they may develop during the course taken. In this respect the metaphor "Climbing the mountain" comes in: wanting to achieve what previously was thought to be hard to accomplish, and also: attaining a higher level of performance, preferably sustained at a high level of performance. We certainly would like to avoid the situation addressed by the tongue in cheek remark of our reviewer about what would happen when one comes down from the mountain. There is usually another, higher and more challenging mountain to climb nearby. Mentoring is therefore not an end in itself, but a way to achievement (Alexander, 2008).

- "Mentoring does not happen by itself"

Our reviewer continues by saying that in mentoring attention is needed to structure, content and context. And we adhere to that explicitly; a reader might rightfully coin that the book pays an overly great attention to conversation, i.e, the talk without specifically addressing structure, content and context. Indeed, the main intention behind the book is specifying how the vehicle of mentoring, the conversation, can be analyzed and understood. Given such an understanding we assert that the mentor (and mentee) can become more aware of how the process works in which they are partaking, as a fundamental step to knowing the content they are addressing, the context in which they operate, and the structure of their mutual involvement. For this reason we started the book with an explication of the nature of knowledge as it relates to mentoring settings.

• "By analyzing talk mentors can become aware"

A mentor's awareness of style, strategy, the other as a person, and the meanings conveyed is a crucial constituent of 'good' mentoring; it is part of mentor professionalism (Chapter 13–15). In order to bring awareness up to the level of professionalism we positioned this awareness at the level of mentor knowledge (Chapter 1) and interpreted it as situated understanding and distributed" knowledge shared and recognized among mentor professionals. What then triggers the knowledge building among mentor professionals? We believe it is analyzing the heart of what they do: that is, talk.

• "Mentoring context enables and constraints"

Mentoring itself provides a context as space for interpersonal reasoning, framed by the wider setting (institutional, programmatic) which provides the affordances to mentor. The close and interactional context of a space for dialogue is a delicate platform affected by authority, norms and reigned by integrity (Chapter 9). We encountered many instances of delicateness in spaces of mentoring in the conversations we analyzed. As Bakhtin (2010) notes (interpersonal reasoning and expressing voice in dialogues creates identity as well as shapes (multiple) identities. Mentors are highly influential in shaping the conversational space. On the other hand, they themselves are 'shaped' by the setting in which they work (Chapter 13). Being part of a professional learning community as a mentor can help (Chapter 15) to design supportive learning environments in mentoring.

• An "important consideration is the relationship between discipline-specific and generic professional training"

As our reviewer notes 2 Chapters (Chapter 11 & 12) specifically address domain specificity in mentoring conversation. What is apparent from these Chapters is that the mentor activity and problems encountered in conversation are so recognizable and to be found across different subject matter areas. Chapter 3 and 5 give evidence of such a communality of issues in mentoring in different (content) settings. This brings us to plead for a profession in a profession (Chapter 13) that can deal with the competences of mentors in different domains.

• "Does mentor education make a difference?"

In connection to the previous issue and in answering the question, yes, the line of thought throughout the book, and specifically the last part, advocates a raising of professionalism in mentoring. Our argument starts by noting that "mentors make a difference" (Zanting et al., 1998). The difference of being a 'good' mentor expresses itself mainly in: guidance, relationship, and integrity (see Chapter 8); and most of these qualities can be acquired through deliberate professional development (and practice).

Our intention is that this book contributes new knowledge to mentoring conversations and to the mentoring profession. But the road ahead is still long and there are many aspects of mentoring we still need to learn more about.

Closely connected to this book, yet going a step further, is creating more knowledge about how analysis of a conversation can help the mentor and mentee to plan future action, and to which extent is the future actions based on learning for the mentee as well as for the mentor. Another issue that still needs to be further developed is how to, first from a research perspective and second from a practical perspective, to find ways to 'routinize' complex conversational analysis systems into more adoptable and feasible systems for examining talk between a mentor and a mentee.

We still need to know more about how mentors can be prepared for, educated to take on mentoring responsibilities, being aware of the fact that mentoring in itself is not necessarily a good thing, it is the quality of mentoring that counts. By analysing mentor conversation we are able to learn what the needs of the mentee are, and not least, what mentoring knowledge and skills are needed to respond to the mentee's needs, so learning can occur. Acknowledging the fact that mentoring is to a large extent context bound, our research and previous research (Tillema, Smith, & Leshem, 2011) suggest there are several generic features of mentoring which need to be further explored. This will be an important contribution to an international debate on on mentor professionalism and education that would lead to an (internationally accepted) profession.

REFERENCES

Alexander R. J. (2008). *Essays on pedagogy*. London, England: Routledge.

Bakhtin, M. M. (2010). *Dialogic imagination*. Austin, TX: University of Texas Press.

Barnes D. (2008). Exploratory talk for learning. In N. Mercer & S. Hodgkinson (Eds.), *Exploring talk in school*. London, England: Sage.

Garvey, B. (2008). Readiness to mentor. *International Journal of Mentoring and Coaching, VI*(2), 06.

Magano, M. D., Mostert, P., & Van der Westhuizen, G. (2010). *Learning conversations: The value of interactive learning*. Johannesburg: Heinemann.

Tillema, H., Smith, K., & Leshem, S. (2011). Dual roles – conflicting purposes: A comparative study on perceptions on assessment in mentoring relations during practicum. *European Journal of Teacher Education, 34*(2), 139–159.

Zanting, A., Verloop, N., Vermunt, J. D., & Van Driel, J. H. (1998). Explicating practical knowledge: An extension of mentor teachers' roles. *European Journal of Teacher Education, 21*(1), 11–28.

CPSIA information can be obtained at www.ICGtesting.com
Printed in the USA
BVOW04*1725040515

398148BV00003B/5/P